MOD

'83

James K. Bell and Adrian A. Cohn

COLLEGE OF SAN MATEO

RHETORIC IN A MODERN MODE

with selected readings

SECOND EDITION

GLENCOE PRESS

A DIVISION OF THE MACMILLAN COMPANY

BEVERLY HILLS, CALIFORNIA

H.L.

for Barbara and for Joan

CONTENTS

READINGS

My Self, the Deepest of the Seas

Men and Women

Turning Points: a World in Crisis

The Classical Mode: Essays for Further Reading

Preface
to the Second Edition

Like the first, the second edition of *Rhetoric in a Modern Mode with Selected Readings* is a book in two parts: a *modern* rhetoric and a *modern* reader. We are republishing our remarks on contemporary rhetoric because there seems to be some real demand—in this age of bright, brummagem, flashily "contemporary" textbooks—for an unpretentious and entirely forthright presentation of the basic techniques of writing expository prose. We believe that the intentions set forth in the Preface to our original *Rhetoric* have steadfastly guided us in this revision: we have tried to make a book that students would read with pleasure and use with confidence, knowing that it did not insist, "This is the way people *ought* to write"—but that it said, instead, "This is the way some good writers *are* writing. This is how you can use their forms."

So, although the terms are old ones, our rhetoric works with new examples to show students, first, how to write a good expository paragraph and, second, how to make an essay that uses paragraph structures. In our first four chapters, we take up four aspects of the paragraph: *unity, development, organization,* and *continuity*. We explain how these work in expository paragraphs and then ask students to write paragraphs that have the same qualities. In our fifth chapter we move quickly from the paragraph to the essay, showing—perhaps for the first time—*how to use the paragraph as a model for the essay*. In short, though we recognize that we have oversimplified the rhetoric of the paragraph in order to eliminate unusual forms and to sharpen distinctions that are sometimes obscured in actual practice, we nevertheless think we have written a lively, honest, practical, *modern* guide to the expository essay whose methods have been tested in our classes with gratifying results.

Besides reinforcing the merits of our first edition by adding many new examples, improving the best exercises, and substantially modifying many others, we have endeavored to strengthen the book as a whole by concluding the rhetoric with a new chapter, "The Art of the Essay," which offers a contrasting perspective of the essay as a flexible, spontaneous, artistic expression of uniquely individual human experiences.

In this chapter we include for study and emulation two essays that serve as ideal examples of the essay as high art: George Orwell's "A Hanging" and "Marrakech."

In the reader, too, we have tried to emphasize the modern by choosing truly contemporary essays (while avoiding ephemeral journalism). To make this even more of a new book, we have reprinted only three essays from the first edition. Moreover, we include for the first time a number of short stories and poems, interesting and relevant not only because of their ideas but also because of the contrasting rhetorical modes they employ. Finally, for further comparison and contrast, we have concluded this second edition of the book with a brief but entirely new selection of classical essays. Thus every selection—worthwhile in and for itself—supplements our rhetoric in one way or another.

It is an article of faith with us that writing is more than mere academic exercise: we believe that writing is a process that leads to discover and commitment. That's why we open our book with Gene Fowler's poem "The Words": "I carry boulders across the day/From the field to the ridge,/and my back grows tired." Perhaps, after the act of creation and discovery, the writer remains "Alone, with heavy arms." But what he has done *matters*.

College of San Mateo
September, 1971

James K. Bell
Adrian A. Cohn

RHETORIC IN A
MODERN MODE

SECOND EDITION

THE WORDS*

I carry boulders across the day
From the field to the ridge,
& my back grows tired.
A few, stubborn, in a field drawn
To old blood by the evening sun
& trembling muscles, remain.
These chafe my hands,
Pull away into the black soil.
I take a drop of sweat
onto my thumb,
Watch the wind furrow its surface,
Dream of a morning
When my furrows will shape this field,
When these rocks will form my house.
Alone, with heavy arms,
I listen thru the night to older farms.

RHETORIC

for life's not a paragraph*
—e.e. cummings

1

UNITY
IN THE
PARAGRAPH

"Life's not a paragraph," the poet says. He means of course, "I don't like rules. I don't want to fit my life into neat, rigid patterns. I've got too much *living* to do."

You may happen to feel the same way about paragraphs—they couldn't really be very important, could they? And you might add, "Besides, I've studied them already. Why do I have to do it all over again?"

No doubt you can think up good answers to both questions. Begin with the easy one: why do you need to review paragraphs? If you answer honestly, you'll probably admit that you can't seem to write consistently *good* paragraphs—especially when your teachers give you subjects like this: "Compare and Contrast the Strategy of Napoleon with that of Wellington and Blucher at the Battle of Waterloo." In part, of course, you may be stumped by the material. But that's not the whole story. Like most students, you probably lack a good *strategy* —a way of getting the material down on paper in an orderly, coherent

* From *Poems: 1923-1954* (New York: Harcourt Brace Jovanovich, Inc., 1954), p. 208. Reprinted by permission.

paragraph. So you'll agree, perhaps, that even though you've *studied* paragraphs, you haven't *mastered* them. You need to learn more about writing before you can handle all your writing assignments smoothly.

Now come back to the other question: "are paragraphs really very important?" To that question we've already given a practical answer; we've already noted that some assignments call for great skill in putting ideas together in paragraphs. Next, consider an equally obvious answer, one we'll hardly need to touch on: you will *never* be able to compose a good essay until you can compose a good paragraph. It's as simple as that.

Finally, we'll give you a teacher's answer to that question; but to be a bit more exact, let's rephrase it. Let's ask, "Is the study of the paragraph important for any reasons that are *not* obvious?"

We think so. We think in fact that you should learn to see the paragraph in two ways: first, as a piece of an essay, a kind of "unitized" container for an idea; second, and perhaps more important, as a brief but complete composition, like an essay but smaller in size. Study the paragraph in both ways; then you'll know more than how to write a paragraph: *you will also get most of the skills you need to plan and write an essay.*

Very emphatically, then, we want to insist that the study of the paragraph is important for this reason. You *can* learn to write a paragraph that faithfully reflects the organization and development of the essay; you *can* carry over to the essay most of what you learn in studying the paragraph. The "transfer," as you'll see, is easy.

We say all this with one qualification: we make these claims only for *expository* prose, the workmanlike, everyday writing that keeps the world's business going. *Expository* prose simply explains. For instance, using expository prose you might explain a process, like the action of a particular chemical on the brain cells; you might explain your reasons for acting in some way, like voting for or against capital punishment; you might explain an attitude, like your feelings toward war. At one time or another in college you'll probably be asked to explain just about everything you know. You'll do that with expository prose, set down in expository paragraphs.

So from the beginning, let's keep in mind this definition of an expository paragraph: *it's a distinct part of an essay, it's begun on a new and usually indented line, and it contains a unified statement of a particular point.*

A *good* expository paragraph has:

1. UNITY—it sticks to a main idea;
2. DEVELOPMENT—it explores the main idea explicitly and concretely;
3. ORGANIZATION—it arranges sentences in an orderly way;
4. CONTINUITY—it shows how these sentences are tied to each other and to the main idea.

UNITY

Aim first of all for unity.

Unity means oneness—and you get it by sticking to your main idea, by making sure every sentence carries its part of the burden instead of drifting off into unrelated ideas.

Take for example the following paragraph. It has unity; it hangs together as a whole. Note that the first sentence states the main idea: "At exam time I learned the sad truth that Americans are at no stage of their career taught how to write." As you read the paragraph, note that the writer explains what happened at exam time to make him come to this opinion. Every sentence turns on this point, his main idea.

At exam time I learned the sad truth that Americans are at no stage in their career taught how to write. I mean this not only in the literary sense but also physically. The student who can type beautifully on his own electric typewriter almost disintegrates when asked to put pen to paper for an hour or two in an examination. The lack of style, the misspelling, and the idiotic punctuation drove me to despair from which I was only rescued by the occasional discovery of first-rate answers and the odd remarks that were unintentionally funny. One student, for example, called Homer's epic "The Achilliad." Another wrote that "St. Augustine was illuminated by divine power." (I had to put the comment, "A.C. or D.C.?") In an essay on the *Song of Roland* a girl wrote: "He charged in against the dragon relying on God to help him, and if He didn't, well that's the way the cookie crumbles." Another girl throughout her answers referred to "sweety-pie Aristotle."

—Richard Gilbert, *A Good Time at UCLA: an English View*[1]

Stick to the main idea and you can't go wrong. This sounds simple enough. But look at how quickly you can stray off into unrelated ideas. Watch what happens as a student argues that we are becoming a nation of cheaters. His first two sentences set up the main idea and give an example to support it—but sentence three catches at *another* idea: the reasons for cheating. This is undoubtedly suggested by the main idea, but it does not carry out the main idea; instead, it drifts off into a little story about last night's "date," splitting the paragraph into two pieces. The sense of unity is lost; the feeling of oneness is broken.

(1) You don't have to look very far to see that just about everyone, in one way or another, cheats, apparently with the approval of their family and friends, which makes them cheaters too. (2) For example, my father pads his expense account every time he goes on a business trip. (3) Of course, one of the reasons Americans cheat is that everything is so expensive. (4) Just last night I took out a girl who wanted an orchid corsage. (5) That was five dollars. (6) And then there was the price of the dinner (ten dollars), admission to the dance (four-fifty), and a snack afterwards (four dollars). (7) All together, she cost me twenty-three-fifty, but we had so much fun it was worth the money. (8) So, like everyone else I cheat too—because I have to.

In short, only sentences 1 and 2 stick to the point; sentences 3-8 skip off into other ideas, and the paragraph loses unity.

EXERCISE   1

The paragraphs below lack unity. In each paragraph, sentence 1 states the main idea, but other sentences depart from the main idea and break unity.

Read through each of these paragraphs. As you read, underline each sentence that departs from the main idea and breaks unity.

A.   (1) When I spent last summer in Greenwich Village, I learned what life was all about. (2) To begin with, I had a rotten childhood. (3) My father was rich, my mother was beautiful, and we lived in a big white house in the best part of Atlanta. (4) Every day somebody made me eat breakfast or study or brush my teeth. (5) Finally I couldn't stand it any longer—it was just too much. (6) So when the chance came to get a ride to New York, I put a flower in my hair and set out, taking only my guitar, my Indian headband, and my little white rat, Micky. (7) At last I could go for days without washing my feet! (8) We got to the Village one chilly dawn and wandered around the streets as the sun came out and the city woke. (9) I couldn't explain it then and I can't explain it now, but I suddenly felt very bad about everything. (10) I guess the first thing I learned about life is that the big city can be very lonely on a cold morning.

B.   (1) Even to kids that are really turned on by life, a car is still an important status symbol. (2) Let me explain why I think so. (3) First, there's the little matter of what a car tells us about a guy's bank account. (4) A beat-up old Chevy says, "The owner of this car has at least $10.00 a week to spend on gas, oil, maintenance, and insurance." (5) But a shiny new Corvette says, "Look! Here's money to burn. This guy is loaded." (6) Naturally, most girls prefer the more expensive car—it takes them to nicer places a lot faster. (7) So the sure test of a girl's principles comes when she has to choose between you and the driver of that Corvette. (8) If she chooses you, and you're *not* driving a Corvette, you can be pretty sure of her character. (9) So there's no doubt about it—the car is still an important status symbol.

C.   (1) There are three reasons why I like Japanese food. (2) When I was growing up I never ate Japanese food, since we lived in a part of Texas where there were no Orientals, but now I really like it. (3) One of the best things about Japanese food is that it consists primarily of meat and vegetables, so that it's not at all fattening. (4) However, most Japanese love rice. (5) One of my Japanese friends has at least two bowls of rice at every meal. (6) Another reason for liking Japanese food is that it's always beautifully served, even at lower-priced restaurants. (7) Every dish is a work of art: the chicken yakitori is presented on a gleaming platter criss-crossed with skewers of meat and vegetables, and the shrimp tempura comes on a lovely little bamboo tray. (8) For the American who wants to serve Japanese food like this, these platters and trays may be purchased at a local import store. (9) My final reason for liking Japanese food is its exotic flavor. (10) There is nothing in American or European cuisine quite like the flavor of *sashimi* (raw fish dipped in soy sauce and horseradish) or *shabu-shabu*, a meat and vegetable dish that you cook right at your own table by swishing the bite-sized pieces in a pan of seasoned boiling water. (11) Also, from the male point of view, Japanese restaurants are attractive for another reason—the beautiful little doll-like wait-resses, who bow and smile shyly as they serve your food. (12) With all this, is there any wonder Japanese food appeals to me?

UNITY AND THE TOPIC SENTENCE

You've heard about it already of course, and you've just finished working with it. But you should now remind yourself: *the sentence that states the main idea of the paragraph, and helps give the paragraph unity, is called the TOPIC SENTENCE.*

Take the paragraph below, for example. The main idea happens to be expressed in the first sentence: "There are three kinds of book owners." This sentence is the topic sentence.

(1) There are three kinds of book owners. (2) The first has all the standard sets and best-sellers—unread, untouched. (3) (This deluded individual owns woodpulp and ink, not books.) (4) The second has a great many books—a few of them read through, most of them dipped into, but all of them as clean and shiny as the day they were bought. (5) (This person would probably like to make books his own, but is restrained by a false respect for their physical appearance.) (6) The third has a few books or many—every one of them dog-eared and dilapidated, shaken and loosened by continual use, marked and scribbled in from front to back. (7) (This man owns books.)
—Mortimer J. Adler, *How to Mark a Book*[2]

Subject and Focus

For most of us, however, that's not much help. Naturally, we need to know what a topic sentence is, but we also need to know something more important: *we need to know how a topic sentence works.*

In exploring this question, let's do only one thing—find out how a topic sentence works by putting one together step-by-step. And to avoid confusion, let's agree to forget all about grammar. *Forget about subjects and predicates; forget about nouns and verbs—because we are not talking about grammar.*

Begin at the beginning. Suppose you are asked to write a paragraph on one of the following *subjects:*

1. Fate
2. Love
3. Democracy
4. Teen-agers
5. Music

The *first* step is to choose a subject—one you know something about, obviously. The *next* step is to say something about your subject in one sentence. That sentence is your topic sentence. Already you can see that it does two things:

1. it lays down your subject;
2. it puts forth your main idea about the subject.

Go back to the five subjects listed above; say something in one sentence about each subject. You might write:

1. Fate
   I don't believe in *fate*.
2. Love
   Love is a dangerous emotion.
3. Democracy
   In a *democracy*, the people govern themselves through their elected representatives.
4. Teen-agers
   Today's *teen-agers* call themselves the "turned-on generation."
5. Music
   Music is interesting and enjoyable.

Now you have some topic sentences (which may or may not be *good* topic sentences—that's a separate question). Clearly each of these topic sentences has two parts: first, a *subject*; second, *something said about the subject.* For convenience, let's call this second part— "something said about the subject"—the FOCUS. We can then say that a topic sentence has two parts: *subject* and *focus.*

In our examples:

1. *Subject:* fate
   Focus: I don't believe in . . .

2. *Subject:* love
   Focus: . . . is a dangerous emotion.

3. *Subject:* democracy
   Focus: In a . . . , the people govern themselves through their elected representatives.

4. *Subject:* teen-agers
   Focus: today's . . . call themselves the "turned-on generation."

5. *Subject:* music
   Focus: . . . is interesting and enjoyable.

Briefly, then: *a topic sentence has a subject and a focus; a topic sentence works by naming a subject and saying something about that subject—in the focus.*

EXERCISE   2

A.   Write out the subject and the focus in each of the following topic sentences.

1. For those who make it to the top, professional boxing can be an extremely lucrative sport.
2. Speech defects are caused not by lazy minds but by physical deformities, or by "faulty sensory perception" in the mouth, which prevents a person's knowing exactly where his tongue is when he is speaking.
3. Japanese gangsters traditionally cover their bodies with tatoos as signs of their courage.
4. Most doctors believe that alcoholism should be treated as a disease, not a crime.
5. The Playmate of the Month always has an interesting hobby as well as other attractive characteristics.
6. Suzy Creamcheese believes that hippies smell bad and use dirty words.
7. Curiously enough, detective novels are often read most enthusiastically by scholars and bookmen such as the poet W. H. Auden.
8. London, in August, was hot, damp, smoggy, and crawling with tourists.
9. The crime rate in big American cities continues to rise steadily.
10. Women's skirts always get shorter during times of prosperity.

B.   Choose five subjects. Then write one topic sentence on each subject.

C.   In each of the topic sentences you wrote for Exercise 2B, underline the subject once, the focus twice.

Limiting the Subject; Sharpening the Focus

Finally, to come round to the point of this discussion: *what makes a good topic sentence?*

You can find the answer to this question by looking at a *bad* topic sentence: "Music is interesting and enjoyable." That's the kind of topic sentence you're likely to start with any time you're given a subject like "music" to write on—and it can only lead to disaster. Take it apart and you'll see why:

> *Subject:* music
> *Focus:* . . . is interesting and enjoyable.

1. *Subject:* music
    Ask yourself, "What do I mean by *music?* What kind of music? Do I mean symphonic music, chamber music, scores for opera and ballet? Do I mean popular dance music, folk music, rock-and-roll, jazz? Do I mean the music of a 'happening'? *How can I cover so many types of music in one paragraph?*"

2. *Focus:* . . . is interesting and enjoyable.
    Ask yourself, "What do I mean by *interesting* and *enjoyable?*" If it will help, look in a dictionary. You will find: "*interesting*—exciting curiosity or attention"; "*enjoyable*—agreeable." And you'll have to admit that *interesting* and *enjoyable* don't say very much about music. They simply express approval, and they are far too vague.

That's the process. You've taken the sentence apart and you've found that "music is interesting and enjoyable" makes a bad topic sentence—*bad because the subject is too broad; bad because the focus is vague.*

The same is true of each of the next examples:

Detective fiction is always very exciting.

Water pollution is a big problem.

The Communist conspiracy is spreading.

Morality is unnatural.

Life began in a strange way.

I believe that divine powers exist everywhere.

Using the same process, you'll find that these too are bad topic sentences—bad because the subject is too broad; bad because the focus is vague.

What lesson can we draw from all this? If you want to write a *good* topic sentence, you need to do two things: *first, limit your subject; second, sharpen your focus.*

Instead of *music*, for example, limit your subject to *folk-rock* or (better still) to *the San Francisco sound*. Instead of *interesting and enjoyable*, sharpen your focus to *appeals mainly to the younger generation* or (better still) *combines the rhythms of rock-and-roll with the lyrics of the folk ballad*. Then you have three topic sentences:

Bad: Music is interesting and enjoyable.

Better: Folk-rock appeals mainly to the younger generation.

Good: The San Francisco sound combines the rhythms of rock-and-roll with the lyrics of the folk ballad.

In short, a good topic sentence has a limited subject and a sharp focus.

EXERCISE 3

Limit the subject and sharpen the focus in each of the following topic sentences. In doing so, you may change the meaning and the wording of the topic sentence in any necessary way. To revise the sentences effectively, you must make conspicuous changes in both subject and focus.

For example:

Original: Modern innovations have revolutionized life.
Revision: The computer center established by the Internal Revenue Service has made it much more difficult for Americans to cheat on their income tax returns.

1. Modern innovations have revolutionized life.
2. Today's fashions are too extreme.
3. English music is the best there is today.
4. Working creates difficulties for students.
5. Foreign cars are better than American cars.
6. Students profit from attending educational events.
7. The study of a foreign language is most interesting.
8. Television is improving.
9. Education is essential to financial success.
10. Sports develop character, agility, strength, and endurance.

Using the Focus to Maintain Unity

When you've limited your subject and sharpened your focus, you're finally ready to put your topic sentence to work in a paragraph. You'll see later that a good topic sentence works for you in many ways. For the moment, make the topic sentence work for you like this: *use the subject to mark off your specific material; use your focus to point out exactly what you will say about that material.*

You'll understand why you must *use* the focus to maintain unity if you stop to consider a rather obvious idea: unless you're just daydreaming on paper, you'll probably stick to your subject. But you can very easily forget about your focus—and shatter the unity of your paragraph. Let's put it this way: you probably wouldn't begin with the subject *love* and end up writing about *slang*; but on the other hand, you conceivably *could* start to explain why you're in favor of love and wind up attacking the image of romantic love drawn by movies and television. Think about what this means: it is not enough just to "stick to your subject"—*you will have to check everything you say in your paragraph to be sure you stick to your focus. You will have to use your focus to hold onto unity. For the focus is the heart of your paragraph.*

To see how this works, let's take the subject "folk-rock music" and write a paragraph about it. Since we can't talk about all of it, let's limit our subject to *"much* folk-rock music." As our next step, we need to decide exactly what we will say about our subject: we need to find a focus. Now, for an audience of older people—those of us who merely listen from the fringes—one thing in particular stands out about recent folk-rock songs: they contain "secret drug messages." Let's use this idea as our focus, then, and let's phrase our topic sentence: "Much folk-rock music contains secret messages about drugs." As we write the paragraph, watch the way we get unity by using the focus "contains *secret* messages about drugs" (and remember that *secret* is a key word):

> Much folk-rock music contains secret messages about drugs. Sometimes the messages are hidden in the titles of the songs. "Love Special Delivery" and "Lucy in the Sky with Diamonds," for example, use the first letters of words in their titles to spell LSD. "Along Comes Mary" and "Acapulco Gold" refer to marijuana—as people "in the know" will be glad to explain: Mary is a code-word for marijuana; Acapulco Gold is a very high grade of marijuana. Other titles that supposedly convey secret messages are "Puff the Magic Dragon" (that delightful children's song), "Mellow Yellow," and "Eight Miles High." But these messages are not restricted to the titles; you can also find them in the lyrics. The messages are there—all you have to do is find them.

Placing the Topic Sentence

You can put it anywhere (or even leave it out)—but the topic sentence fits naturally and works best at the beginning of a paragraph. You should place it there most of the time—and place it elsewhere only for a *good* reason.

UNITY IN THE PARAGRAPH: SUM AND SUBSTANCE

A good expository paragraph has four qualities:

1. UNITY—it sticks to a main idea;

2. DEVELOPMENT—it explores the main idea explicitly and concretely;
3. ORGANIZATION—it arranges sentences in an orderly way;
4. CONTINUITY—it shows how these sentences are tied to each other and to the main idea.

Of these qualities, *unity*—the sense of oneness—is perhaps the most fundamental, since the expository paragraph is by definition *a unified statement of a particular point*.

The sentence that states the main idea of the paragraph, and helps give the paragraph unity, is called the *topic sentence*. A topic sentence works by naming a *subject* and then saying something about that subject in the *focus*. A good topic sentence has a *limited subject* and a *sharp focus*. Since the topic sentence states the main idea of a paragraph, it is usually the first sentence of the paragraph.

EXERCISE 4

A. Write a good topic sentence for each of the following subjects. Be sure to limit your subject and sharpen your focus.

1. Animals
2. Clothes
3. Pollution
4. Marriage
5. Books
6. Dancing
7. Friends
8. The Women's Liberation movement
9. Nature
10. Sports

B. Write a paragraph of about 150 words using one of the topic sentences you wrote for Exercise 4A. Remember to use your focus to maintain unity.

2

DEVELOPMENT IN THE PARAGRAPH

Let us begin with a definition: *development clarifies, illustrates, or proves the main idea stated in the topic sentence.*

Good expository paragraphs have both unity and development. In fact, skillful development helps you to stick to your subject and focus and to keep up the sense of oneness.

Let's look at this idea a little more closely. *Development* is a word we use to explain what happens in a paragraph after the topic sentence. In the topic sentence you *state* your main idea; in the rest of the paragraph you *develop* your main idea in great detail in order to show your reader exactly what you mean. Developing your main idea, then, is a little like blowing up a photograph to make the details clearer. In the paragraph, you do that by using the *techniques of development*. Keep in mind that the purpose of this chapter is to teach you those techniques—after you have learned a few basic principles.

The Importance of Good Development

To see the importance of showing your reader exactly what you mean, study two examples: a paragraph written by a professional and a paragraph written by a student.

Take the good example first. Study the way Jacques Barzun *develops* his main idea in this paragraph. He begins with the subject "literature" (anything written); he says about this subject: "we can't get along without it" (in different words, of course). Then, *to show the reader exactly what he means*, he tells a story about coming home and finding a note written by his window washer.

> Whether it is the records we have to keep in every business and profession or the ceaseless communicating at a distance which modern transport and industry require, the world's work is now unmanageable, unthinkable, without literature. Just see how many steps you can take without being confronted by something written or by the necessity of writing something yourself. Having been away for a couple of weeks during the summer, I find a bill from the window washer, who luckily came on a day when the cleaning woman was in the apartment. He has therefore scribbled below the date: "The windows have been cleaned Wed. 12:30 P.M. Your maid was there to veryfy the statement"—perfectly clear and adequate. One can even appreciate the change in tenses as his mind went from the job just finished to the future when I would be reading this message from the past.
>
> —Jacques Barzun, *English as She's Not Taught*[1]

Here, the first sentence states the main idea; the second sentence *develops* the main idea by saying to the reader, "Isn't this your experience?" The rest of the paragraph *develops* the main idea in more detail by giving an example. So the professional writer *shows the reader exactly what he means*.

Take the poor example next. Study the way a student "develops" his main idea in the following paragraph. His subject is Marcus Welby, hero of the television show *Marcus Welby, M.D.*; the focus reads "is by far the most devoted to his patients." The rest of the paragraph makes a half-hearted effort to develop this idea—*but it does not show the reader exactly what the writer means*.

> Of all the television doctors, Marcus Welby is by far the most devoted to his patients. He gives all his patients careful, understanding attention. He is so devoted that he succeeds in caring for the minds and spirits as well as the bodies of his patients.

The paragraph is not weak because it's short. It's weak because it doesn't say anything except that Marcus Welby is devoted: the idea needs *development*. A more skillful writer would have described specific situations, actions, and details to *show* exactly how devoted

Marcus Welby is. In other words, good expository writing goes beyond the bare, flat assertion of an idea; it brings the idea to life by vivid development.

So it all comes down to this: *use the techniques of development to clarify, illustrate, or prove your main idea. Show your reader exactly what you mean.*

The Secret of Good Development

Actually, most students have heard that they need to develop their ideas. Even the student who wrote on Marcus Welby knew that. What he didn't know is what you're now going to learn: *the secret of good development.*

Let's put it simply. Most of the paragraphs you write will begin with a topic sentence. The topic sentence is a *generalization—a broad statement of the main idea.* The rest of the paragraph *develops* the main idea by using *specific statements.* So the basic principle of good development can be stated briefly: *go from the general to the specific.* But that's only part of the secret. Here's the rest: you must know the *difference* between a general and a specific statement.

General and Specific Statements

That difference is one of the most important things you'll learn in this book. Consciously or unconsciously, good writers always know it; awkward, inept writers never do.

The difference is simply this: a general statement carries *few* details; it pulls many things together into only a *few words.* A specific statement, on the other hand, names *more* details; it lays things out in as many words as necessary. As the words *few* and *more* suggest, the difference between general and specific statements is actually *a difference in degree.* Some statements are *more general* than others; some statements are *more specific* than others.

For example, compare the following statements. They show what we mean by a difference in degree. The first statement is very general; the last statement is very specific; the other two stand somewhere in between.

1. Janet is a good girl.
2. Janet is considerate of her family.
3. Janet helps her parents by earning money at part-time jobs.

4. By selling toys at a local department store, Janet is able to earn twenty dollars a week, all of which she gives to her parents.

Is it clear that these four statements differ in their *degree* of generality? At a high level of generality, the first statement says without explanation that Janet is a good girl; it seems to view her ways of life from a great distance, and so it omits all the details. Now take one step down. The second statement is less general because it includes one detail: "Janet is considerate of her family." Then take one more step. The third statement is less general still (and more specific): it's less general because it explains that Janet *helps* her parents by earning money at part-time jobs. Finally, take the last step. The fourth statement is the least general and most specific of all: the details name Janet's job (selling toys), her employer (local department store), her salary (twenty dollars), and its use (given to her parents).

Think of what this means: *here is the key to good development —understanding the difference between these statements.* Look at them this way:

1. *Most general (least specific):* Janet is a good girl.
2. *Less general (more specific):* Janet is considerate of her family.
3. *Still less general (still more specific):* Janet helps her parents by earning money at part-time jobs.
4. *Least general (most specific):* By selling toys at a local department store, Janet is able to earn twenty dollars a week, all of which she gives to her parents.

To be less precise, we might simply say: "The first two statements are general. The last two statements are specific." *The important point is that you see the difference between general and specific statements.*

Let's study another example:

1. I like novels.
2. I like novels about spies.
3. I like Ian Fleming's novels about James Bond.

You can analyze these statements in this way:

1. I like novels.
   "The novel is a type of literature. When I think of novels, I

think of *Pilgrim's Progress, The Memoirs of a Lady of Pleasure, David Copperfield, Lolita.* This statement pulls many things together into a few words. Obviously this statement is *more general* than the next one."

2. I like novels about spies.
"This statement says something about a smaller group of things. Novels about spies—that suggests *The Great Impostor, The Secret Agent,* and *On Her Majesty's Secret Service.* So this statement is *less general* than the first one. But still it's *more general* than the next one."

3. I like Ian Fleming's novels about James Bond.
"This statement says something about just one group of spy stories. These are the stories about James Bond. So this must be the *least general* of all three statements. Naturally, it's also the *most specific.*"

And, if you wanted, you could write statements at both higher and lower degrees of generality. For instance:

1. I like literature.
2. I like prose fiction.
3. I like novels.
4. I like novels about spies.
5. I like Ian Fleming's novels about James Bond.
6. I like *Casino Royale, Goldfinger,* and *Dr. No.*

In short, the secret of good development can be stated simply: *go from the general to the specific.* You can *use* the secret once you understand the difference between general and specific statements.

EXERCISE 1

In each of the following groups, list the statements in order from the most general to the most specific.

A. 1. The most popular music today is the rock-and-roll music of vocal-instrumental groups such as Iron Butterfly, Canned Heat, The Animals, and Blood, Sweat & Tears.

2. Music is the only universal language.

3. On February 15, 1971, the top tune of the "Big Thirty" national survey was "One Bad Apple" by The Osmunds.

4. The Romantic music of nineteenth-century Europe does not appeal to most young Americans.

B.   1. Television is an important medium of communication.

2. Walter Cronkite, in my opinion, has the most interesting of all the network news programs.

3. There are few really good shows on television.

4. In general, the network news programs are the best shows on television.

C.   1. Humpty Dumpty thought he knew everything about language.

2. "When I use a word," Humpty Dumpty said, in rather a scornful tone, "it means just what I choose it to mean—neither more nor less."

3. Humpty Dumpty was very conceited.

4. "*Brillig* means four o'clock in the afternoon—the time when you begin broiling things for dinner."

D.   1. In civilized countries, money is used as a medium of exchange and value.

2. At last I held ten $100 bills in my hand!

3. Money is the root of all evil.

4. The dollar, equal to 100 cents, is the basic monetary unit of the United States.

E.   1. Love is a basic human emotion, common to virtually all people at all times and in all places.

2. Romantic love is a strong, usually passionate affection for a person of the opposite sex.

3. Eve and Bob fell in love on the evening of Saturday, July 4, as they sat on the roof of a garage watching the fireworks and drinking apple wine.

4. For my cats, Omar and Mephisto, love is a bowl of chopped raw kidney.

F.   1. Most political writing is filled with pretentious diction and meaningless words.

2. A symptom of the decay of the language is the frequent use of clichés and stereotyped expressions such as "Right on!" and "in the fast moving world of today."

3. The English language is decadent.

4. English prose in particular reveals many signs of decadence.

G. 1. In San Francisco, a center of alcoholism in the United States, one out of every five persons drinks excessively.

   2. Americans consume billions of cigarettes and millions of tons of aspirins every year.

   3. A friend of mine takes two dexedrine tablets every morning to wake him up and three 75mg Thorazine Spansules during the day to calm him down; he drinks three double Tanqueray martinis before dinner, two glasses of wine during dinner, and four ounces of cognac after dinner; and then, before he goes to bed, he takes three aspirins and two 100mg phenobarbital capsules to put him to sleep.

   4. We live in a culture that permits us to develop a dependence on drugs.

H. 1. Women are female human beings, distinguished from and naturally inferior to men.

   2. Karen is the freshest, loveliest, sweetest girl I have ever known.

   3. Women are mainly useful as cooks, housekeepers, babysitters, and chauffeurs.

   4. Women play only a modest role in American government.

PARAGRAPH PATTERNS: THREE USES OF THE LEVELS OF GENERALITY

Right away you can make an important use of the difference between general and specific statements: you can study the way paragraphs are developed around them. Once you've done that, you'll be ready to learn the techniques of development.

Pattern 1: A Simple Deductive Arrangement

You know the first pattern already: this kind of paragraph (the most common) begins with a topic sentence—that is, a high-level generalization. Each sentence in the rest of the paragraph states specific details; these sentences are low-level generalizations. To this familiar pattern let's apply an unfamiliar term: *deductive arrangement*. We can then say that most paragraphs are *deductive: they go from general to specific.*

To master this idea, linger for a moment on the word *deductive*. Notice that it comes from a Latin prefix, *de*, meaning "away from, down from," and the verb *ducere*, "to lead." Then remember that *deductive* means "leading away from a generalization."

Here is an excellent example: this paragraph *leads away from a generalization* in the topic sentence and into specific details that develop the main idea: *Peanuts* (the comic strip) "is hitting a high new peak" in popularity:

> *Peanuts* has enjoyed great popularity for a full decade, but the craze is now hitting a high new peak (TOPIC SENTENCE). At scores of colleges, *Peanuts* characters are the biggest people on campus. In Vietnam, pilots fly into combat with Snoopy painted on their planes. Records based on *Peanuts* have sold millions of copies. And even before it opened last week, a new off-Broadway hit musical, *You're a Good Man, Charlie Brown*, had sold tickets to admirers as far away as Nebraska. Dolls, cards, clothes, and other *Peanuts* paraphernalia make up a more than $15 million-a-year business. And in 900 newspapers in the U.S. and Canada and 100 abroad, the misadventures of Charlie, Snoopy and their friends are followed by 90 million readers a day (SPECIFIC DETAILS TO DEVELOP THE MAIN IDEA STATED IN THE TOPIC SENTENCE).
>
> —Jon Borgzinner, *Peanuts' Losers Win at Last*[2]

You can see clearly that this paragraph (like most others) fits the *deductive pattern*.

Pattern 2: A Simple Inductive Arrangement

Our basic rule for good development is "Go from the general to the specific." Occasionally, however, a writer may do exactly the opposite —sometimes to retrace the steps leading to a conclusion, but more often to intrigue the reader by engrossing his attention. *Inductive* paragraphs (Latin *in*, "into," + *ducere*, "to lead") lead *into* a generalization: they place the topic sentence at the end. In the following paragraph, for example, the main idea is stated in the last sentence: "After more of the same we may be tempted to agree with Justice Holmes that 'the chief end of man is to frame general propositions, and no general proposition is worth a damn.'" Before stating this main idea, the writer gives a number of examples of "the generalizations that float into every conversation":

Listen attentively to those around you, and note the generalizations that float into every conversation: Europeans are lazy and shiftless. European girls make good wives. American girls are selfish. Politicians are crooks. Gentlemen prefer blondes. On a somewhat more "intellectual" level, we find: Liberals never think a matter through. Intellectuals always show a lack of practical judgment. Americans are idealists. Americans are materialists. All American men suffer from "momism." Economics is bunk. Modern art is trash. Psychiatrists never bring up their own children properly. In the middle ages everyone was religious. And so on. After more of the same we may be tempted to agree with Justice Holmes that "the chief end of man is to frame general propositions, and no general proposition is worth a damn."

—Lionel Ruby, *Are All Generalizations False?*[3]

So, to get variety and drama, this writer reverses the usual rule "Go from the general to the particular." He develops his topic sentence by specific, concrete details—but he places the topic sentence *at the end of the paragraph*. That is, he follows an *inductive* pattern.

Pattern 3: A Complex Deductive Arrangement

Go back to the beginning of this chapter for a moment. There, you will remember, we studied the *degrees of generality*. We learned that some statements stand at a very high level of generality; that some statements stand at a very low level of generality; and that other statements stand somewhere in between. In putting that knowledge to use, you have studied a *simple deductive pattern* (the most common) and a *simple inductive pattern* (very rare). Both of these patterns work with two levels of generality, as you've just seen. The topic sentence is general, the specific statements much less general. Now we are going to take a very important step: we are going to study a more complex pattern. This pattern uses *three levels of generality*.

Let's describe it briefly. The *complex deductive paragraph* begins with a topic sentence—as you would expect, the most general statement in the paragraph. The *major supports* develop the topic sentence; they set up details that *directly* illustrate the topic sentence— but (and this is *very* important) the major supports stand at an *in-between* level of generality. That means one thing: the *major supports* need statements at a lower level of generality; they need statements that are more specific. For the sake of convenience, let's say they need *minor supports.* These refer *indirectly* to the topic sentence; they refer *directly* to the major supports.

This sounds complicated, but let's see how it works. At the same time, you will also see *why* you often need minor supports as well as major supports.

Major and Minor Supports

Take the following example and try to break it into statements that lie at three different levels of generality. Do it in this way: first, find the topic sentence. Then see which sentences go back *directly* to the topic sentence—these are the major supports. See which sentences go back *indirectly* to the topic sentence—these are the minor supports. You'll see that the minor supports give more details and are therefore more specific; you'll also discover that the minor supports go back directly to the major supports. And then you'll conclude that the major and minor supports, taken *together*, develop the topic sentence. It's simply a matter of using three levels of generality instead of two.

To simplify your analysis, we have put the proper labels on each sentence in our example:

> Our fascination with sounds gives us two interesting if not important sources of English vocabulary (TOPIC SENTENCE). *The first source is onomatopoeia—making up words that sound like what they mean* (MAJOR SUPPORT). For example, the word *buzz* sounds like the action it represents (MINOR SUPPORT). Other onomatopoeic words are *tinkle, hiss, whirr, sizzle, slam* (MINOR SUPPORT). *Besides onomatopoeia, we also form words by reduplication—the repetition of sounds* (MAJOR SUPPORT). Sometimes reduplication merely produces catchy rhyming sounds, as in *honky-tonk, rinky-dink, drunk as a skunk,* and *hodge-podge* (MINOR SUPPORT). But reduplication may also intensify the meaning of a root word; *goody-goody*, for instance, may mean "too good," and a *go-go* girl doesn't simply *go*—she *really* goes (MINOR SUPPORT).

An outline will make the development of this paragraph even clearer:

MAIN IDEA: Our fascination with sounds gives us two sources of English vocabulary.

MAJOR SUPPORT: *Onomatopoeia*

MINOR SUPPORTS: *Buzz, tinkle, hiss, whirr, sizzle, slam*

MAJOR SUPPORT: *Reduplication*
MINOR SUPPORTS: *Honky-tonk, rinky-dink, drunk as a skunk, hodge-podge, goody-goody, go-go girl*

To sum up, we should note that the main idea, at the highest level of generality, is developed through two intermediate levels (the major supports). Then, at the lowest level of generality, the minor supports give examples to illustrate the major supports.

WHEN TO USE MAJOR AND MINOR SUPPORTS

In developing a paragraph, how do you decide whether to use major supports alone or both major and minor supports? Almost always your topic sentence tells you what to do. If your main idea is fairly complex or on a relatively high level of generality, your major supports will probably be too general to stand alone. For example, read the following paragraph. Is it clear? Has the writer shown the reader exactly what he means?

> According to Aristotle, the writer has four general topics that he can adapt to any audience (TOPIC SENTENCE). The first of these Aristotle calls "the possible and the impossible" (MAJOR SUPPORT). The second general topic in Aristotle's list is "whether a thing has happened or not" (MAJOR SUPPORT). The third topic is "whether a thing will happen or not" (MAJOR SUPPORT). The final item in Aristotle's list is "greatness and smallness, including amplification and deprecation" (MAJOR SUPPORT). In short, then, with Aristotle's four general topics before him, the writer can proceed to choose a subject which will interest both himself and his reader: the whole world lies before him—simplified (CONCLUSION).

Although it has a topic sentence, four major supports, and a concluding sentence, this paragraph is *still* too general. It needs to be developed by more specific statements. To clarify the "four general topics" listed in this paragraph, we can rewrite it, giving examples of each topic. In the revised version we will use two minor supports to give examples for each major support. The paragraph is very long, but the minor supports are specific enough to make the whole idea come clear.

> According to Aristotle, a writer has four general topics that he can adapt to any audience (TOPIC SENTENCE). *The first of these Aristotle calls "the possible and the impossible"* (MAJOR SUPPORT). For ex-

ample, the writer might attempt to show that race riots in the United States will hurt the civil rights movement (MINOR SUPPORT). Or, on another subject, the writer might want to demonstrate the possibility that life exists on planets other than earth (MINOR SUPPORT). *A second general topic in Aristotle's list is "whether a thing happened or not"* (MAJOR SUPPORT). For instance, did Lee Harvey Oswald bear sole responsibility for the assassination of President Kennedy? (MINOR SUPPORT). Did the Greeks and Romans discover America? (MINOR SUPPORT) *The third topic in Aristotle's list is "whether a thing will happen or not"* (MAJOR SUPPORT). For example, will the Catholic Church change its stand on birth control? (MINOR SUPPORT) Or, will America be the first country to send a manned spaceship to another planet? (MINOR SUPPORT) *If none of these three general topics will satisfy the writer's need, there is still the final item in Aristotle's list: "greatness and smallness, including amplification and deprecation"* (MAJOR SUPPORT). To what extent did Shakespeare influence the development of tragedy in English literature? (MINOR SUPPORT) Or, at another extreme, how good is Willie Mays compared with the greatest outfielders in the history of baseball? (MINOR SUPPORT) *In short, then, with Aristotle's four general topics before him, the writer can proceed to choose a subject which will interest both himself and his reader: the whole world lies before him—simplified* (CONCLUSION).

Of the three methods of arranging details and generalizations in the paragraph, the simple deductive pattern is certainly the most common, the simple inductive pattern the least common. Almost every paragraph you write will use a simple deductive arrangement. But the more complex pattern described here is as essential to the writer as paper, a pen, and a clear mind.

And there is a reason for this: only the *complex deductive paragraph*—as you will see in Chapter 5—is the perfect model for the expository essay.

EXERCISE 2

Analyze the following *complex deductive* paragraphs by listing each sentence as a topic sentence, major support, or minor support, to show its level of generality.

A. (1) The home during the late fifties began to show signs of supplanting the automobile as the status symbol most favored by Americans for staking their status claims. (2) There are a number of explanations for this change, but the most important one, undoubtedly, is that with the general rise of incomes and installment buying a luxuriously sculptured chariot has become too easily obtainable for the great multitudes of status strivers. (3) A home costs more money, a lot more. (4) Another explanation is the appearance in profusion of mass merchandisers in the home-selling field, who have become skilled —partly by copying mass-selling strategies developed in the automobile field—in surrounding their product with status meanings. (5) Example: "Early American Luxurious Ranch . . . $27,900 & Up." (6) That's in Long Island, not the Texas Panhandle.

—Vance Packard, *The Status Seekers.*[4]

B. (1) As if this perverse fatigue were not bad enough, our tired housewife is distressed by other considerations. (2) First, she feels isolated and peculiar. (3) It is hard for her to believe that anybody else could have anything like this. (4) "You mean other women feel as bad as I do?" she asks incredulously. (5) Secondly, the housewife's fatigue may be accompanied by other symptoms. (6) She may suffer from headaches, dizziness, indigestion, backache, or bowel disorders. (7) Thirdly, the tired housewife is almost always in a state of great anxiety, almost panic. (8) "You can't tell me there isn't anything wrong with me," she exclaims defiantly. (9) "Nobody could feel as bad as I do and not have something serious the matter." (10) The emphasis is on the word "serious." (11) The implied but unspoken adjective is "fatal."

—Walter E. O'Donnell, M.D., *Finally: A Sure Cure for Housewife Fatigue*[5]

C. (1) Some people, for reasons still not clear, are pitched at a much higher level of stimulus hunger than others. (2) They seem to crave change, even when others are reeling from it. (3) A new house, a new car, another trip, another crisis on the job, more house guests, visits, financial adventures and misadventures—they seem to accept all these and more without apparent ill effect. (4) Yet close analysis of such people often reveals the existence in their lives of what might be called stability zones—certain enduring relationships that are carefully maintained despite all kinds of other changes. (5) One scientist I know has run through a series of love affairs, a divorce and remarriage—all within a very short time. (6) He thrives on change, enjoys travel, new foods and new ideas, new movies, plays and books. (7) He has a high intellect and a low threshold of boredom, is impatient with tradition and restlessly eager for novelty. (8) Ostensibly,

he is a walking exemplar of change. (9) When we look more closely, however, we find that he has stayed on the same job for ten years. (10) He drives a battered seven-year-old automobile. (11) His clothes are a few years out of style. (12) His closest friends are longtime professional associates and even a few old college buddies.
—Alvin Toffler, *Coping with Future Shock*[6]

D.   (1) To the golfer, the lure of this "royal and ancient" game is complete and irresistible. (2) He will play anywhere and under any circumstances. (3) On the lush layout near Wankie in Rhodesia, an elephant rifle for protection against dangerous animals is a must. (4) In Victoria Falls, club members share the course with crocodiles from the Zambezi. (5) When the intrepid British explorer Robert Scott went to the South Pole, he took along a shag bag of practice balls and a midiron to work on his approach shots . . . . (6) Certainly no game supposedly played for pleasure gives so much pain to the participants. (7) In the earliest history of golf, men went to jail rather than forgo their regular round. (8) During the 15th century so many Scottish soldiers sneaked away from archery practice to play at the links nearby that the game was temporarily outlawed. (9) In 1593 John Henrie and Pat Rogie were arrested in Edinburgh for "playing of gowlf on the links of Leith every sabbath at the time of the sermonses."

—*Playboy*[7]

E.   (1) According to Robert S. De Ropp in *The Master Game*, there are five levels of human consciousness. (2) The lowest of these is dreamless sleep, characterized by deep narcosis and physiological quietude. (3) In dreamless sleep we know and experience nothing; we are totally unaware of internal and external stimuli. (4) The second stage of human consciousness is sleep with dreams. (5) In the dream state we experience—through purely mental "seeing"—episodic images, accompanied by rapid eye movements, shallow breathing, rapid pulse, and increased blood pressure. (6) The third stage of consciousness is normal everyday awareness of ourselves as human beings; it is, in De Ropp's terminology, "identification." (7) De Ropp also calls it "waking sleep," because he believes that in this state we are "lost" in whatever we happen to be doing or thinking or feeling from moment to moment; hence we are not fully awake or completely free. (8) In the fourth stage of consciousness, however, we reach "self-transcendence," a condition in which we are said to "remember" ourselves. (9) Self-transcendence is an objective separation of awareness from what we are doing, feeling, or thinking: it makes us both actor and observer, and it frees us from the misery and fear imposed by the personal ego in the third stage of consciousness. (10) The fifth level of consciousness is "cosmic" consciousness. (11) Cosmic consciousness is a kind of transcendental identification with the cosmos, a perception of the life and order of the universe. (12) This mode of awareness may occur spontaneously for some men; in others it may be induced by psychedelic drugs or by meditation. (13) To most men, however, it is a room in the human mind to which the door must remain perpetually locked.

THE TECHNIQUES OF DEVELOPMENT

You now know why you need to develop your ideas; you understand the secret of good development; and you have studied the three common ways of arranging general and specific statements in the paragraph. These basic principles have prepared you for the next step: actually *writing* paragraphs using *the techniques of development*.

The techniques of development give you an answer to the question, "How do I know what to say after I have written the topic sentence?" *Use the techniques of development to provide specific details for the main idea stated in the topic sentence.*

The most common and most effective techniques of development are:

1. Descriptive Details
2. Factual Details
3. Illustration
4. Definition
5. Authority: Quotation and Paraphrase

Descriptive Details

Use descriptive details as the basic technique of development

The first rule for every writer is to be as specific as possible. That means that you should try to catch actions, ideas, appearances, tastes, textures, sounds, and smells in *descriptive details*. Descriptive details use *concrete words and expressions—as opposed to abstract words and expressions.*

To see the difference, let's study some definitions and examples. Concrete words name things—for example, *water, rocks, roses, skunks* are concrete words; they almost force your reader to see and touch objects that have real existence. Concrete words bring ideas down to earth. *Abstract words,* by contrast, describe qualities common to a *group* of things—*beauty, toughness, difficulty.* They also name spiritual, intellectual, or emotional states—*honesty, immorality, fear.* Instead of being down to earth, like concrete words, abstract words get very far away from the real world. *So the good writer always searches for the most concrete word as he develops his ideas.*

However, we must make one thing quite clear: words are only *relatively* concrete, or *relatively* abstract—that is, they are rather like general and specific statements. We have seen that some statements are more general, some less general; in the same way, we should note that some words are more abstract, some less abstract. *Only things are truly concrete.*

Take off your wrist watch, for example. Hold it, and you can feel that it's cold and smooth and hard; look at it, and you can see that it has a definite color, shape, and texture. *The watch itself is concrete; the words we use to talk about it are only relatively concrete.* We can, in fact, go from the watch itself up a ladder of words that becomes progressively less concrete and more abstract. We begin with the concrete thing; we call it a *wrist watch*—and already we are less concrete. We can see it as a *timepiece* (more abstract); as a *machine* (still more abstract); or as a *manufactured product* (most abstract). From these words we could climb to the attributes of *manufactured products*—*beauty* or *utility,* for instance; and we would then be *still* more abstract. But the important point is that the most concrete word, like the hardest and brightest diamond, is the best.

Putting concrete words to work, George Orwell uses *descriptive details* (here italicized) to paint the difference between "the filthy little scullery" and the dining room of a Parisian restaurant:

> It was amusing to look round the *filthy little scullery* and think that only a *double door* was between us and the *dining-room.* There sat the *customers* in all their splendour—spotless tablecloths, bowls of *flowers, mirrors* and *gilt cornices* and *painted cherubim*; and here, just a *few feet* away, we in our *disgusting filth.* For it really was *disgusting filth.* There was no time to sweep the *floor* till evening, and

we slithered about in a compound of *soapy water, lettuce-leaves, torn paper* and *trampled food*. A *dozen waiters* with their *coats* off, showing their *sweaty armpits*, sat at the *table* mixing *salads* and sticking their *thumbs* into the *cream pots*. The *room* had a *dirty, mixed smell* of *food* and *sweat*. Everywhere in the *cupboards*, behind the *piles* of *crockery*, were *squalid stores* of *food* that the *waiters* had stolen. There were only *two sinks*, and *no washing basin*, and it was nothing unusual for a *waiter* to wash his *face* in the *water* in which *clean crockery* was rinsing. But the *customers* saw nothing of this. There were a *coco-nut mat* and a *mirror* outside the *dining-room door*, and the *waiters* used to preen themselves up and go in looking the *picture* of cleanliness.

—George Orwell, *Down and Out in Paris and London*[8]

As a final note: *remind yourself to use descriptive details with all the other techniques of development.*

EXERCISE 3

A. Arrange the words in each of the following groups in the order of abstractness. List them from the most abstract to the most concrete.

1. Food   veal chops   beef   Gross National Product
2. Abraham Lincoln   man   President   human being
3. Voice   "Hi!"   sound   vibrations
4. Life   flora   tree   redwood
5. Beauty   women   Sophia Loren   femme fatale
6. Machine   Cadillac   vehicle   car
7. Cattle   livestock   cow   assets
8. College   education   Harvard   school
9. *Saturday Review*   communication   magazine   publication
10. Natural entity   diamond   mineral   jewel

B. Write a very concrete paragraph, developed by descriptive details, on one of the following topics. Begin your paragraph with a sharply focused topic sentence. Be sure that each succeeding sentence is directly related to your focus.

1. Describe the appearance of someone you like very much.
2. Describe the appearance of an unusual room.

3. Describe an effective printed advertisement.
4. Describe a sunset.
5. Describe your car—or the car you would like to have.

Factual Details

Use factual details to present objective historical information or evidence obtained by scientific procedures.

To use factual details properly, you need to be able to distinguish between facts and judgments. The fact is external and objective; the judgment is internal and subjective. The fact represents merely what has happened; the judgment interprets, evaluates, and classifies what happened. The fact is more specific; the judgment is more general. Facts are stated in concrete words; judgments are stated in abstract words.

For instance:

Fact: The Golden Gate Bridge was completed in 1937.
Judgment: The Golden Gate Bridge is the most beautiful bridge in the world.

Fact: Jonathan brought his mother a bouquet of roses.
Judgment: Jonathan loves his mother.

Fact: Lisa has dark eyes, tawny hair, and an olive complexion.
Judgment: Lisa is a beautiful girl.

Fact: The Cincinnati Reds won the pennant in 1970.
Judgment: The Cincinnati Reds are the best team in the National league.

Fact: LSD is a psychedelic drug.
Judgment: LSD is a sure road to self-discovery.

Fact: Gene Fowler has published three books of poetry: *Field Studies, Shaman Songs*, and *Her Majesty's Ship*.
Judgment: Gene Fowler is one of the best young poets writing in America today.

Other statements combine fact and judgment; they overlap both categories.

Her father says Lisa is a beautiful girl.

Some critics have asserted that Gene Fowler is the best young poet writing in America today.

Each of these statements can be verified simply by checking the sources, but each also includes a judgment. In the same way, the following statements lie in a shadowy realm between fact and judgment.

The Rolls Royce Silver Cloud is an expensive car.

Football is a rugged game.

Obviously words like *expensive* and *rugged* are relative terms. For most college English teachers, the Rolls Royce Silver Cloud is a *very* expensive car, but would it seem expensive to an Arabian multimillionaire? Compared with ice hockey, is football a rugged game? But we could show that the Silver Cloud is expensive by quoting facts about its purchase cost and maintenance expenses, just as we could use the number of serious injuries in the National Football League during the last ten seasons to show that football is a rugged game. We can prove both statements by factual details.

In the following paragraph, Sir Julian Huxley combines facts, judgments, and semifactual statements: he asserts in his topic sentence that "Science is exploding even more violently than population"; he supports this semifactual statement in sentences 2, 3, and 4 by statistical evidence (physical fact). In sentence 5 he makes three judgments based on the factual evidence in the paragraph.

(1) Science is exploding even more violently than population. (2) Scientists (including technicians) are multiplying over three times as fast as ordinary people. (3) The 1,000,000 or so scientists now at work constitute over 90 percent of all the scientists who have ever lived, and their numbers may well go up to 20,000,000 or even 30,000,000 by A.D. 1999. (4) The number of scientific journals has increased from one in 1665—*The Philosophical Transactions of the Royal Society*—to about 1000 in 1865, to over 50,000 in 1965, in which nearly 5,000,000 separate articles are published each year; and the rate of increase is itself increasing. (5) If nothing is done about it, science runs the risk of drowning in this torrent of paper; specialization will make scientists in one field more ignorant of work in other fields; and man's advance will be stifled in the mounting mass of unassimilable knowledge that he himself has accumulated.

—Sir Julian Huxley, *The Crisis in Man's Destiny*[9]

In the next paragraph, however, instead of statistics, the writer uses an objective summary of historical fact to develop his discussion of laws governing morality in seventeenth-century Virginia:

> The early laws of Virginia forbade playing cards or throwing dice— doubtless for the good Puritan motive that they "wasted precious time." There was a fine of 50 pounds of tobacco, equivalent to a week's wages, for missing church on Sunday, when neither travel, business, nor loading of ships was allowed. Each Virginia parish was governed by a self-perpetuating vestry and two churchwardens who acted as moral policemen of the parish, like the constables of a New England town. The churchwardens presented to the county court all cases of bastardy, adultery, blasphemy, sabbath-breaking, slander, backbiting, and other "scandalous offences." County courts composed of land-owners appointed by the governor, punished by whipping, stocks, pillory, and ducking stools—rarely, by imprisonment, as that was expensive and took labor out of production. The problem of five-month babies bothered Virginia like other rural societies; for where a man depended on the labor of his children, he could not take the chance of marrying a barren woman. Virginia couples caught that way had to confess premarital intercourse in open congregation while clad in the white sheet of penitence, as in New England or Old England. And there are even cases of adulterers having to wear the scarlet letter A, and of women being punished—but never executed—for witch-craft.
>
> —Samuel Eliot Morison, *The Oxford History of the American People*[10]

In short, then, *use factual details as especially convincing evidence for the main idea stated in the topic sentence.*

EXERCISE   4

A.   Identify each of the following statements as fact or judgment, or as an example of both fact and judgment.

1. Ross Macdonald writes detective novels featuring a private investigator named Lew Archer.

2. *Playboy* is a silly, nasty, pornographic publication.
3. Cigarette packages, as required by federal law, are labeled: "Warning: The Surgeon General has determined that cigarette smoking is dangerous to your health."
4. Cigarette smoking inevitably causes lung cancer, cardiovascular diseases, or emphysema.
5. Only a fool would play the stock market.
6. Will slept for fifteen minutes while his class discussed the social implications of motion pictures.
7. By the year 2000 A.D. the United States will be so densely populated that each of us will have only four square feet of living space.
8. Augustus Toplady, an extremely minor figure in eighteenth century English literature, wrote the hymn "Rock of Ages."
9. As an institution, marriage resembles a prison—easy to enter, impossible to live in, and hazardous to escape from.
10. In the United States, the total yearly cost of automobile accidents rose from $6.4 billion in 1959 to $16.5 billion in 1969.
11. Most automobiles are unsafe at any speed.
12. Members of the women's liberation movement are usually horse-faced, wall-eyed, flat-chested, knock-kneed, and flat-footed.
13. Merle Haggard is a great songwriter and a brilliant musician.
14. He staggered out of a bar; obviously he was drunk.
15. She was so sweet and clean—she smelled of warm apples and ocean-spray.
16. Writing is one of life's great mysteries.
17. I got close enough to him to smell the garlic and wine and to see the open pores in his nose.
18. Negroes have a native ability to dance and make music.
19. It was a terrible storm: four inches of rain fell in two days.
20. The word *paper* is derived from the Greek *papyros*, the name of the reed from which paper was made in ancient Egypt.

B. Write a completely objective report developed by actual details on one of the following topics. Try to report only on what happened without interpreting or evaluating what happened. Although the phrasing of some topics involves judgment words—*dishonest, dull, painful*—these are intended only to guide you toward a subject. In neither your title nor your topic sentence should you use words that betray your feelings or state your opinions. Don't, for instance, entitle your paper "A Painful Event"; you might use, instead, the title "A Childhood Memory."

1. A dishonest act
2. A dull evening
3. A painful event
4. First love
5. A death in the family

Before writing your paper, carefully study the example presented here (on the subject "A Painful Event") to show how a writer can report objectively on events that arouse deep feelings.

A Childhood Memory

A scene I remember most vividly from my childhood occurred one summer afternoon when I was twelve years old. My aunt and uncle and four cousins had come to stay with us, and we boys had spent the afternoon playing baseball in the dusty streets as the temperature rose to 98° on the thermometer by the back door. Suddenly, in the late afternoon, I smelled meat frying; my stomach began to ache, and I ran into the kitchen for a glass of water. My mother was bent over the stove; on the counter, next to the sink, was an empty Spam can. I looked at it, and my mouth watered as I smelled the meat frying. *Spam and gravy, mashed potatoes and salad!* I wondered how many slices of Spam I would get—there were eleven of us, after all, and my father and uncle would serve themselves first. My stomach hurt worse than before. I set the glass of water down and asked my mother where my aunt and uncle were. They were having supper with my grandmother, she said. My stomach stopped hurting so much, but my mouth was dry, and I walked out into the backyard and down the street to the baseball game with a little smile on my face. I walked over to the battered piece of plywood that served for homeplate. Tommy was batting. "Tommy," I said, "listen, Tommy, your mother just called and said you and Ralph and Bobby and Walter have to go to Grandma's house for dinner. She said to hurry." They hurried. Gene and Jerry and I carried the ball and bat back to the house. I had three pieces of Spam, after I told my mother that my cousins had gone to Grandma's for supper. I chewed each piece very slowly, and hungry as I was, it seemed hard to swallow, and I have never eaten Spam again.

C.   Write a brief paragraph (about 150 words) in which you support your opinion, as expressed in the topic sentence, by objective evidence drawn from a recent newspaper or news-magazine article *developed mainly by factual details.* For instance, having read that the war in Vietnam is costing American taxpayers over $2000 per minute, you might express this opinion in your topic sentence: "Certainly there are many good reasons for ending the war in Vietnam, but one of the best reasons, in this period of domestic crises, is that the war is tremendously expensive." In the rest of the paragraph, you would support your opinion by details drawn from an article on the cost of the war.

You may choose an article on any subject, but be sure that the article itself is *objectively developed by factual details.* Note that this assignment will provide a further test of your ability to distinguish between facts and opinions.

Hand in the article with your paragraph.

Illustration

Use illustration to clarify your main idea.

For student writers, *illustration* is probably the most flexible, most practical, and most useful type of development. Combined with descriptive details, illustrations set forth concrete instances— examples, anecdotes, or analogies—to show what the writer means; they give tentative evidence explaining why he holds his opinions. Unlike factual details, illustrations do not *prove* anything; they do what their name implies: they *illustrate.*

MULTIPLE EXAMPLES

An example is a specific instance, a typical case, a piece selected to show the nature or character of the whole.

In developing a paragraph by multiple examples, begin with a sharply focused topic sentence, as usual, and then illustrate the generalization by several specific instances.

Take, for example, the following paragraph. James Harvey Robinson *illustrates* an opinion with multiple examples. His opinion is that all men, including the world's greatest thinkers, indulge in *reverie,* a free association of ideas much like an idle daydream. Obviously, no one can *prove* that all men think in a certain way, but one can offer fairly convincing examples—in this case, Aristotle, Diogenes, and Tennyson:

> . . . The reverie goes on all the time not only in the mind of the mill hand and the Broadway flapper, but equally in weighty judges and godly bishops. It has gone on in all the philosophers, scientists, poets, and theologians that have ever lived. Aristotle's most abstruse speculations were doubtless tempered by highly irrelevant reflections. He is reported to have had very thin legs and small eyes, for which he doubtless had to find excuses, and he was wont to indulge in very conspicuous dress and rings and was accustomed to arrange his hair carefully. Diogenes the cynic exhibited the impudence of a touchy soul. His tub was his distinction. Tennyson in beginning his "Maud" could not forget his chagrin over losing his patrimony years before as the result of an unhappy investment in the Patent Decorative Carving Company. These facts are not recalled here as a gratuitous disparagement of the truly great, but to insure a full realization of the tremendous competition which all really exacting thought has to face, even in the minds of the most highly endowed mortals.
> —James Harvey Robinson, *The Mind in the Making*[11]

Here, in another excellent paragraph, Richard D. Altick uses four examples to show that the greatest literary scholars, two generations ago, were "characters":

> Obviously there is no such person as a "typical" literary scholar, and there never has been. But it is remarkable that the greatest scholars two generations ago were, seemingly without exception, "characters". . . The pioneer medieval scholar and simplified spelling enthusiast F. J. Furnivall liked to scull on the Thames, while his long white whiskers streamed out behind him. The most famous of American scholars, George Lyman Kittredge, who was reputed to dip his beard in laundry bluing, strode across Harvard Square against the lights in defiance of trucks and streetcars ("Look out there, Santy Claus," cried the drivers and motormen), had a marvelous knack of timing his lecture and making his exit from the classroom so that his last word and his students' last glimpse of him chimed with the bell, held midnight conferences over cigars at his home which are fondly remembered by hundreds of his one-time graduate students, and had habits of leisure reading that resulted in the Harvard library's acquiring over the years one of the world's finest collection of detective fiction. An Anglo-Saxon specialist almost killed the graduate study of English in one of our great universities because he insisted on teaching all the courses himself; and another great American medievalist

lost his hat at a meeting of the Modern Language Association many years ago, when he was rosily under the influence, and thereby started a famous legend.

—Richard D. Altick, *The Scholar Adventurers*[12]

EXTENDED EXAMPLES

When a paragraph is developed by *one long example instead of several brief ones*, the writer uses an *extended example*, as in the following paragraph by Jacques Ellul, who argues that "all technical progress contains unforeseeable effects":

> The most elementary example of the unforeseeable effects of technical progress is furnished by drugs. You have a cold in the head; you take an aspirin. The headache disappears, but aspirin has other actions besides doing away with headaches. In the beginning we were really oblivious of these side effects; but, I should imagine, by now everyone has read articles warning against the use of aspirin because of its possible effects, say, on the blood picture. Grave hemorrhages have appeared in people who habitually took two or three aspirins daily. Yet aspirin was thought the perfect remedy a scant ten years ago— on the ground that no side effects were to be feared. Now such effects begin to appear in what was, and is, probably the most harmless of all drugs.
>
> —Jacques Ellul, *Technological Progress Is Always Ambiguous*[13]

Since the extended example offers even less evidence than multiple examples, it does not *prove* the generalization in the topic sentence: instead, it clarifies by putting the general idea in a vivid instance.

ANECDOTE

An anecdote is an example in the form of a story, a brief narrative told to illustrate the writer's point.

Anecdotes differ from extended examples in two important ways. First, anecdotes are frequently (though not always) humorous; second, anecdotes are more dramatic: they paint a scene much like what you might see on stage or in a movie, with people acting and talking in a specific setting. For instance, watch Joseph Wechsberg using an anecdote in his article "The Lore and Lure of Roulette." He has already set the scene: the plush, elegant casinos of Monte Carlo. He has already said that most of the tales of fantastic winnings are mere folklore. But, he believes, "miracles *do* happen in Monte Carlo." He illustrates this topic sentence with an anecdote:

> . . . But miracles *do* happen in Monte Carlo. Years ago at the elegant Summer Sporting Club, where roulette tables are on the terrace, the croupier said, "Rien ne va plus," when a 100-franc chip dropped down from heaven and fell into the slot of number eight. A second later the ball fell into the slot of number eight. A lady on the balcony who had lost all her money had found another chip in her purse, got mad and threw it over the balustrade. She won 3500 francs, came down to collect, stayed at the table and lost everything. That's a true story, and a sad one.
>
> —Joseph Wechsberg, *The Lore and Lure of Roulette*[14]

In "The Vestige of God," Milton Mayer opens with an anecdote to explain what he means by "the irresistible imperative to right action." Because he uses the anecdote to dramatize his point, he places the topic sentence at the beginning of the second paragraph.

> During the Nazi occupation of Norway, a Norwegian schoolgirl, twelve years old, was caught smuggling food to Russian soldiers held as prisoners of war. The camp was only half a mile from school, and the knowledge was notorious that the prisoners were being starved. The girl was brought before a Gestapo interrogator, who asked her if she knew that her activity was illegal. She said she did. Why, then, did she do it? "Because," she said, "I have been taught that I must feed hungry people." "But," said the interrogator, "these Russians are not people; they are beasts." "I was also taught," said the girl, "that I must feed hungry beasts."
>
> In this anecdote—it happens to be true, but no matter—I sense the irresistible imperative to right action . . . .
>
> —Milton Mayer, *The Vestige of God*[15]

HYPOTHETICAL ILLUSTRATION

From time to time you may need to *invent* examples or anecdotes to illustrate your ideas. That is, you may want to use a *hypothetical illustration*. To be quite honest with your reader, you should inform him, either directly or indirectly, that your illustration is faithful to your experience, but not literally true. You might do that directly by writing, "Here is a hypothetical example." Or you might do it indirectly by planting some obvious clue. For instance, the writer of the next paragraph tells us *indirectly* that his example is just a hypothetical case. In defining the word *egghead*, he uses the example of a young man by the name of Jonathan Square. Only the dullest reader could be taken in by this transparent name.

> An egghead is anyone who seems to be so absorbed in the pursuit of knowledge that he hardly sees the obvious pleasures of life—watching *Peyton Place* three times a week, "getting wasted" on Saturday night, and lying to your parents about your reasons for staggering home at three in the morning when curfew is at twelve sharp. Instead of living, the egghead thinks. For example, consider Jonathan Square. Does he ever date girls, go to dances, watch television, or listen to "together" music? The answer is definitely "No!" When I see him in the hall each morning, his head is bent, his feet shuffle lethargically, his back twists into a question mark above the twelve books under his right arm; his appearance unequivocally suggests lofty contemplation. At noon, while everyone else gossips and giggles, Jon Square sits silently in a corner, thumbing the worn pages of a massive philosophy text; from time to time, his eyes glaze over like a lizard's. And what he does in the evening is no secret to anyone; while Mozart tinkles away, or Beethoven blares, Jonathan Square nods and dreams over his books or reflects on the human condition and the sadness of a world without joy.

EXERCISE 5

Choose one of the subjects from one of the groups below for development in a paragraph of 150-200 words. Having chosen a subject, write a sharply focused topic sentence. Then illustrate your topic sentence in the way indicated.

A. Multiple examples
  1. Ideas in contemporary music (use several songs as examples)
  2. A trend in styling the latest cars (use several cars as examples)
  3. Disadvantages of falling in love while attending college (use several students as examples)
  4. The heroes of the young (use several heroes as examples)

B. Extended example
  1. A typical "swinger"

2. The liberal treatment of sex in a recent movie
3. The perfect student
4. An ideal companion

C.   Anecdote
1. How *not* to behave on a date
2. A good way to get revenge on an enemy
3. An event that taught you to respect (or disrespect) policemen
4. One of the cruelest things you ever did

ANALOGY

Like examples and anecdotes, analogies *illustrate.*

Use analogies to explain the unfamiliar in terms of the familiar. That is, use them to explain unfamiliar ideas or describe things in a point-by-point comparison with something your reader will know better.

In some ways, of course, analogies are simply figures of speech that have been stretched out. "Marrying a divorced woman is like buying a used car." That's a figure of speech. If you go on to explain two or three ways in which marrying a divorced woman is like buying a used car, your figure of speech becomes an analogy.

For instance, in the following paragraph John Lear creates a graphic verbal picture of an unfamiliar object, Ranger VII, by drawing an analogy with the familiar dragonfly. An outline of the four points in the comparison briefly summarizes the similarities:

Ranger VII	*Dragonfly*
Camera lenses	Eyes
Taking photographs	Blinking Eyes
Radio antenna	Nose
Stabilizers	Wings

They made a robot in the shape of a dragonfly and named it Ranger VII, thereby expressing their hope that it would range the face of the moon. For eyes, they gave it camera lenses, and taught it how to photograph by blinking the shutters. Near the place where its nose should have been, they put a radio antenna like a saucer, and taught the robot how to send pictures back through the saucer to the earth. When all this was done, they folded the dragonfly's wings, set the mechanical insect on top of a rocket, and fired the rocket into orbit around the earth. Finally they shot the robot out of the orbit, told it to unfold its wings, and pointed it onto a curving path across 243,665 miles of sky. The path ended in a dry lunar lakebed that hadn't been thought important enough to be named.

—John Lear, *What the Moon Ranger Couldn't See*[16]

You can also use an analogy to develop a point in an argument. Here is an example of how that's done. Erich Fromm is trying to prove that one bad decision leads to another bad decision, until finally we are trapped. He writes:

A good illustration of the principle involved here is the game of chess. Assuming that two equally skilled players begin a game, both have the same chance of winning . . . in other words, each has the same freedom to win. After, say, five moves the picture is already different. Both still *can* win, but A, who has made a better move, already has a greater chance of winning. He has as it were more freedom to win than his opponent, B. Yet B is still free to win. After some more moves, A, having continued to make correct moves that were not effectively countered by B, is almost sure to win, but only *almost*. B *can* still win. After some further moves, the game is decided. B, provided he is a skilled player, recognizes that he has no longer the freedom to win; he sees that he had already lost before he is actually checkmated . . . .

—Erich Fromm, *The Heart of Man*[17]

Unless you have a good reason for being subtle, it is best to make a simple point-by-point comparison in an analogy, as in this paragraph comparing an over-dressed woman with a circus horse.

An over-dressed woman is like a circus horse. Just as the circus horse is bedecked with gaudy plumes and fine trappings, so the over-dressed woman turns herself out in flashy furs and tight, shiny dresses. The circus horse is dressed for a performance. In the same way, an over-dressed woman intends to display her "beauty" and to dazzle and delight all her spectators. But, just as the circus horse entertains by its novelty, so the over-dressed woman amuses the people who watch her —not by her loveliness or her grace but by her burlesque of real beauty.

EXERCISE 6

Write a brief paragraph developed by analogy on one of the following subjects. Three or four points of comparison (five or six sentences) will be enough.

1. Falling in love is like . . .
2. Going on a blind date is like . . .
3. Buying a used car is like . . .
4. A college is like . . .
5. Marrying a divorced woman is like . . .
6. Preparing an interesting meal is like . . .
7. Catching a boyfriend (girlfriend) is like . . .
8. Finding a job is like . . .
9. In relation to his subjects, a king is like . . .
10. A student without discipline is like . . .
11. Censorship of books is like . . .
12. Finding a book in the library is like . . .
13. Choosing new clothes is like . . .
14. Learning a foreign language is like . . .
15. Watching television is like . . .
16. Losing a boyfriend (girlfriend) is like . . .
17. Getting out of bed in the morning is like . . .
18. Attending a psychedelic light show is like . . .
19. Pornography is like . . .
20. A hard-working student is like . . .

Definition

"I don't know what you mean by 'glory,' " Alice said.

Humpty Dumpty smiled contemptuously. "Of course you don't— till I tell you. I mean 'there's a nice knock-down argument for you!' "

"But 'glory' doesn't mean 'a nice knock-down argument,' " Alice objected.

"When I use a word," said Humpty Dumpty, in rather a scornful tone, "it means just what I choose it to mean, neither more nor less."

"The question is," said Alice, "whether you *can* make words mean so many different things."

"The question is," said Humpty Dumpty, "which is to be master— that's all."

—Lewis Carroll, *Through the Looking Glass*

Like Humpty Dumpty, we all want to be masters of words— and the first step towards mastery is learning to define them.

Later we'll come to the point of this discussion: *definition is a common, effective technique for developing paragraphs.* At the beginning, however, let's look closely at what a definition does and study some of the ways it can and should be written.

The general rule for defining can be stated simply: *define words by putting them into more concrete words.* Besides this general rule for defining, you should learn the following *methods.*

DEFINITION BY EXAMPLE

Definition by example explains a term by offering a specific instance of it. "Baseball is an example of a game." Such definitions, obviously, are meaningful only insofar as the reader knows something of both the term and the example. For instance, how well do you understand the following definitions?

A folk etymology is a word or a phrase like *Amazon* or *curry favor.*

A blend is a word like *slanguage* or *motel.*

Finnegans Wake is an example of "stream-of-consciousness" novel.

Only the reader who already knows, for instance, that a blend is a combination of two words (i.e., that *slanguage* = *slang* + *language*) will be able to decipher the definition of blend. For many readers, the other definitions would certainly be unclear. We can conclude, then, that definition by example merely hints at the meaning of a word instead of laying it out explicitly.

DEFINITION BY ETYMOLOGY

This kind of defining traces the early history of a word to find its etymology or derivation. In these simple but vivid examples, definition by etymology digs up the concrete ruins buried under some rather abstract terms.

> *Bigot* derives from the Spanish phrase *hombre de bigote*, literally "man with a mustache." Because this phrase characterized a man of spirit—a man who had firm, forceful opinions—the word *bigot* came to mean "a person whose views are fixed, unchangeable, intolerant."
>
> *Chrysostomic*, meaning "eloquent," is a compound of the Greek roots *chrysos*, "gold," and *stomat-*, "mouth." The eloquent man is *chrysostomic*—"a man with a golden mouth."
>
> The Greeks constructed some tombs from a limestone that caused a rapid disintegration of the body; hence *sarco-*, "flesh," and *phagein*, "to eat," were brought together in *sarcophagus*—a "flesh-eating" grave.

Definition by etymology does not give the exact meaning of any term; instead, it makes the term easier to understand by unfolding some concrete details of its history.

DEFINITION BY SYNONYM

The most concise method of definition defines by synonyms (etymologically, "together words"). Here are some examples of definition by synonym:

> *Sleazy* means "dirty, grimy, or filthy."
>
> The slang expression to *sizzle* means "to be electrocuted."
>
> A *fylfot* is a *"swastika."*
>
> *Temulent* means "drunken."

Definition by synonym works by explaining "hard" words with "easy" words. Obviously, since no two words have exactly the same meaning, this kind of defining gives only a close approximation of the meaning of a term.

DEFINITION BY CLASS AND DIFFERENTIATION

The most exact, and consequently the most important kind of definition, is the *logical definition*, which explains the meaning of a term by placing it in a class and then showing how it differs from all other members of that class. For example:

Term	Class	Differentiation
Mononucleosis	is a *disease*	usually transmitted by kissing and characterized by the presence in the blood of an excessive number of cells having a single nucleus; college students are particularly susceptible.
A company man	is an *employee*	usually a white-collar worker, whose loyalty to his employers is greater than his loyalty to his fellow employees.
A jar	is a *container*	made of glass, stone, or earthenware, usually cylindrical, with a large opening and no spout; some jars have handles.

The logical definition views two aspects of the term being defined: first, it views the *general aspect* by fitting the term into a class; second, it views the *particular aspect* by showing the details that make the term different from all other members of that class. Although the examples listed above *separate* these two aspects, a brief logical defiinition may combine them. For instance, Aristotle defines *man* by saying, "Man is a rational animal." This logical definition places the term in the class "animal" (the general aspect) and then distinguishes it from all other members of the class by adding "rational" (the particular aspect). Other brief logical definitions use the same procedure: "a *gaffer* is an old man," for instance, or "a *grimalkin* is an old she-cat."

Errors in Definition

Before writing *any* definitions, you should learn to recognize certain common errors in definition:

1.   *Nonparallel Grammatical Form.* Both the term to be defined and the definition must use the same grammatical structure. That is, verbs should be defined by verbs, nouns by nouns, adjectives by adjectives, adverbs by adverbs, etc.

Noun:
WRONG: *Flirtation* means "to play at love."
RIGHT: *Flirtation* means "the act of playing at love."

Adjective:
WRONG: *Ineffable* means "that which cannot be spoken."
RIGHT: *Ineffable* means "unspeakable."

Verb:
WRONG: To *cogitate* is "thinking."
RIGHT: To *cogitate* is "to think."

One form of this error in defining is so common and so illogical that it requires special attention—the use of *is when* or *is where*. *When* indicates time; *where* identifies location; and neither word should be used in defining unless time or place is part of the definition. A further objection is that such constructions often violate formal grammar and therefore offend your instructor's sense of propriety. It would be indiscrete, of course, to point out to him that Robert Cawdrey, in his *Table Alphabeticall of Hard Words* (1604), used *is-when* and *is-where* definitions whenever he felt so inclined: Cawdrey could hardly spell, either.

WRONG: *Flirtation is when* you play at love.
Flirting is where you play at love.

RIGHT: *Flirtation* is "the act of playing at love."
Flirting is "playing at love."

2. *Circular Definitions.* In the definition, do not repeat the term or a derivative of it. To define *existentialism* as "the philosophy of an existentialist" is not very helpful. And your reader will scarcely understand *lambency* when the term is defined as "the quality of being lambent."

3. *Highly Technical Definitions.* Be sure that your definitions actually clarify instead of obscuring the term. Dr. Johnson's definition of *network*, often quoted to illustrate this point, is beautifully precise and succinct—and virtually impenetrable: "Any thing reticulated or decussated, at equal distances, with interstices between the intersections." And a truly determined pedant could smother a simple term like *bicycle* under a landslide of Latin and Greek by defining it, for instance, as "a conveyance consisting of a tubular ferrous frame, mounted on two macroscopic azoic rims connected by spokes to a central hub and covered by a vulcanized pneumatic hydrocarbon, propelled by the crural dynamism of the rider."

4. *Improper Classification.* In writing a logical definition, you should take care to place the term in a *class* that is neither too general nor too specific.

	Term	Class	Differentiation
TOO GENERAL:	A *sextant* is a	*thing*	used for measuring the altitudes of the stars from a moving ship or airplane.
EXACT:	A *sextant* is an	*instrument*	for measuring the altitudes of celestial bodies from a moving ship or airplane.
TOO SPECIFIC:	A *parody* is a	*poem*	which imitates the language and style of another work for comic effect or in ridicule, often with certain peculiarities greatly heightened or exaggerated.
EXACT:	A *parody* is a	*writing*	which imitates the language and style of another work for comic effect or in ridicule, often with certain peculiarities greatly heightened or exaggerated.

In the examples above, *thing* is too general a class, since it comprehends many diverse concerns, acts, entities, utensils, details, etc. *Instrument*, on the other hand, precisely designates an implement or utensil.

Poem is too specific: as a class, it excludes other kinds of parodies, such as prose parodies; hence the more comprehensive term, *writing*, better serves as the class in this definition. It is important to note, however, that we have still defined only one group of parodies: under a second heading, most dictionaries would also define musical parodies.

5. *Improper Differentiation.* Like the classification, the differentiating details should be neither too specific nor too general. If you define a poet as "a person who writes rhymed, rhythmical lines," your differentiation is *too specific*: it excludes, for example, poets who do not use rhyme. On the other hand, if you define a poet as "a person who creates literature," your differentiation is *too general*, since it does not distinguish poets from other literary artists (novelists, for instance). A poet is better defined as "a person who writes verse."

EXERCISE   7

A.   Indicate which of the methods of definition is used in each of the following: Example, Etymology, Synonym, or Class and Differentiation.

1. *Circumscribe* is a compound of the Latin prefix *circum*, "around," and the root *scribere*, "to write."
2. *Centrifugal Bumble-puppy* is "a children's game played with a chrome-steel tower and a ball thrown so as to land on a platform at the top of the tower, roll down into the interior, fall onto a revolving disc, be hurled through a hole in the casing, and be caught by one of the players surrounding the tower."
3. A *lexicographer* is "A writer of dictionaries; a harmless drudge, that busies himself in tracing the original, and detailing the signification of words."—Samuel Johnson
4. *To decimate* is "to destroy almost completely."
5. A *parable is* "a short, simple story from which a moral may be drawn."
6. Tranquillity means "calmness; peacefulness; serenity; quiet."
7. A *symbol* is something like a flag.
8. *Lilliputian* means "very small; tiny."
9. *Metaphor* derives from Greek *meta-*, "beyond, across," + *pherein,* "to carry."
10. A *metaphor* is "a figure of speech in which one thing is likened to another, different thing by being spoken of as if it were that other."

B.   Identify each error in the definitions below as one of the following types:

Nonparallel grammatical form

Circular definition

Highly technical definition

Improper classification

Improper differentiation

Note: some definitions contain more than one error.

1. A *bed* is "a thing people sleep in."
2. "My only conception of the poet is that he is a person who writes poetry."—Mark Van Doren

3. A *network* is "Any thing reticulated or decussated, at equal distances, with interstices between the intersections."—Samuel Johnson
4. *Mortal* means "to die."
5. A *parody* is "a poem which imitates the language and style of another work for comic effect or in ridicule, often with certain peculiarities greatly heightened or exaggerated."
6. A *genealogist* is when you have your family tree traced back as far as possible.
7. A fork is "an instrument or implement used for eating."
8. *Chimerical* means "relating to or being like a chimera."
9. *To somnambulate* means "walking around in a trance-like state while asleep."
10. An *allegory* is "where a writer tells two stories at the same time, one on a literal level and one on an allegorical level."
11. *Gobbledygook* is "language characterized by altiloquence, turgidity, teratology, orotundity, rodomontade, lexiphanicism, tautology, and bombastic sesquipedalianism.
12. "Hope is the thing with feathers."—Emily Dickinson
13. "Let me therefore define tolerance as tolerating other people even when they don't tolerate you."—E. M. Forster
14. *Vacillating* means "to sway to and fro."
15. A *saw* is "a doo-dad used for cutting."

C.   In your dictionary, find the etymological meaning of each of the following words.

1. Inspect
2. Symposium
3. Manufacture
4. Paragraph
5. Imply

D.   Define each of the following words by synonym. Write a complete sentence and *be sure to use proper parallel structure.*

1. Temerity
2. Verbose
3. To harangue
4. Pungently
5. Euphemistic

E.   Without referring to your dictionary, write a logical definition of *three* of the following terms. Use complete sentences.

1. A fork
2. A guitar
3. A pencil
4. A sportscar
5. A circle

F.   After studying the clues provided in the following sentences, define the term *spadlush* by placing it in a class and then differentiating it from all other members of that class.

1. I put five gallons of gasoline in my *spadlush*.
2. All three tires on my *spadlush* were flat.
3. The sparkplug on my *spadlush* is not arcing.
4. My *spadlush* goes only 35 miles per hour, but it's fun to drive anyway.
5. Driving back in my *spadlush*, I got wet when it started to rain; but the groceries stayed dry in the sidecart.

Writing the Extended Definition

The paragraph developed by definition may combine any of the ways of defining to explain terms in full and adequate detail. Instead of surveying all of the means of extending definitions, we will use three examples to suggest some of the many possible combinations. The first two examples attempt merely to clarify the term; the third argues for the writer's definition, and its purpose is not only to clarify but to convince.

1. Logical Definition + Example with Concrete Descriptive Details

A Happening, in case you don't know it, is the first formless art form. Things just *happen*. For example, eighty naked men come out and squirt each other with fire hoses containing tinted yogurt. Then eighty more naked men come out and light birthday candles in the navels of the first eighty men. Then one girl, clothed, comes out and pulls three thousand feet of sausage casing through her pierced ear. Then eighty more naked men come out and eat a station wagon.

There is, of course, a musical accompaniment to all these fun things. Usually it is "Begin the Beguine," played by 26 trench mortars, a drop forge, and a rooster.

—Max Shulman, *Requiem for a Square*"[18]

2. Etymology + Synonym + Descriptive Details + Quotation (Expert Testimony)

Flirtation is a slippery word, definable as much by your own attitude as by the dictionary. According to Webster it probably derives from the Old French *fleureter*, "to move lightly from flower to flower," and means "to play at love." Playing at love, however, can mean almost anything you choose: from a slightly longer than necessary handshake to a kiss on the lips, from an intellectual conversation to a whispered invitation to lunch; from a meaningful glance across a crowded room to an outright proposition. Essentially it is sexual—not in fact, but in feeling. "Flirting," one wife stated, "is a way of saying, 'I'm a woman and you're a man; I know that you know it and you know that I know it.' "

—Norman M. Lobsenz, *The Innocent Game that Disrupts Marriage*[19]

3. Logical Definition + Etymology + Elaborated Logical Definition + Example

What, therefore, is a cliché? Perhaps intellectual and intelligent opinion has not yet been so far crystallized as to justify a definition. The *Oxford English Dictionary* says that it is "a stereotyped expression, a commonplace phrase." I should . . . like to enlarge on that definition and render it more practical, more comprehensive. The origin of the term may help, for as Littré shows, *cliché* is the substantivized participle of *clicher*, a variant of *cliquer*, "to click"; *clicher* is a die-sinker's term for "to strike melted lead in order to obtain a cast"; hence, a cliché is a stereotyped expression—a phrase "on tap" as it were—and this derivative sense, which has been current in France since the early eighties, came to England *ca.* 1890. *Revenons à nos moutons* (cliché). A cliche is an outworn commonplace; a phrase, or short sentence, that has become so hackneyed that careful speakers and scrupulous writers shrink from it because they feel that its use is an insult to the intelligence of their audience or public: "a coin so battered by use as to be defaced" (George Baker). Clichés range from flyblown phrases ("much of a muchness"; "to all intents and purposes"), metaphors that are now pointless ("lock, stock and barrel"), formulas that have become mere counters ("far be it from me to . . .")—through sobriquets that have lost all their freshness and most of their significance ("the Iron Duke")—to quotations that are nauseating ("cups that cheer but not inebriate"), and foreign phrases that are tags ("*longo intervallo*," "*bete noire*").

—Eric Partridge, *Dictionary of Clichés*[20]

EXERCISE   8

Write a one-paragraph definition (about 150-200 words) of one of the following terms. First, define the term *by class and differentiation* in your topic sentence. Next, explain its *etymology*. Then develop your paragraph in full and adequate detail by an *extended hypothetical example*. For a good illustration of how an extended hypothetical example may be used in such a paragraph of definition, study the paragraph defining *egghead* in the section on *Hypothetical Illustration* (p. 41).

1. Narcissist
2. Hippie
3. Highbrow
4. Lowbrow
5. Teeny-bopper
6. Prude
7. Introvert
8. Lothario
9. Coquette
10. Cynic

Appeal to Authority: Quotation and Paraphrase

Whenever possible, support your opinions by producing expert witnesses to testify for you; that is, use an appeal to authority.

In our time this kind of development is regarded with some suspicion, perhaps because of the unscientific way medieval thinkers bowed to the authority of ancient philosophers. There is, for instance, the story of the medieval scholar who was asked how many teeth his horse had. Instead of looking into the horse's mouth and counting the teeth, as you or I would, he said, "I don't know just off hand, but when I get home, I'll look it up in Aristotle." So long as you don't let your authorities overwhelm you, you can use the appeal to authority as an effective method of development.

For example, in arguing against censorship, you might refer to Milton's famous denunciation of censorship in *Areopagitica*; you might also quote a more recent expert—Walter Lippmann or Supreme Court Justice Woolsey. In that way you can develop your ideas and support your opinions by presenting their details, facts, illustrations, and definitions, either directly *through quotation* or indirectly *by paraphrase*. In the following paragraph from his *Introductory Lecture*, for example, A. E. Housman uses both quotation and paraphrase to support his main idea that "the acquisition of knowledge needs no formal justification."

> The acquisition of knowledge needs no formal justification: its true sanction is a much simpler affair, and inherent in itself. People are too prone to torment themselves with devising far-fetched reasons: they cannot be content with the simple truth asserted by Aristotle: "all men possess by nature a craving for knowledge" . . . . This is no rare endowment scattered sparingly from heaven that falls on a few heads and passes others by: curiosity, the desire to know things as they are, is a craving no less native to the being of man, no less universal through mankind, than the craving for food and drink. And do you suppose that such a desire means nothing? The very definition of the good, says Aristotle again, is that which all desire. Whatever is pleasant is good, unless it can be shown that in the long run it is harmful, or, in other words, not pleasant but unpleasant. Mr. Spencer himself on another subject speaks thus: "So profound an ignorance is there of the laws of life, that men do not even know that their sensations are their natural guides, and (when not rendered morbid by long continued disobedience) their trustworthy guides." The desire of knowledge does not need, nor could it possibly possess, any higher or more authentic sanction than the happiness which attends its gratification.
>
> —A. E. Housman, *Introductory Lecture*[21]

Housman's evidence for his main idea is provided largely by the quotations from Aristotle and the philosopher Herbert Spencer. But Housman also *paraphrases* Aristotle's concept of "the good": he puts the definition into his own words rather than using a direct quotation (hence the absence of quotation marks in that part of the paragraph).

How to Use Quotations and Paraphrases

We will assume that you know enough about your library to find authoritative sources or that you are willing to ask your librarian for help. Having chosen authoritative sources to support your opinions, you should use them *carefully*. That means several things. First, identify every source. You can do this most easily by working the name of your source into the body of your text—by writing, for instance, "According to Aldous Huxley in *Brave New World Revisited*, amphetamine produces undesirable physiological side-effects." Failing to identify your source *weakens* your argument and exposes you to suspicion of plagiarism (the presentation of somebody else's ideas, phrases, or organization as your own). For plagiarism you could receive an *F* on your paper or an *F* for your semester's work; you could even be expelled from school, depending on the policy of your college in such cases. *Do not fail, then, to identify your source.*

Second, choose your quotations with care. You should quote only brief, pointedly relevant passages, and these should be selected for their importance.

Finally, present most of your expert testimony by paraphrase— that is, by putting it into your own words but with the author and title of the source clearly identified. In paraphrasing, do not use even brief phrases worded exactly as in the source; these—if you use them —*must* be put in quotation marks.

To see how quotation and paraphrase from an authoritative source might be used, compare the two following passages. The first is the source; the second is developed by information from the source. In studying the second passage, *note that the source is identified, that only a few striking quotations are used, and that all other information is paraphrased in the writer's own words.*

Source

What is the relationship of *man toward himself*? I have described elsewhere this relationship as "marketing orientation." In this orientation, man experiences himself as a thing to be employed successfully on the market. He does not experience himself as an active agent, as the bearer of human powers. He is alienated from these powers. His aim is to sell himself successfully on the market. His sense of self does not stem from his activity as a loving and thinking individual, but from his socio-economic role. If things could speak, a typewriter would answer the question "Who are you?" by saying "I am a typewriter," and an automobile, by saying "I am an automobile," or more specifically by saying, "I am a Ford," or "a Buick," or "a Cadillac." If you ask a man "Who are you?", he answers "I am a manufacturer," "I am a doctor"—or "I am a married man," "I am the father of two kids," and his answer has pretty much the same meaning as that of the speaking *thing* would have. That is the way he experiences himself, not as a man, with love, fear, convictions, doubts, but as that abstraction, alienated from his real nature, which fulfills a certain function in the social system. His sense of value depends on his success: on whether he can sell himself favorably, whether he can make more of himself than he started out with, whether he is a success . . . .

—Erich Fromm, *The Sane Society*[22]

Quotation and Paraphrase

Another symptom of alienation is the tendency of modern man to view himself as a commodity to be bought and sold on the open market in competition with other commodities. According to Erich Fromm in *The Sane Society*, modern man is related through a "marketing orientation." That is, "His sense of self does not stem from his activity as a loving and thinking individual, but from his socio-economic role." Asked who he is, such a man describes his identity by saying, "I am a clerk," "I am a doctor," or "I am a married man." He speaks, in other words, as though he were a *thing*. Fromm clarifies this similarity by pointing out that if a typewriter could talk and if we asked it the question "Who are you?" it would respond, "I am a typewriter." Fromm concludes, then, that modern man has no sense of value outside of his success in selling himself. Hence his distance from his human centers—hence his alienation.

EXERCISE 9

Choose a subject from the list below and write a topic sentence presenting *both your opinion and one of the most important reasons for holding that opinion.* Make your opposition or your agreement unequivocally clear. For instance, on the subject of divorce you might write, "One of the reasons I am opposed to divorce is that in most cases it brings financial hardship to both the husband and the wife." On the subject of capital punishment you might write, "The best justification of capital punishment is that it keeps convicted murderers from ever killing again." Having selected a subject and composed a topic sentence, write a paragraph (about 150-200 words) developed by an appeal to authority (including both quotation and paraphrase). You will need to go to the library for an appropriate source.

1. The military draft
2. Legalized abortion
3. Guaranteed minimum income
4. Liberal education
5. The use of marijuana
6. Organized religion
7. Capital punishment
8. American involvement in Southeast Asia
9. Divorce
10. Pornography

Development by a Combination of Methods

Although it should be obvious that the types of development we have discussed in this chapter may be used in many possible combinations, let's now say it explicitly: *descriptive details, factual details, multiple examples, extended examples, anecdotes, analogies, definition, and quotation and paraphrase may be combined in many possible ways.* Most paragraphs, in fact, are likely to be developed by a combination of methods. Examples may include descriptive details, factual details, and definition, for instance; and the extended definition may use any of the other methods of development—in any of a large number of combinations.

In the following paragraph, the author develops his topic sentence—"Today no one bestrides our narrow world like a colossus"—by descriptive details, multiple examples, quotation from authority, and factual detail. As something of an expert on the techniques of development, you should be able to pick them out as they weave their way through this paragraph:

> Today no one bestrides our narrow world like a colossus; we have no giants who play roles which one can imagine no one else playing in their stead. There are a few figures on the margin of uniqueness, perhaps: Adenauer, Nehru, Tito, De Gaulle, Chiang Kai-shek, Mao Tse-tung. But there seem to be none in the epic style of those mighty figures of our recent past who seized history with both hands and gave it an imprint, even a direction, which it otherwise might not have had. As De Gaulle himself remarked on hearing of Stalin's death, "The age of giants is over." Whatever one thought, whether one admired or detested Roosevelt or Churchill, Stalin or Hitler, one nevertheless felt the sheer weight of such personalities on one's own existence. We feel no comparable pressures today. Our own President, with all his pleasant qualities, has more or less explicitly renounced any desire to impress his own views on history. The Macmillans, Khrushchevs and Gronchis have measurably less specific gravity than their predecessors. Other men could be in their places as leaders of America or Britain or Russia or Italy without any change in the course of history. Why ours should thus be an age without heroes, and whether this condition is good or bad for us and for civilization, are topics worthy of investigation.
>
> —Arthur M. Schlesinger, Jr., *The Decline of Greatness*[23]

IN BRIEF: THE CONCEPT AND TECHNIQUES OF DEVELOPMENT

The Concept

1. Development clarifies, illustrates, or proves the main idea stated in the topic sentence.
2. Good development depends on your ability to distinguish general statements from specific details.
3. Three paragraph patterns are developed around the difference between general and specific statements:
   (a) *A Simple Deductive Arrangement*—topic sentence plus specific details;
   (b) *A Simple Inductive Arrangement*—specific details plus topic sentence;

(c) *A Complex Deductive Arrangement*—topic sentence plus major and minor supports.

The Techniques

1. *Descriptive Details*—specific actions, appearances, tastes, smells, etc.

2. *Factual Details*—scientific measurements, statistics, historical records, objective accounts

3. *Illustration*—including:
    (a) *Multiple Examples*—typical cases, specific instances
    (b) *Extended Example*—one long example instead of several brief ones
    (c) *Anecdote*—an example in the form of a story; a brief narrative told to illustrate a point
    (d) *Hypothetical Illustrations*—examples or anecdotes *invented* for the occasion
    (e) *Analogy*—point-by-point comparison explaining the unfamiliar in terms of the familiar

4. *Definition*—explaining words, terms, and related concepts through
    (a) Example
    (b) Etymology
    (c) Synonyms
    (d) Class and Differentiation

5. *Appeals to Authority: Quotation and Paraphrase*—use of details, facts, illustrations, definitions, etc., from recognized, credible authorities

EXERCISE 10

Carefully study the development of each of the following paragraphs. Be prepared to discuss these questions about each paragraph:

a. Which sentence is the topic sentence?

b. What pattern does the paragraph follow—a simple deductive pattern, a simple inductive pattern, a complex deductive pattern? How do you know?

c. What techniques of development are used?

1.　　But, I repeat, it is the relationship between birth rate and death rate that is most critical. Indonesia, Laos, and Haiti all had birth rates around 46 per thousand in 1966. Costa Rica's birth rate was 41 per thousand. Good for Costa Rica? Unfortunately, not very. Costa Rica's death rate was less than nine per thousand, while the other countries all had death rates above 20 per thousand. The population of Costa Rica in 1966 was doubling every 17 years, while the doubling times of Indonesia, Laos, and Haiti were all above thirty years. Ah, but, you say, it was good for Costa Rica—fewer people per thousand were dying each year. Fine for a few years, perhaps, but what then? Some 50% of the people in Costa Rica are under 15 years old. As they get older, they will need more and more food in a world with less and less. In 1983 they will have twice as many mouths to feed as they had in 1966, if the 1966 trend continues. Where will the food come from? Today the death rate in Costa Rica is low in part because they have a large number of physicians in proportion to their population. How do you suppose those physicians will keep the death rate down when there's not enough food to keep people alive?

—Paul Ehrlich, *The Population Bomb*[24]

2.　　Grammar is somewhat like a freshly caught fish. Take it in your hand to wash it in the stream; two wriggles, and it is gone. So with grammar, and I speak as one who has gone through the chastening experience of asking himself quite soberly what our grammar is. I have tried to divest myself of old grammatical prejudices beaten into me at an early age, and acquired later with the profligate expenditure of midnight electricity. I have at times thought I had drawn from the deceptive grammatical waters a fine, trim, grammatical fact. I grasped him firmly by the tail, and meant only to clean him up a bit. Two flips, and he was gone.

—Charlton Laird, *The Miracle of Language*[25]

3.　　The second distinguishing mark of Newspeak grammar was its regularity. Subject to a few exceptions which are mentioned below, all inflections followed the same rules. Thus, in all verbs the preterite and the past participle were the same and ended in -ed. The preterite of *steal* was *stealed*, the preterite of *think* was *thinked*, and so on throughout the language, all such forms as *swam, gave, brought, spoke, taken*, etc. being abolished. All plurals were made by adding

-s or -es as the case might be. The plurals of *man, ox, life* were *mans, oxes, lifes.* Comparison of adjectives was invariably made by adding -er, -est (*good, gooder, goodest*), irregular forms and the *more, most* formation being suppressed.

—George Orwell, *1984*[26]

4.   It follows naturally that in the popular consciousness of this country, "un-American" is the ultimate in negation. An anecdote will serve to illustrate this. Several years ago a leading cigarette manufacturer in this country had reason to believe that very damaging reports were being circulated about his product. The reports were such that had they not been stopped, the sale of this brand of cigarettes might have been reduced. The company thereupon inaugurated an extensive advertising campaign, the object of which was to halt these rumors in the most effective way possible. The concocters of the advertising copy evidently concluded after due deliberation that the strongest term of condemnation which could be conceived was "un-American," for this was the term employed in the campaign. Soon the newspapers were filled with advertising rebuking this "un-American" type of depreciation which had injured their sales. From examples such as this we may infer that "American" stands not only for what is forward in history, but also for what is ethically superior, or at least for a standard of fairness not matched by other nations.

—Richard M. Weaver, *Ultimate Terms
in Contemporary Rhetoric*[27]

5.   It is not only that population grows while the water supply remains relatively constant. There is also the fact that in countries like the U.S., the amount of water used per capita has grown enormously since the turn of the century, partly because more people have bathrooms, but mostly as a result of industrial consumption. It takes 110,000 gallons of water to make a ton of steel, for example, and a jetliner needs 1,000 gallons to take off. In 1900, Americans used some 40 billion gallons of fresh water a day. By 1940, when the population had grown by only 74 percent, the usage of water had more than tripled. Today, the rate of consumption has soared to about 350 billion gallons a day—which is getting uneasily close to the country's potential water supply of 515 billion gallons.

—*Water, Water Everywhere—and Now to Drink*[28]

6.   The relative pronoun "which" can cause more trouble than any other word, if recklessly used. Foolhardy persons sometimes get lost in which-clauses and are never heard of again. My distinguished contemporary, Fowler, cites several tragic cases, of which the follow-

ing is one: "It was rumored that Beaconsfield intended opening the Conference with a speech in French, his pronunciation of which language leaving everything to be desired . . . ." That's as much as Mr. Fowler quotes because, at his age, he was afraid to go any farther. The young man who originally got into that sentence was never found. His fate, however, was not as terrible as that of another adventurer who became involved in a remarkable which-mire. Fowler has followed his devious course as far as he safely could on foot: "Surely what applies to games should also apply to racing, the leaders of which being the very people from whom an example might well be looked for . . . ." Not even Henry James could have successfully emerged from a sentence with "which," "whom," and "being" in it . . . .

> —James Thurber, *Ladies' and Gentlemen's Guide to Modern English Usage*[29]

7.   Perhaps the hardest to understand of today's young men and women are the cop-outs—the runaways who find their native culture sordid, corrupt and controlled by a power elite too strong to struggle against. Disgusted by contemporary society but feeling incapable of changing it, the cop-outs withdraw and live apart from society and all its values in enclaves of bohemianism and relative poverty. They work just enough to support themselves, and take pride in the simplicity of their way of life and in their freedom from possessions ("Things own *you*; you don't own them," they explain). They spend their leisure time in various ways—reading, talking, painting, experimenting with drugs, and in general seeking a euphoric state of mind in which they say they feel perfectly free from conflicts, perfectly loving. "I love everybody," says one young man who looks deceptively like a cutthroat. "Sometimes I love so much it makes me dizzy."

> —Morton M. Hunt, *Don't Trust Anyone Over Thirty*[30]

8.   One of the fundamental facts about words is that the most useful ones in our language have many meanings. This is partly why they are so useful: they work overtime (but, as we shall see, not for nothing). Think of all the various things we mean by the word "foot" on different occasions: one of the lower extremities of the human body, a measure of verse, the ground about a tree, twelve inches, the floor in front of the stairs. The same is true of nearly every common noun or verb. The editors of *The American College Dictionary*, in their preliminary investigation of words most frequently used, found 55 distinct senses of the word "point" in 1,100 occurrences of the word, and they distinguished 109 different senses of the word "run."

> —Monroe Beardsley, *On Contexts and Vagueness*[31]

9.   Many years ago a graduate student inconvenienced himself greatly
to come a long distance to see me to ask if I could help him secure
some information about the term "poll tax." He was preparing a
doctor's thesis, he told me, and needed to know how long this term
had been in the language, what its basic meaning was, and what other
meanings it may have had in the course of its use in English. He was
most surprised when I opened the *OED* [*Oxford English Dictionary*]
to the appropriate place and showed him that all he needed to know
about this term had been available within a few feet of his desk in
the school where he was studying. It is not at all likely that any but
the exceptional student will ever need all the information about words
that the larger dictionaries afford, but it is well worth the while of
every student to become acquainted with the fact that such information is available for those who at any time need to make use of it.

                    —Mitford M. Mathews, *The Freshman and His Dictionary*[32]

10.   The heavenly counterpart of tolerance is love. Between the two a
great gulf is set. Love is positive; tolerance negative. Love involves
passion; tolerance is humdrum and dull. Love may explain the universe; tolerance, through common sense and good temper, tries to
avert further disaster from the earth. Yet despite the gulf between,
these two abstractions have problems in common. Love, too, has been
asked to take risks: "Love your enemies, do good to them that hate
you" is a text that has needed a good deal of explanation on the part
of theologians. And love, in a pregnant line of W. H. Auden's, has
been assigned the role which I have here claimed for tolerance: "We
must love one another or die," the line runs. In another poem he tells
us that we must love our crooked neighbor with our crooked heart;
and how else shall we tolerate him?

                    —E. M. Forster, *Toward a Definition of Tolerance*[33]

I took a corkscrew from the shelf:
I went to wake them up myself.
And when I found the door was locked,
I pulled and pushed and kicked and knocked.
And when I found the door was shut,
I tried to turn the handle, but—
There was a long pause.
"Is that all?" Alice timidly asked.
"That's all," said Humpty Dumpty. "Good-bye."

—Lewis Carroll, *Through the Looking Glass*

3

ORGANIZATION
IN THE
PARAGRAPH

Naturally, the piece of the poem Humpty Dumpty recites to Alice means nothing to you: we chopped off the beginning, cut out the middle, and left only the truncated tail. "I tried to turn the handle, but—" That's all.

Something is missing: *the sense of wholeness and completeness, the feeling of order.* And what's not there disturbs us. For we all feel that anything written ought to start at a logical point; ought to go on for a reasonable length; ought to stop when it's over. We demand *organization. We demand the right arrangement, the systematic order of events and ideas.*

But we don't always get it. As your teachers have probably told you often enough by now, students' writing in particular tends to be badly organized. You probably *don't* know which argument to start with, or how to end your papers without sounding like Humpty Dumpty; you probably *don't* know how to make the best possible start, how to place your points in comparison and contrast, or how to analyze a process. In fact, we'd bet that your writing is most aptly described by Sheridan Baker in *The Complete Stylist*: "Many a freshman's essay has no structure and leaves no impression. It's all chaotic middle. It has no beginning, it just begins; it has no end, it just stops, fagged out at two in the morning."[1]

"Well," you ask, "how *should* I do it then?"

That's the question we're going to answer in this chapter.

THE BASIC PRINCIPLE OF ORGANIZATION

This is so obvious that it hardly needs to be repeated—except for the fact that millions of writers, every day, seem to forget it: the simple, basic principle of organization that Aristotle outlined for Greek tragedy. A *whole*, Aristotle said, has a beginning, a middle, and an end. For us, as we study the expository paragraph, that means simply this: *the beginning is the topic sentence; the middle contains the full, logical development of the topic stentence through any of the techniques discussed so far; and the end brings the whole to a conclusion.*

You can see immediately, of course, that we need to ask three questions:

1. What kind of topic sentence leads to the clearest organization?
2. What is the best way to arrange the middle?
3. What makes the best conclusion?

THE TOPIC SENTENCE AS A KEY TO ORGANIZATION

Use the topic sentence to organize your paragraph.

What kind of topic sentence leads to the clearest organization? Let's work out the answer to that question by writing some topic sentences. Suppose that you have been asked to write a paragraph on one of the following subjects:

1. Analyze your reasons for coming to Dwight College.
2. Compare and contrast the differences between high school and college teachers.
3. Explain how to read an entry in a dictionary.

Suppose also that you have chosen the first subject and tried to put your ideas into topic sentences:

1. I came to Dwight College because I didn't know where else to go.
2. I came to Dwight College because there are a lot of pretty girls here.
3. I came to Dwight College for three reasons: its convenient location, its low tuition, and its academic prestige.

Now, the question is: which topic sentence leads to the clearest organization? Perhaps the answer is obvious, but you can work out a good answer by looking closely at the focus in each topic sentence. Do it this way:

1.   I came to Dwight College *because I didn't know where else to go.*
    "I could explain how everybody else was going to Harvard and Yale and I knew I couldn't get in. I could explain how I didn't have any way of deciding which college to go to. I could also explain that I couldn't really choose a college because I didn't know what I wanted to major in. But actually, none of this is going to be very well organized. This topic sentence doesn't seem to lead anywhere."

2.   I came to Dwight College *because there are a lot of pretty girls here.*

    "I could describe all the pretty girls I know here—Linda, Susan, Martha, Janet, Jill, Lisa. I could also say that I *knew* there would be more pretty girls here than at Harvard or Yale. But truthfully, I don't think this paragraph is going to be very well organized, either."

3.   I chose Dwight College *for three reasons: its convenient location, its low tuition, and its academic prestige.*

    "If I use this topic sentence, I know there will be three parts to my paragraph. *First, location.* I can point out that I live only two miles away and that my dad goes by here on his way to work, so I don't need to drive a car. *Second, low tuition.* I can point out that Dwight charges only $200 a year, but I'd have to pay $1,950 at Yale or $1,760 at Harvard. *Third, academic prestige.* Everybody knows that two Nobel Prize winners did their undergraduate work here. And I just read that about 30 percent of the graduates go on for advanced degrees. Besides, there's that poet . . . . Pretty clearly, this topic sentence will work best. The focus says, *three reasons: location, tuition, prestige.* My paragraph will be *organized* around these three reasons."

We can conclude, then, in answer to our question, that *the best topic sentence is one that gives clear signals for organization. It does this by outlining the parts of the paragraph in the focus.*

Look at two other examples of good topic sentences. These too include clear signals for organization in the focus. The signals are italicized.

> The greatest difference between high school and college teachers is their *method of teaching*; the greatest similarity is their *interest in the students.*

> To read an entry in a dictionary, you should *begin with the pronunciation, check the etymology, and then find the meaning which fits the context of the word you are studying.*

The first of these sentences leads to a *two-part paragraph*: part one uses descriptive details and examples to show the difference between high school and college teachers; part two uses descriptive details and examples to show the similarity. The second topic sentence leads to a *three-part paragraph*: part one comments on pronunciation; part two on etymology; part three on meaning in relation to context. Both topic sentences give clear signals for organization.

In short, then, good organization begins with a carefully phrased topic sentence—one that outlines the organization of the paragraph.

THE EFFECTIVE CONCLUSION

Most paragraphs used as parts of essays have no "concluding" sentence. The reason for this is, of course, that these paragraphs lead on to something else in the essay. But the paragraph written as a short composition—the kind of paragraph you have written so far—usually does have a sentence that we can label "conclusion." There are no simple rules for such a sentence; you will have to be guided by your own good sense. We will simply remind you that at the end of any composition you have your final chance to impress your reader. Even in writing a "one-paragraph essay" you will probably want to use this opportunity. To do so, *end with a sentence that restates your main idea (in deductive paragraphs) or draws a logical conclusion from the evidence you have presented (in inductive paragraphs).*

Consider only one example of the effective conclusion in the paragraph. Here, Vance Packard begins with the following topic sentence: "The early nineteen fifties witnessed the beginnings of a revolution in American advertising: Madison Avenue became conscious of the *unconscious*." In the concluding sentence he cleverly rephrases this idea by substituting *ad* for Madison Avenue and *id* (the source of our unconscious desires) for the *unconscious*: "The ad is being tailored to meet the needs of the id."

> The early nineteen fifties witnessed the beginning of a revolution in American advertising: Madison Avenue became conscious of the *unconscious*. Evidence had piled up that the responses of consumers to the questions of market researchers were frequently unreliable—in other words, that people often don't want what they say they want. Some years ago, for instance, a great automobile company committed one of the costliest blunders in automobile history through reliance on old-style "nose counting" methods. Direct consumer surveys indicated that people wanted a sensible car in tune with the times—without frills, maneuverable and easy to park. A glance at today's cars—elongated, fish-finned and in riotous technicolor—shows how misleading were the results of the survey. Errors of this sort convinced manufacturers and advertisers that they must take into account the irrationality of consumer behavior—that they must carry their surveys into the submerged areas of the human mind. The result is a strange and rather exotic phenomenon entirely new to the market place—the use of a kind of mass psychoanalysis to guide campaigns of persuasion. The ad is being tailored to meet the needs of the id.
>
> —Vance Packard, *The Ad and the Id*[2]

DESIGNING THE MIDDLE

Good organization never "just happens"—it's planned that way: it comes about through deliberate, intelligent, careful *design*.

To find the best organization, you need to answer two questions:

1. How can I make my organization interesting?
2. How can I make my organization clear?

The first question you can answer easily; the second is much more difficult but—as you'll see—not impossible. We'll take up each question in turn.

Using Climactic Arrangement

The answer to the first question lies in the psychology of human interest. If a play begins with the most dramatic moment in the script and becomes less and less dramatic as it crawls to the last word, most of the audience will head for the nearest pub at the end of Act I— if they're still awake. So your solution to the problem of interest should be the same as the playwright's: *use climactic arrangement.*

In designing the middle of your paragraph, use climactic arrangement like this: *go from your least significant, least important idea to your most significant, most important idea.* For instance, examine your reasons for going to Dwight College. Ask yourself, "Which is the most important reason—low tuition, convenient location, academic prestige?" Then arrange these reasons in the order of importance. Most of us would go from *location* to *tuition* to *academic prestige.* In writing the paragraph, we might even suggest to our reader that we are using the order of importance by beginning our discussion of each reason in this way: "One reason . . . ." "A more important reason . . . ." "The most important reason . . . ."

For interest, *use climactic arrangement.*

Finding the Clearest Order

Our more important and more difficult question is "How do I make my organization clear?" The answer: *for some subjects use natural order; for all other subjects use logical order.*

Natural Order

For some subjects use natural order. There are two kinds of natural order: *the order of space and the order of time.*

The Order of Space

Whenever an assignment requires that you describe a concrete object—a statue, a room, the cover of a magazine, a landscape—your subject contains a natural arrangement: *the order of space.* A room, for instance, can be described in a clockwise or a counterclockwise direction; from the inside or the outside; from the center or a corner; from a fixed or a moving point; from the floor to the ceiling. A person can be described from head to foot; from foot to head; from a central point to either extremity. In other words, *the order of space shows how elements are related to each other in space; such order is built into assignments requiring that you describe things or people.*

Look at a simple example first. The next paragraph uses the order of space to arrange details in the description of a person; it begins with the head and concludes with the feet of the subject—a clear, rather mechanical approach. Because the details are put in climactic order, the organization is also interesting:

> I began to believe that teachers are human beings—with human *weaknesses*—when I saw Professor Frog. As he walked into Biology 10 that first morning, I thought, "Good grief—he dresses that way *deliberately.*" Even then I knew the thick red hair couldn't really be his own. I followed it with my eyes as it crawled slowly towards his left ear. Then I took stock of the rest of him. He was wearing an electric-blue sport coat with high padded shoulders. He also wore a vest, in shocking magenta, buttoned haphazardly over a little-girl-pink tie that sparkled with game birds and cattails. His banana-yellow trousers came almost to the tops of his tennis shoes, but there was space enough there for me to see that the orange sock on his right foot didn't quite match the green one on his left foot.

Then look at a more complex example: T. E. Hotchner's description of Ernest Hemingway. Hotchner scans Hemingway's appearance in this order: pants, belt, shirt, shoes, hair, and mustache. Next, in some detail, he describes the dominant impression: Hemingway was "massive." Finally, Hotchner concludes with a much more important point: Hemingway "radiated" *enjoyment.* Despite the complexity of this paragraph, the arrangement of details is both interesting and clear:

> Hemingway . . . was wearing khaki pants held up by a wide old leather belt with a huge buckle inscribed GOTT MIT UNS, a white linen sport shirt that hung loose, and brown leather loafers without socks. His hair was dark with gray highlights, flecked white at the temples, and he had a heavy mustache that ran past the corners of his mouth, but no beard. He was massive. Not in height, for he was only an inch over six feet, but in impact. Most of his two hundred pounds was concentrated above his waist: he had square heavy shoulders, long hugely muscled arms (the left one jaggedly scarred and a bit misshapen at the elbow), a deep chest, a belly-rise but no hips or thighs. Something played off him—he was intense, electro-kinetic, but in control, a race horse reined in. He stopped to talk to

one of the musicians in fluent Spanish and something about him hit
me—*enjoyment*: God, I thought, how he's *enjoying* himself! I had
never seen anyone with such an aura of fun and well-being. He
radiated it and everyone in the place responded. He had so much
more in his face than I had expected to find from seeing his photographs.

—A. E. Hotchner, *Papa Hemingway*[3]

Remember, then: *to organize a description, use the natural order
—the order of space.*

EXERCISE   1

Using the order of space, write a descriptive paragraph (150-200
words) on one of the following subjects. Try to keep the most important, most striking details for the end. Remember to begin with a
sharply focused topic sentence and to use concrete descriptive details
in developing your paragraph.

1. An antique shop
2. The locker room after a physical education class
3. A painting
4. Your room
5. A pet

The Order of Time

Less frequently you will meet subjects with another kind of
natural order—*the order of time.*

When you are asked to write a narrative, a story, or an anecdote,
you will need to use the order of time—to show how things happened
one after another *in time.* To do that, simply describe what happened,

selecting details for interest, of course, and using words like *first, next,* then, and *finally* to show the chronological relationship of events.

Here is a beautiful example: George Orwell's story of shooting an elephant. The elephant, temporarily mad, had killed a native; and as a member of the Indian Imperial Police, Orwell had the job of finding the beast and killing him. He writes:

> When I pulled the trigger I did not hear the bang or feel the kick—one never does when a shot goes home—but I heard the devilish roar of glee that went up from the crowd. In that instant, in too short a time, one would have thought, even for the bullet to get there, a mysterious, terrible change had come over the elephant. He neither stirred nor fell, but every line of his body had altered. He looked suddenly stricken, shrunken, immensely old, as though the frightful impact of the bullet had paralyzed him without knocking him down. At last, after what seemed a long time—it might have been five seconds, I dare say—he sagged flabbily to his knees. His mouth slobbered. An enormous senility seemed to have settled upon him. One could have imagined him thousands of years old. I fired again into the same spot. At the second shot he did not collapse but climbed with desperate slowness to his feet and stood weakly upright, with legs sagging and head dropping. I fired a third time. That was the shot that did it for him. You could see the agony of it jolt his whole body and knock the last remnant of strength from his legs. But in falling he seemed for a moment to rise, for as his hind legs collapsed beneath him he seemed to tower upwards like a huge rock toppling, his trunk reaching skywards like a tree. He trumpeted, for his first and only time. And then down he came, his belly towards me, with a crash that seemed to shake the ground even where I lay.
>
> —George Orwell, "Shooting an Elephant"[4]

Remember, then: *to organize a narrative, use the natural order —the order of time.*

EXERCISE 2

Using the order of time, write a narrative paragraph (150-200 words) on one of the following subjects. Try to capture the most interesting, most striking moments. Remember to begin with a sharply focused topic sentence and to use concrete descriptive details in developing your paragraph.

1. An act of prejudice
2. Shoplifting
3. An exciting day
4. A trip
5. Hurt feelings

LOGICAL ORDER

Besides the natural orders of space and time, there is only one other kind of clear organization: *logical order.*

Logical order simplifies complex ideas and gives shape to formless impressions; it reduces a chaotic swirl of thoughts to a smooth and intelligible flow of connected ideas. It is the essential ingredient of good expository prose.

For most subjects, you can use one of three kinds of logical order: *analysis, classification, comparison-contrast.*

Analysis
For most writing assignments, use analysis.

We are going to apply the term very broadly—almost in its etymological meaning "to loosen up." We are going to define analysis *as the process of dividing a whole into its parts; as a way of "loosening up" anything to separate it into its basic elements or internal divisions; as a way of finding the parts of any whole.*

Let's study some examples to see exactly what we do in analyzing something. If we analyze a filter-tipped cigarette, for instance, we separate it into three parts: tobacco, paper, and filter. If we analyze a certain type of filter, we separate it into a cover, charcoal granules, and a compressed fibre. If we analyze a magazine, we separate it into articles, stories, "departments," poems, cartoons, and advertisements. If we analyze a story in a magazine, we separate it into setting, plot, characters, and theme. If we analyze a character in a story, we separate him into *his* basic parts: appearance, attitude toward politics, religious beliefs, typical behavior, and so on.

Analysis, then, "loosens up" an idea, an object, an organization, an argument; it separates things into their basic parts—and finds order where there doesn't seem to be any.

Steps in an Analysis. How do you make an analysis?

Suppose that you have been given a typical assignment—you have been asked to analyze the student body at Dwight College. Your problem is to break this whole—the student body—into its basic parts. As you think about the problem, you begin to make notes.

Student Body Made Up Of:

> conservatives
> moderates
> liberals
>
> *or*
>
> good students
> average students
> poor students
>
> *or*
>
> "swingers"
> "squares"
>
> *or*
>
> members of fraternities and sororities
> students living at home
> students with rooms off campus
>
> *or*
>
> students with cars
> students without cars
>
> *or*
>
> male students
> female students

At this point you realize, of course, that you have found six different ways to analyze the student body—and that you can use any of these six ways to *organize* your paper on the student body of Dwight College. At the same time, you have discovered *the three basic steps in an analysis:*

1. *Find a clear basis of division.* In your notes you have used the following bases of division: *politics, scholastic success, social habits, living arrangements, automobiles,* and *sex.* With a little more thought

you could have found many other ways to divide the student body at Dwight College.

2.   *Follow the basis of division consistently.* You did that when you wrote, for instance, "good students, average students, poor students." Obviously, you would not analyze the student body by saying that it consists of "good students, average students, *girls*, poor students."

3.   *Carry out the division until it includes all the basic parts.* Logically, your division must be complete. You can't divide the student body into "average students, poor students"; you can't divide it into "liberals, moderates"—unless, of course, there are no *good students* and no *conservatives.*

While you were uncovering the basic steps in an analysis, you undoubtedly noticed one more thing: *any whole can be analyzed in many different ways, depending on how it's seen.* Take your English class as an example. Your instructor might divide it into good, average, and bad students; a sociologist might divide it into upper-class, middle-class, and working-class people; and a psychologist might divide it into extroverts and introverts. So your basis of division will reflect your interests and your purpose.

Typical Subjects for Analysis. You can organize almost any writing assignment by analysis. Here are some of the ways you can use analysis:

1.   *To organize an argument.* Any argument can be analyzed into "reasons for" or "reasons against." If you are asked to attack or defend the sale of *Playboy* on campus, for instance, you should set up your organization around *reasons*, like this:

> *Playboy* should be sold on campus because—
> a. *Playboy* features stories and articles by some of the best writers in America;
> b. *Playboy* deals with important moral problems;
> c. *Playboy* is concerned with contemporary social issues.

2.   *To organize a discussion of causes.* Any condition or state of affairs can be explained by an analysis of its causes. Suppose your subject is *student apathy and campus politics.* You can set up your organization around *causes*, like this:

> The majority of students at Dwight College are apathetic about campus politics because—
> a. most of them live at home and are not involved in campus life;

b. many of them feel that their vote wouldn't make any difference;

c. most of them think that campus politics are trivial matters, when compared with the business of getting an education.

3. *To organize an explanation of a system or institution or mechanism.* The government of a state can be analyzed into judicial, legislative, and executive branches. A college can be analyzed into administrative, faculty, and students. A watch can be analyzed into springs, wheels, jewels, case, hands, etc. For such subjects you can set up your organization around the *divisions,* like this:

Dwight College is an institution made up of—
a. administration,
b. faculty,
c. students.

4. *To organize an explanation of a process.* Any process can be divided into the separate steps it requires. For a *process analysis* you can set up your organization around the *steps,* like this:

There are four steps in frying snapping turtle—
a. slice the meat into thin strips,
b. salt and pepper each strip,
c. melt a tablespoonful of butter in a frying pan over medium heat,
d. add strips of meat and fry until tender.

5. *To organize a discussion of anything with a history.* Writing about the English language, for example, you can set up your organization around *historical periods,* like this:

Scholars recognize three periods in the development of the English language—
a. Anglo-Saxon Period (450-1100 A.D.),
b. Middle English Period (1100-1450 A.D.),
c. Modern English Period (1450 A.D.—).

Writing the Paragraph of Analysis. To be sure, there are many ways to write the paragraph organized by analysis. One is the professional's way—rather loose and informal, for the most part; another is the way of the learner—tighter and more rigidly controlled. You can learn much from the way of the professional, but—for practice— you should try to write in the way of the learner.

Take the professional's way first. Watch Gilbert Highet in the following paragraph. In discussing the qualities of a good teacher, Highet analyzes the *purposes* served by humor. The paragraph is organized like this:

MAIN IDEA: Humor serves many purposes.

MAJOR SUPPORT: Humor keeps students alive and attentive.

MAJOR SUPPORT: Humor helps give a true picture about many important subjects.

MINOR SUPPORTS: Multiple examples.

Highet writes:

> One of the most important qualities of a good teacher is humor. Many are the purposes it serves. The most obvious one is that it keeps the pupils alive and attentive because they are never quite sure what is coming next. Another is that it does in fact help to give a true picture of many important subjects. Suppose you are discussing English literature in the early nineteenth century. If you confine yourself to talking about Wordsworth's lyrical simplicity, and Shelley pinnacled dim in the intense inane, you will be giving an incomplete picture of the group; whereas if you also d-d-describe Ch-Charles Lamb as both f-funny and ch-charming, and bring out the weird boyish comedy of some of Wordsworth's other poems, and read some of Byron's rougher letters, you will then establish the idea that these men are rich and varied and human personalities, not "classics" cast in a single mold of solid bronze, and you can proceed all the better to explain both the nobility of their achievement and the sadness of their failures.
> —Gilbert Highet, *The Art of Teaching*[5]

Take the learner's way next. Use a model for the paragraph of analysis: *begin with a topic sentence that announces the parts of the whole; use each major support to describe one part of the whole; use one or more minor supports to develop each major support; and end with a summary sentence.*

This sounds complicated, but a little discussion and practice will prove that it's very simple. Here is the outline for our first model paragraph:

MAIN IDEA: The typical teen-ager has three main characteristics: *he's affluent, he's educated, he's casual about sex.*

MAJOR SUPPORT: *he's affluent,*

MINOR SUPPORTS: statistics on teen-age spending

MAJOR SUPPORT: *he's educated,*

MINOR SUPPORTS: statistics on education

MAJOR SUPPORT: *he's casual about sex.*

MINOR SUPPORT: anecdote on teen-age attitude toward sex

SUMMARY SENTENCE: Although individuals certainly vary, the typical teen-ager seems to have three main characteristics.

The model paragraph reads like this:

It seems to older adults that the typical teen-ager today has three main characteristics: *he's affluent, he's educated, he's casual about sex* (TOPIC SENTENCE ANNOUNCING THE PARTS OF THE WHOLE). *First of all, the teen-ager is affluent: he has a lot of money to spend* (MAJOR SUPPORT DESCRIBING ONE PART OF THE WHOLE). Recent statistics show, for instance, that each year teen-agers are now spending $570 million on toiletries, $1.5 billion on entertainment, and $3.6 billion on women's clothes alone. All together, they spend close to $12 billion (MINOR SUPPORTS TO DEVELOP THE MAJOR SUPPORT). *The typical teen-ager is also educated—at least better educated than his parents were* (MAJOR SUPPORT DESCRIBING PART OF THE WHOLE). More teen-agers go to school and stay there than ever before. In 1900 only 13 percent of them were enrolled in school; now about 95 percent of them are in high school, and about half of those will go to college (MINOR SUPPORTS TO DEVELOP THE MAJOR SUPPORT). *A third striking characteristic of the typical teen-ager is that he's casual about sex* (MAJOR SUPPORT DESCRIBING THE LAST PART OF THE WHOLE). This is hard to prove, but it's rather neatly illustrated by a story I read in a recent issue of *Time*: as a practical joke, a 16-year-old boy calmly announced at the dinner table that his girl friend was pregnant. Before his shocked parents could say anything, his 13-year-old brother reacted. "My God," he said. "You'll lose your allowance" (MINOR SUPPORTS TO DEVELOP THE LAST MAJOR SUPPORT). *So, although individuals certainly vary, the typical teenager seems to have three main characteristics* (SUMMARY SENTENCE).

Next, study a *process analysis* organized around the *steps* in the process:

According to S. I. Hayakawa in *Language in Thought and Action*, there are four steps in writing a dictionary: (1) *collecting words,* (2) *alphabetizing and sorting the collection,* (3) *studying each word in context,* and (4) *writing definitions of each word based on its contexts* (TOPIC SENTENCE ANNOUNCING THE PARTS OF THE

WHOLE). *The first step is collecting words* (MAJOR SUPPORT DE-
SCRIBING ONE PART OF THE WHOLE). Editors do this by reading all
the important literature that might include words they want to define.
As they read, they write down each of these words on a separate card.
Below the word, they write the sentences in which it appears, since
they must collect words in context (MINOR SUPPORTS TO DEVELOP
THE MAJOR SUPPORT). *Once they have gathered all their words—on
perhaps millions of cards—the editors are ready for the second step:
sorting and alphabetizing the cards* (MAJOR SUPPORT DESCRIBING
ANOTHER PART OF THE WHOLE). They arrange the cards so that
each word will be represented by a whole group of cards giving many
examples of its use (MINOR SUPPORT TO DEVELOP THE MAJOR
SUPPORT). *Next, the editors study each word in context* (MAJOR
SUPPORT DESCRIBING ANOTHER PART OF THE WHOLE). As they
discover the possible meanings of a word, they group the cards around
those meanings (MINOR SUPPORT TO DEVELOP THE MAJOR SUP-
PORT). *Only then can they take the final step: writing definitions*
(MAJOR SUPPORT DESCRIBING THE LAST PART OF THE WHOLE).
In writing definitions, the editors can use only what the cards tell them
about the meaning of each word; that is, they must define their words
in context (MINOR SUPPORT TO DEVELOP THE MAJOR SUPPORT).
*You can see, then, that defining words plays only a small part in the
production of a modern dictionary; before that, vast amounts of
money, time, and energy go into collecting, sorting, and studying
words* (SUMMARY SENTENCE).

In short, the model paragraph of analysis uses a paragraph pattern that you knew all along: *the complex deductive pattern.* And
you can't go wrong in writing your paragraphs of analysis if you remind yourself of these simple requirements: *begin with a topic sentence that announces the parts of the whole; use each minor support
to describe one part of the whole; use one or more minor supports to
develop each major support; and end with a summary sentence.*

EXERCISE   3

A.   Write a paragraph (about 150-200 words) on one of the following subjects. Be sure to follow the model for the paragraph organized
by analysis.

1. The characteristics of love
2. Aims of women's liberation movements
3. Reasons for attending college
4. What is a liberal (conservative)?
5. Disadvantages of attending_____High School
6. Why students drop out of college
7. A moral code accepted by college students
8. Qualities of a good job
9. Why parents dislike rock-and-roll
10. What is maturity?

B. Write a process analysis (about 150-200 words) on one of the following subjects. Be sure to follow the model for the paragraph organized by analysis.

1. How to make a dress
2. How to fix a flat tire
3. How to get your parents to give you what you want
4. How to get a date
5. How to wait on a customer
6. How to make French bread
7. How to diagnose a strange noise under the hood of a car
8. How to meet strangers
9. How to train a dog (horse, child, etc.)
10. How to handle an embarrassing situation

Classification

Another common and useful kind of logical order is *classification*. *Classification works by sorting things into groups.* It is so closely related to analysis that it is sometimes seen as an aspect of the same process, but there is a difference. While analysis divides a whole into its parts, classification brings together similar things to show what they have in common. You will understand the difference if you first analyze and then classify something—a book, for instance. If you *analyze* a book, you take it apart in some systematic way; if you *classify* a book, you place it in a category with other books. For example, if you *analyze* Ian Fleming's *Thrilling Cities*, you can find that it is divided into thirteen chapters, each dealing with one or more cities. But if you *classify* the same book, you can group it with other travel books—Boswell's *Journal of a Tour to the Hebrides* and Arthur Frommer's *Europe on 5 Dollars a Day*, perhaps.

So classification differs from analysis in this significant way. However, there are also some striking similarities. For one thing, whether you are classifying or analyzing, your results may well look the same. In his book *The Status Seekers*, for instance, Vance Packard sorts people into five classes grouped under two headings:

The Diploma Elite
1. The Real Upper Class
2. The Semi-Upper Class

The Supporting Classes
3. The Limited-Success Class
4. The Working Class
5. The Real Lower Class

On the other hand, we could also say that he analyzes society—seen as a whole—into two major parts, which are subdivided into their minor parts: the results, essentially, are the same.

We are going to note, very briefly, two other important similarities. First, the steps in making a classification are much like those in making an analysis. Suppose that you have been asked to classify types of cars, for instance. You might classify them according to price, with these results: "high-priced cars, medium-priced cars, low-priced cars." In making this classification, you take three steps:

1. *Find a clear basis of classification.* Your basis of classification is "price."
2. *Follow the basis of classification consistently.* That is, use "price" as your only basis of classification. Obviously, you couldn't classify cars by saying, "There are high-priced, low-priced, and sports cars."
3. *Carry out the classification until it's complete.* Obviously, you wouldn't classify cars by saying, "There are two types of cars —high-priced cars and low-priced cars." You must also include "medium-priced cars."

The other similarity simplifies the job of actually writing a paragraph organized by classification: you can use the same paragraph pattern. In writing the paragraph organized by classification, *begin with a topic sentence that announces the groups in the classification;*

use each major support to describe one group; use one or more minor supports to develop each major support; and end with a summary sentence.

In the following paragraph, you can see exactly how it's done:

Words derived from proper nouns fall into two distinct categories: *words that have their origin in the names of individuals and words that develop from place names* (TOPIC SENTENCE). *Words in the first category often come from mythology or literature* (MAJOR SUPPORT). Take only one example—*procrustean*, from the name of Procrustes, the mythical highwayman who robbed travelers and then placed them on a special bed. If they were too short for the bed, he stretched them out; if they were too long, he cut them off. Hence, *procrustean*: "tending to produce conformity—often by violent means," as in "the *procrustean* schools of America" (MINOR SUPPORTS). *Words in the second category come from the names of places that for some reason or another have stamped their impression on history* (MAJOR SUPPORT). *Sybaritic* is an excellent example: it comes from the name of an ancient Greek city in Southern Italy, Sybaris, whose inhabitants were notorious for a strange mixture of human passions. Sybaritic men loved horses, drunken parties, and other men. They were (almost literally) sitting ducks for their savage neighbors, who coveted the Sybarites' horses and didn't hesitate to slit a few thousand Sybaritic throats in order to get them. So the neighbors got the horses and the Sybarites left only their name to history. To this day *sybaritic* conjures up an image of the person who loves luxury and pleasure—in a slightly effeminate way (MINOR SUPPORTS). *Although these two examples don't begin to suggest the wonderful variety of words derived from proper nouns, they aptly illustrate the categories: words that have their origin in the names of individuals and words that develop from place names* (SUMMARY SENTENCE).

Of course, as the professional writes it, the paragraph organized by classification is likely to be much more casual than this. Here is a typical example—a paragraph that classifies "pot smokers":

Pot smokers nowadays comprise three broad groups (TOPIC SENTENCE). *First there are the prisoners of the ghetto, who turn to marijuana to escape the grinding despair of their circumstances* (MAJOR SUPPORT). Since they live in neighborhoods where narcotics are also available, these are the pot users most likely to graduate to heroin, the most pervasive eradicator of consciousness (MINOR SUPPORT). *Then there are the samplers and the chronic potheads* (MAJOR

SUPPORT). The sampler is usually a middle-class youngster who tries an occasional marijuana joint to see if the drug really does heighten his awareness and appreciation of music, philosophy, art—and people. The chronic pothead may come from the same background; he feels empty and alienated from the world around him. The pothead, says Columbia's Liebert, "takes marijuana regularly and compulsively. It fills a definite need to relieve an intolerable tension and depression." And Rand's McGlothlin says persistent users "will be less achievement-oriented, less competitive" (MINOR SUPPORTS).[6]

As you read, you probably noticed these differences between the model paragraph and this example. In the model paragraph, the topic sentence names the groups in the classification; in the example, the topic sentence says only "three broad groups." In the model paragraph, each group is described in a separate major support; in the example, the first group is described in one major support and the other two groups are described together in another major support. Finally, the model paragraph ends with a summary sentence; the example does not have a summary sentence.

Again, we suggest that you follow the model paragraph until you have mastered the form: *begin with a topic sentence that announces the groups in the classification; use each major support to describe one group; use one or more minor supports to develop each major support; and end with a summary sentence.*

EXERCISE   4

Write a paragraph (about 150-200 words) on one of the following subjects. Be sure to follow the model for the paragraph organized by classification.

1. Types of rock groups (or singers)
2. Types of girls (or boys) you like or dislike
3. Types of students at your school
4. Types of activities you enjoy
5. Types of cars

Comparison-Contrast

A third kind of logical order is *comparison-contrast. Comparison points out similarities; contrast points out differences.* Often, however, we use both comparison *and* contrast to organize a discussion of things that are different in some ways and similar in others. For the sake of convenience—and because they have much in common—let's speak of the three processes as *comparison-contrast.*

Use comparison-contrast to analyze two (or more) things at one time in order to show their similarities or their differences or both.

The Paragraph of Comparison. Use comparison to analyze two (or more) things at one time in order to show their *similarities.* Study the following paragraph as an example. Here Alan Moorhead shows the similarities between Australia and the United States. He expresses his main idea in the first sentence: "the two countries are much alike." In the rest of the paragraph he lists specific similarities.

> Despite the great discrepancy in population and resources the two countries are much alike. In area—3,000,000-odd square miles— they are the same; they share a very similar temperate climate; both are Christian democracies; both speak the same language and observe the English system of common law; both entered modern history as British colonies and have built up their populations by dispossessing the native inhabitants and establishing European migrants in their place. There may even be a temperamental bond between the two peoples inasmuch as they both had to start from scratch and both feel young, free, and independent—resurgents from the older, more sophisticated civilization of Europe and Asia.
>
> —Alan Moorhead, *The Affinity with Australia*[7]

The Paragraph of Contrast. Use contrast to analyze two (or more) things at the same time in order to show their *differences.*

Look carefully at the following example—a paragraph that contrasts the Pueblo Indians with the Dobus (who live on the Dobu Islands off the coast of New Guinea). The main idea, stated in the first sentence, is that the Pueblos differ from the Dobus in three important ways. Each of the three major supports names one of those ways; the minor supports say something more specific about the Pueblos and something *in contrast* about the Dobus (as the "contrast words" *on the other hand, however,* and *but* suggest). There is no summary sentence—but there *might* be one, of course. Clearly the paragraph pattern looks much like that of the model paragraph organized by analysis:

> According to Ruth Benedict in *The Patterns of Culture*, the Pueblos and the Dobus differ in three important ways (TOPIC SENTENCE). *First, they differ in the basic structure of their societies* (MAJOR SUPPORT). The Pueblos have a peaceful, cooperative society (MINOR SUPPORT). The Dobus, on the other hand, are "lone wolves"; the normal Dobu is sneaky, suspicious and aggressive instead of peaceful and cooperative (MINOR SUPPORT). *Second, as you would expect, the Pueblos and the Dobus differ in their attitudes toward sexual behavior* (MAJOR SUPPORT). The Pueblos are not jealous about "sexual rights" and do not punish infidelity (MINOR SUPPORT). The Dobus, however, are viciously jealous: the in-laws spy on married people constantly, and any infidelity brings swift, brutal punishment (MINOR SUPPORT). *Finally, the Pueblos and the Dobus differ in their attitudes toward material success* (MAJOR SUPPORT). The Pueblos make no display of political or economic power (MINOR SUPPORT). But the Dobus are fiercely proud of such success: like the old-time Captains of American Industry, they worship property and will go to any extreme—including fraud and murder—to get what they want (MINOR SUPPORT).

The Paragraph of Comparison and Contrast. Use the paragraph of comparison and contrast to analyze two (or more) things that are *different* in some ways, and *similar* in other ways.

Here is an excellent example—a paragraph that compares *and* contrasts the "hippies" with the subculture that comes before them, the "beats." The main idea, again, is stated in the first sentence: "there has been a startling transformation in bohemia." The first major support leads into a brief discussion of *similarities* between hippies and beats; these similarities are developed in a minor support. The second major support introduces a discussion of the *differences*; these are developed in several minor supports. Again, there is no summary sentence, but the pattern closely resembles that of the model paragraph of analysis.

> The immediate progenitors of the hippies were the beats of the 1950s, but there has been a startling transformation in bohemia (TOPIC SENTENCE). *Many of the same elements were present in the beat generation* (MAJOR SUPPORT): scorn for prevailing sexual mores, a predilection for pot and peyote, wanderlust, a penchant for

Oriental mysticism on the order of Zen and the Veda (MINOR SUP-
PORT). *Yet the contrasts are even more striking* (MAJOR SUPPORT).
San Francisco's North Beach was a study in black and white; the
Haight-Ashbury is a crazy quilt of living color (MINOR SUPPORT).
Black was a basic color in the abstract-expressionist painting of the
beats; hippiedom's psychedelic poster art is blindingly vivid (MINOR
SUPPORT). The progressive jazz of the beats was coolly cerebral; the
acid rock of the hippies is as visceral as a torn intestine (MINOR SUP-
PORT).[8]

Arranging Details in Comparison-Contrast Paragraphs. In paragraphs organized by comparison-contrast, place your details in one of
two ways: *"point-by-point"* or *"block-by-block."*

Suppose for example that you are contrasting the culture of the
Pueblo Indians with that of the Dobus. You can discuss the differences between them point-by-point, or you can discuss the Pueblos in
one part of your paragraph and the Dobus in the next. You might
make a rough outline showing the arrangement of details in each of
these two plans:

Point-by-Point Organization

Pueblos	peaceful, cooperative
Dobus	violent, aggressive
Pueblos	tolerant of sexual infidelity
Dobus	jealous and possessive
Pueblos	indifferent to political and economic display
Dobus	fiercely proud of political and economic success

Block-by-Block Organization

Pueblos
   peaceful, cooperative
   tolerant of sexual infidelity
   indifferent to political and economic success

Dobus
   violent, aggressive
   jealous, possessive
   fiercely proud of political and economic success

In writing the paragraph organized point-by-point, you would
discuss one point at a time, dealing with the Pueblos in one sentence
and the Dobus in the next. Look back at the model paragraph of contrast to see how that is done.

In writing the paragraph organized block-by-block, you would discuss the Pueblos in the first part of the paragraph and the Dobus in the next part, like this:

> According to Ruth Benedict in *The Patterns of Culture*, the Pueblo Indians are different from the Dobus in three important ways (TOPIC SENTENCE). *Take the Pueblos first* (MAJOR SUPPORT). The Pueblos have a very cooperative, peaceful society (MINOR SUPPORT). They are not jealous about sexual rights and they do not punish infidelity (MINOR SUPPORT). Moreover, they make no display of political or economic power (MINOR SUPPORT). *The Dobus are different in every way* (MAJOR SUPPORT). To begin with, they are a violent, aggressive people (MINOR SUPPORT). Unlike the Pueblos, they are intensely jealous: the in-laws spy on married people constantly, and any infidelity is met with swift, brutal punishment (MINOR SUPPORT). Also, the Dobus are fiercely proud of political and economic success: like the old-time Captains of American Industry, they worship property and will go to any extreme—including fraud and murder—to get what they want (MINOR SUPPORT).

Probably you see already which of these two arrangements works best: differences (or similarities) are sharper and clearer when the details are placed point-by-point. *For most comparison-contrast paragraphs, then, use a point-by-point arrangement.*

EXERCISE   5

Write a paragraph (about 150-200 words) on one of the following subjects. Organize your paragraph by comparison, contrast, or comparison *and* contrast.

1. Country and city life
2. Two sports
3. Successful and unsuccessful students
4. Two friends
5. Sexual attitudes

A FINAL WORD

And when I found the door was shut
I tried to turn the handle, but—

Organization is never easy. Our minds are cluttered—like junk-shops. Our ideas are jumbled; our experiences are quick and deceptive. But with care and hard work, you should be able to find an interesting and clear organization for almost any subject. It will help if you remember the principles laid down in this chapter:

1. Good organization demands *form*: a beginning, a middle, and an end.
2. For the most interesting arrangement of the middle, use climactic order.
3. For the clearest arrangement of the middle, follow the natural orders of space and time whenever possible.
4. When your subject doesn't have a natural order, use logical order: analysis, classification, comparison-contrast.

EXERCISE 6

Study the organization of each of the following paragraphs to find which of these orders is used:

Natural Order	*Logical Order*
Space	Analysis
Time	Classification
	Comparison
	Contrast
	Comparison *and* Contrast

Then answer the questions at the end of each paragraph.

1.   The electric organs of the eel are in three pairs: the Large Organs, the Bundles of Sachs, and the Organs of Hunter . . . . The first of these is functionally the most important, and begins at about one-fifth of the length of the fish behind the snout, continuing unchanged

to a point about two-thirds the length of the fish behind the snout. From this place on it tapers off and the resulting space is taken up by the Bundles of Sachs, which grow in size as the large organs diminish. The Bundles are responsible for the small discharges [of electricity] apparently used for locating food. The third pair of organs, those of Hunter, start at the same level as do the Large Organs and run to the end of the tail. In cross-section these are very small and their discharge is irregular and appears to be a function of that of the Large Organs . . . .

—Christopher Coates, *The Kick of an Electric Eel*[9]

a. Which sentence is the topic sentence? Is it a good topic sentence? Why?
b. List each major support.
c. List each minor support.
d. Which order is used in this paragraph?

2.   The seventeenth-century English clergyman Thomas Fuller thought that there were four kinds of students. First, he said, there are the "ingenious and industrious" students. These are the good students, who learn easily and work hard—students to be used "with all gentleness" by the schoolmaster. Then there are the "ingenious and idle" students. They're smart, certainly; but they won't work, Fuller says— unless they're whipped. Next, there are the "dull and diligent" students. They work hard but learn slowly. However, like wine, they improve with age, and Fuller thinks their dullnss should be borne with rather than punished. Finally, there are the "invincibly dull and negligent" students. Let them go, Fuller says: "All the whetting in the world can never set a razor's edge on that which hath no steel in it." If they "will not serve for scholars," they will make "excellent merchants and mechanics."

a. Which sentence is the topic sentence?
b. List each major support.
c. List each minor support.
d. Which order is used in this paragraph?

3.   So it happens that our colleges are divided into two cultural groups whose values tend to meet only in the most tangential ways. The faculty group is made up of men and women not particularly distinguished as smooth dancers but, rather, dedicated to books; so

dedicated, in fact, that they are willing to live on academic salaries in return for the freedom of having their reading interfered with by students, most of whom are only taking the course because they have to. The student group does share the same campus with the faculty group, but tends to center around the jukebox in the snack bar rather than around the library. Professor Jones is eager to explain the Greek aorist and to show its connection with the Latin ablative absolute, but what the girls really want out of Greek Week is a good date for the dance. Let the faculty praise great minds; the girls are there to get married, most of them as per the advertised standard.

—John Ciardi, *The Unfading Beauty: a Well-filled Mind*[10]

a. Which sentence is the topic sentence?
b. List each major support.
c. List each minor support.
d. Which order is used in this paragraph?

4.   The next day General Littlefield summoned me to his office. He was swatting flies when I went in. I was silent and he was silent too, for a long time. I don't think he remembered me or why he had sent for me, but he didn't want to admit it. He swatted some more flies, keeping his eyes on them narrowly before he let go with the swatter. "Button up your coat!" he snapped. Looking back on it now I can see that he meant me although he was looking at a fly, but I just stood there. Another fly came to rest on a paper in front of the general and began rubbing its hind legs together. The general lifted the swatter cautiously. I moved restlessly and the fly flew away. "You startled him!" remarked General Littlefield, looking at me severely. I said I was sorry. "That won't help the situation!" snapped the General, with cold military logic. I didn't see what I could do except offer to chase more flies toward his desk, but I didn't say anything. He stared out the window at the faraway figures of co-eds crossing the campus toward the library. Finally, he told me I could go. So I went. He either didn't know which cadet I was or else he forgot what he wanted to see me about. It may have been that he wished to apologize for having called me the main trouble with the university; or maybe he had decided to compliment me on my brilliant drilling of the day before and then at the last moment decided not to. I don't know. I don't think about it much any more.

—James Thurber, *University Days*[11]

a. Does this paragraph have a topic sentence? Explain.
b. Which order is used in this paragraph?

5.   *Goldfinger* is probably the most obvious reworking of early myth. Auric Goldfinger, who drives a gold car, carries his money in solid gold, dreams of robbing Fort Knox, and likes his women gold-plated all over, is a reincarnation of King Midas. Midas was tone deaf and earned a pair of ass's ears for misjudging a music contest between Pan and Apollo; Goldfinger, when Bond first meets him, is wearing a hearing aid and sunning himself with a set of tin wings resembling a pair of long, slightly pointed ears. Midas' barber, unable to contain the secret of his master's aural adornment, whispered his message into a hole. Later a reed grew and told the secret to all passersby. James Bond, in Goldfiger's captivity, must foil the planned robbery of Fort Knox; he tapes his message to an airplane toilet seat, the only hole available, and thus transmits it to the outside world.

                     —George Grella, *James Bond: Culture Hero*[12]

a. Which sentence is the topic sentence?
b. Which order is used in this paragraph?

4

CONTINUITY
IN THE
PARAGRAPH

Continuity means literally "holding together." It's what gives your writing a sense of smoothness as you go from one idea to the next. You get continuity by good organization, because the clear, logical arrangement makes the order of thought easy to follow. But you also get it from the language you use to *tell* your reader how your ideas fit together—you get it in *transitions*.

Transitions are like bridges: they carry your reader across the gaps between sentences and paragraphs. Find the meaning in the etymology: *trans*, "across"; *-ition*, "going"; *trans-ition*—"going across." *So a transition is a word or a phrase that connects ideas. Within the paragraph, transitions show how sentences are tied to each other and to the main idea.*

Learn to use three common transitional devices:

1. Pronoun reference
2. Repetition of important words
3. Transitional expression

PRONOUN REFERENCE

First, learn to use pronoun reference to achieve continuity.

Take the following paragraph as an example of the way pronouns can be used to tie sentences together in the paragraph. Here, Henry Steele Commager begins with the topic sentence "The American is optimistic, self-confident, and self-satisfied." In the rest of the paragraph Commager gets continuity by using the word *he* (and its variants *his* and *him*) to refer back to *the American*. Note that the pronoun appears at or near the beginning of most of the sentences, and that there is never any doubt about what word the pronoun refers back to:

> The American is optimistic, self-confident, and self-satisfied. *He* takes for granted that *his* is the best of all countries, the happiest and most virtuous of all societies, the richest and most bounteous of all economies. *He* knows that Providence has favored *him* in the past and *he* takes for granted that *he* will continue to be the object of special dispensation. Collectively *he* has never known defeat, or prolonged misery, and only colored Americans—who are usually left out of calculations—have known oppression. *He* is not indifferent to the past, as long as it is American, and is inclined to believe that history began in 1607 or—if *he* is a Yankee—in 1620. Although less sure of progress than *his* fathers or grandfathers, *he* is confident that if there is progress, it will be under American leadership and bear the American imprint. Accustomed to seeing *his boldest* plans and most sanguine anticipations realized, *he* believes that they will continue to be fulfilled—but with that belief goes a suspicion that in these matters *he* is no longer the free agent *he* was during the period of relative immunity from European affairs.
>
> —Henry Steele Commager, *Portrait of the American*[1]

REPETITION OF IMPORTANT WORDS

Second, learn to repeat important words to achieve continuity.

In one shining paragraph from his essay "The Culture of Machine Living," Max Lerner gets continuity by repeating the word *standardized* (as well as by using clear pronoun reference). He has placed his topic sentence at the end of the preceding paragraph:

"Someone with a satiric intent could do a withering take-off on the rituals of American standardization." Now, he writes:

> Most American babies . . . are born in *standardized* hospitals, with a *standardized* tag put around them to keep them from getting confused with other *standardized* products of the hospital. Many of them grow up in uniform rows of tenements or suburban houses. They are wheeled about in *standard* perambulators, shiny or shabby as may be, fed from *standardized* bottles with *standardized* nipples according to *standardized* formulas, and tied up with *standardized* diapers. In childhood they are fed *standardized* breakfast foods out of *standardized* boxes with pictures of *standardized* heroes on them. They are sent to monotonously similar schoolhouses, where almost uniformly *standardized* teachers ladle out to them *standardized* information out of *standardized* textbooks . . . .
> —Max Lerner, *The Culture of Machine Living*[2]

But that is, after all, a *tour de force*, a highly polished display of technical virtuosity—and you are not very likely to want to imitate its methods. For a more practical example of the way word repetition can be used to tie sentences together, look closely at this paragraph: it gets continuity by repeating the words *reality, teachers, students,* and *system*:

> Theorists can keep *reality* at arm's length for long periods of time. *Teachers* and administrators can't. They are closeted with *reality* all day long. In many instances they are co-prisoners with electronic-age *students* in the old pencil box cell. And it is the best *teachers* and the best *students* who are in the most trouble because they are challenging the *system* constantly. It is the *system* which has to come under scrutiny. *Teachers* and *students* can say, in the words of the Late, Late Show, "Baby, this thing is bigger than both of us." It won't be ameliorated by a few dashes of good will or a little more hard work . . . .
> —John M. Culkin, S.J., *A Schoolman's Guide to Marshall McLuhan*[3]

TRANSITIONAL EXPRESSIONS

Finally, *learn to use transitional expressions to achieve continuity.*
Transitional expressions are words and phrases that, for the most part, have only one job in the language: to show how events or

ideas or things are related to one another. Alone, they mean nothing: empty words, these are. Suppose someone walks up to you and says, "In the first place, however, thus, consequently, nevertheless, last!" See?

But as gimmicks and gadgets of language they are most useful. They underline infinitely important relationships; they give you an extraordinarily exact way of showing how sentences in a paragraph are related to the main idea and to each other.

Pull the transitional expressions from this paragraph, for example—and see how little sense is left:

Contrast: introduces contrasting conclusion

Addition: shows how one thing happens after another

Result: introduces conclusion drawn from preceding paragraphs

Addition: introduces explanation for preceding statement

Addition: introduces further explanation

Result: introduces conclusion drawn from details in this paragraph

Thus, in the perspective of biology, war first dwindles to the status of a rare curiosity. Further probing, however, makes it loom large again. For one thing, it is a form of intra-specific struggle, and as such may be useless or even harmful to the species as a whole. Then we find that one of the very few animal species that make war is man; and man is today not merely the highest product of evolution, but the only type still capable of real evolutionary progress. And, war, though it need not always be so harmful to the human species and its progress, indubitably is so when conducted in the total fashion which is necessary in this technological age. Thus war is not merely a human problem; it is a biological problem of the broadest scope, for on its abolition may depend life's ability to continue the progress which it has slowly but steadily achieved through more than a thousand million years.

—Sir Julian Huxley, *War as a Biological Phenomenon*[1]

As you write, then, keep before you this "catalog" of transitional expressions, organized around the relationships they usually bring out:

Addition   additionally, again, also, and also, and then, as well, besides, beyond that, equally important, first (second, third, fourth, finally, last, lastly, *etc.*), for one thing, further, furthermore, in addition, likewise, moreover, next, now, on top of that, over and above that

Comparison	in the same way, likewise, similarly
Contrast	after all, although this may be true, and yet, be that as it may, but, even so, for all that, however, in contrast, in other circumstances, in spite of that, nevertheless, nonetheless, on the contrary, on the other hand, otherwise, still, yet
Emphasis	above all, certainly, especially, in any event, in fact, in particular, indeed, most important, surely
Exemplification	as an example, as an illustration, for example, for instance, in other words, in particular, that is
Place	above that, at this point, below that, beyond that, here, near by, next to that, on the other side, outside, within
Reason	for this purpose, for this reason, to this end
Result	accordingly, as a consequence, as a result, consequently, for that reason, hence, inevitably, necessarily, that being the case, then, therefore, thus
Summary	as has been noted, as I have said, finally, in brief, in other words, in short, in sum, lastly, on the whole, to be sure, to sum up
Time	after a while, afterward, at last, at length, at once, briefly, by degrees, eventually, finally, first, (second, third, etc.), gradually, immediately, in a short time, in the future, in the meantime, instantaneously, later, meanwhile, promptly, soon, suddenly

USING TRANSITIONAL DEVICES

In most paragraphs, *mix your transitional devices: combine pronoun reference, repetition of important words, and transitional expressions to achieve the most effective continuity.*

The reason for the mixture is quite simple: repetition dulls, but variety sharpens, interest. Look at the next paragraph, for example, where the writer balances pronoun reference (*we, us, our*), repetition of important words (*teen-agers, teen-years, teens*), and transitional expressions (*for instance, on the other hand*)—to get continuity *and* interest.

Pronoun (referring back to *teen-agers*)

Pronoun

Transitional expression

Pronoun

Pronoun

Transitional expression

Important word

Pronoun

Pronoun

Repetition of important word

Repetition of important word

Pronoun

Pronoun

Pronoun

And since we [*teen-agers*] are so new, many people have some very wrong ideas about us. For instance, the newspapers are always carrying advice-columns telling our mothers how to handle us, their "bewildered maladjusted offspring," and the movies portray us as half-witted bops; and in the current best sellers, authors recall their own confused, unhappy youth. On the other hand, speakers tell us that these teen-years are the happiest and freest of our lives, or hand us the "leaders of tomorrow, forge on the future" line. The general opinion is that teen-agers are either car-stealing, dope-taking delinquents, or immature, weepy adolescents with nothing on our minds but boys (or girls as the case may be). Most adults have one of two attitudes toward the handling of teens —some say that only a sound beating will keep us in line; others treat us as mentally unbalanced creatures on the brink of insanity, who must be pampered and shielded at any cost.

—Judith D. Matz, *The New Third Age*[5]

In brief, don't make your reader jump desperately from one idea to another, like a flea changing dogs; use your transitions to *carry* him across the gaps between sentences. *Get continuity in orderly arrangement; point out the continuity with transitional devices—pronoun reference, repetition of important words, and transitional expressions.*

EXERCISE   1

For each of the following paragraphs, list the transitional devices used to connect one sentence with another. Identify each device as *pronoun reference, repetition of important words,* or *transitional expression.*

1.   I suspect that lifetime chastity, the cult of virginity, is a characteristic of the sophisticated and complex cultures that we call civiliza-

tion: it would hardly seem either possible or worthwhile to the more primitive cultures closer to nature. Yet such cultures do have a variety of religious controls over sexual behavior. Sex may be taboo before or during special activities such as fishing, hunting or war. Sex may be required in relation to ceremonies to insure fertility of crops. Either food or sex may get involved in ideas of sacrifice, and the sacrifice may involve either abstention or indulgence. Thus we find cults of temple prostitution on the one hand, and of chastity on the other; ceremonies which require that no food be eaten, and others at which participants must eat.

—Marston Bates, *Man, Food and Sex*[6]

2.   We are, of course, surrounded by shams. Until recently the schools were full of them—the notion that education can be had without tears, that puffed rice is a better intellectual diet than oatmeal, that adjustment to the group is more important than knowing where the group is going, and that democracy has made it a sin to separate the sheep from the goats. Mercifully, these are much less evident now than they were before Sputnik startled us into our wits.

In front of the professor are the shams of the learned fraternity. There is the sham science of the social scientist who first invented a speech for fuddling thought and then proceeded to tell us in his lock-jawed way what we already knew. There is the sham humanism of the humanist who wonders why civilization that once feasted at his table is repelled by the shredded and desiccated dishes that often lie on it today. There is the sham message of the physical scientist who feels that his mastery of nature has made him an expert in politics and morals, and there are all the other brands of hokum which have furnished material for satire since the first quacks established themselves in the first cloisters.

—Alan Simpson, *The Marks of an Educated Man*[7]

3.   To climb to the top in the business world, the experts tell us, you need to have the proper birth, the right education, and a gregarious personality. So far as birth is concerned, you almost have to be a white, Anglo-Saxon, Protestant male: Negroes, Jews, and women seldom reach the top in the business world. The right education, of course, means a *college* education. If you don't have a diploma, you are eliminated from the best positions almost automatically. If you can jump these two hurdles, there's still another: you need a gregarious personality. You *must* be able to get along with the rest of the herd. You *must* be liked by everyone. And you must *seem* to like everyone else. In other words, smile a lot—whether you feel like it or not. If you're

a white, Anglo-Saxon, Protestant male, start climbing: you shouldn't have far to go.

—James K. Bell

4.   Many teachers feel that exams take all the fun out of teaching. They turn friends into enemies, make the classroom a battlefield, and set the hostile troops against their leader . . . . Exams create an impassable gulf between instructor and student. No matter how informal, friendly, and relaxed things had been in the past, they will never be quite the same again. The instructor knows that he must sit in judgment on his students. The little girl with the cute legs in the front row may never smile at him again nor will the tall fellow in the heavy sweater come up after class. Exams turn everything upside down in the instructor's mind. The stupid-looking lout who sits in the back row and jokes with his neighbor writes the best examination of all. The students who look interested and come to him afterward turn in poor papers. With a heavy heart the young instructor gives C's and D's to his favorites and A's and B's to parts of the anonymous sea of faces which seemed completely bored during the class hour. At judgment day both the instructor and his class have been found wanting. No longer is he the genial and easygoing fellow who keeps his class amused during the period (they all used to say it was "the shortest hour on campus"). Nor are they his eager and alert students, ready to take down his every word and cherish it until the ink fades and the paper turns yellow. . . . They have learned that their instructor is like all the rest, a teacher at heart.

—Robert Sommer, *The Class War*[8]

5.   In this wise, the American garden is a cultural cognate of the Trobriand Island yam-house. A Trobriander builds his yam storage hut in such a way that passers-by can estimate how many yams are inside it. There are wide gaps between the beams so that one may see the quality of the fruit; of course the best yams are placed up forward. Especially excellent yams are decorated and hung up outside the hut. But the chief of a Trobriand village need not go to these lengths. His position is established regardless of the size of his yams. Similarly, an American whose prestige derives from more secure foundations can afford to ignore or even flaunt the community lawn-and-garden standards. Not long ago, for instance, missile scientist Werner von Braun, whose professional achievements afford him all the distinction he can want, bought a house and promptly poured a thick layer of grass-green concrete over the front yard—probably gaining, in the process, even more esteem than if he had chosen to raise rare plants.

—Norman M. Lobsenz, *Some Masks of Pleasure*[9]

EXERCISE   2

In the following paragraphs, list an appropriate *transitional expression* for each blank space.

1.   As of today, I am fed up with the food served in the campus dining hall. My disenchantment started in September—the day I bit into a hamburger to find myself staring at a long strand of grey hair that trailed out of the meat, through the mayonnaise, and over the edge of the bun. _____, I was not much surprised by the little things I came across in October and November: bugs in the salad and a bobby pin in the meatloaf, _____. _____ in December the food was worse—and a little dirtier. For Christmas dinner, _____, the cook gave me a thin slice of rolled turkey, straight out of the can, and dished up a cockroach in my rice pudding. _____ that was excusable (nobody is perfect), but what happened today is not: I had already eaten most of my clam chowder before I found it, at the bottom of the bowl, nestled among the diced potatoes and the chopped onions: one band-aid, slightly used.

2.   During the nineteenth century a whole literature developed around the dewy-eyed and innocent South Seas maiden who was seduced by the white man and then abandoned to a life of misery and regret. This was based on a misreading of Polynesian character. _____, the girl was not abandoned; she had the family, the tribe, the island to return to. _____, she did not put as much into the affair as the white man imagined—she could not, it was a psychological impossibility. Sex does not mean this to the Polynesian. _____, there was no misery to the situation as such. An individual white *tane* (man) might be miserable to live with but his Polynesian vahine could not be made miserable simply because she had lived with him. Once over, the affair continued only in the tortured imagination of the white man.

—Eugene Burdick, *The Polynesian*[10]

3.   According to Ray Brown, a San Francisco sports car expert, the Corvette Fastback is a more economical buy than the Jaguar XKE. _____, the original investment in a Corvette is less: currently, the most expensive model sells for about $5,000—compared with about $5,500 for the Jaguar two-door Roadster (base price without options). _____ _____ the Corvette costs less to maintain—a lot less. Mr. Brown estimates that a Corvette with a 327 cu. in. engine can be maintained for about $5.00 to $7.00 a month,

whereas maintenance on the XKE averages about $35.00 a month and may run as much as $50.00. Mr. Brown explained this difference by pointing out, first, that the high-performance engine in the Jaguar requires much more frequent and more careful tuning, and, second, that parts for imported cars are 100 percent to 150 percent more expensive than parts for American-made cars. _____ the Corvette is a more economical buy for another reason: it has, comparatively, a higher resale value. _____, the Corvette that cost $5,000 originally can be sold for about $4,200 one year later; but the Jaguar XKE that cost $5,500 is worth only $4,300 one year later. In other words, in one year the Corvette depreciates by $800 and the Jaguar by $1,200. For the more economical deal, _____, buy a Corvette: it costs less to begin with, it's cheaper to maintain, and it gives you a better return on your investment when you sell it.

4.   There are at least three reasons why a girl should have a college education: it can give her greater financial gain, a better family life, and richer personal resources. _____, the girl who has a college education is likely to find a better job and make more money. A typist, _____, may earn only $300 a month. A research chemist, _____, may earn more than $15,000 a year. _____, the college-educated girl is likely to have a better family life. _____, she'll be able to communicate with her husband, since she knows more about ideas and about life than the woman who drops out of school in the tenth grade and spends most of her time washing diapers and watching television. _____, the college-educated woman can influence her children's education by taking an intelligent, informed interest in it. _____—and perhaps most important of all—is the fact that a college education gives a woman richer personal resources than she would otherwise have. It gives her a taste for ideas and a knowledge of history, art, philosophy, music, science and so on—something to think about during the long, empty days she spends cleaning house and waiting for her children and husband to come home in the evening. For these three reasons—greater financial gain, a better family life, and richer personal resources—every woman should try to get a college education.

5

FROM PARAGRAPH TO ESSAY

An *essay*, says Dr. Johnson in his famous *Dictionary* (1755), is "A loose sally of the mind; an irregular, indigested piece; not a regular and orderly composition." His definition inadvertently but rather exactly fits the kind of essays scratched out of a black void and tortured onto paper again and again by American college students: feats of self-mutilation performed in morbid despair, frenzied recklessness, or plucky determination.

Against all odds the thing is finally done!

But loose. Irregular. Indigested.

In rare moments of lucidity, an occasional student undoubtedly asks, "Why am I *doing* this to myself?"

Though the mysterious process by which the deed is finally consummated lies beyond our ultimate grasp, there are nevertheless occasions when we all *must* write, spinning out words to tie down vaguely defined ideas, miraculously encountering new thoughts in a maze of words, perceptions, distractions, daydreams. The accomplishment is miraculous—even when badly done.

But it need not be badly done. It need not be loose, irregular, indigested. It need not come with painful laboriousness. Because, curiously enough, there are parts of this miracle that we can understand: like other arts, writing has its own technology. Its mechanics are primitive, as unsophisticated as a brush and a tube of paint. But they are also simple and clear. Teachers can teach them. Students can learn.

You can learn to write two kinds of essays: the "perfectly" organized essay, built on a formula for organization (the pattern laid down in this chapter), and then the more artful "irregular" and "indigested" essay which Dr. Johnson so succinctly defined. The perfectly organized essay gives you a model to follow until you have mastered the principles of organization in the standard expository essay and are ready to experiment with forms of your own.

In this chapter, then, we treat the essay as a formal exercise with rigid limitations and little room for individuality. In the next chapter, however, we treat essay writing as an art, with the freedom, flexibility, and personal integrity of an art, where "Each man," as Emerson has said ". . . is justified in his individuality."

ORGANIZING THE ESSAY

The formula for the perfectly organized expository essay goes like this: *The organization of certain essays is exactly like the organization of certain paragraphs—paragraphs that begin with a topic sentence, use both major and minor supports, and end with a summary sentence.*

When you "expand"* a paragraph of this sort into an essay, this is what happens:

1. The *topic sentence* becomes the *thesis statement* of the essay.
2. Each *major support* becomes a *topic sentence* for a new paragraph in the essay.
3. Each *minor support* provides details to develop its new para-

---

* The essay, obviously, covers a good deal more material than a paragraph; for that reason, you need to add ideas and evidence to the essay that you couldn't possibly force into a paragraph. So, we use the notion of "expanding" a paragraph into an essay mainly as a teaching technique; we don't propose that you see it as the *only* way to organize an essay. And, of course, we are not at all interested here in the long essay; instead, we aim at the brief, tightly organized essay (500-750 words), put into four or five paragraphs.

graph in the essay. (With the help of a lot more material, obviously.)

4. The *summary sentence* becomes the *concluding paragraph* in the essay.

Linger for a moment on these similarities. Think of what they mean: you *already* know how to organize an essay—*perfectly!*

But just in case this is too much to grasp all at once, study the diagram below. It sums up what happens when a typical "complex deductive paragraph" grows into an essay.

Paragraph		Essay	
I. *Topic Sentence*	becomes	I. *Thesis Statement*	(paragraph 1)
II. *Major Support*	becomes	II. *Topic Sentence* ⎫	
A. *Minor Support*	becomes	A. *Development* ⎬	(paragraph 2)
B. *Minor Support*	becomes	B. *Development* ⎭	
III. *Major Support*	becomes	III. *Topic Sentence* ⎫	
A. *Minor Support*	becomes	A. *Development* ⎬	(paragraph 3)
B. *Minor Support*	becomes	B. *Development* ⎭	
IV. *Summary Sentence*	becomes	IV. *Concluding Paragraph*	(paragraph 4)

There is nothing magic about the numbers here, by the way: *the formula works just as well for paragraphs with three or four major supports and fewer (or more) minor supports.* The diagram just happens to show a paragraph with two major supports, each developed by two minor supports. The topic stentence becomes the thesis statement in paragraph 1; the major supports become the topic sentences for paragraphs 2 and 3; the minor supports provide details to develop paragraphs 2 and 3; the summary sentence becomes the concluding paragraph. As a result, we have a *four*-paragraph essay. If we had started with a paragraph developed through *three* major supports, we would have wound up with a *five*-paragraph essay. It's as simple as that. The important thing is not *NUMBERS*—but the basic, simple, beautifully clear *FORM* of the model paragraph as it grows into a model essay.

Now, let's see how it works. Look closely at the next paragraph, for example. It exactly fits the pattern of our model paragraph as we diagrammed it above. This paragraph begins with a topic sentence:

> According to many authorities, the federal government is waging an undeclared war on privacy—particularly through two of its agencies, the Internal Revenue Service and the Department of Justice.

It has two major supports:

1. To begin with, many agents of the Internal Revenue Service are trained to use sensitive electronic equipment in undercover surveillance work.
2. But none of this is quite as dangerous as the threat to privacy posed by the Justice Department itself.

The paragraph develops each of these major supports with two minor supports, as you will see. And it ends with a summary sentence:

All in all, there is enough evidence to convince many people that the government, through these two agencies in particular, is making an unwarranted attack on our privacy.

Read the paragraph carefully:

According to many authorities, the federal government is waging an undeclared war on privacy—particularly through two of its agencies, the Internal Revenue Service and the Department of Justice (TOPIC SENTENCE). *To begin with, many agents of the Internal Revenue Service are trained to use sensitive electronic equipment in undercover surveillance work* (MAJOR SUPPORT). At its school in Washington, D.C., the agents study "Surreptitious Entry," "Microphone Installation," and "Amplifiers and Recorders" (MINOR SUPPORT). Putting this training to use, agents in the field have been known to "bug" conference rooms and telephones—sometimes in violation of federal law (MINOR SUPPORT). *But none of this is quite as dangerous as the threat to privacy posed by the Justice Department itself* (MAJOR SUPPORT). First, the Justice Department is computerizing vast files of information scraped together by assorted snoopers (MINOR SUPPORT). For example, numerous Congressmen have reported their conviction that their telephones have been tapped by the FBI (MINOR SUPPORT). *All in all, there is enough evidence to convince many people that the government, through these two agencies in particular, is making an unwarranted attack on our privacy* (SUMMARY SENTENCE).

The paragraph is stuffed; it *has* to become an essay: the subject teems with important ideas; the evidence is overwhelming. And this is where the fun comes in, because we can let our minds play with words and ideas and implications. To begin with, we can actually introduce our thesis statement—instead of shutting our eyes and jumping into a topic sentence. Also, we can unfold our evidence in all its convincing power—instead of jabbing a finger at it in passing.

Finally, we can really make something of our conclusion: we can draw the implications of our evidence in bold detail.

Before we do all this, stop long enough to remember that:

1. Our topic sentence becomes the thesis statement in the first paragraph of our essay.
2. Our two major supports become topic sentences for two new paragraphs in our essay.
3. Our minor supports provide details to develop the two new paragraphs in our essay. (And we'll add more details, of course.)
4. Our summary sentence becomes the concluding paragraph in our essay (with more emphasis on implications).

So, it works like this:

THE WATCHFUL EYE

From the age of uniformity, from the age of Big Brother, from the age of doublethink—greetings!
—George Orwell, *1984*

INTRODUCTORY QUOTATION *(optional)*

In *1984*, he was everywhere you were, watching with a watchful eye. Look up at a wall in a silent, empty street, and the eyes of Big Brother met yours; move, and the eyes followed you. In your room they watched, too, from the blank "telescreen." In your office, in the long bureaucratic hallways, in a rest room, in a bar—the eyes were everywhere, always. "You had to live," Orwell says, "—did live, from habit that became instinct—in the assumption that every sound you made was overheard and, except in darkness, scrutinized." Would you like to live like this? Of course not. If you value your privacy, you don't want *anyone* to invade it, for any reason. *But the fact of the matter is that the federal government is waging an undeclared war on privacy—particularly through two of its agencies, the Internal Revenue Service and the Justice Department.*

THESIS STATEMENT

To begin with, many agents of the Internal Revenue Service are trained to use sensitive electronic equipment in undercover surveillance work. According to Senator Edward V. Long in his book *The Intruders*, the IRS has set up a school in Washington, D.C., where agents learn to install microphones and tap telephones, for example. The official curriculum for the school lists courses in

TOPIC SENTENCE

"Surreptitious Entry," "Microphone Installation," and
"Amplifiers and Recorders."[1] What's more, IRS agents
actually *use* these skills. For instance, agents in the field
have been known to tap telephones, in violation of the
Constitution and of federal law,[2] and to maintain conference rooms equipped with two-way mirrors and con-
cealed microphones.[3]

But none of this is quite as dangerous as the threat   TOPIC
to privacy posed by the Justice Department itself. Vast   SENTENCE
files are now being computerized on thousands of Amer-
icans.[4] According to officials in the Department, files are
being kept on Black militants, opponents of the war in
Viet Nam, members of left-wing as well as right-wing
extremist organizations, and liberal political officials—
as well as moderates—who are thought to condone or
encourage civil disobedience.[5] Moreover, numerous
Congressmen have reported their conviction that their
telephones have been tapped by the FBI.[6] "There is no
doubt about it," one Congressman insists.[7] According to
Representative Hale Boggs, ". . . the fear of phone tap-
ping is as dangerous as the fact, for it can only chill the
kind of free discourse we must have if we are to continue as a free society."[8]

The war on privacy is not, of course, a simple matter   CONCLUSION
of governmental "spying" on innocent citizens. The government *must* apprehend criminals; it *must* detect crime,
when it can, for the protection of all of us. At the same
time, we cherish our right to privacy—and we don't
want to lose it. All in all, there is enough evidence to
convince many people that the government, through
these two agencies in particular, is making an unwarranted and dangerous attack on this right to privacy.
Surely the time has come for all of us to say, *"Don't
look—we'd rather be free."*

Looking back, you can see that many of your problems are
solved: *because the essay really is like a paragraph.* Look at your
thesis statement. It closely resembles the carefully phrased, very concrete topic sentence you have already learned to write. And like a
good topic sentence, your thesis statement gives clear signals for organization: "particularly through *two* of its agencies, *the Internal
Revenue Service and Justice Department.*" You know that the Internal Revenue Service will be the subject of one paragraph in your

essay, and that the Justice Department will be the subject of the next paragraph.

Once you have written the introduction, then, you write two more paragraphs, organized and developed as usual. *For there's nothing new here.* The middle paragraphs can be organized in any of the ways you already know; they can be developed through any of the techniques of development that you already know. So, these two paragraphs are exactly like the paragraphs you have been writing all along. There's no summary sentence, of course—but there might be: it's a matter of emphasis, as we pointed out in Chapter 3.

Finally, your concluding paragraph works much like the summary sentence: it sums up important points. And the important point in this essay is not just that our privacy is, perhaps, threatened, but that we ought to *do* something because it is. In the last paragraph, then, you dwell on the implications of your ideas—you hand your reader a message to take away with him: *THE* message of the essay.

But there are still a few unanswered questions, like these:

1. How do you get continuity between paragraphs?
2. What makes the best introduction?
3. What makes the best conclusion?

We'll answer these three questions in the rest of this chapter.

EXERCISE 1

With more details, the following paragraphs could be expanded into essays. In each paragraph

a. Find the sentence that would become the *thesis statement* in an essay.
b. Find the sentences that would become *topic sentences* for new paragraphs in an essay.
c. Find the sentence that would become the *concluding paragraph* in an essay.

A. (1) Movies are currently rated in four categories, according to the audiences for which they are appropriate. (2) The first rating is

General Audience (G), designating movies suitable for the family. (3) Such films include *Hello, Dolly! True Grit!, 2001: A Space Odyssey,* and *The Andromeda Strain.* (4) The second rating is Qualified General (GP), which means that such movies might be appropriate to children but that parental guidance is advised. (5) Examples include *Butch Cassidy and the Sundance Kid, Love Story, Patton,* and *Valley of the Dolls.* (6) For more mature audiences, the rating is Restricted (R), which would comprehend movies suitable for mature teenagers as well as for adults. (7) The films in this group are often characterized by their serious and candid treatment of sex and violence, as in *Joe,* which concludes—after an all-night drug-inspired orgy—with a massacre of hippies; or by their comic preoccupation with sex, as in *Bob and Carol and Ted and Alice* and *There's a Girl in My Soup.* (8) Finally, there is the rating Adults Only (X), for films restricted to those over eighteen. (9) X-rated films, as in *Beyond the Valley of the Dolls, Coming Apart, Damned,* and *Daughter,* deal explicitly and almost exclusively with sexual material. (10) Thus, while the rating system does not offer a flawless guide for motion picture audiences, it is certainly superior to no system at all: parents in particular will want to take advantage of it.

B.   (1) While it is almost impossible to define poetry, several notable attempts to do so were made by nineteenth century poets. (2) Edgar Allen Poe emphasized that the essence of poetry is beauty. (3) "I would define the poetry of words as the rhythmical creation of beauty," Poe wrote. (4) "Its sole arbiter is taste." (5) He added that poetry had little or nothing to do with intellect, conscience, duty, or truth. (6) William Wordsworth, on the other hand, saw poetry in terms of feeling. (7) "Poetry is the imaginative expression of strong feeling, usually rhythmical . . . the spontaneous overflow of powerful feelings recollected in tranquility." (8) Another Romantic, Percy Bysshe Shelley, seemed, in his definition of poetry, to stress the most exalted experiences of superior men. (9) "Poetry," he wrote, "is the record of the best and happiest moments of the best and happiest minds." (10) A fourth poet, the eminent Victorian Matthew Arnold, thought of poetry as more rational and intellectual. (11) He defined poetry as "a criticism of life under the conditions fixed for such criticism by the laws of poetic truth and beauty." (12) After all these studied and sophisticated definitions, however, I believe we are still at a loss to say for sure what poetry *is*: it eludes logical definition so persistently that perhaps one can only offer an example, saying as he does so, "*This* is a poem."

C.   (1) It is well-known, as Dr. Spock has taught several generations of mothers now, that children go through fairly predictable stages of development; it is not so well known that adults also go through stages, though the stages are not as sharply outlined or clearly predictable. (2) We might call them characteristic *ages* instead. (3) According to a charming medieval poem entitled *The Parlement of the Thre Ages* ("The Debate of the Three Ages"), there are three distinct periods in the life of men. (4) The first is represented, in the poem, by Youth. (5) Youth is thirty, he dresses in fanciful green clothes, and he loves women, dancing, chess, hunting, and story telling. (6) The second period is represented by Middle Age. (7) Middle Age, dressed in staid, sedate gray, is sixty years old. (8) He says it is foolish to squander money on fine clothes, as Youth has done, and to squander time on frivolous pursuits like women, dancing, games, and sports. (9) He says that only one thing matters in this life—money: land, houses, cattle, tenants, and cold cash. (10) The third period is represented by Old Age, who is dressed in solemn black. (11) Old Age is a hundred years old; when he talks, he mumbles and drools; he is wizened, twisted, and ugly. (12) He is near death. (13) But he makes himself understood: he too was once young and in love with love; once middle-aged and in love with money. (14) Now, as he feels death stalk him, he has realized that only religion counts, since no one—not one of the good, great, wise, and proud men who have ever lived—has escaped death. (15) "Confess your sins!" he tells his companions! (16) "Death is just behind you!" (17) And after such words he dramatically illustrates his point by dying, "as dead as a doornail," the poet says. (18) He was not a very good poet, perhaps—but he advances an interesting thesis, and maybe a true one: now that I have *passed* thirty, I far prefer Benjamin Franklin's picture on a dull-green one hundred dollar bill to the glossiest reproductions of the sexiest Playmates in all of Bunnyland.

CONTINUITY BETWEEN PARAGRAPHS

To get continuity between paragraphs, use one of these traditional devices:

1. Repetition of important words

2. Transitional expressions
3. Sentences of transition
4. Paragraphs of transition

Repetition of Important Words

First, use repetition of important words—as you would to get continuity *within* a paragraph.

Take these two paragraphs, for example, from F. L. Lucas' essay "What Is Style?" The first paragraph begins, "*Clarity* comes before *brevity*"; the second, "But *clarity* and *brevity* . . . are only a beginning." The repetition of important words ties the two paragraphs together:

> *Clarity comes before brevity*, but it is a fallacy that wordiness is necessarily clearer. Metternich when he thought something he had written was obscure would simply go through it crossing out everything irrelevant. What remained, he found, often became clear. Wellington, asked to recommend three names for the post of Commander-In-Chief, India, took a piece of paper and wrote three times—"Napier." Pages could not have been clearer—or more forcible. On the other hand the lectures and the sentences of Coleridge became at times bewildering because his mind was often "wiggle-waggle"; just as he could not even walk straight on a path.
>
> But *clarity and brevity*, though a good beginning, are only a beginning. By themselves they may remain bare and bleak. When Calvin Coolidge, asked by his wife what the preacher had preached on, replied "Sin," and, asked what the preacher had said, replied, "He was against it," he was brief enough. But one hardly envies Mrs. Coolidge.
>
> —F. L. Lucas, *What Is Style?*[9]

Transitional Expressions

Second, use transitional expressions—just as you would to get continuity *within* a paragraph.

Consider the last paragraphs of Robert Jungk's essay "World without Walls." He has already built his case: industrial spying goes on almost everywhere. He has already shown that the average American employee does exactly what he's expected to do—because he knows he's being watched. Now, Mr. Jungk takes up the consequences of this conformity, for the individual in the first paragraph, for the nation in the second; and the two paragraphs are strung together on the word *thus:*

> This standard mask of the "jolly good fellow," of the "easy going guy," of the "sweet girl," grows onto some of them as a second face. It is no longer a question of the inner conscience, of a true impulse of the soul, but of codes of behavior coming from the outside. To judge how the wind from the heights of the directors' office will blow, how the potential giver of an order would like the salesman to behave, to guess how a superior pictures the man whom he will promote, this is the most important asset in the battle for a living. In place of rules and regulations imposed by the authorities appears a far stricter self-censorship. Be sure to do nothing striking or unusual, which could be regarded as neurotic, as egotistical, as maladjusted or perhaps even revolutionary.
>
> *Thus* in the "world without walls" which has increasingly come to be, the type of man on which America's greatness was based is becoming rarer and rarer; the strong, free man guided by his own conscience, constantly searching for something new. Since four out of five Americans today are employees (as against one in five a hundred years ago), a profound alteration in the national character is taking place, a contradiction of the democratic tradition and a cause of concern to every friend of America.
>
> —Robert Jungk, *World without Walls*[10]

Sentences of Transition

Third, use a *sentence* of transition—from time to time.

The sentence of transition makes a complete statement that connects what has gone before with what is to come. In our model essay, for example, we might have tied together paragraphs two and three with such a sentence. If we had, the first sentence in paragraph three would have made the transition; the *second* sentence would have been our topic sentence, like this:

> So, the Internal Revenue Service does not always respect the citizen's right to privacy—and the same is true of the Justice Department (SENTENCE OF TRANSITION). In fact, the Justice Department poses an even more dangerous threat to privacy (TOPIC SENTENCE).

Paragraphs of Transition

Finally, use a *paragraph* of transition—from time to time.

The paragraph of transition is one whole paragraph, usually quite short (sometimes only one sentence). Its job is to connect two parts of an essay: that is, it ties together what has gone before and what is to come. You won't see this kind of paragraph very often— especially in brief essays—but it is used, and you ought to know about it.

Here is an example: in his essay "On Privacy: The American Dream, What Happened to It," William Faulkner begins by describing this dream, in very careful detail. In much of the rest of the essay he explains what happened to the dream. He ties together these two parts of his essay with this transitional paragraph:

> Something happened to the Dream. Many things did. This, I think, is a symptom of one of them.[11]

In the next paragraph he begins his analysis of the symptom.

There are, of course, still other ways to make the transition from one paragraph to another. But if you can use these four—the repetition of important words, transitional expressions, sentences of transition, and paragraphs of transition—continuity between paragraphs will be one of your strong points.

WRITING THE INTRODUCTION

In the first paragraph of your essay, you should try to do two things:

1. interest your reader;
2. state your thesis.

The basic technique is simple: don't begin by taking two steps backward; instead, dive into your subject. In doing so, you can catch the attention of your reader in many ways, a few of which we will comment on here. When you have him "hooked," give him your thesis immediately—at the end of the first paragraph, if possible.

Narrative Introductions

The narrative introduction begins with a brief story; it shows people *acting*, as in this opening paragraph from an essay on college students during the Great Depression of the 1930's. The thesis is stated at the beginning of the second paragraph:

> Across the campus of Oklahoma A. and M. College moved a weird procession. At the front was an ancient open flivver, sufficiently battered to be termed "collegiate." In its front seat were two boys; in its back seat a bale of hay. There followed another car, differing from the first only in the number and kind of dents in its fenders and body. It was also manned by two boys. Its back seat was occupied by a large crate of protesting poultry. Then came a fifth boy leading a Jersey cow. The cow refused to be influenced by the obvious impatience of the motorized portion of the procession, so it was hours later when the strange group finally arrived in front of a house on the outskirts of the college town. The poultry was given a back yard coop in which to live and, presumably, to lay eggs. The cow was tethered in an adjoining field. Then from some recesses in the battered hulls of the flivvers the boys pulled out some 200 quarts of canned fruits and vegetables and a dozen cured hams. With meat and vegetables in the cellar and prospective eggs and milk in the back yard, the five were ready for higher education.
>
> *College students have probably developed more ingenious ways of beating the depression than any other group in America . . . .*
> —Gilbert Love, *College Students Are Beating the Depression*[12]

Or look at this narrative opening: it uses a brief, humorous incident to set the stage for the thesis statement at the end of the second paragraph. (Actually, the concept is one paragraph; the paragraph division occurs because of the dialogue.)

> On vacation in rural New England, the president of an Eastern university woke up one night with sharp abdominal pains. He got to the nearest hospital, where a local technician took a sample of his blood and confirmed the doctor's verdict: appendicitis. Everything was being readied for the operation, when the surgeon learned that his patient, like himself, was a Rotarian. At this news he paused.
>
> "Better do that blood test again," he said thoughtfully. "The lab girl isn't very good." A fresh sample was taken, and this time the white count proved normal. His appendix in fine shape—he had nothing more than indigestion—the educator left the hospital with his faith in Rotarians unshaken. *But he vowed never again to place blind trust in a medical laboratory.*
> —Maya Pines, *Danger in our Medical Labs*[13]

Expository Introductions

The expository opening begins by explaining or describing. Sometimes the expository opening paragraph is little more than a thesis statement. In that case, the writer often tries to capture his reader's interest with a startling thesis statement or a bit of catchy phrasing, as in this paragraph from Welles Hangen's "Stirrings Behind the Wall: East Germany's Muted Revolution":

> Robert Havemann, the scientist, could never be compared to Galileo, but Robert Havemann the heretic is more remarkable. *He has refused to recant.*[14]

And sometimes it is a carefully detailed description:

> Look at him. A tall, lanky, young man, aged thirty, with a ready boyish smile and charm that is almost a tool. Blue-gray eyes, a handsome face, a sensitive mouth, blond hair. He likes flashy clothes, Italian shoes, tight trousers, colorful sweaters. Does he really come from Moscow, or from Saint Germain des Pres, Via Veneto, or Greenwich Village? Why is he the idol of Soviet youth, who recite his poems by heart? Why do the Russians first promote him at home, send him abroad on almost official assignments—and then suddenly unleash the whole Soviet propaganda apparatus in an attempt to destroy him? Is he a showman or poet, prophet or opportunist, rebel or Soviet propagandist-at-large? *Who are you, Evgeny Evtushenko?*
> —Michel Gordey, *Consider Me a Communist*[15]

Another way to get the interest of your reader in an expository introduction is to begin with a direct quotation—sometimes from a literary source, sometimes from a central figure expressing an important idea or attitude in your essay. Look at the next paragraph, for example: a direct quotation introduces the subject and at the same time leads to the thesis statement in the last sentence in the paragraph.

> "It's not my fault! Nothing in this lousy world is my fault, don't you see that? I don't want it to be and it can't be and it won't be." This outcry comes from Kerouac's Sal Paradise, but it expresses the deep conviction of multitudes of irresponsibles in the age of self-pity. *It is a curious paradox that, while the self is the center of all things, the self is never to blame for anything.*
> —Robert Elliot Fitch, *The Irresponsibles*[16]

Finally, we come to the type of expository opening paragraph that gets interest by presenting facts and figures of a rather startling nature, as in this opening paragraph:

> Over one million Americans have already been slaughtered in highway accidents. A million more will be killed over the next 15 years. *Irate safety experts say that fully two-thirds of all traffic victims could be spared their lives if auto manufacturers could place less emphasis on "styling" and more on "crash-worthiness."*
>
> —Ralph Ginzburg, *S.O.B. Detroit*[17]

In brief, the good introduction, like a short skirt or a flashy car, gets attention: it says, "Look!" But it does more than that, of course —for it also leads to the thesis statement, usually the last sentence of the first paragraph or the first sentence of the second paragraph; and on your thesis statement hangs all the rest of the essay.

EXERCISE 2

A.   Write an opening paragraph for a 500-word essay on one of the following subjects. Be as interesting, as dramatic, and as informed as possible. Place your thesis statement at the end of the paragraph— and underline it to show that it really *is* your thesis statement. *Remember that your thesis statement should outline your essay for you, so that your reader can see immediately how many paragraphs you intend to write and what the subject of each paragraph will be.*

1. The dangers of cigarette smoking or of using another drug
2. Reasons for or against getting married
3. Causes of racial prejudice
4. Advantages or disadvantages of working your way through college
5. Reasons for supporting or not supporting the women's liberation movement
6. Rebellion of the young
7. The police
8. Conscientious objectors
9. Professorial tenure
10. Guaranteed minimum income

B.   Write a brief paragraph explaining what the thesis statement you wrote in part A of this exercise commits you to do in the rest of your essay. In particular, explain how many paragraphs you would write for the body of your essay, and what would be the subject of each paragraph.

WRITING THE CONCLUSION

The concluding paragraph of the essay should provide an exit for both the reader and the writer.

The last paragraph should drive home your main points by summarizing or repeating your thesis. And under *no* circumstances should you introduce a new idea in the last paragraph, for, naturally, your reader would expect further development of such a point.

To get into the final paragraph, use appropriate transitional words: *then, finally, thus, in short, therefore* (but not *in conclusion—* please).

Here is the final paragraph from Russell Lynes's "Highbrow, Lowbrow, Middlebrow." His thesis is that it isn't wealth or family that makes prestige these days: it's high thinking. He begins and ends his essay with a reference to his grandmother. The implied transitional word is *thus.*

> If life for grandmother, who wouldn't dine with the Cartiers, was simple in its social distinctions, life is becoming equally simple for us. The rungs of the ladder may be different, it may even be a different ladder, but it's onward and upward just the same. You may not be known by which fork you use for the fish these days, but you will be known by which key you use for your *Finnegan's Wake.*[18]

Here is the concluding paragraph from Aaron Copland's *What to Listen for in Music.* His transitional word is *then.* His thesis is that the whole listening process will become clearer if we break it up into its basic parts through active listening.

> What the reader must strive for, then, is a more *active* kind of listening. Whether you listen to Mozart or Duke Ellington, you can deepen your understanding of music only by being a more conscious

and more aware listener—not someone who is just listening, but someone who is listening *for* something.[19]

And here is the concluding paragraph from Richard Hanser's "A Plea for Literary Mayhem." His transitional word *thus* is implied. His thesis is that literary feuds should be carried on with vigor.

> A revival of the gentle art of literary mayhem would do us far more good in the way of excitement and vitality than harm in battered reputations and bruised sensibilities. An infusion into our republic of letters of the kind of frontier vigor which once prompted man to shoot from the hip when crossed or challenged would be a most salutary thing.[20]

Finally, here is a concluding paragraph from Robert Benchley's "Throwing Back the European Offensive." His transitional phrase, *whichever way*, refers back to the two methods he has recommended to combat the menace of returning travelers.

> Whichever way you pick to defend yourself against the assaults of people who want to tell you about Europe, don't forget that it was I who told you how. I'm going to Europe myself next year and if you try to pull either of these systems on *me* when I get back, I will recognize them at once, and it will just go all the harder with you. But of course, *I* will have something to tell that will be worth hearing.[21]

IN CONCLUSION

Writing the expository essay can be easy if you remember that it is simply an expanded paragraph. That is:

1. The thesis statement organizes the essay in much the same way as the good topic sentence organizes the paragraph.
2. The paragraph topic sentences in the body of the essay are much the same as the major supports in the paragraph.
3. Paragraph development within the body of the essay is just as urgent as it is when you write the paragraph as a self-contained composition.
4. Transitions between paragraphs are just as necessary as they are between sentences in the paragraph.
5. Concluding paragraphs in the essay do essentially the same job that concluding sentences do in the paragraphs.

Finally, essays require an introductory paragraph that

1. Catch the interest of the reader.
2. Set the stage for the thesis statement, ideally located near the end of the introductory paragraph.

EXERCISE   3

Write a 500-word essay on one of the topics in part A of Exercise 3. Underline your thesis statement twice. Underline the topic sentence of each paragraph in the body of your essay once. Finally, in the margin of your paper, label your concluding paragraph "Conclusion."

If a man does not keep pace with his companions, perhaps
it is because he hears a different drummer.
—Henry David Thoreau

6

THE ART
OF THE
ESSAY

It is the fate of those who toil at the lower employments of life, to be rather driven by the fear of evil, than attracted by the prospect of good; to be exposed to censure, without hope of praise; to be disgraced by miscarriage, or punished for neglect, where success would have been without applause, and diligence without reward.

Among these unhappy mortals is the writer of dictionaries. . . .
—Samuel Johnson, *Preface to the Dictionary*

After the show, McLuhan calls to the M.C., the woman at the microphone—she was clothed, by the way—he calls her over to our table and says to her, "I have something you can use in your spiel."

"What's that?" she says. Her face starts to take on that bullet-proof smile that waitresses and barmaids put on to cope with middle-aged wiseguys.

"Well, it's this," says McLuhan. . . . "You can say, you can tell them"—and here his voice slows down as if to emphasize the utmost significance—"The topless waitress is the opening wedge of the trial balloon!"

Then he looks at her with an unfathomable smile.

Her smile, however, freezes. The light goes out in her eyes. She

suddenly looks like an aging pole-axed ewe. She stares at McLuhan
without a word or an expression—
   But of course!
   —*what if he is right?*
                                        —Tom Wolfe, *What if He Is Right?*[1]

An essay, according to Thrall, Hibbard, and Holman in *A Handbook
to Literature*,[2] is "a moderately brief prose discussion of a restricted
topic." But, like all definitions of the essay, this one too is unsatisfactory. The term comprehends such a variety of prose discussions—
letters, narratives, descriptive ventures, anecdotes, critical analyses,
moralizing exhortations, sermons, character sketches, historical dis-
sertations, reflective pieces, biographical studies, editorials, and entirely personal revelations—that the mind hedges around definitions
as a hopeless, thankless task.

   It is also a pointless task.

   Do not ask, then, "What is an essay?"—especially in an essay on
"The Art of the Essay." After endless discussion, we would only have
thrown up a barrier of words around a perfectly innocent and resolutely independent term. We can say that an essay *is* pretty much
what it *wants* to be—a prose vehicle for ideas or perceptions, with no
predetermined form. After that we can only give examples: "Here is
a nice aphoristic piece of Henry David Thoreau. Over there is a slice
of studied elegance from Dr. Johnson. And here—well, here is Tom
Wolfe!"

   It is useful, moreover, to assert that the *essence* of all definitions
of the essay is wrong. It is partially true, as Nathaniel Bailey says in
his dictionary (*Universal Etymological Dictionary of the English Language,* 1721) that an essay is "a short discourse or treatise on some
subject." But such definitions lead us to think of the essay as something we write in school because the teacher tells us to. They lead us
to think of the essay *merely* as a more or less organized discussion of
an assigned topic.

   This is where they fail us: because the essay is also art. In its
highest and best sense, as a form of serious art, the essay is subtle,
powerful, infinitely variable—a kind of poetic fiction. *Fiction* comes
from Latin *fictio,* which meant "making" or "counterfeiting": that is,
the creation of an image faithful to an original. The essay as poetic
fiction, then, discovers, portrays, and communicates the deepest intel-

lectual, emotional, and spiritual meanings of human experiences. Thus it can be—*is*—an art.

But it is useful to dissent: "Yes, the essay can, perhaps, be an art. But most essays are like chairs—they are functional, their main purpose is to hold things up—people or ideas—so we hardly think of essays as we think of a picture or a poem."

And we would agree, for a simple reason: traditionally, men have written two kinds of essays. Let us call them *formal essays*, in the Greek mold, and *informal essays*, in the French manner. As they are customarily written, the formal essay tends to be "merely" useful; the informal essay more frequently aspires to the condition of art.

Now the Greeks wrote a kind of "essay" marked by lucid, logical form, in which an argument was developed point by point or an idea was anatomized systematically. This is the kind of essay we encouraged you to write—in a carefully structured set-form—in Chapter 5. It is a distinct type of essay with a recognizable historical tradition, ranging from Aristotle's *Poetics*, through Cicero's *De Oratore* and *De Legibus*, to Edgar Allan Poe's "The Philosophy of Composition" in America and to the work of many nineteenth-century English essayists, including T. B. Macaulay, Thomas De Quincy, Thomas Carlyle, Walter Pater, and Matthew Arnold. The list is very long—and most distinguished. And it certainly includes men of genius who raised the formal essay to the level of art.

On the other hand, there is the informal essay, in the French manner. Let us use the term "in the French manner" because this kind of essay, as a distinct type of prose writing, was fashioned and popularized by a Frenchman, Michel Eyquem de Montaigne (1533-92), whose first collection of *Essais*—written after he retired from business and politics to devote himself to "the contemplative life"—was published in 1580. Montaigne said, "Others look before them; I look within myself," and he wrote in answer to the question *Que sais-je?*—("What do I know?")—"Myself am the groundwork of my book." He selected the term *essai* for these prose excursions into his mind because he wanted to emphasize the tentative, exploratory nature of his efforts. Hence *essai*—"a trial," "an attempt," an effort to make discoveries.

Montaigne's essays, like other informal essays, fit Dr. Johnson's definition of the essay as "A loose sally of the mind." Other distinguished informal essayists include such writers as Francis Bacon, Abraham Cowley, Sir Thomas Browne, Ben Jonson, Izaak Walton,

Joseph Addison, Richard Steele, Samuel Johnson, Charles Lamb, and, in our own time, brilliant stylists like James Thurber, George Orwell, and Tom Wolfe. The informal essays written by these men are often personal and self-revelatory; confidential and unconventional; free from stiffness and pretense; humorous, droll, and witty, or grave, sober, and earnest; often tentative and incomplete. They often imply far more than they say. And they may have what the critics call "a rambling structure."

Harsh criticism? That interpretation is misleading. One thing that makes an essay informal, in fact, is that it has no *planned* structure that marches with a neat, tidy, trim step along perfectly straight streets. No, its organization *grows* out of the writer's material. A fancy term is convenient here: the informal essay, when it approaches art, has *organic form*. *Organic*: growing from within, not superimposed. In other words, its organization reflects the writer's experience, the twists and turns of his mind, the pattern his eye perceives.

Besides "rambling structure" or organic form, the informal essay is characterized by less conventional language and development. The style of the informal essay may be eccentric, playful, grotesque, wildly colloquial, and possibly obscene. Depending on the subject and the audience, *anything* goes. Here is Tom Wolfe again, in "The Pump House Gang":

> All these kids, 17 of them, members of the Pump House crowd, are lollygagging around the stairs down to Windansea Beach, La Jolla, California, about 11 A.M., and they all look at the black feet, which are a woman's pair of black street shoes, out of which stick a pair of old veiny white ankles, which lead up like a senile cone to a fudge of tallowy, edematous flesh, her thighs, squeezing out of her bathing suit, with old faded yellow bruises on them, which she probably got from running eight feet to catch a bus or something. She is standing with her old work-a-hubby, who has on *san*dals: you know, a pair of navy-blue anklet socks and these sandals with big, wide, new-smelling tan straps going this way and that, *for keeps*. Man, they look like orthopedic sandals, if one can imagine that. Obviously, these people come from Tucson or Albuquerque or one of those hincty adobe towns. All these hincty, crumbling black feet come to La Jolla-by-the-sea from the adobe towns for the weekend. They even drive in cars all full of thermos bottles and mayonnaisey sandwiches and some kind of latticework wooden-back support for the old crock who drives and Venetian blinds on the back window.[3]

The techniques of the informal essay are also wide-open. In fact, many of them are borrowed from fiction. The informal essay may rely heavily on scene-setting (dramatizing a scene instead of merely writing *about* it), on detailed description, on vivid action, on dialogue. Here is John Steinbeck in "How to Tell Good Guys from Bad Guys":

> I have observed the physical symptoms of television-looking on children as well as on adults. The mouth grows slack and the lips hang open; the eyes take on a hypnotized or doped look; the nose runs rather more than usual; the backbone turns to water and the fingers slowly and methodically pick the designs of brocade furniture. Such is the appearance of semiconsciousness that one wonders how much of the "message" of television is getting through to the brain. This wonder is further strengthened by the fact that a television-looker will look at anything at all and for hours. Recently I came into a room to find my eight-year-old son Catbird sprawled in a chair, idiot slackness on his face, with the doped eyes of an opium smoker. On the television screen stood a young woman of mammary distinction with ice-cream hair listening to a man in thick glasses and a doctor's smock.
>
> "What's happening?" I asked.
>
> Catbird answered in the monotone of the sleeptalker which is known as television voice, "She is asking if she should dye her hair."
>
> "What is the doctor's reaction?"
>
> "If she uses Trutone it's all right," said Catbird. "But if she uses ordinary or adulterated products, her hair will split and lose its golden natural sheen. The big economy size is two dollars and ninety-eight cents if you act now," said Catbird.
>
> You see, something was getting through to him. He looked punch drunk but he was absorbing. I did not feel it fair to interject a fact I have observed—that natural golden sheen does not exist in nature . . . .[4]

Enough: the point is made. The problem now is to attempt the art on your own—to *write* an informal essay.

We therefore conclude this chapter with three essays, the first two of which are offered for study, analysis, discussion, and emulation. They are "A Hanging" and "Marrakech," written on relevant and significant subjects by George Orwell, one of the most highly esteemed and influential essayists of our time. You are invited, of course, to use as many of his techniques as possible on subjects of your own choosing. But we also hope that, like Thoreau, you will hear "a different drummer"—your own. That like Montaigne, you will be the "groundwork" of your own writing. And that you will remember, as Persius is supposed to have observed, "Out of nothing, nothing can come. . . ."

The final essay, by a student, Bill Albin, illustrates what you *can* do if you live up to these expectations. Mr. Albin, as you will see, writes a strongly individual informal essay. He hears a different drummer. "Himself" forms his subject. And he knows, clearly, that something must be made of experience, for "out of nothing, nothing can come."

ESSAY 1

George Orwell (Eric Arthur Blair, 1903-1950) is probably the greatest essayist of our time. His command of style, reflected in the most exact attention to telling details and the nicest sense of colloquial English, enlivens all he wrote, from the novels like *Down and Out in Paris and London*, *Burmese Days*, *Animal Farm*, *1984*, *Coming Up for Air*, *A Clergyman's Daughter*, and *Keep the Aspidistra Flying*, to the essays and memoirs like *Homage to Catalonia*, *Shooting an Elephant and Other Essays*, and *Such, Such Were the Joys*. The things of value, Orwell says in "Why I Write," are always political: "it is invariably where I lacked a *political* purpose that I wrote lifeless books and was betrayed into purple passages, sentences without meaning, decorative adjectives and humbug generally."

"A Hanging," like "Shooting an Elephant," captures a "political" experience Orwell had during the early 1920's, when he spent five years as a member of the Imperial Police in Burma. In this informal essay—certainly a work of art—Orwell describes a hanging he witnessed officially. He doesn't say much, directly, about what he felt—but every word carries a burden of meaning. As the body of the dead man hangs a hundred yards from Orwell and his party—a group of jesting, swaggering men—Orwell himself laughs and drinks with the executioners. But Orwell's views on capital punishment thrust at us with a twist of irony. Suddenly we *know*. We know how "unspeakably wrong" the execution was, and we know it in the torn tangle of our emotions.

His techniques? Orwell approaches each essay as an individual work of art. His technique here is to present an apparently objective account of a hanging: in only one passage does he directly betray his own feelings—a passage you will want to discover for yourself at the dramatic moment when Orwell realizes how intensely and poignantly *alive* the prisoner is. For the rest, Orwell *implies* an attitude as he chooses details like "sodden morning" and "sickly light" to suggest his feelings and invoke ours. The structure of the essay is a simple narrative; that is, Orwell tells the story in straight chronological fashion. But the narrative is so artfully presented with economy and aptness that its apparent simplicity is deceptive, and the incongrous details established, from the very beginning, a savagely ironic tone that pervades the entire essay. And we sense that these are real people, brought alive by action and speech, in a real—and terrible—story.

In brief, the techniques are artful: description, action, dialogue in a succinct, well-told story. You can imitate them effectively, once you have studied the essay in all its complex simplicity, using as best you can the questions for study and discussion we have provided at the end of it. You will be a better writer for having done so.

A HANGING

—George Orwell

[1]   It was in Burma, a sodden morning of the rains. A sickly light, like yellow tinfoil, was slanting over the high walls into the jail yard. We were waiting outside the condemned cells, a row of sheds fronted with double bars, like small animal cages. Each cell measured about ten feet by ten and was quite bare within except for a plank bed and a pot for drinking water. In some of them brown silent men were squatting at the inner bars, with their blankets draped round them. These were the condemned men, due to be hanged within the next week or two.

[2]   One prisoner had been brought out of his cell. He was a Hindu, a puny wisp of a man, with a shaven head and vague liquid eyes. He had a thick, sprouting moustache, absurdly too big for his body, rather like the moustache of a comic man on the films. Six tall

Indian warders were guarding him and getting him ready for the gallows. Two of them stood by with rifles and fixed bayonets, while the others handcuffed him, passed a chain through his handcuffs and fixed it to their belts, and lashed his arms tight to his sides. They crowded very close about him, with their hands always on him in a careful, caressing grip, as though all the while feeling him to make sure he was there. It was like men handling a fish which is still alive and may jump back into the water. But he stood quite unresisting, yielding his arms limply to the ropes, as though he hardly noticed what was happening.

[3]   Eight o'clock struck and a bugle call, desolately thin in the wet air, floated from the distant barracks. The superintendent of the jail, who was standing apart from the rest of us, moodily prodding the gravel with his stick, raised his head at the sound. He was an army doctor, with a grey toothbrush moustache and a gruff voice. "For God's sake hurry up, Francis," he said irritably. "The man ought to have been dead by this time, Aren't you ready yet?"

[4]   Francis, the head jailer, a fat Dravidian in a white drill suit and gold spectacles, waved his black hand. "Yes sir, yes sir," he bubbled. "All iss satisfactorily prepared. The hangman iss waiting. We shall proceed."

[5]   "Well, quick march, then. The prisoners can't get their breakfast till this job's over."

[6]   We set out for the gallows. Two warders marched on either side of the prisoner, with their rifles at the slope; two others marched close against him, gripping him by arm and shoulder, as though at once pushing and supporting him. The rest of us, magistrates and the like, followed behind. Suddenly, when we had gone ten yards, the procession stopped short without any order or warning. A dreadful thing had happened—a dog, come goodness knows whence, had appeared in the yard. It came bounding among us with a loud volley of barks and leapt round us wagging its whole body, wild with glee at finding so many human beings together. It was a large wooly dog, half Airedale, half pariah. For a moment it pranced round us, and then, before anyone could stop it, it had made a dash for the prisoner and, jumping up, tried to lick his face. Everyone stood aghast, too taken aback even to grab at the dog.

[7]   "Who let that bloody brute in here?" said the superintendent angrily. "Catch it, someone!"

[8]   A warder, detached from the escort, charged clumsily after the dog, but it danced and gambolled just out of his reach, taking everything as part of the game. A young Eurasian jailer picked up a handful of gravel and tried to stone the dog away, but it dodged the stones and came after us again. Its yaps echoed from the jail walls. The prisoner, in the grasp of the two warders, looked on incuriously, as though this was another formality of the hanging. It was several minutes before someone managed to catch the dog. Then we put my handkerchief through its collar and moved off once more, with the dog still straining and whimpering.

[9]   It was about forty yards to the gallows. I watched the bare brown back of the prisoner marching in front of me. He walked clumsily with his bound arms, but quite steadily, with that bobbing gait of the Indian who never straightens his knees. At each step his muscles slid neatly into place, the lock of hair on his scalp danced up and down, his feet printed themselves on the wet gravel. And once, in spite of the men who gripped him by each shoulder, he stepped slightly aside to avoid a puddle on the path.

[10]   It is curious, but till that moment I had never realized what it means to destroy a healthy, conscious man. When I saw the prisoner step aside to avoid the puddle I saw the mystery, the unspeakable wrongness, of cutting a life short when it is in full tide. This man was not dying, he was alive just as we are alive. All the organs of his body were working—bowels digesting food, skin renewing itself, nails growing, tissues forming—all toiling away in solemn foolery. His nails would still be growing when he stood on the drop, when he was falling through the air with a tenth-of-a-second to live. His eyes saw the yellow gravel and the grey walls, and his brain still remembered, foresaw, reasoned—reasoned even about puddles. He and we were a party of men walking together, seeing, hearing, feeling, understanding the same world; and in two minutes, with a sudden snap, one of us would be gone—one mind less, one world less.

[11]   The gallows stood in a small yard, separate from the main grounds of the prison, and overgrown with tall prickly weeds. It was a brick erection like three sides of a shed, with planking on top, and above that two beams and a crossbar with the rope dangling. The hangman, a grey-haired convict in the white uniform of the prison, was waiting beside his machine. He greeted us with a servile crouch as we entered. At a word from Francis the two warders, gripping the

prisoner more closely than ever, half-led half-pushed him to the gallows and helped him clumsily up the ladder. Then the hangman climbed up and fixed the rope round the prisoner's neck.

[12]   We stood waiting, five yards away. The warders had formed in a rough circle round the gallows. And then, when the noose was fixed, the prisoner began crying out to his god. It was a high, reiterated cry of "Ram! Ram! Ram! Ram!" not urgent and fearful like a prayer or cry for help, but steady, rhythmical, almost like the tolling of a bell. The dog answered the sound with a whine. The hangman, still standing on the gallows, produced a small cotton bag like a flour bag and drew it down over the prisoner's face. But the sound, muffled by the cloth, still persisted, over and over again: "Ram! Ram! Ram! Ram! Ram!"

[13]   The hangman climbed down and stood ready, holding the lever. Minutes seemed to pass. The steady, muffled crying from the prisoner went on and on, "Ram! Ram! Ram!" never faltering for an instant. The superintendent, his head on his chest, was slowly poking the ground with his stick; perhaps he was counting the cries, allowing the prisoner a fixed number—fifty, perhaps, or a hundred. Everyone had changed color. The Indians had gone grey like bad coffee, and one or two of the bayonets were wavering. We looked at the lashed, hooded man on the drop, and listened to his cries—each cry another second of life; the same thought was in all our minds: oh, kill him quickly, get it over, stop that abominable noise!

[14]   Suddenly the superintendent made up his mind. Throwing up his head he made a swift motion with his stick. "Chalo!" he shouted almost fiercely.

[15]   There was a clanking noise, and then dead silence. The prisoner had vanished, and the rope was twisting on itself. I let go of the dog, and it galloped immediately to the back of the gallows; but when it got there it stopped short, barked, and then retreated into a corner of the yard, where it stood among the weeds, looking timorously out at us. We went round the gallows to inspect the prisoner's body. He was dangling with his toes pointed straight downwards, very slowly revolving, as dead as a stone.

[16]   The superintendent reached out with his stick and poked the bare brown body; it oscillated slightly. "He's all right," said the superintendent. He backed out from under the gallows, and blew out a deep breath. The moody look had gone out of his face quite suddenly. He

glanced at his wrist-watch. "Eight minutes past eight. Well, that's all for this morning, thank God."

[17]   The warders unfixed bayonets and marched away. The dog, sobered and conscious of having misbehaved itself, slipped after them. We walked out of the gallows yard, past the condemned cells with their waiting prisoners, into the big central yard of the prison. The convicts, under the command of warders armed with lathis, were already receiving their breakfast. They squatted in long rows, each man holding a tin pannikin, while two warders with buckets marched round ladling out rice; it seemed quite a homely, jolly scene after the hanging. An enormous relief had come upon us now that the job was done. One felt an impulse to sing, to break into a run, to snigger. All at once everyone began chattering gaily.

[18]   The Eurasian boy walking beside me nodded towards the way we had come, with a knowing smile: "Do you know sir, our friend (he meant the dead man) when he heard his appeal had been dismissed, he pissed on the floor of his cell. From fright. Kindly take one of my cigarettes, sir. Do you not admire my new silver case, sir? From the boxwalah, two rupees eight annas. Classy European style."

[19]   Several people laughed—at what, nobody seemed certain.

[20]   Francis was walking by the superintendent, talking garrulously: "Well, sir, all hass passed off with the utmost satisfactoriness. It was all finished—flick! like that. It iss not always so—oah, no! I have known cases where the doctor wass obliged to go beneath the gallows and pull the prissoner's legs to ensure decease. Most disagreeable!"

[21]   "Wriggling about, eh? That's bad," said the superintendent.

[22]   "Ach, sir, it iss worse when they become refractory! One man, I recall, clung to the bars of hiss cage when we went to take him out. You will scarcely credit, sir, that it took six warders to dislodge him, three pulling at each leg. We reasoned with him. 'My dear fellow,' we said, 'think of all the pain and trouble you are causing to us!' But no, he would not listen! Ach, he wass very troublesome!"

[23]   I found that I was laughing quite loudly. Everyone was laughing. Even the superintendent grinned in a tolerant way. "You'd better all come out and have a drink," he said quite genially. "I've got a bottle of whisky in the car. We could do with it."

[24]   We went through the big double gates of the prison into the road. "Pulling at his legs!" exclaimed a Burmese magistrate suddenly,

and burst into a loud chuckling. We all began laughing again. At that moment Francis' anecdote seemed extraordinarily funny. We all had a drink together, native and European alike, quite amicably. The dead man was a hundred yards away.

Study and Discussion

Vocabulary and Style

A.   In your dictionary find the meaning of the following words:
1. sodden (para. 1)
2. puny (para. 2)
3. wisp (para. 2)
4. desolately (para. 3)
5. Dravidian (para. 4)
6. volley (para. 6)
7. pariah (para. 6)
8. gambolled (para. 8)
9. Eurasian (para. 8)
10. servile (para. 11)
11. abominable (para. 13)
12. timorously (para. 15)
13. garrulously (para 20)
14. refractory (para. 22)
15. amicably (para. 24)

B.   In paragraph 2, study Orwell's style. How would you describe the length and construction of the sentences, the relative concreteness of the nouns, the force of the verbs, the exactness of the adjectives and adverbs, and the vividness of his figures of speech?

Rhetoric

1. What method of organization does the author use in this essay?
2. What technique of development is used most often in this essay?
3. For the most part, the author's main idea is implied by his choice of words and his arrangement of details. But there is one direct statement of the thesis. Where *is* the thesis stated? Is it more effective there than it would be in the usual positions? Why?
4. Orwell's strategy is simple and effective: instead of arguing in expository prose that capital punishment is inhumane, he dramatizes its inhumanity by narrating one specific hanging. Do you think his approach is more convincing than the expository approach? Why?

CONTENT

1. What details does the author emphasize in the description in paragraph 1? Which words suggest Orwell's attitude toward the condemned man and toward the hanging?

2. In paragraph 2, what is the effect of each of the following details:
   a. "a puny wisp of a man";
   b. "with a shaven head and vague liquid eyes";
   c. "a thick sprouting moustache . . . rather like the moustache of a comic man on the films";
   d. "rifles . . . fixed bayonets . . . chain . . . handcuffs";
   e. "like men handling a fish . . ."

3. Why is the superintendent of the jail in a hurry to get the hanging over with? What is ironic about this reason?

4. What kind of dog is "half Airedale, half pariah"? How does the dog behave toward the prisoner? Why does the author bring the dog into the essay at all? How does the dog respond to the actual hanging?

5. What do the details in paragraph 9 emphasize about the prisoner?

6. Why does the author feel that capital punishment is wrong?

7. How do the witnesses respond to the prisoner's cries? Why do they want the hangman to hurry? Do they feel sorrow for the prisoner?

8. In paragraph 15, Orwell uses two clichés: "dead silence" and "as dead as a stone." Are the clichés justified? Why?

9. What is ironic about the superintendent's examination of the body?

10. What is ironic about Francis' talk in paragraphs 18, 19, 20, and 22?

11. What is ironic about the final scene—described in Paragraph 24?

IDEAS AND IMPLICATIONS

1. Did you notice that the author never tells us what crime the prisoner had committed? How would you interpret this significant omission? Does it say anything, indirectly, about the penalty of death generally?

2. Is the author's point a valid one—or does he evoke sympathy

for the inhumanity dealt the prisoner and forget all about the suffering of the victims?

3. Do you think Orwell would be in favor of a more humane form of capital punishment? A fast-acting poison administered during sleep, for instance?

Writing Suggestions

The important point about "A Hanging" is that it is *not* a formal expository or argumentative essay of the type you were asked to write in Chapter 5. Certainly, you will want to reinforce what you learned in that chapter by frequent practice, but probably before you do so, you should attempt an informal, personal essay with an *organic* form ("rambling structure"). Thus we do not believe that you should now write an expository analysis of Orwell's techniques, or a formal argument for or against capital punishment.

Instead, *using* as many of Orwell's techniques as possible, you should write on a significant experience of your own: make yourself your subject. Above all, do not try to fake a "political" experience like the one you read about in "A Hanging." Be honest. Your experiences may be limited, but much of them are meaningful, all of them are human, and some of them are worth writing about.

What about the pathetically cruel and stupid fifth-grade teacher that you and your classmates taunted and tortured? What about the money you stole when you were twelve years old? What about the kitten that died after you had loved and fed and played with it?

The possibilities, you see, are almost endless.

ESSAY 2

In "Marrakech," as in "A Hanging," Orwell has, in the broadest sense, a *political* purpose: the description of a way of being known to oppressed minorities everywhere, at all times. He uses many of the same techniques—dialogue and action, for instance—to develop the thesis of this essay: that people whose skins are the color of the earth are simply invisible to the white man. But the basic structure of "Marrakech" is different, as one would expect: organic form grows out of the writer's material. Here, then, Orwell does not simply tell a single story to persuade us to accept an idea. Instead, his approach is mainly descriptive: he sets a series of five scenes, each a kind of story in miniature, each of which emphasizes the "invisibility of these people." There is an opening, but no introduction; there is an ending, but no conclusion: he moves us into and out of these pictures without observing the formal niceties. And he leaves us with a terrifying image shimmering in the light of a blistering African day.

> "As the corpse went past the flies left the restaurant table in a cloud and rushed after it, but they came back a few minutes later."

And so we begin: detail piles on detail, until we see the misery sketched into these faces, smell the stench of the city streets, bear the burdens borne by haggard old women. The details are astonishingly vivid, and they are intensified by the lash of similes and metaphors that cut across our eyes: "sore-eyed children cluster everywhere . . . like clouds of flies"; old men with warped legs work "in dark fly-infested booths that look like caves."

The prose is lucid, "like a window pane," to use Orwell's own simile for good prose. Look through it. You'll see how *they* live.

MARRAKECH

—George Orwell

[1]   As the corpse went past the flies left the restaurant table in a cloud and rushed after it, but they came back a few minutes later.

[2]   The little crowd of mourners—all men and boys, no women—threaded their way across the market-place between the piles of pomegranates and the taxis and the camels, wailing a short chant over and over again. What really appeals to the flies is that the corpses here are never put into coffins, they are merely wrapped in a piece of rag and carried on a rough wooden bier on the shoulders of four friends. When the friends get to the burying-ground they hack an oblong hole a foot or two deep, dump the body in it and fling over it a little of the dried-up, lumpy earth, which is like broken brick. No gravestone, no name, no identifying mark of any kind. The burying-ground is merely a huge waste of hummocky earth, like a derelict building-lot. After a

month or two no one can even be certain where his own relatives are
buried.

[3]   When you walk through a town like this—two hundred thousand inhabitants, of whom at least twenty thousand own literally
nothing except the rags they stand up in—when you see how the
people live, and still more how easily they die, it is always difficult
to believe that you are walking among human beings. All colonial
empires are in reality founded upon that fact. The people have brown
faces—besides, there are so many of them! Are they really the same
flesh as yourself? Do they even have names? Or are they merely a
kind of undifferentiated brown stuff, about as individual as bees or
coral insects? They rise out of the earth, they sweat and starve for a
few years, and then they sink back into the nameless mounds of the
graveyard and nobody notices that they are gone. And even the graves
themselves soon fade back into the soil. Sometimes, out for a walk, as
you break your way through the prickly pear, you notice that it is
rather bumpy underfoot, and only a certain regularity in the bumps
tells you that you are walking over skeletons.

[4]   I was feeding one of the gazelles in the public gardens.

[5]   Gazelles are almost the only animals that look good to eat
when they are still alive, in fact, one can hardly look at their hind-
quarters without thinking of mint sauce. The gazelle I was feeding
seemed to know that this thought was in my mind, for though it took
the piece of bread I was holding out it obviously did not like me. It
nibbled rapidly at the bread, then lowered its head and tried to butt
me, then took another nibble and then butted again. Probably its
idea was that if it could drive me away the bread would somehow
remain hanging in mid-air.

[6]   An Arab navvy working on the path nearby lowered his heavy
hoe and sidled slowly towards us. He looked from the gazelle to the
bread and from the bread to the gazelle, with a sort of quiet amaze-
ment, as though he had never seen anything quite like this before.
Finally he said shyly in French:

[7]   "I could eat some of that bread."

[8]   I tore off a piece and he stowed it gratefully in some secret
place under his rags. This man is an employee of the Municipality.

[9]   When you go through the Jewish quarters you gather some
idea of what the medieval ghettoes were probably like. Under their
Moorish rulers the Jews were only allowed to own land in certain

restricted areas, and after centuries of this kind of treatment they have ceased to bother about overcrowding. Many of the streets are a good deal less than six feet wide, the houses are completely window-less, and sore-eyed children cluster everywhere in unbelievable num-bers, like clouds of flies. Down the centre of the street there is gen-erally running a little river of urine.

[10]   In the bazaar huge families of Jews, all dressed in the long black robe and little black skull-cap, are working in dark fly-infested booths that look like caves. A carpenter sits crosslegged at a prehistoric lathe, turning chair-legs at lightning speed. He works the lathe with a bow in his right hand and guides the chisel with his left foot, and thanks to a lifetime of sitting in this position his left leg is warped out of shape. At his side his grandson, aged six, is already starting on the simpler parts of the job.

[11]   I was just passing the coppersmiths' booths when somebody noticed that I was lighting a cigarette. Instantly, from the dark holes all round, there was a frenzied rush of Jews, many of them old grand-fathers with flowing grey beards, all clamouring for a cigarette. Even a blind man somewhere at the back of one of the booths heard a rumour of cigarettes and came crawling out, groping in the air with his hand. In about a minute I had used up the whole packet. None of these people, I suppose, works less than twelve hours a day, and every one of them looks on a cigarette as a more or less impossible luxury.

[12]   As the Jews live in self-contained communities they follow the same trades as the Arabs, except for agriculture. Fruit-sellers, potters, silversmiths, blacksmiths, butchers, leatherworkers, tailors, water-carriers, beggars, porters—whichever way you look you see nothing but Jews. As a matter of fact there are thirteen thousand of them, all living in the space of a few acres. A good job Hitler wasn't here. Perhaps he was on his way, however. You hear the usual dark rumours about the Jews, not only from the Arabs but from the poorer Europeans.

[13]   "Yes, mon vieux, they took my job away from me and gave it to a Jew. The Jews! They're the real rulers of this country, you know. They've got all the money. They control the banks, finance—every-thing."

[14]   "But," I said, "isn't it a fact that the average Jew is a labourer working for about a penny an hour?"

[15]   "Ah, that's only for show! They're all moneylenders really. They're cunning, the Jews."

[16]   In just the same way, a couple of hundred years ago, poor old women used to be burned for witchcraft when they could not even work enough magic to get themselves a square meal.

[17]   All people who work with their hands are partly invisible, and the more important the work they do, the less visible they are. Still, a white skin is always fairly conspicuous. In northern Europe, when you see a labourer ploughing a field, you probably give him a second glance. In a hot country, anywhere south of Gibraltar or east of Suez, the chances are that you don't even see him. I have noticed this again and again. In a tropical landscape one's eye takes in everything except the human beings. It takes in the dried-up soil, the prickly pear, the palm tree and the distant mountain, but it always misses the peasant hoeing at his patch. He is the same colour as the earth, and a great deal less interesting to look at.

[18]   It is only because of this that the starved countries of Asia and Africa are accepted as tourist resorts. No one would think of running cheap trips to the Distressed Areas. But where the human beings have brown skins their poverty is simply not noticed. What does Morocco mean to a Frenchman? An orange-grove or a job in Government service. Or to an Englishman? Camels, castles, palm trees, Foreign Legionnaires, brass trays, and bandits. One could probably live there for years without noticing that for nine-tenths of the people the reality of life is an endless, back-breaking struggle to wring a little food out of an eroded soil.

[19]   Most of Morocco is so desolate that no wild animal bigger than a hare can live on it. Huge areas which were once covered with forest have turned into a treeless waste where the soil is exactly like broken-up brick. Nevertheless a good deal of it is cultivated, with frightful labour. Everything is done by hand. Long lines of women, bent double like inverted capital L's, work their way slowly across the fields, tearing up the prickly weeds with their hands, and the peasant gathering lucerne for fodder pulls it up stalk by stalk instead of reaping it, thus saving an inch or two on each stalk. The plough is a wretched wooden thing, so frail that one can easily carry it on one's shoulder, and fitted underneath with a rough iron spike which stirs the soil to a depth of about four inches. This is as much as the strength of the animals is equal to. It is usual to plough with a cow and a donkey yoked together. Two donkeys would not be quite strong enough, but on the other hand two cows would cost a little more to

feed. The peasants possess no harrows, they merely plow the soil several times over in different directions, finally leaving it in rough furrows, after which the whole field has to be shaped with hoes into small oblong patches to conserve water. Except for a day or two after the rare rainstorms there is never enough water. Along the edges of the fields channels are hacked out to a depth of thirty or forty feet to get at the tiny trickles which run through the subsoil.

[20] Every afternoon a file of very old women passes down the road outside my house, each carrying a load of firewood. All of them are mummified with age and the sun, and all of them are tiny. It seems to be generally the case in primitive communities that the women, when they get beyond a certain age, shrink to the size of children. One day a poor old creature who could not have been more than four feet tall crept past me under a vast load of wood. I stopped her and put a five-sou piece (a little more than a farthing) into her hand. She answered with a shrill wail, almost a scream, which was partly gratitude but mainly surprise. I suppose that from her point of of view, by taking any notice of her, I seemed almost to be violating a law of nature. She accepted her status as an old woman, that is to say as a beast of burden. When a family is travelling it is quite usual to see a father and a grown-up son riding ahead on donkeys, and an old woman following on foot, carrying the baggage.

[21] But what is strange about these people is their invisibility. For several weeks, always at about the same time of day, the file of old women had hobbled past the house with their firewood, and though they had registered themselves on my eyeballs I cannot truly say that I had seen them. Firewood was passing—that was how I saw it. It was only that one day I happened to be walking behind them, and the curious up-and-down motion of a load of wood drew my attention to the human being beneath it. Then for the first time I noticed the poor old earth-coloured bodies, bodies reduced to bones and leathery skin, bent double under the crushing weight. Yet I suppose I had not been five minutes on Moroccan soil before I noticed the overloading of the donkeys and was infuriated by it. There is no question that the donkeys are damnably treated. The Moroccan donkey is hardly bigger than a St. Bernard dog, it carries a load which in the British Army would be considered too much for a fifteen-hands mule, and very often its pack-saddle is not taken off its back for weeks together. But what is peculiarly pitiful is that it is the most willing creature on earth, it follows its master like a dog and does not need

either bridle or halter. After a dozen years of devoted work it suddenly drops dead, whereupon its master tips it into the ditch and the village dogs have torn its guts out before it is cold.

[22]   This kind of thing makes one's blood boil, whereas—on the whole—the plight of the human beings does not. I am not commenting, merely pointing to a fact. People with brown skins are next door to invisible. Anyone can be sorry for the donkey with its galled back, but it is generally owing to some kind of accident if one even notices the old woman under her load of sticks.

[23]   As the storks flew northward the Negroes were marching southward—a long, dusty column, infantry, screw-gun batteries, and then more infantry, four or five thousand men in all, winding up the road with a clumping of boots and a clatter of iron wheels.

[24]   They were Senegalese, the blackest Negroes in Africa, so black that sometimes it is difficult to see whereabouts on their necks the hair begins. Their splendid bodies were hidden in reach-me-down khaki uniforms, their feet squashed into boots that looked like blocks of wood, and every tin hat seemed to be a couple of sizes too small. It was very hot and the men had marched a long way. They slumped under the weight of their packs and the curiously sensitive black faces were glistening with sweat.

[25]   As they went past a tall, very young Negro turned and caught my eye. But the look he gave me was not in the least the kind of look you might expect. Not hostile, not contemptuous, not sullen, not even inquisitive. It was the shy, wide-eyed Negro look, which actually is a look of profound respect. I saw how it was. This wretched boy, who is a French citizen and has therefore been dragged from the forest to scrub floors and catch syphilis in garrison towns, actually has feelings of reverence before a white skin. He has been taught that the white race are his masters, and he still believes it.

[26]   But there is one thought which every white man (and in this connection it doesn't matter twopence if he calls himself a socialist) thinks when he sees a black army marching past. "How much longer can we go on kidding these people? How long before they turn their guns in the other direction?"

[27]   It was curious, really. Every white man there had this thought stowed somewhere or other in his mind. I had it, so had the other onlookers, so had the officers on their sweating chargers and the white N.C.O.'s marching in the ranks. It was a kind of secret which we all knew and were too clever to tell; only the Negroes didn't know it.

And really it was like watching a flock of cattle to see the long column, a mile or two miles of armed men, flowing peacefully up the road, while the great white birds drifted over them in the opposite direction, glittering like scraps of paper.

Study and Discussion

VOCABULARY AND STYLE

A. In your dictionary find the meaning of the following words:

1. wailing (para. 2)
2. bier (para. 2)
3. hummocky (para. 2)
4. derelict (para. 2)
5. navvy (para. 6)
6. sidled (para. 6)
7. ghettoes (para. 9)
8. frenzied (para. 11)
9. clamouring (para. 11)
10. desolate (para. 19)
11. mummified (para. 20)
12. galled (para. 22)

B. List all the verbs in paragraphs 2 and 3. Would you say that Orwell's style is marked by his use of short, powerful, active verbs?

C. Find as many figures of speech as possible in this essay. Is the author's figurative language original, forceful, and effective? Show how at least one figure of speech is effective in its context.

RHETORIC

1. What method of development is used most often in this essay?
2. Why are the opening and closing paragraphs especially effective? What do they have in common?
3. The thesis of this essay is implied in paragraph 3 and stated in paragraphs 17, 21, and 22. In your own words, what is it?
4. This essay consists of a number of "scenes" that are related to each other because they all make the same point. How many scenes are there?
5. In your opinion, does the lack of transitions between the scenes weaken the essay? Or does it have sufficient continuity without transitions? Why?

CONTENT

1. What does the author mean when he says, "All colonial empires are founded upon that fact" (para. 3)? Explain in your own words.

2. What point does he make in describing the burial scene? In describing the incident in the public garden?
3. What kind of life do the Jews live in the ghetto? What "dark rumours" are heard about the Jews?
4. Why is it that we don't *see* the natives in "the starved countries" of Asia and Africa?
5. Why did the Moroccans plow with a cow and a donkey yoked together? What does this detail tell us about the lives of these people?
6. Why did the old woman scream when the author gave her a five-sou piece?
7. Why is it that Europeans feel more pity for mistreated donkeys than for the people themselves?
8. What is the point of the last incident described in this essay?
9. How are the last five paragraphs related to the rest of the essay? The last sentence comments on the final section, but could it in any way be a comment on the essay as a whole?

IDEAS AND IMPLICATIONS

1. Orwell is writing about English colonialism in Africa. Do his observations have any relevance for America today? If so, what?
2. If you live in the South—or have ever lived or visited there— would you say that the author's description of the lives of African natives could be applied with some accuracy to the lives of the Southern Negroes?
3. Do you think the author's approach to the problems of prejudice is effective? Would this be a better essay if he argued *against* prejudice instead of describing and narrating scenes that reflect it?
4. Have you read anything else by George Orwell—*1984* or *Animal Farm*, for instance? If so, does this essay have anything in common with those books? What?

Writing Suggestions

1.   Write an essay in which you use Orwell's techniques in "Marrakech" to arouse indignation over any social problem of which you have direct knowledge or experience, or which you can make an

opportunity at first hand. Try, in particular, to imitate the *structure* of "Marrakech"—that is, the organization into scenes with few or no transitions between them.

2. Write an informal essay on any other subject of your own choosing, using any techniques and any structure that you find appropriate.

ESSAY 3

Bill Albin is not a professional writer. He wrote this essay when he was a student at the College of San Mateo in 1967. Since it was not written for an English class—and he had no formalities to observe— he felt free to let go with language and structure. There are no restraints except those imposed by his own sense of art; it is, then, an informal essay. Perhaps it is not *profoundly* artful. But it has individuality, integrity, consistency, and many of the typical qualities of the informal essay.

BINGE

—Bill Albin

Of all the places to hang up—Susanville. Al and I are sitting alongside the road where the town begins and ends. That's nowhere. The population-elevation sign is Al's back rest; I've spent the night face down in the tar weed, our common ground. The big asphalt strip is beside us, and all around are the rusty cans that belong to the road. What a place to hang up—but it's as good as any.

A year ago Al and I were buddies. We both lived in Menlo Park and once in a while we'd shake off together at the Big O (a beer joint in Menlo). We both walked the same razor edge 'til Al split. I stayed because I still had a couple of reasons. Al quit right in the middle of the game. He wasn't winning or losing, he just put everything down and walked away. He didn't fall with a crash. It was as if he slipped slowly down and settled on his bottom. So this is it. Susanville. No reason to get up. No place to go.

I'm here to visit Al—maybe I'll stay. I'm not here to help him because I don't know how. I came here to shake off with him, that's all.

We bought three gallons of red wine. We've been drinking and talking. We talk and drink 'til one of us passes out. Al has just shut off and I'm looking around and thinking. It's good; I'm blowing my mind. It's like sitting in a junk yard and being a piece of the junk, a real feeling of belonging. Today Al and I have our finger extended to the world. It's O.K. because I don't have a reason anymore either.

God, the sun's bright. I wish it would go away. It's another day. Who cares?

Al's coming around now. He's still holding the bottle of embalming fluid. Hell, he looks good; he's so bashed up. With a stupid yellow smile he hands me the jug. Down and around we go again. We're going to crash—why not? Maybe if I dive again I'll come up with something.

A day later, one hundred yards down the road, sitting under a bridge in a dry gulch. At least we can't see the sun. We started for town yesterday afternoon but we stopped here for a last drink and went under again.

Now we're out of juice so we have to go into Susanville. So we carry our heads back to the world. We get into town and some dandy hayseed offers to buy us a cup of coffee. What a bummer. He tries to straighten us out and sell us on a new kind of life. He throws his pitch and then asks Al, "Why?" Al answers, "No reason." Now the Good Samaritan becomes a frustrated farmer. He gulps his coffee down and leaves saying, "Got to go tend my pigs." Al's wearing his big stupid yellow smile and leaning back in his chair. I guess old Al wouldn't want to tend any pigs.

It's been a groove. Al's got it made, he doesn't have a cage to rattle, and he's bent to nowhere. I'm going back to my jungle. The angel of nil is staying here on his cloud or in his hell, or what ever it is for him. It's been a groove. I blew my mind into a new frame. I'm not going to look for a reason or try to answer the why. The word's out, the answer is, "Why not?" and the reason is, no reason. We're waiting for a bus where it doesn't stop and we have no fare. It's a hysterically sad joke with no punch line.

Al and I split. We're both ready to bury ourselves in our ways. There is no answer if there is no reason. I wish I could hang it up.

NOTES TO THE RHETORIC

CHAPTER 1

1. *Harper's Magazine*, April 1965.
2. *Saturday Review*, July 6, 1940, p. 11.

CHAPTER 2

1. *The Atlantic Monthly*, December 1953.
2. *Life*, March 17, 1967, p. 74.
3. *The Art of Making Sense* (Philadelphia, Pa.: J. B. Lippincott Company, 1954).
4. New York: Pocket Books, 1961, p. 53.
5. *Ladies' Home Journal*, April 1967, p. 74.
6. *Playboy*, March 1970, p. 90.
7. "Golf," *Playboy*, August 1965, pp. 94-95.
8. New York: Pocket Books, 1954, p. 78.
9. *Playboy*, January 1967, p. 214.
10. New York: Oxford University Press, 1965, pp. 90-91.
11. New York: Harper & Row, Publishers, 1921.
12. New York: The Macmillan Company, 1960, p. 4.
13. John Wilkenson, trans., *Technology and Culture*, Fall 1962.
14. *Playboy*, January 1967, p. 116.
15. *What Can a Man Do?* W. E. Gustafson, ed. (Chicago: University of Chicago Press, 1964).
16. *Saturday Review*, September 5, 1964, p. 35.
17. New York: Harper & Row, Publishers, 1964, pp. 135-36.
18. "On Campus with Max Shulman," *The San Matean*, April 21, 1967.
19. *Redbook*, April 1967, p. 64.
20. New York: The Macmillan Company, 1950.
21. New York: Cambridge University Press, 1937, p. 26.
22. New York: Holt, Rinehart & Winston, Inc., 1955.
23. *The Saturday Evening Post*, November 1, 1958, p. 25.
24. New York: Ballantine Books, 1968.
25. New York: Fawcett World Library, 1965, pp. 156-57.
26. *1984* (New York: Harcourt Brace Jovanovich, Inc., 1949).

27. *The Ethics of Rhetoric* (New York: Henry Regnery Company, 1953).
28. *Newsweek,* July 31, 1967.
29. *The New Yorker,* 1929.
30. *Redbook,* June 1967, pp. 120-21.
31. *Thinking Straight: Principles of Reasoning for Readers and Writers* (2nd ed.; Englewood Cliffs, N. J.: Prentice-Hall, Inc., 1956).
32. *College Composition and Communication,* December 1955.
33. *The New York Times Magazine,* February 22, 1953, p. 13.

CHAPTER 3

1. New York: Thomas Y. Crowell Co., 1966, p. 27.
2. *Harper's Bazaar,* August 1967, p. 97.
3. New York: Random House, Inc., 1966, p. 6.
4. *Shooting an Elephant and Other Essays* (New York: Harcourt Brace Jovanovich, Inc., 1945).
5. New York: Random House, Inc. (Vintage Books), 1957, p. 53.
6. "The Medical View: Not What the Doctor Ordered," *Newsweek,* July 24, 1967, p. 47.
7. *Saturday Review,* October 8, 1966, p. 43.
8. "The Hippies," *Time,* July 7, 1967, p. 20.
9. *Atlantic Monthly,* October 1947.
10. *Glamour,* 1959.
11. *My Life and Hard Times* (New York: Harper & Row, 1933, 1961).
12. *The New Republic,* May 30, 1964.

CHAPTER 4

1. *Years of the Modern* (New York: David McKay Company, Inc., 1949).
2. *America as a Civilization* (New York: Simon & Schuster, Inc., 1957).
3. *Saturday Review,* February 4, 1967, pp. 51-52.
4. *On Living in a Revolution* (New York: Harper & Row, 1942).
5. *American Judaism,* Winter 1964-65.
6. *The American Scholar,* XXVII, 4, Autumn 1958.
7. *Context,* I, No. 1 (Spring 1961).
8. *Expertland* (New York: Doubleday & Company, Inc., 1963).
9. *Is Anybody Happy?* (New York: Doubleday & Company, Inc., 1962).

10. *The Blue of Capricorn* (Boston, Mass.: Houghton Mifflin Company, 1961).

CHAPTER 5

1. Senator Edward V. Long, *The Intruders* (New York: Frederick A. Praeger, Inc., 1967), p. 116. Senator Long presents much of the same information in his article, "Big Brother in America," *Playboy*, January 1967.
2. *The Intruders*, pp. 113-16.
3. *Ibid.*, p. 119.
4. *Time*, March 8, 1971, pp. 38-39.
5. San Francisco *Chronicle*, "Sunday Punch," April 11, p. 2.
6. San Francisco *Chronicle*, April 7, 1971, p. 13.
7. *Ibid.*
8. *Ibid.*
9. *Holiday*, XXVII, March 1960.
10. *Tomorrow is Already Here*, Marguerite Waldman, trans. (New York: Simon & Schuster, Inc., 1954).
11. *Harper's Magazine*, July 1955.
12. *School and Society*, XXXVIII, June 10, 1933.
13. *Harper's Magazine*, October 1963, p. 84.
14. *Harper's Magazine*, May 1965.
15. *Harper's Magazine*, October 1963.
16. *Odyssey of the Self-Centered Self* (New York: Harcourt Brace Jovanovich, Inc., 1960, 1961).
17. *Fact*, May-June 1964.
18. *The Tastemakers* (New York: Harper & Row, Publishers, 1949, 1954).
19. New York: McGraw-Hill Book Company, 1939, 1957.
20. *Saturday Review*, April 11, 1953.
21. *The Early Worm* (New York: Harper & Row, Publishers, 1927).

CHAPTER 6

1. The New York Herald Tribune, Inc., 1965. Reprinted in *The Pump House Gang* (New York: Farrar, Straus & Giroux, Inc., 1968).
2. William Flint Thrall and Addison Hibbard, *A Handbook to Literature* (New York: The Odyssey Press, 1936); revised and enlarged by C. Hugh Holman (The Odyssey Press, 1960). We would like to acknowledge here that we are indebted to this source for a few minor details in our discussion of the essay in this chapter.

3. *The Pump House Gang* (New York: Farrar, Straus & Giroux, Inc., 1968).

4. Copyright © 1955 by John Steinbeck. Appeared originally in *The Reporter*. Reprinted by permission of McIntosh and Otis, Inc.

READINGS

CONTENTS

My Self, the Deepest of the Seas

Men and Women

Turning Points: a World in Crisis

The Classical Mode: Essays for Further Reading

My Self, the Deepest of the Seas

CRISIS
OF
SELF

WHO AM I?

MARYA MANNES   Who am I? That question vexes great numbers of young people these days, both on and off college campuses, as they strive to discover their identity. Once upon a time, Marya Mannes writes, the search for self among young people was not nearly so self-conscious. Today, however, there are complications: young people "stand naked and exposed in too large a world." In her analysis of the problem, the author relies rather extensively on generalizations based on personal experience; but the essay is also developed by descriptive detail and illustration. Miss Mannes, a free-lance writer, is the author of Message from a Stranger, War in Anger, *and* Subverse. *Most recently she wrote a novel entitled* They, *which deals with a social take-over by the young.*

[1]   Who are you? You singly, not you together. When did it start— that long day's journey into self? When do you really begin to know

what you believe and where you're going? When do you know that you
áre unique—separate—alone?

[2]   The time of discovery is different for everybody. Some people
find themselves in early childhood, some in middleage, some—the
tragic ones—never.

[3]   I suggest that the first recognition comes when others try to tell
you what you are. And although what happened in my generation is
supposed to have no relevance to what happens in yours, I know when
it happened to me.

[4]   I may have been six years old when aunts and uncles and cousins used to say: "You look just like your mother!" or "You're the image
of your brother!"

[5]   Now, for reasons that have nothing to do with duty or discipline in that distant day, I loved my family. I loved them because
they were interesting, handsome, talented, and loving people. I was
lucky. But in spite of that, I felt an immediate, instinctive resistance to
any suggestion that I was like them or like anybody else. I didn't want
to be like anybody else. I was Me. Myself. Separate. Alone.

[6]   This is probably as good a time as any to say that if I use the
first-person pronoun—if I refer from time to time to my own long,
arduous, bumbling journey into self—it is not because of narcissism,
but because I have always believed that the particular is more illuminating than the general. Perhaps my dependence as a writer on direct
observation rather than on scholarly research, on living example rather
than on sociological method, is the natural result of illiteracy. I never
went to college and therefore know much less than you people do.
About books, I mean. Or the sciences.

[7]   But since the laboratory for the study of man is clearly life itself, then I have studied hard in the act of living, of looking, of feeling; involvement rather than detachment; doing as well as being.

[8]   We were talking of the first discoveries of uniqueness—of being
oneself and no one else. Not your father, not your mother, not your
sister, not your brother. I. Me.

[9]   It is then—when you begin not only to know it, but act it—that
society moves in. Society says it wants people to be different but it
doesn't really mean it. Parents like to believe their children are different
from other children—smarter, of course, better-looking and so forth—
but most parents are secretly disturbed when their children are *really*
different—not like others at all. In fact, very early they start to pigeonhole you in certain ways.

[10]   Take the difference of sex, for instance. Little girls are pink, little boys are blue. Little girls want dolls, little boys want trains.

[11]   For a long time, for instance, the word "tom-boy" to a girl held undertones of worry and disapproval. All it meant was that the girl liked to play ball, climb trees, and skin her knees instead of wearing frilly dresses and curtseying. The companion word for boys, of course, was "sissy"—meaning the kid liked music and poetry and hated fighting. These ignorant and damaging labels have now been discredited, thanks largely to you and the more enlightened members of our society. But there is still, alas, a large Squareland left where growing girls are told from the age of twelve onward not only by their mothers but by the mass media that marriage is the only valid female goal and that Career is a dirty word.

[12]   Even now—even when you here know how silly it is (at least, I hope you do), most parents hear wedding bells the minute a girl is born, most parents see an executive office when a boy is born, and the relentless conditioning starts on its merry way. Educate a girl for the marriage market, educate a boy for success. That you, as a human being, as a separate identity, may not want or fit in with either of these goals is considered not a sign of independence but of deviation—pointing to the couch or—in social terms—failure.

[13]   That is why these same parents—and they are still a majority—are bewildered, depressed, or plain horrified when their adolescents openly refuse to accept these goals or to share any common identity with any past. Who on earth, their parents moan, will marry this stringy girl with her false eyelashes and shuffling gait? Who will employ this bearded boy with his grunts and records, his pop and pot? On the other end, how gratified are parents when their clean-cut athletic sons get high marks and their clean and pretty daughters marry the clean-cut boys who get good jobs?

[14]   You know, I pity you. I pity you for reasons you might not suspect. I pity you because your search for self has been made so self-conscious. You are overexposed in and by the mass media, which never for one instant night and day stop telling you what you are and who you are. With us, decades ago, there was no radio and no television. As adolescents we seldom read papers (they never reported on us) or magazines. The word "teenager," thank God, never existed. From twelve to seventeen we were painful to our parents and not very attractive to ourselves. Our skins and bodies did strange things and we felt strange things. The world paid no attention to us. It didn't interview us,

quote us, and ask our advice. We didn't expect it to. We had twenty-five to fifty cents a week to spend for allowance (rich kids got a dollar), but who needed it? Books were in the house or you could borrow them, movies were a quarter, and if you were lucky your family took you to occasional plays or concerts. School was sometimes boring, but we expected it to be. Nobody told us learning ought to be fun. When it was—well, great!

[15]   Nothing much external happened, except for trips with the family and meetings with friends. There was a lot of unfilled, unstructured, unplanned free time—with no messages coming in from anywhere to distract us, no entertainment at arm's length, no guidance counselors or psychiatrists to tell us what was bugging us. We had a vast amount of inner space to fill by ourselves. In this inner space there was room and time for that very tender, very vulnerable thing called "I" to be born—and grow.

[16]   For there are really two births—the first physical, the second spiritual. Both share something in common: Premature expulsion, premature exposure, can damage both foetus and soul. The prenatal fluid that protects the foetus until it is ready for air has its counterpart in the secret world of the yet unborn identity.

[17]   Now I want to make it quite clear that this secret world of child and adolescent is not a matter of protection from reality. Just because a child may grow up in the relative security of home and school and neighborhood doesn't mean that the human comedy-tragedy is not a part of daily life. You are not cut off from experience because the world you live in is physically small. On the contrary, you can be put off from real experience because the world has become too large.

[18]   And that is precisely why I pity you. You stand naked and exposed in too large a world, and that prenatal sac of your soul has been so repeatedly punctured by external influences, persuasions, and pressures that it must take superhuman will to keep yourself intact. Many of you don't. Or at least you find the only answer to a fragmented self in a fragmented life—or a withdrawal from life.

[19]   How, in any case, are you ever going to know what you are or who you are when these hundreds of voices are doing the job *for* you? How do you know how much of what you think and do is what you *really* think and want to do, or how much is the feedback from what you hear about yourselves—daily, hourly? A lot of it, of course, is true.

[20]   You *are* the new power, if only in numbers. You *are* rich, if only in dollars. You *are* smarter than your parents, if only in acquired

knowledge. A lot of you take drugs and pills or cop out in communal huddles, living on handouts. I question whether you are more interested in sex than we were, or even more active. The difference here is that it's now so easy to come by, in beds as well as in books, that it may mean less. Obstacles are great aphrodisiacs.

[21]   I would like to think that those of you who hate war are a majority. I would like to think that those of you who believe that sweeping changes must be made in our whole social, legal, political and economic life are a majority and an acting majority at that.

[22]   Whatever you are, you can't do anything about making a better society and a better world until you are a productive human being. And you can't be a productive human being, sorting the world out, until you sort yourself out.

[23]   Until you really attain an expansion of consciousness—not of another world, through hallucination, but of this world, through illumination. Not long ago Professor Lettwin, that dynamic, free-wheeling bear of M.I.T., told an audience of high-school students and undergraduates in Boston that in order to do what they wanted to do—to change the disastrous drift of society—they would have to keep their wits about them. You must be conscious, he exhorted, you must at all times keep your sense of judgment intact. Anything that blurs, that weakens your judgmental values will, in time, make you ineffective. Only your judgment, consciously arrived at, only the intellect and senses in the service of human compassion—will take you where you want to go—where this new society *must* go.

[24]   This I would also passionately advocate. As a long-time rebel, a seeker of new adventures, a destroyer of old myths, I have come to believe that this total awareness is the greatest single attribute of identity, and most preciously to be guarded. That it can be chemically achieved I would very much doubt. For moments, maybe. For the long haul, no. It is one thing—and who doesn't need it?—to seek escape from the pain of total awareness—in drink or pot. It is another to take the quick exit from reality with the distinct possibility that you may not make the reentry back. Or that if you do, you may never be yourself— your real, your useful, your creative self—again. Fly Now—Pay Later.

[25]   The price of conscious awareness is stiff—but not that stiff. The price is a very hard look at yourself—alone, and not bolstered by a crowd, a tribe—or even—a wife. And here is where I'm going to stick this already battered neck further out—on the institution of matrimony.

[26]   Your parents, I would imagine, consider your generation in-

comprehensible, sometimes frightening, and certainly unconventional. Everything you wear, grow on your face or head, think, believe, do, is way out of their norm.

[27]   Except marriage. In a world of undreamed-of scope and opportunity and choice, most of you do exactly what your parents did in a much more limited world. You rush to the altar to tie the legal tie from the age of eighteen onward to a girl no older. Here you are in the full flower of body and mind (and I speak of both sexes) and with the only pure freedom of action you will ever know again, and you tie yourself to one mate and one hearth before you know who you are.

[28]   If you're lucky, you will find yourselves *through* each other— the ideal nature of love, the true—and rare—blessing of marriage.

[29]   If you're not lucky—and the evidence would call you a majority—you will be two half-persons, half-grown, prematurely bound, inhibiting each other's growth, choking up the road to your full development as a human being.

[30]   Many of our laws and institutions, as you well know, have not yet caught up with reality . . . the fact that men and women cannot be codified. So long as we do others no harm, how we choose to live is our own affair, and ours alone. How *you* choose to live is yours alone. And if you are able to bring about an intelligent society—I avoid the word "great"—one of the most important things you will have to do is remove the senseless stigmas that still prevail against single men or single women, and against whatever kind of love is the product of deep inner need.

[31]   One of your great influences already is that in your new sense of community—in part forced upon you by isolation from your elders— you have managed to blur already many of the lines of demarcation— between races, between sexes, between thought and feeling, between feeling and action—which have trapped the former generations in patterns of sterility. The best of you have not only discovered your conscience, but are living it.

[32]   But apart from the terrible issues of the day—to which the best of you address your conscience—war in Vietnam, the brutal war in the streets—how much are you living it as individuals, how much in group conformity?

[33]   How brave, how independent are you when you are alone? I ask this chiefly of my own sex, for I wonder whether girls now really know and want the chances and choices that are open to them, or whether they have been so conditioned by history and habit that they

slip back into the old patterns of their mothers the minute they graduate. Oddly enough, this supposed choice between marriage and a career never bothered my generation as much as it seems to have bothered the postwar ones. And I lay the blame for it on a mass media—mainly television, advertising, and women's magazines—which maintain the fiction that the only valid goal for women is marriage and children and domesticity (with a little community work thrown in), and that women who demand and seek more than this from life are at best unfulfilled and at worst unfeminine. It is about time that we realized that many women make better teachers than mothers, better actresses than wives, better mistresses than housekeepers, better diplomats than cooks. Just as many men are better rakes than lawnmowers and better dreamers than providers. We have lost a great deal of talent and wasted a great many lives in the perpetuation of these myths that are called "the role of men" or "the role of women." And just as you have managed to dissipate some of them in your dress, I hope you will dissipate others in your lives. The only thing you need to aspire to, the only ultimate identity you must discover, is that of a human being. The sex, believe it or not, is secondary.

[34]   But in the search for this human identity, I urge you to remember one thing. I said before that our first recognition of it comes when we know we are not like anybody else, that we are unique. That is so.

[35]   But we did not spring into this world through galactic explosion—we did not even burst from the head of Zeus.

[36]   We came from somewhere. Not just the womb of our mothers and the seeds of our fathers but from a long, long procession of identities—whose genes we possess.

[37]   Whether we like it or not, we bear the past inside us. Good or bad, it cannot be excised, it cannot be rejected . . . it should not be. Humanity is a continuous process, and without a past there is no future.

[38]   In your worship of Now, in your fierce insistence that only the present exists, that you are new on the face of the earth, owing nothing to history—you are cheating yourself. You are not only denying evolution but limiting your future.

[39]   You may say you have nothing in common with the preceding generation, you may lay the blame for the present entirely on their shoulders and on the mistakes of the past. But what of the others who came before? What of the great rebels, the great innovators, the great

voices without which no light, no truth would ever have prevailed? Much of what poets and philosophers and artists and scientists said ten centuries ago is as valid now as it was then. Where would you be, where would we be, without them?

[40]   On a much humbler level, I remember the photograph albums so many families kept when I was a child. There, in our own, were these strange faces and strange clothes of the dead who preceded me: the tall, gaunt old baker in Poland, the opera singer in Germany, the immigrant furniture dealer in New York, the violinist in Breslau, the general near Kiel, the incredible web of cells and genes contained in my own self.

[41]   It took me more than twenty years to realize that they lived in me, that I was part of them, and that in spite of distance, time, and difference, I was part of them. I was not, in short, alone.

[42]   And neither are you. I suppose what I am asking for here is that, along with your pride of generation, you somehow maintain compassion for those who preceded you as well as for those who will come after you.

[43]   If you will, this is a community just as important as any living community of your own age and time, and if you deny your connection with it, you deny evolution, you deny the human race.

[44]   Don't play it too cool. The ultimate pattern of life is immense, there are other worlds in other galaxies that may have far transcended ours, and if you aren't turned on more by a shower of meteors than by an electric circus, you're half dead already.

[45]   You won't find yourself in a crowded room. You may find yourself under the crowded sky of night, where—if you attach yourself to a single star—you will discover that you are one of many millions, but still—One.

[46]   Listen to your own drum and march to it. You may fall on your face—but then, anybody who never does is—Nobody!

STUDY AND DISCUSSION

Vocabulary

In your dictionary find the meaning of any of the following words you do not know:

1. arduous (para. 3)   2. bumbling (para. 6)
3. narcissism (para. 6)   4. to pigeonhole (para. 9)

5. prenatal fluid (para. 16)
7. inhibiting (para. 29)
9. lines of demaracation (para. 31)
11. galactic (para. 35)
13. excised (para. 35)

6. aphrodisiacs (para. 20)
8. stigmas (para. 30)
10. perpetuation (para. 33)
12. Zeus (para. 35)

Rhetoric

1. The first paragraph of this essay is highly effective. Explain why.
2. Why is para. 9 vital to the development of this essay?
3. What methods of development are used in paras. 14, 18, 23, and 40?
4. In the first sentences in each of the following paragraphs, identify the transitional devices: 5, 7, 9, 12, 17, 29, 32, and 42.
5. In para. 6, Marya Mannes writes that she believes "the particular is more illuminating than the general." What effect does this statement have on the predominant rhetorical method she has chosen to use in this essay?
6. Could this essay also be a speech? Is it possible that it was originally intended as an address to be delivered to a group of young people—say, a graduating class? Point to examples in the text that corroborate this supposition.

Content

1. What does Marya Mannes consider to be "the only thing you need to aspire to. . . ?" Why is it important?
2. What keeps people from achieving it?
3. What solutions does the author offer for a better society? How can you become a part of it? What price is exacted in the process?
4. Whom does Mannes blame for the immense job of type-casting that she feels has tied so many of us to unfulfilling roles?
5. What, above all, does she warn young people away from?

Ideas and Implications

1. Have you found what Marya Mannes says is true, namely that "society says it wants people to be different but it really doesn't mean it . . ."?
2. Can you imagine living in a world in which the word, teenager, simply didn't exist? What do you suppose your life from 12 to 20 would be like? Has the Teenage Culture put pressure on you (made you date or wear make-up before you really wanted to, for instance, or forced you into consuming unwanted products)? Can you cite some actual examples of the tyranny of self-consciousness either in your own life or on campus?
3. Agree or disagree with the statement in para. 30 that "men and women cannot be codified."

4. "How brave, how independent are you when you are alone?" Mannes
   asks in para. 33. Answer her.
5. Is Mannes correct when she says that "humanity is a continuous process and without a past there is no future"? To what extent do you feel
   formed by your progenitors? How warmly do you feel toward your great
   grandfather or great grandmother? Do they smile down benevolently
   upon you from That Great Geriatrics Ward In The Sky during moments
   of intense personal crisis? In other words, does knowing that they once
   existed soothe you as it seems to soothe Mannes?

INDIAN CAMP

ERNEST HEMINGWAY Couvade *is an anthropological term which describes the custom, in some cultures, of a laboring woman's husband miming the actual act of labor while his wife gives birth. In a sense, the following story is "about" a couvade, such as the young Ernest Hemingway might actually have witnessed in the back country of northern Michigan where his father, who was a doctor, vacationed in the early part of this century.*

"Indian Camp," of course, is about a great many other issues, motives and motivations, too. Underlying its surface simplicity are themes that, when examined, go very deep indeed into the human heart and soul.

One of this story's major ironies comes in its last sentence. In order to appreciate it in all its dimensions, it is important to know that this story is, by Hemingway's own admission, largely autobiographical—"Nick Adams" is the name Hemingway gave to his young self. It is important for you to know, too, that Hemingway's father shot himself and that, in 1961, Ernest Hemingway, perhaps the most celebrated author this country has yet produced, also committed suicide.

Born in 1898, Ernest Miller Hemingway wrote some of the most influential fiction of this century. He is the author of, among other books, In Our Time *(from which this story is taken),* The Sun Also Rises, A Farewell to Arms, Death in the Afternoon, For Whom the Bell Tolls, *and* The Old Man and the Sea, *which won him The Nobel Prize for Literature in 1952.*

[1]   At the lake shore there was another rowboat drawn up. The two Indians stood waiting.

[2]   Nick and his father got in the stern of the boat and the Indians shoved it off and one of them got in to row. Uncle George sat in the stern of the camp rowboat. The young Indian shoved the camp boat off and got in to row Uncle George.

[3]   The two boats started off in the dark. Nick heard the oarlocks of the other boat quite a way ahead of them in the mist. The Indians rowed with quick choppy strokes. Nick lay back with his father's arm around him. It was cold on the water. The Indian who was rowing them was working very hard, but the other boat moved further ahead in the mist all the time.

[4]   "Where are we going, Dad?" Nick asked.

[5]   "Over to the Indian camp. There is an Indian lady very sick."

[6]   "Oh," said Nick.

[7]   Across the bay they found the other boat beached. Uncle George was smoking a cigar in the dark. The young Indian pulled the boat way up on the beach. Uncle George gave both the Indians cigars.

[8]   They walked up from the beach through a meadow that was soaking wet with dew, following the young Indian who carried a lantern. Then they went into the woods and followed a trail that led to the logging road that ran back into the hills. It was much lighter on the logging road as the timber was cut away on both sides. The young Indian stopped and blew out his lantern and they all walked on along the road.

[9]   They came around a bend and a dog came out barking. Ahead were the lights of the shanties where the Indian barkpeelers lived. More dogs rushed out at them. The two Indians sent them back to the shanties. In the shanty nearest the road there was a light in the window. An old woman stood in the doorway holding a lamp.

[10]   Inside on a wooden bunk lay a young Indian woman. She had been trying to have her baby for two days. All the old women in the camp had been helping her. The men had moved off up the road to sit in the dark and smoke out of range of the noise she made. She screamed just as Nick and the two Indians followed his father and Uncle George into the shanty. She lay in the lower bunk, very big under a quilt. Her head was turned to one side. In the upper bunk was her husband. He had cut his foot very badly with an ax three days before. He was smoking a pipe. The room smelled very bad.

[11]   Nick's father ordered some water to be put on the stove, and while it was heating he spoke to Nick.

[12]   "This lady is going to have a baby, Nick," he said.

[13]   "I know," said Nick.

[14]   "You don't know," said his father. "Listen to me. What she is going through is called being in labor. The baby wants to be born and she wants it to be born. All her muscles are trying to get the baby born. That is what is happening when she screams."

[15]   "I see," Nick said.

[16]   Just then the woman cried out.

[17]   "Oh, Daddy, can't you give her something to make her stop screaming?" asked Nick.

[18]   "No. I haven't any anaesthetic," his father said. "But her

screams are not important. I don't hear them because they are not important."

[19]   The husband in the upper bunk rolled over against the wall.

[20]   The woman in the kitchen motioned to the doctor that the water was hot. Nick's father went into the kitchen and poured about half of the water out of the big kettle into a basin. Into the water left in the kettle he put several things he unwrapped from a handkerchief.

[21]   "Those must boil," he said, and began to scrub his hands in the basin of hot water with a cake of soap he had brought from the camp. Nick watched his father's hands scrubbing each other with the soap. While his father washed his hands very carefully and thoroughly, he talked.

[22]   "You see, Nick, babies are supposed to be born head first but sometimes they're not. When they're not they make a lot of trouble for everybody. Maybe I'll have to operate on this lady. We'll know in a little while."

[23]   When he was satisfied with his hands he went in and went to work.

[24]   "Pull back that quilt, will you, George?" he said. "I'd rather not touch it."

[25]   Later when he started to operate Uncle George and three Indian men held the woman still. She bit Uncle George on the arm and Uncle George said, "Damn squaw bitch!" and the young Indian who had rowed Uncle George over laughed at him. Nick held the basin for his father. It all took a long time.

[26]   His father picked the baby up and slapped it to make it breathe and handed it to the old woman.

[27]   "See, it's a boy, Nick," he said. "How do you like being an interne?"

[28]   Nick said, "All right." He was looking away so as not to see what his father was doing.

[29]   "There. That gets it," said his father and put something into the basin.

[30]   Nick didn't look at it.

[31]   "Now," his father said, "there's some stitches to put in. You can watch this or not, Nick, just as you like. I'm going to sew up the incision I made."

[32]   Nick did not watch. His curiosity had been gone for a long time.

[33]   His father finished and stood up. Uncle George and the three Indian men stood up. Nick put the basin out in the kitchen.

[34]   Uncle George looked at his arm. The young Indian smiled reminiscently.

[35]   "I'll put some peroxide on that, George," the doctor said.

[36]   He bent over the Indian woman. She was quiet now and her eyes were closed. She looked very pale. She did not know what had become of the baby or anything.

[37]   "I'll be back in the morning," the doctor said, standing up.

[38]   "The nurse should be here from St. Ignace by noon and she'll bring everything we need."

[39]   He was feeling exalted and talkative as football players are in the dressing room after a game.

[40]   "That's one for the medical journal, George," he said. "Doing a Caesarian with a jack-knife and sewing it up with ninefoot, tapered gut leaders."

[41]   Uncle George was standing against the wall, looking at his arm.

[42]   "Oh, you're a great man, all right," he said.

[43]   "Ought to have a look at the proud father. They're usually the worst sufferers in these little affairs," the doctor said. "I must say he took it all pretty quietly."

[44]   He pulled back the blanket from the Indian's head. His hand came away wet. He mounted on the edge of the lower bunk with the lamp in one hand and looked in. The Indian lay with his face toward the wall. His throat had been cut from ear to ear. The blood had flowed down into a pool where his body sagged the bunk. His head rested on his left arm. The open razor lay, edge up, in the blankets.

[45]   "Take Nick out of the shanty, George," the doctor said.

[46]   There was no need of that. Nick, standing in the door of the kitchen, had a good view of the upper bunk when his father, the lamp in one hand, tipped the Indian's head back.

[47]   It was just beginning to be daylight when they walked along the logging road back toward the lake.

[48]   "I'm terribly sorry I brought you along, Nickie," said his father, all his post-operative exhilaration gone. "It was an awful mess to put you through."

[49]   "Do ladies always have such a hard time having babies?" Nick asked.

[50]   "No, that was very, very exceptional."

[51] "Why did he kill himself, Daddy?"
[52] "I don't know, Nick. He couldn't stand things, I guess."
[53] "Do many men kill themselves, Daddy?"
[54] "Not very many, Nick."
[55] "Do many women?"
[56] "Hardly ever."
[57] "Don't they ever?"
[58] "Oh, yes. They do sometimes."
[59] "Daddy?"
[60] "Yes."
[61] "Where did Uncle George go?"
[62] "He'll turn up all right."
[63] "Is dying hard, Daddy?"
[64] "No, I think it's pretty easy, Nick. It all depends."
[65] They were seated in the boat, Nick in the stern, his father rowing. The sun was coming up over the hills. A bass jumped, making a circle in the water. Nick trailed his hand in the water. It felt warm in the sharp chill of the morning.
[66] In the early morning on the lake sitting in the stern of the boat with his father rowing, he felt quite sure that he would never die.

STUDY AND DISCUSSION

1. Briefly analyze Hemingway's style. What are its typical qualities? Is it effective, in your opinion? Is it appropriate to this story? Why or why not?

2. Why is the Indian woman's husband lying in the bunk above her? Granted that he has had an "accident," what are his apparent motives for remaining near his wife?

3. What is the attitude of Nick's father toward the operation? In your opinion, what does Hemingway want us to think of Nick's father?

4. What does Uncle George do during the operation? Does he contribute anything to the story? That is, is he an essential character, or could his place be taken by someone totally anonymous?

5. How do you interpret the laughter of the young Indian in paragraph 25?

6. Why does Uncle George say to the doctor, "Oh, you're a great man, all right"? What attitude does this statement imply?

7. In your opinion, why does the Indian commit suicide? Does his act

make sense to you? Is it noble, or meaningful—or is it merely "crazy"?

8. Is there any significance in the fact that this story begins in darkness and ends at daylight? Why should Hemingway want the story to take place at night?

9. Uncle George does not go back in the boat with Nick and his father. Why not, apparently? Compare his response to the birth and death with Nick's.

10. At the end of the story, Nick feels "quite sure" that he will never die. Why does he feel this way? In your opinion, has he been changed by this incident? Has he learned anything from it? What seems to be his final response to the entire incident?

11. What point do you think Hemingway intends to make in this story?

DOVER BEACH

MATTHEW ARNOLD   Matthew Arnold (1822-1888), an eminent Victorian poet, essayist, and literary critic, spent most of his adult life as a professor of poetry at Oxford and as an inspector for the British school system. Arnold believed in "the pursuit of total perfection by means of getting to know . . . the best that has been thought and said in the world." For that reason he looked upon literature—poetry in particular—not as esthetic experience but as "a criticism of life." Besides his poetry, Arnold's most distinguished publications include Essays in Criticism, Culture and Anarchy, *and* Discourses in America.

In "Dover Beach" (1867), Arnold meditates on the nature of the universe and man's relation to it: he listens to the waves striking the beach at Dover on the southern coast of England and hears in them "the eternal note of sadness"—the same sound Sophocles heard centuries ago on the Aegean seacoast—but endowed now with a new significance because Arnold thinks of it as the "melancholy, long, withdrawing roar" of the retreating sea of faith. Modern man, he says, has nothing to believe in: the universe is indifferent, and mankind itself is blind, savage, and ignorant. The poem concludes with a haunting image of the speaker and his love alone "as on a darkling plain."

You might do well to read this poem through several times; about the second or the third, its music ought to start resounding in your inner ear.

The sea is calm to-night,
The tide is full, the moon lies fair
Upon the Straits;—on the French coast, the light
Gleams, and is gone; the cliffs of England stand,
Glimmering and vast, out in the tranquil bay.   5
Come to the window, sweet is the night air!
Only, from the long line of spray
Where the sea meets the moon-blanched land,
Listen! you hear the grating roar
Of pebbles which the waves draw back, and fling,   10
At their return, up the high strand,
Begin, and cease, and then again begin,
With tremulous cadence slow, and bring
The eternal note of sadness in.

Sophocles long ago
Heard it on the Aegean, and it brought
Into his mind the turbid ebb and flow
Of human misery; we
Find also in the sound a thought,
Hearing it by this distant northern sea.   20

The sea of faith
Was once, too, at the full, and round earth's shore
Lay like the folds of a bright girdle furled;
But now I only hear   25
Its melancholy, long, withdrawing roar,
Retreating to the breath
Of the night-wind, down the vast edges drear
And naked shingles of the world.

Ah, love, let us be true   30
To one another! for the world, which seems
To lie before us like a land of dreams,
So various, so beautiful, so new,
Hath really neither joy, nor love, nor light,
Nor certitude, nor peace, nor help for pain;   35
And we are here as on a darkling plain
Swept with confused alarms of struggle and flight,
Where ignorant armies clash by night.

STUDY AND DISCUSSION

Vocabulary
If you don't already know them, consult your dictionary for the meaning
of the following words and proper names:

1. moon-blanched (line 8)
2. strand (line 10)
3. tremulous (line 13)
4. cadence (line 13)
5. Sophocles (line 16)
6. Aegean (line 16)
7. turbid (line 18)
8. girdle (line 23)
9. drear (line 27)
10. darkling (line 35)
11. alarms (line 36)

Content
1. What feelings does Arnold present in the first six lines?
2. Whom does the speaker address, apparently, when he says, "Come to the window"? What, in your opinion is the situation in this poem?
3. Why does the speaker hear "The eternal note of sadness" in the sound of the waves?
4. What does the sea appear to symbolize in the first two sections of the poem?
5. Arnold once described Sophocles as a man "who saw life steadily and saw it whole." In your opinion, why does Arnold refer to Sophocles in this poem? How is Sophocles supposed to have interpreted the sound of the waves?
6. What do you think Arnold means by "The sea of faith"? What does he say has happened to the sea of faith? How could Arnold's opinion have been influenced by Charles Darwin's book *On the Origin of Species by Means of Natural Selection* (1859)?
7. What are "the vast edges drear/And naked shingles of the world"?
8. Why does Arnold say, "Ah, love, let us be true/To one another"? Does he contradict the sense of this request when he asserts that the world "Hath really neither joy, nor *love,* nor light"?
9. What is "a darkling plain"? What image does Arnold present in the last two lines? In your opinion, is it an effective conclusion to the poem? Why or why not?
10. "Just because man loves God is no reason to believe that God loves man in return," wrote Nietzsche, a contemporary of Arnold's and a man who could be called the father of modern philosophy. To what extent would you say that "Dover Beach" reflects this judgment?

PERSONAL INTEGRITY

SHOOTING AN ELEPHANT

GEORGE ORWELL   In "Shooting an Elephant," as in "A Hanging" and in "Marrakech," George Orwell has a political purpose. His intention in this essay is to show not merely that imperialism is an "evil thing" but that "when the white man turns tyrant it is his own freedom that he destroys." In our view, the essay raises another issue, however—the personal, individual problem of maintaining one's integrity against external pressures to conform. As you read about Orwell's confrontation with this problem, note again the utter lucidity of his style and his fine attention to significant descriptive details.

For a note on the author's life, see the introduction to "A Hanging" in Chapter 6 of the rhetoric section of this book.

[1]   In Moulmein, in lower Burma, I was hated by large numbers of people—the only time in my life that I have been important enough for this to happen to me. I was sub-divisional police officer of the town, and in an aimless, petty kind of way anti-European feeling was

very bitter. No one had the guts to raise a riot, but if a European woman went through the bazaars alone somebody would probably spit betel juice over her dress. As a police officer I was an obvious target and was baited whenever it seemed safe to do so. When a nimble Burman tripped me up on the football field and the referee (another Burman) looked the other way, the crowd yelled with hideous laughter. This happened more than once. In the end the sneering yellow faces of young men that met me everywhere, the insults hooted after me when I was at a safe distance, got badly on my nerves. The young Buddhist priests were the worst of all. There were several thousands of them in the town and none of them seemed to have anything to do except stand on street corners and jeer at Europeans.

[2]   All this was perplexing and upsetting. For at that time I had already made up my mind that imperialism was an evil thing and the sooner I chucked up my job and got out of it the better. Theoretically —and secretly, of course—I was all for the Burmese and all against their oppressors, the British. As for the job I was doing, I hated it more bitterly than I can perhaps make clear. In a job like that you see the dirty work of Empire at close quarters. The wretched prisoners huddling in the stinking cages of the lock-ups, the grey, cowed faces of the long-term convicts, the scarred buttocks of the men who had been flogged with bamboos—all these oppressed me with an intolerable sense of guilt. But I could get nothing into perspective. I was young and ill-educated and I had had to think out my problems in the utter silence that is imposed on every Englishman in the East. I did not even know that the British Empire was dying, still less did I know that it is a great deal better than the younger empires that are going to supplant it. All I knew was that I was stuck between my hatred of the empire I served and my rage against the evil-spirited little beasts who tried to make my job impossible. With one part of my mind I thought of the British Raj as an unbreakable tyranny, as something clamped down, in *saecula saeculorum*,[1] upon the will of prostrate peoples; with another part I thought that the greatest joy in the world would be to drive a bayonet into a Buddhist priest's guts. Feelings like these are the normal by-products of imperialism; ask any Anglo-Indian official, if you can catch him off duty.

[3]   One day something happened which in a roundabout way was enlightening. It was a tiny incident in itself, but it gave me a better

---

[1] *saecula saeculorum*, Latin for "time out of mind."

glimpse than I had had before of the real nature of imperialism—the real motives for which despotic governments act. Early one morning the sub-inspector at a police station the other end of the town rang me up on the 'phone and said that an elephant was ravaging the bazaar. Would I please come and do something about it? I did not know what I could do, but I wanted to see what was happening and I got on to a pony and started out. I took my rifle, an old .44 Winchester and much too small to kill an elephant, but I thought the noise might be useful *in terrorem.*[2] Various Burmans stopped me on the way and told me about the elephant's doings. It was not, of course, a wild elephant, but a tame one which had gone "must." It had been chained up, as tame elephants always are when their attack of "must" is due, but on the previous night it had broken its chain and escaped. Its mahout,[3] the only person who could manage it when it was in that state, had set out in pursuit, but had taken the wrong direction and was now twelve hours' journey away, and in the morning the elephant had suddenly reappeared in the town. The Burmese population had no weapons and were quite helpless against it. It had already destroyed somebody's bamboo hut, killed a cow and raided some fruit-stalls and devoured the stock; also it had met the municipal rubbish van and, when the driver jumped out and took to his heels, had turned the van over and inflicted violences upon it.

[4]   The Burmese sub-inspector and some Indian constables were waiting for me in the quarter where the elephant had been seen. It was a very poor quarter, a labyrinth of squalid bamboo huts, thatched with palm-leaf, winding all over a steep hillside. I remember that it was a cloudy, stuffy morning at the beginning of the rains. We began questioning the people as to where the elephant had gone and, as usual, failed to get any definite information. That is invariably the case in the East; a story always sounds clear enough at a distance, but the nearer you get to the scene of events the vaguer it becomes. Some of the people said that the elephant had gone in one direction, some said that he had gone in another, some professed not even to have heard of any elephant. I had almost made up my mind that the whole story was a pack of lies, when we heard yells a little distance away. There was a loud, scandalized cry of "Go away, child! Go away this instant!" and an old woman with a switch in her hand came round the corner of a hut, violently shooing away a crowd of naked

[2] *in terrorem*, Latin for "as a means of provoking fright; an instrument of terror."
[3] *mahout*, trainer and rider.

children. Some more women followed, clicking their tongues and exclaiming; evidently there was something that the children ought not to have seen. I rounded the hut and saw a man's dead body sprawling in the mud. He was an Indian, a black Dravidian coolie, almost naked, and he could not have been dead many minutes. The people said that the elephant had come suddenly upon him round the corner of the hut, caught him with its trunk, put its foot on his back and ground him into the earth. This was the rainy season and the ground was soft, and his face had scored a trench a foot deep and a couple of yards long. He was lying on his belly with arms crucified and head sharply twisted to one side. His face was coated with mud, the eyes wide open, the teeth bared and grinning with an expression of unendurable agony. (Never tell me, by the way, that the dead look peaceful. Most of the corpses I have seen looked devilish.) The friction of the great beast's foot had stripped the skin from his back as neatly as one skins a rabbit. As soon as I saw the dead man I sent an orderly to a friend's house nearby to borrow an elephant rifle. I had already sent back the pony, not wanting it to go mad with fright and throw me if it smelt the elephant.

[5]   The orderly came back in a few minutes with a rifle and five cartridges, and meanwhile some Burmans had arrived and told us that the elephant was in the paddy fields below, only a few hundred yards away. As I started forward, practically the whole population of the quarter flocked out of the houses and followed me. They had seen the rifle and were all shouting excitedly that I was going to shoot the elephant. They had not shown much interest in the elephant when he was merely ravaging their homes, but it was different now that he was going to be shot. It was a bit of fun to them, as it would be to an English crowd; besides they wanted the meat. It made me vaguely uneasy. I had no intention of shooting the elephant—I had merely sent for the rifle to defend myself if necessary—and it is always unnerving to have a crowd following you. I marched down the hill, looking and feeling a fool, with the rifle over my shoulder and an evergrowing army of people jostling at my heels. At the bottom, when you got away from the huts, there was a metalled road and beyond that a miry waste of paddy fields a thousand yards across, not yet ploughed but soggy from the first rains and dotted with coarse grass. The elephant was standing eight yards from the road, his left side towards us. He took not the slightest notice of the crowd's approach. He was tearing

up bunches of grass, beating them against his knees to clean them and stuffing them into his mouth.

[6] I had halted on the road. As soon as I saw the elephant I knew with perfect certainty that I ought not to shoot him. It is a serious matter to shoot a working elephant—it is comparable to destroying a huge and costly piece of machinery—and obviously one ought not to do it if it can possibly be avoided. And at that distance, peacefully eating, the elephant looked no more dangerous than a cow. I thought then and I think now that his attack of "must" was already passing off; in which case he would merely wander harmlessly about until the mahout came back and caught him. Moreover, I did not in the least want to shoot him. I decided that I would watch him for a little while to make sure that he did not turn savage again, and then go home.

[7] But at that moment I glanced round at the crowd that had followed me. It was an immense crowd, two thousand at the least and growing every minute. It blocked the road for a long distance on either side. I looked at the sea of yellow faces above the garish clothes—faces all happy and excited over this bit of fun, all certain that the elephant was going to be shot. They were watching me as they would watch a conjurer about to perform a trick. They did not like me, but with the magical rifle in my hands I was momentarily worth watching. And suddenly I realized that I should have to shoot the elephant after all. The people expected it of me and I had got to do it; I could feel their two thousand wills pressing me forward, irresistibly. And it was at this moment, as I stood there with the rifle in my hands, that I first grasped the hollowness, the futility of the white man's dominion in the East. Here was I, the white man with his gun, standing in front of the unarmed native crowd—seemingly the leading actor of the piece; but in reality I was only an absurd puppet pushed to and fro by the will of those yellow faces behind. I perceived in this moment that when the white man turns tyrant it is his own freedom that he destroys. He becomes a sort of hollow, posing dummy, the conventionalized figure of a sahib.[4] For it is the condition of his rule that he shall spend his life in trying to impress the "natives," and so in every crisis he has got to do what the "natives" expect of him. He wears a mask, and his face grows to fit it. I had got to shoot the elephant. I had

[4] sahib, master; an Indian form of respect used when addressing a Britisher.

committed myself to doing it when I sent for the rifle. A sahib has got to act like a sahib; he has got to appear resolute, to know his own mind and do definite things. To come all that way, rifle in hand, with two thousand people marching at my heels, and then to trail feebly away, having done nothing—no, that was impossible. The crowd would laugh at me. And my whole life, every white man's life in the East, was one long struggle not to be laughed at.

[8]   But I did not want to shoot the elephant. I watched him beating his bunch of grass against his knees, with that preoccupied grand-motherly air that elephants have. It seemed to me that it would be murder to shoot him. At that age I was not squeamish about killing animals, but I had never shot an elephant and never wanted to. (Somehow it always seems worse to kill a *large* animal.) Besides, there was the beast's owner to be considered. Alive, the elephant was worth at least a hundred pounds; dead, he would only be worth the value of his tusks; five pounds, possibly. But I had got to act quickly. I turned to some experienced-looking Burmans who had been there when we arrived, and asked them how the elephant had been behaving. They all said the same thing: he took no notice of you if you left him alone, but he might charge if you went too close to him.

[9]   It was perfectly clear to me what I ought to do. I ought to walk up to within, say, twenty-five yards of the elephant and test his be-havior. If he charged, I could shoot; if he took no notice of me, it would be safe to leave him until the mahout came back. But also I knew that I was going to do no such thing. I was a poor shot with a rifle and the ground was soft mud into which one would sink at every step. If the elephant charged and I missed him, I should have about as much chance as a toad under a steam-roller. But even then I was not thinking particularly of my own skin, only of the watchful yellow faces behind. For at that moment, with the crowd watching me, I was not afraid in the ordinary sense, as I would have been if I had been alone. A white man mustn't be frightened in front of "natives"; and so, in general, he isn't frightened. The sole thought in my mind was that if anything went wrong those two thousand Burmans would see me pursued, caught, trampled on and reduced to a grinning corpse like that Indian up the hill. And if that happened it was quite probable that some of them would laugh. That would never do. There was only one alternative. I shoved the cartridges into the magazine and lay down on the road to get a better aim.

[10]   The crowd grew very still, and a deep, low, happy sigh, as of

people who see the theatre curtain go up at last, breathed from innumerable throats. They were going to have their bit of fun after all. The rifle was a beautiful German thing with cross-hair sights. I did not then know that in shooting an elephant one would shoot to cut an imaginary bar running from ear-hole to ear-hole. I ought, therefore, as the elephant was sideways on, to have aimed straight at his ear-hole; actually I aimed several inches in front of this, thinking the brain would be further forward.

[11]   When I pulled the trigger I did not hear the bang or feel the kick—one never does when a shot goes home—but I heard the devilish roar of glee that went up from the crowd. In that instant, in too short a time, one would have thought, even for the bullet to get there, a mysterious, terrible change had come over the elephant. He neither stirred nor fell, but every line of his body had altered. He looked suddenly stricken, shrunken, immensely old, as though the frightful impact of the bullet had paralysed him without knocking him down. At last, after what seemed a long time—it might have been five seconds, I dare say—he sagged flabbily to his knees. His mouth slobbered. An enormous senility seemed to have settled upon him. One could have imagined him thousands of years old. I fired again into the same spot. At the second shot he did not collapse but climbed with desperate slowness to his feet and stood weakly upright, with legs sagging and head drooping. I fired a third time. That was the shot that did for him. You could see the agony of it jolt his whole body and knock the last remnant of strength from his legs. But in falling he seemed for a moment to rise, for as his hind legs collapsed beneath him he seemed to tower upward like a huge rock toppling, his trunk reaching skywards like a tree. He trumpeted, for the first and only time. And then down he came, his belly towards me, with a crash that seemed to shake the ground even where I lay.

[12]   I got up. The Burmans were already racing past me across the mud. It was obvious that the elephant would never rise again, but he was not dead. He was breathing very rhythmically with long rattling gasps, his great mound of a side painfully rising and falling. His mouth was wide open—I could see far down into caverns of pale pink throat. I waited a long time for him to die, but his breathing did not weaken. Finally I fired my two remaining shots into the spot where I thought his heart must be. The thick blood welled out of him like red velvet, but still he did not die. His body did not even jerk when the shots hit him, the tortured breathing continued without a pause. He was

dying, very slowly and in great agony, but in some world remote from me where not even a bullet could damage him further. I felt that I had got to put an end to that dreadful noise. It seemed dreadful to see the great beast lying there, powerless to move and yet powerless to die, and not even to be able to finish him. I sent back for my small rifle and poured shot after shot into his heart and down his throat. They seemed to make no impression. The tortured gasps continued as steadily as the ticking of a clock.

[13]   In the end I could not stand it any longer and went away. I heard later that it took him half an hour to die. Burmans were bringing dahs[5] and baskets even before I left, and I was told they had stripped his body almost to the bones by the afternoon.

[14]   Afterwards, of course, there were endless discussions about the shooting of the elephant. The owner was furious, but he was only an Indian and could do nothing. Besides, legally I had done the right thing, for a mad elephant has to be killed, like a mad dog, if its owner fails to control it. Among the Europeans opinion was divided. The older men said I was right, the younger men said it was a damn shame to shoot an elephant for killing a coolie, because an elephant was worth more than any damn Coringhee coolie. And afterwards I was very glad that the coolie had been killed; it put me legally in the right and it gave me a sufficient pretext for shooting the elephant. I often wondered whether any of the others grasped that I had done it solely to avoid looking a fool.

STUDY AND DISCUSSION

Vocabulary
Consult your dictionary for any of the following words which might prove unfamiliar:

1. nimble (para. 1)   2. imperialism (para. 2)
3. prostrate (para. 2)   4. despotic (para. 3)
5. "must" (para. 3)   6. labyrinth (para. 4)
7. miry (para. 5)   8. garish (para. 7)
9. senility (para. 11)

[5] *dahs* are crude litters much in use for transport throughout the East.

Rhetoric
1. In what paragraph is the thesis stated? Which sentence states the thesis most exactly?
2. What method of organization is used in the essay as a whole?
3. What method of development is used most extensively in this essay?

Content
1. What signs of hatred did Orwell meet with in Burma?
2. Explain Orwell's attitude toward imperialism.
3. What were Orwell's contradictory feelings about the Burmese?
4. In para. 3, Orwell says that this incident revealed "the real motives for which despotic governments act." In your own words, what are those motives?
5. Explain the Burmans' interest in seeing the elephant shot.
6. Why wasn't Orwell frightened of the elephant?
7. Why did Orwell shoot the elephant? Explain in detail.
8. Why was Orwell glad that the coolie had been killed?

Ideas and Implications
1. Do you blame Orwell for acting as he did, or do you believe that he ought to have approached the elephant to see if it was still dangerous? Explain your reasoning.
2. What do you think of Orwell's motives in general? Is it usually best to do things "solely to avoid looking a fool"? Or should one be himself no matter what the consequences?
3. In your opinion, why does Orwell describe the death agony of the elephant in such detail? Is he merely being gruesome, or is the description justified by the essay as a whole?
4. In your opinion, does Orwell truly succeed in showing "the real motives for which despotic governments act"? If he doesn't, what *are* the motives for which they act?
5. What can you conclude about a system which values an elephant's life more highly than a human being's? What can an elephant, in other words, do that a man can't?
6. What do you suppose the younger Europeans—Orwell's peers—were like on the basis of what is said about them in para. 14?
7. Is there any similarity between the British occupation of Burma and our "presence" in Southeast Asia?

LIKE A BAD DREAM

HEINRICH BÖLL (translated by Leila Vennewitz)   Heinrich Böll is one of the most prominent of post-War German writers. Among his most widely praised novels have been Billiards at Half-past Nine *and* The Clown. *In the following story, Böll's mastery of the short-story form is singularly evident. Like Hemingway's, his style is spare and his narrative proceeds without the use of many evident transitional devices. And, like Hemingway, Böll is able to delve deep into the often murky realms of human motivation. Unlike Hemingway, Böll is a deeply religious man— something which will be evident to the discerning reader after even a light perusal of this story.*

Which, we hope, will not be all the attention you give it. Like a Bad Dream, with its author's preoccupation about the lack of any but material values in the society that has emerged in Western Germany from the rubble of World War II, is worthy of and will repay the closest possible reading you can give it.

[1]   That evening we had invited the Zumpens over for dinner, nice people; it was through my father-in-law that we had got to know them: ever since we have been married he has helped me to meet people who can be useful to me in business, and Zumpen can be useful: he is chairman of a committee which places contracts for large housing projects, and I have married into the excavating business.

[2]   I was tense that evening, but Bertha, my wife, reassured me. "The fact," she said, "that he's coming at all is promising. Just try and get the conversation round to the contract. You know it's tomorrow they're going to be awarded."

[3]   I stood looking through the net curtains of the glass front door, waiting for Zumpen. I smoked, ground the cigarette butts under my foot, and shoved them under the mat. Next I took up a position at the bathroom window and stood there wondering why Zumpen had accepted the invitation; he couldn't be that interested in having dinner with us, and the fact that the big contract I was involved in was going to be awarded tomorrow must have made the whole thing as embarrassing to him as it was to me.

[4]   I thought about the contract too: it was a big one, I would make 20,000 marks on the deal, and I wanted the money.

[5]   Bertha had decided what I was to wear: a dark jacket, trousers a shade lighter and a conservative tie. That's the kind of thing she learned at home, and at boarding school from the nuns. Also what to offer guests: when to pass the cognac, and when the vermouth, how to arrange dessert. It is comforting to have a wife who knows all about such things.

[6]   But Bertha was tense too: as she put her hands on my shoulders, they touched my neck, and I felt her thumbs damp and cold against it.

[7]   "It's going to be all right," she said, "You'll get the contract."

[8]   "Christ," I said, "it means 20,000 marks to me, and you know how we need the money."

[9]   "One should never," she said gently, "mention Christ's name in connection with money!"

[10]   A dark car drew up in front of our house, a make I didn't recognize, but it looked Italian. "Take it easy," Bertha whispered, "wait till they've rung, let them stand there for a couple of seconds, then walk slowly to the door and open it."

[11]   I watched Mr. and Mrs. Zumpen come up the steps: he is slender and tall, with graying temples, the kind of man who fifty years ago would have been known as a "ladies' man"; Mrs. Zumpen is one of those thin dark women who always make me think of lemons. I could tell from Zumpen's face that it was a frightful bore for him to have dinner with us.

[12]   Then the doorbell rang, and I waited one second, two seconds, walked slowly to the door and opened it.

[13]   "Well," I said, "how nice of you to come!"

[14]   Cognac glasses in hand, we went from room to room in our apartment, which the Zumpens wanted to see. Bertha stayed in the kitchen to squeeze some mayonnaise out of a tube onto the appetizers; she does this very nicely: hearts, loops, little houses. The Zumpens complimented us on our apartment; they exchanged smiles when they saw the big desk in my study, at that moment it seemed a bit too big even to me.

[15]   Zumpen admired a small rococo cabinet, a wedding present from my grandmother, and a baroque Madonna in our bedroom.

[16]   By the time we got back to the dining room, Bertha had dinner on the table; she had done this very nicely too, it was all so attrac-

tive yet so natural, and dinner was pleasant and relaxed. We talked about movies and books, about the recent elections, and Zumpen praised the assortment of cheeses, and Mrs. Zumpen praised the coffee and the pastries. Then we showed the Zumpens our honeymoon pictures: photographs of the Breton coast, Spanish donkeys, and street scenes from Casablanca.

[17]   After that we had some more cognac, and when I stood up to get the box with the photos of the time when we were engaged, Bertha gave me a sign, and I didn't get the box. For two minutes there was absolute silence, because we had nothing more to talk about, and we all thought about the contract; I thought of the 20,000 marks, and it struck me that I could deduct the bottle of cognac from my income tax. Zumpen looked at his watch and said: "Too bad, it's ten o'clock; we have to go. It's been such a pleasant evening!" And Mrs. Zumpen said: "It was really delightful, and I hope you'll come to us one evening."

[18]   "We would love to," Bertha said, and we stood around for another half-minute, all thinking again about the contract, and I felt Zumpen was waiting for me to take him aside and bring up the subject. But I didn't. Zumpen kissed Bertha's hand, and I went ahead, opened the doors, and held the car door open for Mrs. Zumpen down below.

[19]   "Why," said Bertha gently, "didn't you mention the contract to him? You know it's going to be awarded tomorrow."

[20]   "Well," I said, "I didn't know how to bring the conversation round to it."

[21]   "Now look," she said in a quiet voice, "you could have used any excuse to ask him into your study, that's where you should have talked to him. You must have noticed how interested he is in art. You ought to have said: I have an eighteenth-century crucifix in there you might like to have a look at, and then. . . ."

[22]   I said nothing, and she sighed and tied on her apron. I followed her into the kitchen; we put the rest of the appetizers back in the refrigerator, and I crawled about on the floor looking for the top of the mayonnaise tube. I put away the remains of the cognac, counted the cigars: Zumpen had smoked only one. I emptied the ashtrays, ate another pastry, and looked to see if there was any coffee left in the pot. When I went back to the kitchen, Bertha was standing there with the car key in her hand.

[23]   "What's up?" I asked.

[24]   "We have to go over there, of course," she said.

[25]   "Over where?"

[26]   "To the Zumpens," she said, "where do you think?"

[27]   "It's nearly half past ten."

[28]   "I don't care if it's midnight," Bertha said, "all I know is, there's 20,000 marks involved. Don't imagine they're squeamish."

[29]   She went into the bathroom to get ready, and I stood behind her watching her wipe her mouth and draw in new outlines, and for the first time I noticed how wide and primitive that mouth is. When she tightened the knot of my tie I could have kissed her, the way I always used to when she fixed my tie, but I didn't.

[30]   Downtown the cafes and restaurants were brightly lit. People were sitting outside on the terraces, and the light from the street lamps was caught in the silver ice-cream dishes and ice buckets. Bertha gave me an encouraging look; but she stayed in the car when we stopped in front of the Zumpens' house, and I pressed the bell at once and was surprised how quickly the door was opened. Mrs. Zumpen did not seem surprised to see me; she had on some black lounging pajamas with loose full trousers embroidered with yellow flowers, and this made me think more than ever of lemons.

[31]   "I beg your pardon," I said, "I would like to speak to your husband."

[32]   "He's gone out again," she said, "he'll be back in half an hour."

[33]   In the hall I saw a lot of Madonnas, gothic and baroque, even rococo Madonnas, if there is such a thing.

[34]   "I see," I said, "well then, if you don't mind, I'll come back in half an hour."

[35]   Bertha had bought an evening paper; she was reading it and smoking, and when I sat down beside her she said: "I think you could have talked about it to her too."

[36]   "But how do you know he wasn't there?"

[37]   "Because I know he is at the Gaffel Club playing chess, as he does every Wednesday evening at this time."

[38]   "You might have told me that earlier."

[39]   "Please try and understand," said Bertha, folding the newspaper. "I am trying to help you, I want you to find out for yourself how to deal with such things. All we had to do was call up Father and he would have settled the whole thing for you with one phone call, but I want you to get the contract on your own."

[40]   "All right," I said, "then what'll we do: wait here half an hour, or go up right away and have a talk with her?"

[41]   "We'd better go up right away," said Bertha.

[42] We got out of the car and went up in the elevator together. "Life," said Bertha, "consists of making compromises and concessions."

[43] Mrs. Zumpen was no more surprised now than she had been earlier, when I had come alone. She greeted us, and we followed her into her husband's study. Mrs. Zumpen brought some cognac, poured it out, and before I could say anything about the contract she pushed a yellow folder toward me: "Housing Project Fir Tree Haven," I read, and looked up in alarm at Mrs. Zumpen, at Bertha, but they both smiled, and Mrs. Zumpen said: "Open the folder," and I opened it; inside was another one, pink, and on this I read: "Housing Project Fir Tree Haven—Excavation Work." I opened this too, saw my estimate lying there on top of the pile; along the upper edge someone had written in red: "Lowest bid."

[44] I could feel myself flushing with pleasure, my heart thumping, and I thought of the 20,000 marks.

[45] "Christ," I said softly, and closed the file, and this time Bertha forgot to rebuke me.

[46] "*Prost,*" said Mrs. Zumpen with a smile, "let's drink to it then."

[47] We drank, and I stood up and said: "It may seem rude of me, but perhaps you'll understand that I would like to go home now."

[48] "I understand perfectly," said Mrs. Zumpen, "there's just one small item to be taken care of." She took the file, leafed through it, and said: "Your price per square meter is thirty pfennigs below that of the next-lowest bidder. I suggest you raise your price by fifteen pfennigs: that way you'll still be lowest and you'll have made an extra four thousand five hundred marks. Come on, do it now!" Bertha took her pen out of her purse and offered it to me, but I was in too much of a turmoil to write; I gave the file to Bertha and watched her alter the price with a steady hand, re-write the total, and hand the file back to Mrs. Zumpen.

[49] "And now," said Mrs. Zumpen, "just one more little thing. Get out your check book and write a check for three thousand marks; it must be a cash check and endorsed by you."

[50] She had said this to me, but it was Bertha who pulled our check book out of her purse and made out the check.

[51] "It won't be covered," I said in a low voice.

[52] "When the contract is awarded, there will be an advance, and then it will be covered," said Mrs. Zumpen.

[53] Perhaps I failed to grasp what was happening at the time. As

we went down in the elevator, Bertha said she was happy, but I said nothing.

[54]   Bertha chose a different way home, we drove through quiet residential districts, I saw lights in open windows, people sitting on balconies drinking wine; it was a clear, warm night.

[55]   "I suppose the check was for Zumpen?" was all I said, softly, and Bertha replied, just as softly: "Of course."

[56]   I looked at Bertha's small, brown hands on the steering wheel, so confident and quiet. Hands, I thought, that sign checks and squeeze mayonnaise tubes, and I looked higher—at her mouth, and still felt no desire to kiss it.

[57]   That evening I did not help Bertha put the car away in the garage, nor did I help her with the dishes. I poured myself a large cognac, went up to my study, and sat down at my desk, which was much too big for me. I was wondering about something. I got up, went into the bedroom and looked at the baroque Madonna, but even there I couldn't put my finger on the thing I was wondering about.

[58]   The ringing of the phone interrupted my thoughts; I lifted the receiver and was not surprised to her Zumpen's voice.

[59]   "Your wife," he said, "made a slight mistake. She raised the price by twenty-five pfennigs instead of fifteen."

[60]   I thought for a moment and then said: "That wasn't a mistake, she did it with my consent."

[61]   He was silent for a second or two, then said with a laugh: "So you had already discussed the various possibilities?"

[62]   "Yes," I said.

[63]   "All right, then make out another check for a thousand."

[64]   "Five hundred," I said, and I thought: It's like a bad dream—that's what it's like.

[65]   "Eight hundred," he said, and I said with a laugh: "Six hundred," and I knew, although I had no experience to go on, that he would now say seven hundred and fifty, and when he did I said "Yes" and hung up.

[66]   It was not yet midnight when I went downstairs and over to the car to give Zumpen the check; he was alone and laughed as I reached in to hand the folded check. When I walked slowly back into the house, there was no sign of Bertha; she didn't appear when I went back into my study; she didn't appear when I went downstairs again for a glass of milk from the refrigerator; and I knew what she was

thinking; she was thinking: he has to get over it, and I have to leave him alone; this is something he has to understand.

[67]   But I never did understand. It is beyond understanding.

STUDY AND DISCUSSION

1. At the beginning of the story, the narrator tells us, "I have married into the excavating business." Does such a statement tell you anything about his values? If so, what? What do you think of these values?
2. Why are the Zumpens in a position to help the narrator and his wife? What sort of people are the Zumpens? What do they look like? What social class do they belong to? Why do they come to dinner at all?
3. What evidence is there that the narrator and his wife come from different levels of society?
4. Why do the Zumpens exchange smiles when they see the narrator's large desk in his study?
5. Throughout the story there are references to religious images—baroque Madonnas, an eighteenth century crucifix, etc. What use does Böll make of these objects in the story?
6. Compare and contrast the character and behavior of the narrator and his wife in this story. What do they have in common? How do they differ? Who seems stronger? Which character do you like better? Why? In general, what are your feelings about them?
7. Twice in this story the narrator thinks of kissing his wife but doesn't. Why not?
8. "Life," said Bertha, "consists of making compromises and concessions." To what extent is this true of the lives lived in this story? Do you believe it is necessary to compromise in order to succeed?
9. Why are the Zumpens so little surprised to see the narrator and his wife again?
10. What, *specifically*, is the bad dream referred to in the title of this story?
11. What is it, at the end of the story, that the narrator doesn't understand?
12. In this story, material values dominate all others. What values are most important in your opinion? Would you personally make the kind of compromises these people make?

LIFE
STYLES

THE SECULAR HERETICS

J. H. PLUMB   The hippie life style is nothing new in history, as J. H. Plumb, a British scholar, finds in a lively examination of the past. But, he wonders, what imprints will the hippie and his life style leave on society? In his analysis, Dr. Plumb makes wide use of factual detail and illustration. Occasionally he resorts to contrast and comparison of such detail to make his point more vivid. A professor at Christ's College, Cambridge, Dr. Plumb has contributed to magazines such as Spectator, Listener, Saturday Review, *and* American Heritage. *In addition, he has written a number of books including* The First Four Georges, Men and Centuries, *and* The Renaissance. *Despite his great number of publications, he has found time to be a dedicated student of American culture.*

[1]   In late February, 1967, a stark-naked man stood near the sanctuary of the Glide Memorial Church in San Francisco; about him men and women, waving incense, chanted to the throb of the Congo drums; topless belly-dancers wove in and out; psychedelic colors flashed across the church; and time and time again the sad, humanity-haunted face

of Christ was projected above the crowd. Adolescents caressed and loved by the altar or withdrew to another room provided with a plastic bed. And so it went on until the early hours of the morning, when the church elders "lost their cool" and called it a day.

[2]   In Cologne, about 1325, the Brethren of the Free Spirit met in their luxurious secret chapel. There a live Christ celebrated mass, a naked preacher exhorted the brethren to return to primeval innocence, to strip, to love; for those who had become one with God there could be no sin, no church, no property. Love and the ecstatic experience was all. The church of the pope and the kingdoms of princes were evil. Take from them all that was needed, cheat them, lie to them, for innocence and love were beyond crime as well as beyond sin. The celebrants responded to the preacher and loved hard, there and then. What better place than a church for copulation that was beyond sin?

[3]   In Hampshire, in 1649, William Franklin and his soul mate and bed companion Mary Gadbury found God within themselves, gave up work, lived in voluntary poverty, rejected sin, and encouraged their little flock of Ranters to revel in obscenity, promiscuity, and drink. They were not alone—little bands of these religious "hippies" buzzed like wasps' nests throughout Cromwell's England. They were eventually stifled, not by the savage laws of the Commonwealth, but by their first cousins, the Quakers, whose early philosophy was hip with a difference. The first Quakers sometimes walked naked through the villages of Leicestershire, both to show disapproval of the accepted world of materialism and darkness and to proclaim their salvation and their purity as children of light. They, too, rejected the religious establishment as well as the differences of social status, wearing their hats in church to demonstrate the one and calling all men "thou" to prove the other. And they would not pay tithes. They went to jail. Nor would they take oaths or fight, so off to jail they went again. And although they eschewed physical love outside marriage, the love of all men and women, whatever suffering it might bring, lay at the heart of their creed.

[4]   Much of the content of hippie philosophy has a long history in such religious heresies. Take promiscuity clothed in an aura of religiosity: this stretches back through the Ranters and the Free Brethren and the Spiritual Libertines and almost to Adam himself. The hippies, ignorant of history, are but a part of a chain stretching back into the Middle Ages and beyond. Why do these philosophies, heresies, call them

what you will, recur so frequently in Western society? And is the present-day hippie world illumined by the light of the past?

[5]   The hippies are secular heretics, for they reject the moral principles of society, claiming to return to a purer, less hypocritical morality. What this new secular heresy has in common with religious heresies of the past, to which it possesses so many resemblances, is that it has occurred in a very affluent society. The Brethren of the Free Spirit, who were so like the hippies, flourished in the prosperous towns of Flanders and the Rhine, where society and the church had grown materialistic, given to wanton luxury and guilt-free extravagance. Also, as now, it was a time of war and of social dislocation. And the same conditions prevailed in England in the days of the Ranters and early Quakers. The philosophy of the market place had spread like bindweed over ancient morality and stifled it; political and social anarchy, with turbulence and riot, combined with seemingly meaningless civil war, gave a loathsome luminosity to the material world in the eyes of the Ranters and Quakers. Better get right out of it and dwell with the brethren, led by the inner light.

[6]   Such antipathy to the material world and to the world of government, order, discipline, and force goes deeper than heresy, however. It is a constant theme in most religions. Sometimes the church has contained it and been revivified by it. Think of Saint Francis, the son of a prosperous merchant, who divested himself of all material things and treated all that lived—birds and beasts and insects—as aspects of God. He pursued poverty like a lover and preferred the broken, the tormented, the simple, and the foolish. A hippie-saint if ever there was one. He and his followers battened on the conscience of the material world that they despised—taking the food, the alms, the shelter, as the hippies do in Haight-Ashbury. Indeed, some founders of religion seem uncomfortably close to the hippies. Beyond Saint Francis looms a larger, more formidable figure, who amid the vast riches and stupendous power of the Roman Empire had no use for it, nor for riches, nor for strife, nor for hypocrisy; who preferred a prostitute to a prude. In the West religion that is intense, personal, and deeply felt has always been at odds with the world it has to live in.

[7]   Yet no matter how closely one compares this new secular heresy —with its total rejection of the principles and morality of the middle-class establishment—to the religious heresies and movements of the past, or indeed sees it as a part of the cycle of rejection of the material-

ism that has been a constant factor in Western life and thought, there remain very important differences. The hippie world is compounded not only of social heresy but of acid. Here, surely, is the break with the past.

[8]   Drugs date back at least to the neolithic revolution, when men first discovered wine and beer; both were given sacred and ritualistic functions, which they have maintained. This is true of all communities, primitive and advanced, communist or capitalist. Almost the whole of humanity has been sodden, at some time or another, with alcohol. And its use is deeply embedded in social rituals. Billions of gallons of wine, spirits, and beer are needed to sustain the social conventions of group activity. Minor drugs and narcotics, after much initial opposition, also secured social acceptance and became a part of the social ritual. After all, James I of England hated tobacco as much as Harry Anslinger hates hemp, and coffeehouses were thought by Charles II to be dens of decadence and political treachery; but the public craving would not be denied.

[9]   Artists, particularly from the nineteenth century onward, sought powerful hallucinations through drugs. Opium, laudanum, ether, and hashish became popular in bohemian and artistic circles in nineteenth-century Europe, a process that reached its zenith in Rimbaud, who deliberately attempted a *déreglement de tous les sens*[1] and wrote psychedelically of the colors of vowels. But this experimentation was a means to art—an attempt to heighten consciousness for art's sake—not a way of life.

[10]   In the hippies, therefore, two historical strands have intertwined in an odd way—social heresy and the artist's quest for heightened perception through drugs. The need for the latter is, of course, due to the absence of God. Ecstasy and elation could be achieved by the mystical heretic through ritual, fasting, contemplation, or flagellation, as long as they were intensified by a sense of God within and without. For the hippie, God scarcely exists, having been replaced by a vague sense of the oneness of humanity that is quite insufficient to create the heightened consciousness needed for hallucinations or ecstatic experience.

[11]   The hippies' ancestry, however, is European rather than American, which, perhaps, is one of the reasons why their impact in

---

[1] *déreglement de tous les sens*, an almost exact quote from a letter of Rimbaud's in which he explained his poetic method as "a (systematic) upheaval of all the senses." Arthur Rimbaud (1854-1891) was a French poet of hallucinatory genius.

America has been so shocking. During the nineteenth century the American artist occasionally toyed with decadence or drugs, but, like Poe, he was an oddity. There were no Coleridges, no Baudelaires, no Rimbauds, no Verlaines, no Wildes, not even a Byron or a Shelley. In America the need to fly from materialism, from the grossness of a conscious world, was assuaged by the West, either actively or imaginatively. Nature, wild and untamed, was there in abundance to soothe a Thoreau or to ease a Parkman. Nothing was easier in nineteenth-century America than to contract out of urban, commercial civilization. Now it is impossible, as it has been in Europe for many centuries. Not because there are not enough ponds for putative Thoreaus or Oregon Trails for embryonic Parkmans, but because myth has grown feebler; myths can only be sustained and given meaning by the needs of society. This aspect of American life—half dream, half reality—has lost its social dynamic. Pioneer America is meaningless not only to hippies but to the nation at large. It has been commercialized into package tours down the Grand Canyon or up the Santa Fe Trail. Escape is easier within oneself. Indeed, there is nowhere else to go.

[12]   Furthermore, America is beginning to be afflicted with those ills that beset Italian and Flemish towns of the late Middle Ages—a contraction of opportunity for their middle class or their artisan young. Medieval heretics were often drawn, as were the early Quakers, from the class of skilled artisans in times of depression and economic contraction or in periods of rapid social and technological change that proved inimical to their crafts. The hippies are largely the waste products of extensive university education systems; they are the dropouts who are creatively or intellectually unsuited to the intense competitive system of a Horatio Alger America. The acceptance of failure and the withdrawal from society are deeply satisfying solutions to anxiety— especially if there is the ultimate safety net of middle-class parents. Religious heresy was rare among the abject poor: they preferred saints and miracles. And hippies are not common in the black ghettos of America.

[13]   And therein lies a danger; for although individuals and groups can opt out of the political and moral structures of society, the majority of the nation cannot. And opting out changes nothing but the individual. No religious heresy of total or partial withdrawal from society has changed a nation for better or worse. Advancement in social and political justice can only come through political action, revolution, or civil war, as indeed the history of America demonstrates. If the hippies

develop a philosophy of active civil disobedience, the picture may change. If they do not, there will be enormous *political* danger in the growth of hippiedom. The aesthetes and decadents, as well as many sensitive liberals, withdrew likewise from active politics in the Germany of the twenties and early thirties. Politics for them were corrupt, violent, and dishonest; withdrawal seemed to possess a higher morality, to be a more sensitive reaction. A withdrawal of a large segment of the younger generation of the middle class from participation in politics may easily lead, as it did in Germany, to a situation ripe for totalitarian politics. One of the most disquieting aspects of the hippie world is the cultivation of the American Indian and the turning away from the Negro and his problems—which create the central crisis of American politics. Lucy may be in the Sky with Diamonds but it is the Negro in the ghetto who matters.

[14] But will this secular heresy grow? After all, medieval heresies rarely lasted. They were quickly rendered ineffective if not obliterated. They were sporadic fires that only ravaged briefly the healthy body of the church. And even the Ranters were quietly absorbed by the Quakers, who disciplined themselves to live alongside, if not within, the society they despised. Other, less ecstatic and more socially oriented heresies, however, such as those that occurred at the Reformation, established themselves successfully. Printing in the fifteenth century broke down the localization of medieval heresy; social dislocation and economic change in the sixteenth century gave new heresies opportunities for growth and victory denied to heresy in the Middle Ages.

[15] Indeed, the potential for the growth of heresy is in direct proportion to the means of communication that are available. At the present time secular heresy has an even greater communications system at its command than that enjoyed by Luther and his allies. Hippies are news, to be exploited by all means of modern communication—press, radio, television, and films. Hence their message and their way of life spread like a virus, leaping from state to state, from country to country, from continent to continent, in the briefest possible time. And they provide by their dress, their buttons, their posters, paint, and pot, quick bucks for the commercially adroit. The consumer society they hate fertilizes their growth. And like the great religious heresies of the Reformation, which succeeded in establishing themselves as orthodoxies, this new secular heresy has begun to spread internationally in a way the beats never did; nor for that matter did the London teddy boys or the mods or rockers. Groups of hippies have emerged in London, in Cam-

bridge, in Oxford, even in the provincial towns of England. Leicester has its flower people, and its park has witnessed its first love-in. The Provos in Holland will soon be riding their white bicycles with tulips in their hair and bells on their handle bars. Already there are feeble attempts—and they will grow stronger—to give these seemingly spontaneous growths international organization and common propaganda.

[16]   The success of any religious or secular heresy requires a social context that will nurture and strengthen it. In return, it must meet the aspirations of and create the opportunities for not merely a handful of folk but considerable and diverse sections of a community. This was true for Christanity, for Lutheranism, for Calvinism, for the Quakers, Unitarians, Mormons, Methodists, and the rest, all of which began as heresies. It is as true of intellectual heresy as it is of religious. Is there a resonance between the hippies and new situations in our society that may echo louder and clearer in the near future? Maybe. Youth has achieved a freedom and an affluence that in previous societies were limited to the aristocracy and to very small sections of the rich middle class. What was once the privilege of a narrow segment of society has acquired a mass basis. Throughout history, youth—especially its elite in intelligence and creativity—has rarely been drawn to the adult world, but it has been forced to accept it and to obey it. The weight of society was too great, the structure of family life too firm, and the acceptance of the Christian morality of the churches too widespread for rebellion and rejection on the part of more than a few gifted individuals clustered in small groups. Most children and adolescents accepted, worked, obeyed, and joined the adults. Those days may be over.

[17]   The opportunity for youth to rebel successfully is made easier because society itself is no longer sure of either its institutions or its morality. After all, both were derived from a largely agrarian and craft-based society. The unitary family proved a remarkably viable basic unit in preindustrial society, and so did the extended family in the Orient. In the early stages of industralization the family proved adequate, though far weaker; but it may be doubted if it will survive into a world molded by technology and science. Certainly its sanctions are crumbling at every level. Few fathers today possess a tenth of the authority of their grandfathers, either over workers or children, and the father is the core of the family as we know it. To the sensitive young the social structure of the adult world must seem hypocritical and luminous with decay, as ripe for revolution as the czardom of Nicholas II. And I suspect that this attitude is acquiring the force of truth in

Moscow as well as New York. Because social institutions have lasted ten thousand years does not mean that they are eternal: ten thousand years is a very brief span in the history of mankind.

[18] The family as an institution may have reached a danger point, just as the aristocracy did in 1789 or the Roman Catholic Church at the time of the Reformation. The situations, oddly enough, are not dissimilar. Institutions that are unsure of themselves, given to practices that do not agree with their avowed ideals, often crumble before a sharp radical attack, as long as this attack has a wide base. And this is the current situation between youth and its social targets in the adult world— marriage, monogamy, family life. It may not be too farfetched to conceive of the Western world being caught up in a new type of social upheaval: a social-revolutionary young attacking the institutions not of political life but of adult living. Possible, but, I think, unlikely.

[19] For the hippies do not possess the most important weapon in all revolutionary movements—a coherent ideology that interlocks belief and action, that combines philosophy with the strategy and tactics of action. If one looks back at the successful historical movements or the triumphant political and social revolutions of the past, one sees that they have always possessed a strong intellectual content as well as deep emotional drives. An active ideology—coherent, rational within its own principles—marks Calvinism as well as communism, the Quakers as well as the Jacobins. But the hippie world is a flight from the intellect and all that the intellect implies. It does not wish to dominate reality but to flee from it: to mock the adult world, not capture and change it. It possesses attitudes but not an ideology.

[20] The hippie movement relates most closely to those ecstatic heresies of the Middle Ages that were also savagely anticlerical, that dwelt with bitterness on the riches, the greed, the corruption, of the clergy as opposed to the simplicity and poverty of Christ: the contrast between the reality and the ideal. In this; the hippies' criticism by implication and by action of the straight world—its self-indulgence, its hypocrisy, its materialism—may lie their greatest contribution to society. The alarming gulf between avowed intention and action—as in Vietnam—is leading to moral bankruptcy. The American dream, like America's manifest destiny, is dissolving, giving way to a future not of hope but of nightmare. If the hippies force us to look at ourselves morally and spiritually naked, then well and good; but they may provoke a blinder and less sensitive reaction. They are playing as dangerously with social passions as any heretic played with religious passions

in the Middle Ages. And remember how society turned on *them*, how its inquisitors rooted them out, tortured them, burned them, extirpated their women and children, purged society of its danger. America, faced by insoluble problems, made frantic by riot and by the prospect of moral defeat, may vent its spleen and crush all liberal attitudes, using as one of its excuses the social nonconformity of the hippies. Heresies without ideology or the discipline necessary for political action have usually ended in disaster.

[21]   The hippies are a part of a social and historical process, and many strands are united in their beliefs and actions; but so far in man's long history, no movement that has ignored power has ever succeeded, and all groups who have made a cult of social anarchy have either been defeated or destroyed. In the absence of a political creed and of a program the hippies must be regarded as a symptom, not a social force— they are a living phantom bred by the decadent hypocrisy of so much of America's social and political morality.

STUDY AND DISCUSSION

Vocabulary

In your dictionary find the meaning of each of the following words that you do not already know:

1. primeval (para. 2)	2. ecstatic (para. 2)
3. promiscuity (para. 3)	4. eschewed (para. 3)
5. heresies (para. 4)	6. Libertines (para. 4)
7. heretics (para. 5)	8. bindweed (para. 5)
9. luminosity (para. 5)	10. antipathy (para. 6)
11. neolithic (para. 8)	12. assuaged (para. 11)
13. putative (para. 11)	14. sporadic (para. 14)
15. obliterated (para. 14)	16. orthodoxies (para. 15)
17. resonance (para. 16)	18. luminous (para. 17)
19. monogamy (para. 18)	20. coherent (para. 19)

Rhetoric

1. Paragraphs 1-3 make an extremely effective opening. Why?
2. What transitional devices are to be found in the first sentences of the following paragraphs: 10, 11, 12, 13, 14, 15, 19?
3. What methods of development are used in paragraphs 1-3, 5, 11, 15?
4. What patterns of organization are employed in paragraphs 5 and 12?

Content

1. What does the secular heresy of the hippie have in common with the religious heresies of the past?
2. Does the use of drugs by hippies have a parallel in the past? Were they used for the same purpose?
3. Why has the impact of the hippie been so shocking in America?
4. For what reasons may we expect the hippie movement to grow?
5. Why does the author see "enormous *political* danger in the growth of hippiedom"?
6. As things now stand, what is the highest good we can expect from the hippie movement? The worst?

Ideas and Implications

1. Why is it that so many religious heresies involved protest against the moral code as well as religious practices?
2. The hippies are accused of being ignorant of history both here and in other essays. Do you think they should be more aware of history? If they were, what changes do you think might occur in the hippie philosophy?
3. The author insists that the hippies are secular heretics. Others insist their heresy is really religious in nature. What do you think?
4. Marya Mannes in "Who Am I?" writes of her youth as a serene, secure experience within a rather tightly knit family. In para. 17 of this essay, Plumb writes that in the face of a world molded by technology and science the family as an institution may have reached a danger point, that it is in danger of crumbling. Is it possible that the family unit has actually weakened so much in so short a time? Or do you feel the family unit is worth saving? If it is, what do you feel must be done to save it?
5. Do you feel, as the author does, that the hippie movement will induce a period of conservative reaction, a period of repression?

GIRL GETTING EDUCATED AT
NOON ON SUNDAY

HERBERT GOLD   Herbert Gold, a resident of the San Francisco Bay Area, writes short stories, essays, and novels. His books include Birth of a Hero, Salt, Fathers, Love and Like, *and* The Age of Happy Problems. *He is a frequent contributor to* Playboy *and other popular periodicals.*

In "Girl Getting Educated at Noon on Sunday," Gold turns to one of the scenes he knows best: "hip" San Francisco, setting for a delicious tale about a professor of French from San Francisco State who picks up a young and beautiful girl at an "acid-rock" dance and takes her home for the night—or longer. It is a funny and touching account of a collision between two different styles of life.

[1]   "Would you have dinner with me one night this week?" he asked the girl at a pause in the foaming, churning breakers of sound. It rose, it rose again, it fell, it rose, and then there was a pause.

[2]   "No," she answered, smiling sweetly.

[3]   "But I thought—you seem—that look on your face—" She had a way of fixing her eyes against his as they danced. She had a way of moving against the way he moved.

[4]   "Sure I grok you," she said.

[5]   Slightly comforted and emboldened, he nevertheless gave up and thought he might as well be a scientist about it. "What did I do wrong?" he asked. "Nothing," she said. The amplified sitar, the electric violin, the wired harpsichord and the pile-driving rhythm instruments were being launched once more to another victory against the stoned and the stunned. There was a willingness to be overcome.

[7]   "You have a friend?"

[8]   "Nothing special," she said. "I came here with a group—all friends."

[9]   "Then why not?"

[10]   She stood a little sideways, gazing at him with her clear sweet hilarious smile, as the acid-rock music of the Salvation Auditorium in San Francisco crested once again. He liked her eyes—smile wrinkles at the corners of the eyes of a girl who couldn't have been more than

22. He liked the healthy slim California look: silk blouse, checked
Carnaby pants, slouching healthy spine—a gutsy challenging teasing
funny chick. Good style.

[11]   "Then why not?" he asked again.

[12]   "I don't make dates. *Plots*, no. I don't make that scene," she
said.

[13]   He frowned. "What a drag."

[14]   "But I'll go home with you now," she said, without changing
the expression but leaning now from right to left instead of from left
to right. "Cuba, *si*—plans, no."

[15]   He had her by the elbow and was pushing through the crowd
toward the door. He was thinking: We both must smell of smoke. He
was thinking: But no beer, that was another generation. He was thinking: Oh, man, let's get out of here, and lucky the car is parked nearby,
before she changes her mind. *Tu penses, donc tu n'es pas*—think a little
less, please. This is the time to shut it off.

[16]   The Anonymous Artists of America, a strong acid-rock group,
was pouring its ardent heart and amplified soul into a song called
When I Was Worried:

> *When I was worried*
> *You made the stars turn pink*
> *When I was worried*
> *You taught me not to think*
> *You said you'd make me feel real fine*
> *Just sign here on the dotted line*
> *And then you made me love you,*
> *Dr. Swain.*

[17]   Or maybe the song was called *Dr. Swain*. The dance at the
Salvation Auditorium south of Mission Street in San Francisco had
not yet come to the scheduled feature attraction: silent Zen contemplation of stones, pennies and corncobs by everyone seated in a circle.
However, in the meantime, while waiting to draw up legs in the man-
dala posture, there was pop and op body painting, there were strobe
lights changing everyone into stop-action dancers, there was the band,
there was the drip, bubble and bounce light show, there were two projectors doing bits of film, there were Hell's Angels and Berkeley students, there were free apples, free licorice, there were posters and
petitions to sign and costumes and the dreamy joy-making of people
in every known variety of high. Including horniness. The previous

number had been introduced by the bushy-bearded leader of the band as "an oldie but a goodie, a dusty diamond, a pearl of some kind of price. . . . Some a you folks out there might remember gettin' pregnant to this song, 'way back in nineteen and sixty-four." The way his beard grew, it looked as if he were walking upside down. He was wearing ecstatic dress—swirls, spangles, silks. The crowd included everything, even clean-shaven gawkers. Including Jim Curtis, just looking around tonight and just finding this girl, this lovely sweet funny girl whose name he didn't even know yet. He would get her outside before he would ask her to repeat her name. He hadn't been able to hear it over the Anonymous Artists of America. It would be better, perhaps, to ask it when they were already on their way.

[18]   "I only," she was saying. "I only," she was explaining. "I only," she murmured sweetly at him, "go with people I grok by accident. Dating is a drag."

[19]   "Yeah, sure," he said, thinking this was a time to emphasize the areas of agreement.

[20]   "Sometimes it means you're lonely. Sometimes it means you're going home with Dr. Swain, say, or nobody else, and that's *something* else. But I'd rather make it by myself than play that girlie-girl-girl game, the cop-out sex game, you know?"

[21]   "Sure, yeah," he said, being on the safe side. He would disagree later. Now was still the time to be agreeable, even a little more. "Jeez, they're a good band," he said.

[22]   "They're coming up strong. Write their own songs, communal 'em together, too."

[23]   "Who's Dr. Swain?"

[24]   She gave him her first puzzled and disappointed look. It crossed her charmed, pleased, healthy, sinewy face like a cloud; it made her body bend another way, backward and looking, as if she were wearing bifocal granny glasses, octagonally dubious. What had he done wrong? How had he let her down? "You don't know who Dr. Swain is?" she asked.

[25]   He walked on without answering. He would not compound his sin. He would wait and see if maybe Dr. Swain came to mind. As a matter of fact, he knew lots of doctors—surgeons, internists, Ph.D.s in various fields, particularly the Romance area—and he himself was a professor of French at San Francisco State; but how could a chap know everybody, such as Dr. Swain? It's a big country—the scene is big. She seemed to forgive and forget his failure; for, a moment later,

emerging from the convolutions of fret, he found her still by his side.

[26]   Out through the crowd; out into the crowd waiting on the sidewalk, the kids without the $2.50 to get past the guards, the white cops brooding, the kids selling revolutionary buttons (YELLOW POWER, SUPPORT VIET ROCK, MARCEL PROUST IS A YENTA), the musicians from the next group, the Santa Fe Weed, unloading their cargo of horns, strings and fuse boxes from their paisley-painted hearse, the astonished winos, relics of pre-mind-expansion, stunned in the doorways, an urban-renewal expert with a clipboard, counting the traffic, the Negro cops watching, the idlers noticing, the pile-up of cycles and Vespas and Hondas, the sports cars slowing down, the teeny-boppers giggling in duos, hoping to be invited in. Air, blessed sea-drift air of San Francisco. Jim took a deep breath. A noise of revving entered with the air, but it was oxygen, all the same. The lungs can take vibration. The girl—*his* girl—was smiling at a spade cat in spats, opera slippers and a long white double-breasted parking-attendant coat with the words RENT-A-TRIP stenciled in psychedelic-ecstatic script above the pocket. Jim's lungs could not take this vibration.

[27]   Uncool was his spirit.

[28]   An effort. Wars are won by the steady. A moral equivalent of war must be fought by new forms of steady.

[29]   Uncool to cool, *over,* he thought.

[30]   Abruptly, Jim Curtis had one of those ideas that provide a turning point of sorts—for an evening or for a life, depending on the energy of the decision and the richness of deposit it leaves after combustion. He swung round on the crowded sidewalk, a sidewalk like a Turkish bazaar, and, half facing her, put his arm about the girl whom he was escorting to his apartment and, instead of asking her name, he took her chin in his hand, pressed it upward gently and kissed her; and then, not dislodging his mouth, he slipped around and they slipped together and kissed deeply there amid the murky crowd. Someone nearby was saying mumble-mumble-mumble. Jim did not care to listen. He was kissing. When they separated, the girl said, "It does good to kiss someone now and then."

[33]   "Yes, it does good," he said.

[34]   "I didn't expect that," she said.

[35]   "Neither did I."

[36]   She smiled sweetly. "You probably didn't hear my name," she said. "Sue Cody."

[37]   "I'll tell you my name, too," he said, and told her. She moved

her lips, as if she had trouble remembering names, though she could always recall the face of the man who had kissed her. She looked as if she had not very often been kissed; felt, squeezed, taken home, rumpled, jumped on, yes, but not, like this, just kissed on the street by a man delighted with silk blouse, narrow pants, graceful dancer's slouch; well-articulated spine. However the clothes clung to her, he realized that he had thought until kissing her that she was a slender, willowy colt of a girl. Well, she was a slender and willowy colt, but she was also opulent. And smart. And funny. (You can tell all that from a kiss? he asked himself.) And crazy. (From a kiss? You can tell? Jim?)

[38]   "Mumble-mumble-mumble," she said, and smiled radiantly. "And just think of Buffalo Bill; that way, you can remember my name," she said.

[39]   "Wha'?"

[40]   "Think about it, Fred. It'll come to you."

[41]   "You're tough, aren't you?"

[42]   For answer she said nothing. She slid over toward him as close as she could. She took hold of his arm. She was humming *When I Was Worried.* Well, that's a hard tune to keep. She was clever, she had music in her, probably mathematics, too; or she had heard it a lot. And *tough,* to her age, he recalled, it means boss, it means very fine.

[43]   It was one of those easy drives home, knowing that the mystery is to be unraveled and no fright in it. Pleasure, not pride; pleasure, not anxious lust; joy in the certain slide of present and coming events. There was a nimbus of fog about the street lamps. A few deep baying notes reverberated from the Golden Gate—freighters, fog. Tonight Jim liked himself. This was a surprising pleasure, too.

[44]   It does good to kiss a girl, he thought. And a strong acid-rock moll is used to going home with strange men, perhaps, but not so used to being kissed impulsively first on the wide space of sidewalk in front of the Salvationist Building. Oh, Sue Cody. I like you, he thought. She was making Jim like himself. That's a nice way to begin a friendship and end an evening.

[45]   It sort of occurred to him that like maybe they would just go up to his place and scramble some eggs in wine and talk and drink a bit of wine or smoke a bit of pot (he kept it with his collection of Rimbaud, Verlaine, René Char, Henri Michaux and St. John Perse). Just that. Maybe no more. A girl who took to a kiss so sweetly might understand. It was a way to dissolve nervousness: Go slow. Sure, she would

understand; but then, it was not necessary to go slow, she had understood so well already, he had understood her so well, it was not necessary to understand, he was not nervous—not, not, not nervous—well,
not very nervous. Instead of 10 percent delight and 90 percent nervousness, which was the usual proportion on first meetings, it was only 10
percent nervousness and 83 percent delight. The minority seven percent was divided among curiosity (five percent), residual panic (one
percent) and fatherly concern, hypoglycemia, itchy nose and effort to
recall cleanliness of undershorts (trace factors).

[46] "Let's kiss again. I grok that," she was saying.

[47] "Can't. Driving."

[48] "Mind if I—"

[49] "Go right ahead. I'll keep my eye glued to the road and my
mighty hands on the wheel. My iron will enables me to respond without moving."

[50] He paused at the intersection. Her breath was upon his cheek
and her merry eyes were examining his jaw line. In the throbbing neon
of a corner bar (DAS GUPTA SUTRA, did it say? Could it say that? Could
a bar get away with an Indian raga neon sign?), she was acquainting
herself with his profile ("Jim Curtis, not Fred," she was saying), and
then she was tenderly pressing her lips to his cheek, she was leaning
over the gearshift, her hands were exploring, her . . .

[51] "Wait!" he said.

[52] She pouted.

[53] "My iron will," he said, "even with all my steel on the side of
the National Safety Council, we are about to become a mere statistic
in the annals of sober driving, if you keep that up."

[54] "You don't love me," she said.

[55] "I want to stay alive in order to get you home and jump on
your bones," he said.

[56] This sentimental comment seemed to console her.

[57] "What's my name?" she asked. "Quick!"

[58] "Suecody-as-in-Buffalo-Bill."

[59] "Right. Very good. I don't have a phone, it's a drag. But we're
here, aren't we, 'cause you stopped the wheels, and that's what counts."

[60] "We're here," he said, meaning they were there. The top of
Twin Peaks, where he lived, lay shrouded in wisps of fog, thick rolling
stretches and then layers of clear mountain air. They were washed in
the damp ocean currents slowly drifting through the Golden Gate on
a mild October evening. Smoke and noise and confusion were being

rinsed away; hair would smell good; he took his time leading her up
the walk to the hare-brained wooden steps. It was a house broken up
into apartments—a dental student, a secretary who voted to the right
but bounced on her bed with hippies, the shrewd old lady who owned
the building. Jim's apartment was the best one, the one with a fireplace
and a view of the cool city. Hang up the painted bodies, he wanted to
tell her (Sue Cody, he would remember the name); hang up the rock
bands and the strobe lights, hang up the Goodwill Industries clothes,
hand up the hang-ups, we're home.

[61]   "We're home," he said.

[62]   "I grok it here," she answered.

[63]   "You're not here yet."

[64]   "Close enough. I grok it."

[65]   He switched on lights and lit the fireplace. He burned real
oak logs, not pressed sawdust. He was pleased that she could see his
books and papers on his desk. He was hoping she couldn't hear the
rhythmic sound of the right-wing hippie upstairs. He had met her in
such a frivolous way, he wanted her to think him serious. If he had
met her at school—a graduate student, a secretary—he would have
hoped for the good luck to impress her as frivolous. "Play against my
type, whatever it is," he said.

[66]   "What?"

[67]   "I'm mumbling to myself. I live alone and get to talking to
myself."

[68]   "Well, you're not alone now, are you? Let's kiss again."

[69]   Hand on tight pants and nothing beneath them. Hand on
silken blouse. Gentle mouth and hard right hand. Gentle left hand
rubbing and hard mouth. "Oh, good, good," he said.

[70]   She broke away, laughing. "Do you know what you're doing?"
she asked.

[71]   "Trust me."

[72]   "But I could feel your heart pounding."

[73]   "That's all right, trust me."

[74]   "Gee, Jim. Jim, that's a, you're a. I mean a funny person.
Again!"

[75]   And they kissed and he made a sweet slip-slip-slipping sound
as he pulled the blouse out. He tugged, it caught, it gave, she greedily
explored him. "Would you believe I never kissed like this before?" she
asked.

[76]   "Don't say would-you-believe," he said.

[77]   "I never did. More, more," she said.

[78]   Later, he thought, he would try to figure her out. Now was not the time for that. She was shameless without clothes on. He switched off the light and she stood at the window, looking out at the dim and deserted street. No one could see in, but still, how did she know that? She stood naked in the window, musing over the bushes gently swaying in the wind and fog, while he fled to the bathroom. He spent a few minutes there.

[79]   She called to him: "What's that noise upstairs?"

[80]   "Thump-thump?" he asked.

[81]   "Right."

[82]   "Never mind," he said.

[83]   "Groovy," she said. "You hear me? I like your house."

[84]   He waited before returning. He wanted a space of silence. Let her look out the window; let her absorb the quiet of Twin Peaks and being with this man, Jim Curtis, who he was. He wanted to be easy with her, all organs easy and relaxed, ready to play. When he returned, she was still naked in the window, in the light of the street, bathed in a bluish suffusion that seemed to come from within her flesh rather than from the fog-diffused glow.

[85]   "You look blue," he said.

[86]   "It's from inside. You've heard about bions? My bions are glowing."

[87]   "It's the light off the street."

[88]   "You don't know what bions are, friend, and that's why I dare say it. Dirty, dirty, *dirty* talk, in a way. It means I like you." She said *like* instead of *grok*.

[89]   "Bions?" he asked.

[90]   "Let's now," she said, suddenly hoarse, tugging at him. "Oh, you're sweet and I like you."

[91]   "Sue."

[92]   Returning to himself by her side, Jim wondered if it would be all right to ask her for a *date* in, say, five minutes. To meet again in this bed in five minutes. Or would that be uncool? Or should he go all the way and propose meeting also tomorrow, no matter what she felt like tomorrow? Dare he make a plan with her? Dare he ask her to make a plan?

[93]   Here he was, her body opened to him, joyful to him, and he could do nothing with it, with her—perhaps—but tomorrow was the

great question, and tomorrow and tomorrow, where she said she lived only by impulse and happenstance.

[94] "Would you?" he asked.

[95] "Would I what?" she said.

[96] "Never mind. Later."

[97] "Do you like music, maybe?" she suggested. One toe moved as if to prod him off the bed toward his rig.

[98] "Yes, sure."

[99] "You got any raga-rock? The Four Tops' freak-out of *Reach Out I'll Be There?* Any folk backlash soul? *The Ballad of the Green Bra?*"

[100] "Uh," he said, "the Jean-Paul Kreder Ensemble doing *Chants de la Renaissance?* There's *Perdre le Sens devant Vous,* there's. . . ."

[101] Silence. "Well, any Beatle record is OK. *Rubber Soul.*"

[102] There would always be the danger with this girl of her taking over. That was the second danger. The first was that she would just disappear into thin unamplified raga-rock in the distant air. Danger made Jim's nose itch. He was looking for danger. The moral equivalent of war was suddenly this gear-laden, eyes-aslant, body-greedy young lady. He wanted to open her up to the world beyond tripping and Motown records: to Jim Curtis.

[103] He was not sure he could manage. To persuade her that she needed him, but for what? To learn French? What else did he know that she didn't know?

[104] Maybe he could just give up. Senator Everett Dirksen, he thought, plays it cool. . . . Well, he would follow his nose, and where his nose led him—ah, that was nice.

[105] She was sighing. "Nice, nice," she was saying, "oh, yes."

[106] He forgot all his ideas and plans. She was delicious.

[107] An hour later, she sat up suddenly and pulled the sheet over them both. "You don't have to take me home," she said, "if you don't mind my spending the night here."

[108] *"Mind?"* he said incredulously.

[109] "Well, some men, they like to be alone afterward, I don't know, I met a boy one time he had to change the sheets and all. You never know when you'll find a freaky kind. He had all sorts of ideas he wanted to try out, but afterward—clean sheets, no me. I didn't grok that."

[110] "Sh."

[111]   "Another one, he wanted a full meal sent up by the Chinese Chinkaroony Kitchen. Wow. Not a snack—*food* food. And then he had a frozen pizza, it was more like a waffle with cheese. I'm used to a guy he wants his morning gruel before he goes out into the rice fields, but—And then the *real* freak, he—"

[112]   "Never mind, I don't want to hear," he said.

[113]   "Yeah, I suppose," she said into the dark. "Maybe you're sleepy. Am I losing my mystery, talking so much?"

[114]   He laughed and rolled over upon her and kissed her cheek, licked her cheeks, kissed and butted her gently, and she giggled and sang, " 'When I was worried, You taught me not to think,' " and pretty soon they must have both been asleep, because he heard a dawn bird twittering. The fog lay heavy outside. They had never drawn the curtains. He should get up or the sun would wake them. He would get up soon. He would get up right away to draw the curtains. He was sleeping.

[115]   Hours later, when she saw his eyes open, one at a time, it turned out that she had been waiting for his two eyes so she could say, "You know what? You taught me to sleep with a man, to *sleep*. I was comfortable. I was lying there in the crook of your elbow—"

[116]   She had been lying there, warm and obedient, asleep, yes, from when he almost got up to pull the curtains.

[117]   "It's not bad," he said, "to do that."

[118]   "No," she said submissively, "it's not bad to do that, either."

[119]   She didn't make dates, but she would stay home with him now. She didn't make plans, but she would search in his eyes with the love-me look, the I-love-you look, eyes glowing and sweet, tender for real, feeling for real, desire for real, all there for him now. No, she would tell him nothing much about who she was. ("Well, you know . . ." she said.) No, she would make no promises for the future. "It's so beautiful right now, let's not think ahead, let me now, let me do that now, let me, oh, let me sweet—"

[120]   *It's not so bad to do that.*

[121]   It was nearly noon.

[122]   What if she was right and he was wrong? What if her way, no plans, was the right way, and his way, think ahead, think about protecting her, think about the future, was the wrong way? He had taught her to kiss, true; he had taught her to sleep sweetly, tightly rolled against him, all right, yes; but what if she could teach him about snatching joy on the run? He would be grateful. He caressed her body,

thinking this over. He rubbed her tummy. She was saying shyly, "Can we kiss again?"

[123]   She tasted good. Her skin shone with good health. "Wild rice, no sugar, but honey, no candy, fruits but not too much, whole-grain cereals, good things like that, what's grown in the area—corn—"

[124]   "It's a good thing, that's all. It's not the macrobiotic eating."

[125]   She giggled.

[126]   "Now should we get up?"

[127]   "If," she said, sighing, "you want to."

[128]   It was that reluctant sighing remark that led him into his false step. It was his own fault, but it was her sigh that led him. Was she tired? Was she disappointed? "Was I . . . ?" he asked. "Was it . . . ?"

[129]   She smiled with that bright alertness he recalled from the stranger he had met less than a day earlier. "Well," she said, "I've known boys who came more often than you,"—she marshaled her ideas briskly—"but I don't know, it's nice with you."

[130]   "You're the second best in that department I've ever known," he said maliciously, furiously. "You're the third or fourth prettiest girl I've ever met, and in the sack, you know, making it, you're fairly close to the top—maybe even second, as I said. Or third, anyway. You like that? You like that, kid?"

[131]   "Oh," she said.

[132]   "Use a little imagination. Look: Other person here! Me human being! Me no Tarzan—me sentient critter! Me jealous, me proud, me—"

[133]   She stroked him gently. "You nice boy," she said. "Look, all I meant was—oh, I hate to go out on a limb about anything—I *like you.*"

[134]   He looked at her straight in the eyes, as he had done only a few hours ago, already it seemed an age ago, finding each other in the crowd on the dance floor. Yet what did he know about her? What else did he know about her, Buffalo Bill Sue Cody whatever-her-name? "I like you very much," he said.

[135]   "I like you very much," she repeated in a tone like his.

[136]   And they both laughed together.

[137]   "It sounds like hypnotism," she said, "we say it so often, but it feels good. Oh, it do."

[138]   "It isn't necessary to tell the whole truth," he said. "Let me explain this situation to you—this sort of situation. You can express the good part, that's enough."

[139]   She looked hurt. "But weren't you asking me? I did say something wrong, Dr. Swain?"

[140]   She poked him. She wanted him to giggle along with her.

[141]   He swung his legs down to the floor. He sat, slightly slumped, on the edge of the bed. She stroked his spine, thinking about the massage, about yoga, about sport, about all the things that told her that his posture spelled discouragement in a questioning curve of spine. He was sulking. He was disappointed. He was wondering what had got him into this. He was jealous. He was thinking about a future of deception. He was going to ask her to be kind. He was about to ask her to be loyal and faithful. He was about to try to make her forget everything but him. He was making trouble for himself. He was making trouble for her.

[142]   She was following his eyes avidly. She was ready for the new stage. She was obedient to him, as she had been obedient to her Negro, her Mexican, her hip nonpainters and media-mix experts. She was a sweet girl. She grokked him for more than the moment.

[143]   And so she could learn to be miserable; that is, to fall in love. The afternoon sun lay aslant on their still, willing bodies.

STUDY AND DISCUSSION

1. "Acid-rock" seems to play a very important role in this story—not merely because Jim Curtis meets Sue Cody at the Salvation Auditorium and from there takes her home to his apartment, but because the music itself seems to shape and reflect the world of Sue Cody and, by implication, of other people like her. What seems to be Herbert Gold's attitude toward the "rock scene" and the life style associated with it? How is his attitude expressed? What use does he make of the rock scene in this story? Do you think Gold's picture is accurate and valid—or is it highly distorted?

2. Carefully analyze the behavior and attitudes of Jim Curtis. What sort of person is he? What does he want from life and why? How does he see himself? How does he respond to Sue Cody? Is he honest with her? Why does he suddenly kiss her after they leave the auditorium? What does he want from her, finally? What do you think he will get?

3. What can you learn about Jim Curtis by studying his apartment?

4. What is the story told from his point of view instead of Sue's?

5. Study in detail the behavior and attitudes of Sue Cody. What does she

want from life and why? By what moral system does she live? How does she view herself? How does she view Jim Curtis? What, finally, is her attitude toward Jim? Why? In the last two paragraphs, what is implied about her future relationship with Jim Curtis?

6. Explain the title of this story, giving special attention to the words *Educated, Noon,* and *Sunday.*

7. This story dramatizes the collision of two people who represent diametrically opposed life-styles. With which of these philosophies of life —or ways of living—does the author seem to identify, if either? Which do you personally consider superior? Why? Which of the two main characters seems to be living a better life? Which of the two do you like better? Why?

Men and Women

LOVE
AND
MARRIAGE

ANTIDOTES FOR THE NEW PURITANISM

ROLLO MAY   "Our dilemma, therefore, is that enlightenment has not at all solved the sexual problems in our culture," writes Rollo May, one of our foremost philosopher-psychoanalysts in the fifth paragraph of this essay, which we hope you will find as cogent as we do. It takes as its assumption the idea that Puritanism (with a capital "p") harms us all by depriving us of our capacity to enjoy the gift of life. As you read this piece, you might reflect upon the nature of puritanism itself and why it evolved as a once-dominant ethic. In other words, if it was good enough— if it actually was—for our ancestors, why is it no longer so today?

The following excerpt is taken from Dr. May's influential book, Love and Will.

[1]   There are several strange and interesting dilemmas in which we find ourselves with respect to sex and love in our culture. When psychoanalysis was born in Victorian times half a century ago, re-

213

pression of sexual impulses, feelings, and drives was the accepted mode. It was not nice to feel sexual, one would not talk about sex in polite company, and an aura of sanctifying repulsiveness surrounded the whole topic. Freud was right in pointing out the varied neurotic symptoms to which this repression of sex gave birth.

[2]   Then, in the 1920s, a radical change occurred almost overnight. The belief became a militant conviction in liberal circles that the opposite of repression—sex education, freedom of talking, feeling, and expression—would have healthy effects, and was obviously the only stand for the enlightened person. According to Max Lerner, our society shifted from acting as though sex did not exist to placing the most emphasis on sex of any society since the Roman.

[3]   Partly as a result of this radical change, we therapists rarely get nowadays in our offices patients who exhibit repression of sex in the pre-World War I Freudian sense. In fact we find just the opposite in the people who come for help: a great deal of talk about sex, a great deal of sexual activity, practically no one complaining of any cultural prohibitions over his going to bed as often or with as many partners as he wishes.

[4]   But what our patients *do* complain of is lack of feeling and passion—so much sex and so little meaning or even fun in it! Whereas the Victorian person didn't want anyone to know that he or she had sexual feelings, now we are ashamed if we do not. Before 1910 if you called a lady "sexy," you insulted her; nowadays the lady accepts the adjective as a prized compliment. Our patients often have problems of impotence or frigidity, but they struggle desperately not to let anyone know they *don't* feel sexually. The Victorian nice man or woman was guilty if he or she did perform sexually; now we are guilty if we *don't.*

[5]   One dilemma, therefore, is that enlightenment has not at all solved the sexual problems in our culture. To be sure, there are important positive results of the new enlightenment, chiefly in increased freedom for the individual. And some external problems are eased— sexual knowledge can be bought in any bookstore, contraception is available almost everywhere outside Boston, and external societal anxiety has lessened. *But internalized anxiety and guilt have increased.* And in some ways, these are more morbid, harder to handle, and impose a heavier burden upon the individual man and woman than external anxiety and guilt.

[6]   A second dilemma is that the new emphasis on technique in sex and love-making backfires. It often seems to me that there is an inverse relationship between the number of how-to-do-it books perused by a person, or rolling off the presses in a society, and the amount of sexual passion or even pleasure experienced by the persons involved. Nothing is wrong with technique as such, in playing golf or acting or making love. But the emphasis beyond a certain point on technique in sex makes for a mechanistic attitude toward love-making, and goes along with alienation, feelings of loneliness, and depersonalization.

[7]   The third dilemma I propose is that our highly vaunted sexual freedom has turned out to be a new form of puritanism. I define puritanism as a state of alienation from the body, separation of emotion from reason, and use of the body as a machine. These were the elements of moralistic puritanism in Victorian times; industrialism expressed these same characteristics of puritanism in economic guise. Our modern sexual attitudes have a new content, namely, full sexual expression, but in the same old puritan form—alienation from the body and feeling, and exploitation of the body as though it were a machine.

[8]   In our new puritanism bad health is equated with sin. Sin used to be "to give in to one's sexual desires"; now it is "not to have full sexual expression." A woman used to be guilty if she went to bed with a man; now she feels vaguely guilty if after a certain number of dates she still refrains. And her partner, who is always completely enlightened—or at least pretends to be—refuses to allay her guilt and does not get overtly angry at her sin of "morbid repression," her refusal to "give." This, of course, makes her "no" all the more guilt-producing for her.

[9]   All this means, of course, that people have to learn to perform sexually but at the same time not to let themselves go in passion or unseemingly commitment—which latter may be interpreted as exerting an unhealthy demand on the partner. *The Victorian person sought to have love without falling into sex; the modern person seeks to have sex without falling into love.*

[10]   Recently I amused myself by drawing an impressionistic picture of the attitude of the contemporary enlightened person toward sex and love. I call it the portrait of the new sophisticate:

> [11]   The new sophisticate is not castrated by society but, like Origen, is self-castrated. Sex and the body are for him not something to be and live out, but tools to be cultivated like a TV announcer's voice. And like all genuine Puritans (very passionate men under-

neath) the new sophisticate does it by devoting himself passionately to the moral principle of dispersing all passion, loving everybody until love has no power left to scare anyone. He is deathly afraid of his passions unless they are kept under leash, and the theory of total expression is precisely his leash. His dogma of liberty is his repression; and his principle of full libidinal health, full sexual satisfaction, are his puritanism and amount to the same thing as his New England forefathers' denial of sex. The first Puritans repressed sex and were passionate; our new man represses passion and is sexual. Both have the purpose of holding back the body, both are ways of trying to make nature a slave. The modern man's rigid principle of full freedom is not freedom at all but a new strait-jacket, in some ways as compulsive as the old. He does all this because he is afraid of his body and his compassionate roots in nature, afraid of the soil and his procreative power. He is our latter-day Baconian devoted to gaining power *over* nature, gaining knowledge in order to get more power. And you gain power over sexuality (like working the slave until all zest for revolt is squeezed out of him) precisely by the role of full expression. Sex becomes our tool like the caveman's wheel, crowbar, or adz. Sex, the new machine, the *Machina Ultima*.

[12]   It is not surprising that, confronted by these dilemmas, people become more and more concerned about the technical, mechanical aspects of the sexual act. The questions typically asked about the act of love-making are not whether there was passion or meaning or even pleasure, but how well did one perform? Even the sexologists, whose attitude is generally the more the merrier, are raising their eyebrows these days about the anxious overemphasis on achieving the orgasm and the great importance attached to "satisfying" the partner. The man makes a point of asking the women if she "made it," or is she "all right," or uses some other such euphemism for an experience for which obviously no euphemism is possible. We men are reminded by Simone de Beauvoir and other women who try to interpret the love act to us, that this is the last thing in the world a woman wants to be asked at that moment.

[13]   I often get the impression, amid the male flexing of sexual biceps, that men are in training to become sexual athletes. But what is the great prize of the game? Now it is well known in psychotherapeutic circles that the overconcern with potency is generally a compensation for feelings of impotence. Men and women both are struggling to prove their sexual power. Another motive of the game is to overcome their own solitariness. A third motive is often the desperate endeavor to

escape feelings of emptiness and the threat of apathy: they pant and quiver to find an answering quiver in someone else's body to prove their own is not dead. Out of an ancient conceit we call this love.

[14]   The struggle to find an identity is also a central motive in acting out these sexual roles—a goal present in women as well as men, as Betty Friedan in *The Feminine Mystique* made clear. The point I wish to emphasize here is the connection between this dilemma about potency and the tendency in our society for us to become machines or ledger books even in bed. A psychiatrist colleague of mine tells me that one of his patients brought in the following dream. "I was in bed with my wife. Between us was my accountant. He was going to make love to my wife. Somehow it seemed all right."

[15]   Along with the overemphasis upon mechanism there goes, understandably enough, a lessening of passion and of feeling itself, which seems to take the form of a kind of anaesthesia in people who otherwise can perform the mechanical aspects of the sexual act very capably. This is one reason we therapists get a good number of patients these days with problems of impotence, frigidity, and simple lack of feeling in the sexual act. We psychiatrists often hear the disappointed refrain, "We made love, but it wasn't much good."

[16]   Sex is the "last frontier," David Riesman meaningfully wrote fifteen years ago in *The Lonely Crowd*. Gerald Sykes in the same vein spoke of sex as the "last green thing." It is surely true that the zest, adventure, the discovering of vast new areas of feeling and passion in one's self, the trying out of one's power to arouse feelings in others— these are indeed "frontier experiences." They are normally present as part of the psycho-sexual development of every individual, and the young person rightly gets a validation of himself from such experiences. Sex in our society did in fact have this power in the several recent decades since the 1920s, when almost every other activity was becoming "other-directed," jaded, emptied of zest and adventure.

[17]   But for various reasons—one of them being that sex had to carry by itself the weight for the validation of the personality on practically all other levels as well—the frontier freshness and newness and challenge of sex were more and more lost. We are now living in the post-Riesman age, and are experiencing the difficult implications of the "other-directed," radar behavior. The "last frontier" has become a teeming Las Vegas and no frontier at all.

[18]   Young people can no longer get a bootlegged feeling of personal identity out of the sexual revolt, since there is nothing left to re-

volt against. A study of drug addition among young people, published recently in the *New York Times*, reports the young people are saying that the revolt against parents and society, the "kick" of feeling their own "oats" which they used to get from sex, they now have to get from drugs. It is not surprising that for many youngsters what used to be called lovemaking is now so often experienced as a futile "panting palm to palm," in Aldous Huxley's predictive phrase, and that they tell us that it is hard for them to understand what the poets were talking about.

[19]   Nothing to revolt against, did I say? Well, there is obviously one thing left to revolt against, and that is sex itself. The frontier, the establishing of identity, can be, and not infrequently is for the young people, a revolt against sexuality entirely. A modern Lysistrata[1] in robot's dress is rumbling at the gates of our cities, or if not rumbling, at least hovering. As sex becomes more machine-like, with passion irrelevant and then even pleasure diminishing, the problem comes full circle, and we find, *mirabile dictu*, a progression from an *anaesthetic* attitude to an *antiseptic* one. Sexual contact itself then tends to be avoided. The sexual revolution comes finally back on itself not with a bang but a whimper.

[20]   This is another and surely least constructive aspect of the new puritanism: it returns, finally, to an ascetic attitude. This is said graphically in a charming limerick that seems to have sprung up on some sophisticated campus:

> The word has come down from the Dean,
> That with the aid of the teaching machine,
>   King Oedipus Rex
>   Could have learned about sex
> Without ever touching the Queen.

[21]   What are the sources of these dilemmas? Perhaps if we can get some idea of what went wrong, we shall rediscover values in sex and love that will have genuine relevance for our age.

[22]   The essential element, I propose, in the dilemmas we have been discussing is the *banalization of sex and love*. Does not the tendency to make sex and love banal and vapid run through our whole

---

[1]*Lysistrata* refers to the 5th-century B.C. comedy of the same name by Aristophanes in which the women, tired of a long, costly, enervating war between two Greek city states, stage a "love-out"—no more sex—until the men come to their senses and stop the slaughter.

culture? The plethora of books on the subject have one thing in common—they oversimplify sex and love, treating the topic like a combination of learning to play tennis and buying life insurance.

[23]   I have said above, describing the modern sophisticated man's dilemmas about sex, that he castrates himself "because he is afraid of his body, afraid of his compassionate roots in nature, afraid of the soil and his procreative powers." That is to say, something much more potent is going on in sexuality than one would gather from the oversimplified books on sex and love—something that still has the power to scare people. I believe banalization serves as a defense against this anxiety.

[24]   The widespread tendency among young people to "go steady" —premature monogamy, as it has been called—is an egregious illustration of our point. In my frequent visits to different college campuses for lectures, I have discussed this phenomenon with students, and something like the following seems to be going on. In our insecure age when all values are in flux, at least "the steady" is steady. Always having a date with the same fellow or girl on Saturday night, dancing with this same person through the entire party at college dances, always knowing this one is available, allays the anxiety of aloneness. But it also gets boring. This leads naturally enough to early sexuality: sex at least is something we can do when we run out of conversation—which happens often when the partners have not developed enough in their own right to be interesting very long to each other as persons. It is a strange fact in our society that what goes into building a relationship—the sharing of tastes, fantasies, dreams, hopes for the future and fears from the past—seems to make people more shy and vulnerable than going to bed with each other. They are more wary of the tenderness that goes with psychological and spiritual nakedness than they are of the physical nakedness in sexual intimacy.

[25]   Now substituting premature sexuality for meaningful intimate relationship relieves the young person's anxiety, but at the price of bypassing opportunity for further development. It seems that going steady, paradoxically, is related to promiscuity. I define "promiscuity" with Webster as the indiscriminate practice of sexuality whether with one person or a number: sex is indiscriminate when used in the service of security, or to fill up an emotional vacuum. But promiscuity is a lonely and alienating business. This loneliness becomes one of the pushes toward early marriage. Grasping each other in marriage gives a kind of security—a legal and social security at least—which tempo-

rarily allays loneliness, but at the price of the haunting dread of a boring marital future. *Each step in this pattern has within it the banalization of sex and love.*

[26]   Now the question rarely asked is, are not these young people—possibly wiser in their innocence than their culture in its sophistication—fleeing from some anxiety that is only too real? I propose that what scares them, like what scares our "new sophisticate," is an element in sex and love which is almost universally repressed in our culture, namely the *tragic, daimonic element.*

[27]   By "daimonic"—which I hasten to say does not refer to little "demons"—I mean the natural element within an individual, such as the erotic drive, which has the power to take over the whole person. The erotic urge pushes toward a general physiological aim, namely sexual release. But it can push the individual into all kinds of relationships without relation to the totality of his self.

[28]   But the potentially destructive effects of the daimonic are only the reverse side of the person's constructive vitality, his passion and other potentially creative activities. The Greeks used the term "daimon" to describe the inspired urges of the poet. Socrates, indeed, speaks of his "daimon" as his conscience. When this power goes awry—when one element takes over the total personality and drives the person into disintegrative behavior—it becomes "demon possession," the historical term for psychosis. The daimonic can be either creative or destructive, but either way it certainly is the opposite to banalization. The repression of the daimonic, tragic aspects of sex and love is directly related to their banalization in our culture.

[29]   The daimonic is present in all nature as blind, ambiguous power. But only in man does it become allied with the tragic. For tragedy is the self-conscious, personal realization of being in the power of one element; thus the Greeks defined tragedy as "inordinate desire," "pride," "reaching beyond just boundaries." We have only to call to mind Romeo and Juliet, Abelard and Héloise, Tristan and Isolde, Helen of Troy, to see the power of sexual love to seize a man and woman, lift them up into a whirlwind that defies rational control and may destroy not only themselves but others at the same time. These stories are told over and over again in Western classic literature, and passed down from generation to generation, for they come from a depth of human experience in sexual love that is profoundly significant. It is a level largely unmentioned in our day, much to the impoverishment of our talk and writing about sex and love.

[30]   If we are to overcome banalization, we must take sex and love on several different dimensions at once. Consider, as an analogy, Mozart's music. In some portions of his music Mozart is engaged in elegant play. In other portions his music comes to us as pure sensuous pleasure, giving us a sheer delight. But in other portions, like the death music at the end of *Don Giovanni*, Mozart is profoundly shaking: we are gripped by fate and the daimonic as the inescapable tragedy rises before us. If Mozart had only the first element, play, he would sooner or later be banal and boring. If he presented only pure sensuality, he would become cloying; or if only the fire and death music, his creations would be too heavy. He is great because he writes on all three dimensions; and he must be listened to on all these levels at once.

[31]   Sexuality and love similarly have these three dimensions. Sex not only can be play, but probably an element of sheer play should be fairly regularly present. By this token, casual relationships in sex may have their gratification or meaning in the sharing of pleasure, tenderness, and so on. But if one's whole pattern and attitude toward sex is only casual, then sooner or later the playing itself becomes boring. The same is true about sensuality, obviously an element in any gratifying sex: if it has to carry the whole weight of the relationship, it becomes cloying. If sex is only sensuality, you sooner or later turn against sex itself. The third element, the daimonic and tragic, we emphasized here because that is the one almost wholly repressed in our culture, a fact that has much to do with the banalization of sex and love in our day. In a book like Erich Fromm's *Art of Loving*, for example, the daimonic, tragic element is completely missing.

[32]   An appreciation of the tragic and daimonic side of sex and love can help us not only to avoid oversimplification but to love better. Let me illustrate the constructive use of the daimonic. Every person, as a separate individual, experiences aloneness and strives to overcome his loneliness, this striving usually being some kind of love. Sexuality and love require self-assertion: if the person is not to some extent an individual in his own right, he will not only have nothing to give, nothing to relate with, but will be unable to assert himself and therefore unable to be genuinely part of the relationship. Both the man and woman need self-assertion in order to breach the separateness and make some kind of union with each other. Thus there is truth in the vernacular expressions about needing to "let oneself go" and "give oneself over" to the sexual act—or to any creative experience for that matter.

[33]   The psychotherapist Dr. Otto Rank once remarked in his latter

years of pratice that practically all the women who came to him had problems because their husbands were not assertive enough. Despite the oversimplified sound of this sentence, it contains a telling point: our effete cultivation of sex can make us so intellectual and detached about it that the simple power of the act evaporates, and we lose—and this loss is especially serious for women—the important elemental pleasure of "being taken," being "carried away." But the self-assertive power must be integrated with the other aspects of one's own personality, and with the total person of the mate; otherwise it becomes daimonic in the destructive sense.

[34]   Let us now summarize some values, potential and actual, in sexual love. There is, first, the overall value of enrichment and fulfilment of personality. This comes from expansion of one's awareness of one's self, one's feelings, one's experience of his capacity to give sexual pleasure and other feelings to the other person, and achieve thereby an expansion of meaning in interpersonal relationship. This fulfilment carries us beyond what we are at any given moment; I become in a literal sense more than I was. The most powerful symbol imaginable for this fulfilment is procreation—the possibility that a new being may be conceived and born. The "birth," however, can and does refer at the same time to the birth of new aspects of one's self.

[35]   Tenderness is a second value, a tenderness that is much more than indicated in that most unpoetic of all words, "togetherness." The experience of tenderness comes out of the fact that the two persons, longing as all individuals do to overcome the separateness and isolation to which we are all heir because we are individuals, can participate in a relationship that for the moment is not two isolated selves but a union. In this kind of sexual intercourse, the lover often does not know whether a particular sensation of delight is felt by him or by his loved one—and it doesn't make any difference anyway. A sharing takes place which is a new gestalt, a new being, a new field of magnetic force. A gratifying sexual relationship thus has the gestalt of a painting—the various parts, the colors, feelings, forms, unite to become a new whole.

[36]   There is the third value which occurs ideally at the moment of climax in sexual intercourse. This is the point when the lovers are carried not only beyond their personal isolation, but when a shift in consciousness seems to occur that unites them also with nature. In Hemingway's novel, *For Whom the Bell Tolls*, the older woman, Pilar, waits for the hero, Robert Jordan, and the girl he loves when they have

gone ahead into the mountain to make love; and when they return, she asks, "Did the earth move?" The shaking of the earth seems to be a normal part of the momentary loss of awareness of the self and the surging up of a sudden consciousness that includes the "earth" as well. There is an accelerating experience of touch, contact, union to the point where for a moment the awareness of separateness is lost, blotted out in a cosmic feeling of oneness with nature. I do not wish this to sound too "ideal," for I think it is a quality, however subtle, in all love-making except the most depersonalized sort. And I also do not wish it to sound simply "mystic," for despite limitations in our awareness, I think it is an inseparable part of actual experience in the love act.

[37]   This leads us immediately to the fourth value, sex and love as the affirmation of the self. Despite the fact that many people in our culture use sex to get a short-circuited, ersatz sense of identity, sexual love can and ought to provide a sound and meaningful way to the sense of personal identity. We emerge from love-making normally with re- newed vitality, a vitality which comes not from triumph or proof of one's strength but from the expansion of awareness. Probably in love-making there is always some element of sadness—as, to use our previous analogy, there is in practically all music no matter how joyful—in the reminder that we have not succeeded absolutely in losing our separate- ness, nor is the infantile hope that we could recover the womb made into reality, and even our increased self-awareness can also be a poig- nant reminder that none of us ever overcomes his loneliness completely. But by one's replenished sense of one's own significance in the love act he can accept these unavoidable human limitations.

[38]   A final value inheres in the curious phenomenon in love-mak- ing: that to be able to give to the other person is essential to one's own full pleasure in the act. This sounds like a banal moralism in our age of mechanization of sex and "release of tension" in sexual objects. But it is not sentimentality but a point which anyone can confirm in his own ex- perience in the love act, that to give is essential to one's own pleasure. Many patients in psychotherapy find themselves discovering, generally with some surprise, that something is missing if they cannot "do some- thing for," give something to the partner—the normal expression of which is the giving in the act of intercourse itself. Just as giving is essential to one's own full pleasure, the ability to receive is necessary in the love interrelationship also. If you cannot receive, your giving will be a domination of the partner. Conversely, if you cannot give, your receiving will leave you empty. The paradox is demonstrably true that

the person who can only receive becomes empty, for he is unable actively to appropriate and make his own what he receives. I speak, thus, not of receiving as a passive phenomenon, but of *active receiving*: one knows he is receiving, feels it, absorbs it into his own experience whether he verbally acknowledges it or not, and is grateful for it.

STUDY AND DISCUSSION

Vocabulary
Should you be unfamiliar with any of the following words, by all means consult your local dictionary:

1. sanctifying (para. 1)	2. vaunted (para. 7)
3. dogma (para. 11)	4. libidinal (para. 11)
5. euphemism (para. 12)	6. banalization (para. 22)
7. plethora (para. 22)	8. monogamy (para. 24)
9. egregious (para. 24)	10. disintegrative (para. 28)
11. psychosis (para. 28)	12. cloying (para. 30)
13. effete (para. 33)	14. gestalt (para. 35)
15. ersatz (para. 37)	16. replenished (para. 37)
17. to inhere (para. 38)	

Rhetoric
1. Rollo May does not rely, throughout his essay, on the more conventional modes of rhetorical analysis. What method does he favor? Refer, in particular, to paras. 5 and 11.
2. What evidence does May give in support of his claim, in para. 5, that "internalized anxiety and guilt have increased" in this day and age?
3. By what rhetorical method are paras. 5, 6, and 7 organized?
4. What is the function of para. 11 in the essay taken as a whole?
5. How does para. 21 work in the total structure of May's essay?

Content
1. What, in your own words, is "the new puritanism"?
2. Define "the daimonic, tragic element" in sexual love.
3. How does this element prove productive? Or, conversely, why does May feel that its lack in our society dehumanizes us?
4. Are there any dangers inherent in "the daimonic, tragic element"? If so, what are they?
5. What is the ultimate alternative which May gives the "mechanization"

of sexual love? How, in other words, does he feel that we can escape
its tyranny?

6. What is the bind that May mentions in para. 38 when he talks about
the inability to either give or receive?

Ideas and Implications

1. In para. 37, May writes that "none of us ever overcomes his loneliness
completely." How do you feel about your loneliness—is it a necessary
condition to your being an individual?

2. Do you think that May is correct when he implies that much of our
love-making is a defense against our existential loneliness?

3. Does loneliness drive people to extremes? Has it ever driven you into "a
mistake"? Do you think that it creates an aura of unbearable tension
within you? How would you define *tension*; how would Rollo May?
Does he ever define it in this article?

4. In what ways do you release tension? Have you ever used sex as a ten-
sion-release? Do you feel that it is wrong to use sex in such a way?
Why? Or why not?

5. Do you believe that our society is preoccupied with sex? Over-preoc-
cupied, perhaps? If so, what might some of the reasons for our obsession
with it be?

6. Is there a difference, in your opinion, between a sex act and a sexual
experience? What would the difference(s) be?

SONNET 116

*WILLIAM SHAKESPEARE   In "Sonnet CXVI," William Shakespeare
(1564-1616) explores the very nature and essence of love: its utter perma-
nence and inflexible endurance. Since Shakespeare uses language most
imaginatively, you will need to bring an agile, imaginative mind to the
poem; and since he uses words very exactly, you will also need to use a*

*dictionary. But careful study of Shakespeare's imagery and language will
be repaid by an enriched understanding of the poem.*

Let me not to the marriage of true minds
Admit impediments. Love is not love
Which alters when it alteration finds,
Or bends with the remover to remove:
Oh, no! it is an ever-fixèd mark,
That look on tempests and is never shaken;
It is the star to every wandering bark,
Whose worth's unknown, although his height be taken.
Love's not Time's fool, though rosy lips and cheeks
Within his bending sickle's compass come;
Love alters not with his brief hours and weeks,
But bears it out even to the edge of doom.
      If this be error and upon me proved,
      I never writ, nor no man ever loved.

STUDY AND DISCUSSION

1. What do you think Shakespeare means by "the marriage of true minds"?
   Is *marriage* meant literally here? In what sense does he use *true*?
2. What are *impediments*? Why should there be no impediments to the
   marriage of true minds? After you have studied each of the questions on
   this poem, try to determine what specific impediments Shakespeare
   considers in this sonnet.
3. Paraphrase lines 2, 3, and 4. (Note line 5.)
4. *Mark*, in line 5, has many, many possible meanings. Study the word in
   your dictionary and then try to decide which of these meanings best fits
   the context ("looks on tempests and is never shaken").
5. What is a *bark*? How could love be a "star" to a "bark"?
6. How do you interpret the statement "Love's not Time's fool"? What does
   Time do to "rosy lips and cheeks"? Try to paraphrase lines 9 and 10.
7. *Doom* (line 12) is Doomsday. What is supposed to happen at Doomsday? What is the relationship between love and Doomsday?
8. What is Shakespeare saying in the last two lines?
9. Lines 1-4, 5-8, 9-12, and 13-14 form organizational units within the
   poem. Does each unit express a different idea and develop a different
   image? Discuss.

somewhere i have never
travelled,gladly beyond

e. e. cummings   *e. e. cummings, one of the best known and most popular poets in twentieth-century America, wrote fiction, drama, and poetry. His books include the novel* The Enormous Room, *many slim volumes of poetry, and* Poems: 1922-1954. *In his poems, cummings is often romantic, sentimental, and extremely emotional—qualities that hide under a deceptively modern veneer of experimental typography.* "Somewhere i have never travelled, gladly beyond" *is typically romantic in its use of language and its attempt to achieve poetic effects by transcending rational statement. Except for its use of lower-case letters and its omission of periods, however, it is rather conventional in typography. Its structure, too, is conventional: cummings uses five four-line stanzas each of which is virtually self-contained. The poem is not quite typical of cummings, then; but it may represent him at his best, nevertheless. It is a tender, lyrical piece.*

somewhere i have never travelled,gladly beyond
any experience,your eyes have their silence:
in your most frail gesture are things which enclose me,
or which i cannot touch because they are too near

your slightest look easily will unclose me
though i have closed myself as fingers,
you open always petal by petal myself as Spring opens
(touching skilfully,mysteriously)her first rose

or if your wish be to close me,i and
my life will shut very beautifully,suddenly,
as when the heart of this flower imagines
the snow carefully everywhere descending;

nothing which we are to perceive in this world equals
the power of your intense fragility:whose texture
compels me with the colour of its countries,
rendering death and forever with each breathing

(i do not know what it is about you that closes
and opens;only something in me understands
the voice of your eyes is deeper than all roses)
nobody,not even the rain,has such small hands

1. "Somewhere i have never travelled" is a love poem, obviously. Which phrases describe the qualities that the speaker likes best about his lover?
2. How does the lover affect him? (Note particular the references to closing and unclosing.) Do you think this is a good way to describe the effects of love?
3. This poem does not make a very rational statement about love. Compare it, for instance, with Shakespeare's "Sonnet CXVI." What, then, does cummings *seem* to be saying about the experience of love?
4. What do you think of the last line of the poem? Does it make sense? Discuss it in detail, especially in reference to the rest of the poem.

COLORS OF LOVE

*GENE FOWLER   Gene Fowler, who lives and works in the San Francisco Bay Area, has been a night-club comic, a soldier, a door-to-door salesman, a convicted armed robber, a prison inmate, and, more recently, a research assistant at the University of California's School of Criminology at Berkeley. He is now an established poet and critic. Since 1965 he has published three books of poetry—*Field Studies, Shaman Songs, *and* Her Majesty's Ship—*and hundreds of poems, short stories, and essays.*

*"Colors of Love" and "Eulogy," both from Fowler's first collection of verse, *Field Studies, *are touching but unsentimental pictures of situations in which love—or a loved one—has been lost. In "Colors of Love" the speaker looks across a room "fashioned" by love, seeing the girl with whom he has shared love; he is separated from her by some undefined distance; he speaks of her "restless" tears and "running feet" in lines that glow with colors ("burnt sienna," "deep blues," "chinese reds"). The room is "silent/ at its windows."*

In "Eulogy," less is said but more is implied. A eulogy, remember, is speech or writing in praise of a person, especially someone who is dead. The poem, then, pictures a room that is, or seems, empty, soundless, still as death. A sound without pictures—the sound of a loved one—intrudes for moment, then vanishes like a sudden memory. The room seems to wait for death.

Reprinted by permission of the author.

You look up
from our book (its pages

well thumbed)

& your tears
        grow restless
in the burnt sienna room
our love
fashioned.

Beautiful young men with
homely faces
        thread tapestries

on guitars
        tapestries that color
your breasts with deep
blues, chinese reds,

tapestries to show you
a copper sun
over flowers gently played
        (whose leaves speak

softly to your running feet)

& your tears

                restless
in the burnt sienna room,
silent
at its windows.

1. Who seems to be speaking in this poem?
2. Who is addressed as "you"?
3. What significance does "our book" have in the poem?

4. What is "burnt sienna"? How can a room be described thus? What feelings are suggested by that color? In what sense can a room be "fashioned" by love?
5. How do you account for the presence of "Beautiful young men" in this poem? Is the poem necessarily set at a party, for instance?
6. How would you explain the references to "tears" and "running feet"?
7. What is implied by the final image of the room "silent/at its windows"?

EULOGY

GENE FOWLER

The room,
soundless, is larger than before.
The paper is impersonal.

Footsteps, laughter,
the light voice: I love you.
The register is wrong;
The sound doesn't touch the room.

The dust motes wait
for an exhaled breath to move them.
The paper, too, will yellow.

STUDY AND DISCUSSION

1. Why is the room "larger than before?"
2. In what sense can the paper be "impersonal"?
3. Assume that the lines
   Footsteps, laughter,
   the light voice: I love you

represent a memory from the past. Why is the "register" wrong now? Why doesn't the sound "touch the room"?

4. Describe the image presented in lines 8 and 9. What does the image imply about the room?

5. What does the last line suggest—not merely about the room but perhaps about everything?

MARRIAGE AS A WRETCHED INSTITUTION

MERVYN CADWALLADER   Mervyn Cadwallader is probably right when he says that although most of us know about the hazards of marriage, most of us defy the odds and plunge on into it anyway. In the following essay, he examines some of the reasons that so many of us rush in where angels fear to tread . . . of course, angels by their very nature are immune to societal and biological pressures. Do you envy them? Do you think, after reading this piece, that the author does?

Mervyn Cadwallader, born in 1926, is a professor of sociology and the humanities at San Jose State College in California where he also serves as Director of its Experimental Program in Humanities and Science. He has been married three times himself and is the father of one child.

[1]   Our society expects us all to get married. With only rare exceptions we all do just that. Getting married is a rather complicated business. It involves mastering certain complex hustling and courtship games, the rituals and the ceremonies that celebrate the act of marriage, and finally the difficult requirements of domestic life with a husband or wife. It is an enormously elaborate round of activity, much more so than finding a job, and yet while many resolutely remain unemployed, few remain unmarried.

[2]   Now all this would not be particularly remarkable if there were no question about the advantages, the joys, and the rewards of married life, but most Americans, even young Americans, know or have heard that marriage is a hazardous affair. Of course, for all the increase in divorce, there are still young marriages that work, unions made by young men and women intelligent or fortunate enough to find the kind of mates they want, who know that they want children and how to love them when they come, or who find the artful blend between giving and receiving. It is not these marriages that concern us here, and that is not the trend in America today. We are concerned with the increasing number of others who, with mixed intentions and varied illusions, grope or fling themselves into marital disaster. They talk solemnly and sincerely about working to make their marriage succeed, but they are very

aware of the countless marriages they have seen fail. But young people in particular do not seem to be able to relate the awesome divorce statistics to the probability of failure of their own marriage. And they rush into it, in increasing numbers, without any clear idea of the reality that underlies the myth.

[3]   Parents, teachers, and concerned adults all counsel against premature marriage. But they rarely speak the truth about marriage as it really is in modern middle-class America. The truth as I see it is that contemporary marriage is a wretched institution. It spells the end of voluntary affection, of love freely given and joyously received. Beautiful romances are transmuted into dull marriages, and eventually the relationship becomes constricting, corrosive, grinding, and destructive. The beautiful love affair becomes a bitter contract.

[4]   The basic reason for this sad state of affairs is that marriage was not designed to bear the burdens now being asked of it by the urban American middle class. It is an institution that evolved over centuries to meet some very specific functional needs of a nonindustrial society. Romantic love was viewed as tragic, or merely irrelevant. Today it is the titillating prelude to domestic tragedy, or, perhaps more frequently, to domestic grotesqueries that are only pathetic.

[5]   Marriage was not designed as a mechanism for providing friendship, erotic experience, romantic love, personal fulfillment, continuous lay psychotherapy, or recreation. The Western European family was not designed to carry a lifelong load of highly emotional romantic freight. Given its present structure, it simply has to fail when asked to do so. The very idea of an irrevocable contract obligating the parties concerned to a lifetime of romantic effort is utterly absurd.

[6]   Other pressures of the present era have tended to overburden marriage with expectations it cannot fulfill. Industrialized, urbanized America is a society which has lost the sense of community. Our ties to our society, to the bustling multitudes that make up this dazzling kaleidoscope of contemporary America, are as formal and superficial as they are numerous. We all search for community, and yet we know that the search is futile. Cut off from the support and satisfactions that flow from community, the confused and searching young American can do little but place all of his bets on creating a community in microcosm, his own marriage.

[7]   And so the ideal we struggle to reach in our love relationship is that of complete candor, total honesty. Out there all is phony, but within the romantic family there are to be no dishonest games, no hypocrisy,

no misunderstanding. Here we have a painful paradox, for I submit that total exposure is probably always mutually destructive in the long run. What starts out as a tender coming together to share one's whole person with the beloved is transmuted by too much togetherness into attack and counterattack, doubt, disillusionment, and ambivalence. The moment the once-upon-a-time lover catches a glimpse of his own hatred, something precious and fragile is shattered. And soon another brave marriage will end.

[8]   The purposes of marriage have changed radically, yet we cling desperately to the outmoded structures of the past. Adult Americans behave as though the more obvious the contradiction between the old and the new, the more sentimental and irrational should be their advice to young people who are going steady or are engaged. Our schools, both high schools and colleges, teach sentimental rubbish in their marriage and family courses. The texts make much of a posture of hard-nosed objectivity that is neither objective nor hardnosed. The basic structure of Western marriage is never questioned, alternatives are not proposed or discussed. Instead, the prospective young bride and bridegroom are offered housekeeping advice and told to work hard at making their marriage succeed. The chapter on sex, complete with ugly diagrams of the male and female genitals, is probably wedged in between a chapter on budgets and life insurance. The message is that if your marriage fails, you have been weighed in the domestic balance and found wanting. Perhaps you did not master the fifth position for sexual intercourse, or maybe you bought cheap term life rather than a preferred policy with income protection and retirement benefits. If taught honestly, these courses would alert the teen-ager and young adult to the realities of matrimonial life in the United States and try to advise them on how to survive marriage if they insist on that hazardous venture.

[9]   But teen-agers and young adults do insist upon it in greater and greater numbers with each passing year. And one of the reasons they do get married with such astonishing certainty is because they find themselves immersed in a culture that is preoccupied with and schizophrenic about sex. Advertising, entertainment, and fashion are all designed to produce and then to exploit sexual tension. Sexually aroused at an early age and asked to postpone marriage until they become adults, they have no recourse but to fill the intervening years with courtship rituals and games that are supposed to be sexy but sexless. Dating is expected to culminate in going steady, and that is the beginning of the end. The dating game hinges on an important exchange. The male

wants sexual intimacy, and the female wants social commitment. The game involves bartering sex for security amid the sweet and heady agitations of a romantic entanglement. Once the game reaches the going-steady stage, marriage is virtually inevitable. The teen-ager finds himself driven into a corner, and the one way to legitimize his sex play and assuage the guilt is to plan marriage.

[10]   Another reason for the upsurge in young marriages is the real cultural break between teen-agers and adults in our society. This is a recent phenomenon. In my generation there was no teen culture. Adolescents wanted to become adults as soon as possible. The teen-age years were a time of impatient waiting, as teen-age boys tried to dress and act like little men. Adolescents sang the adults' songs ("South of the Border," "The Music Goes Round and Round," "Mairzy Doats"—notice I didn't say anything about the quality of the music), saw their movies, listened to their radios, and waited confidently to be allowed in. We had no money, and so there was no teen-age market. There was nothing to do then but get it over with. The boundary line was sharp, and you crossed it when you took your first serious job, when you passed the employment test.

[11]   Now there is a very definite adolescent culture, which is in many ways hostile to the dreary culture of the adult world. In its most extreme form it borrows from the beats and turns the middle-class value system inside out. The hip teen-ager on Macdougal Street or Telegraph Avenue can buy a costume and go to a freak show. It's fun to be an Indian, a prankster, a beat, or a swinging troubadour. He can get stoned. That particular trip leads to instant mysticism.

[12]   Even in less extreme forms, teen culture is weighted against the adult world of responsibility. I recently asked a roomful of eighteen-year-olds to tell me what an adult is. Their deliberate answer, after hours of discussion, was that an adult is someone who no longer plays, who is no longer playful. Is Bob Dylan an adult? No, never! Of course they did not want to remain children, or teens, or adolescents; but they did want to remain youthful, playful, free of squares, and free of responsibility. The teen-ager wants to be old enough to drive, drink, screw, and travel. He does not want to get pushed into square maturity. He wants to drag the main, be a surf bum, a ski bum, or dream of being a bum. He doesn't want to go to Vietnam, or to IBM, or to buy a split-level house in Knotty Pines Estates.

[13]   This swing away from responsibility quite predictably produces frictions between the adolescent and his parents. The clash of

cultures is likely to drive the adolescent from the home, to persuade him to leave the dead world of his parents and strike out on his own. And here we find the central paradox of young marriages. For the only way the young person can escape from his parents is to assume many of the responsibilities that he so reviles in the life-style of his parents. He needs a job and an apartment. And he needs some kind of emotional substitute, some means of filling the emotional vacuum that leaving home has caused. And so he goes steady, and sooner rather than later, gets married to a girl with similar inclinations.

[14]   When he does this, he crosses the dividing line between the cultures. Though he seldom realizes it at the time, he has taken the first step to adulthood. Our society does not have a conventional "rite of passage." In Africa the Masai adolescent takes a lion test. He becomes an adult the first time he kills a lion with a spear. Our adolescents take the domesticity test. When they get married they have to come to terms with the system in one way or another. Some brave individuals continue to fight it. But most simply capitulate.

[15]   The cool adolescent finishing high school or starting college has a skeptical view of virtually every institutional sector of his society. He knows that government is corrupt, the military dehumanizing, the corporations rapacious, the churches organized hypocrisy, and the schools dishonest. But the one area that seems to be exempt from his cynicism is romantic love and marriage. When I talk to teen-agers about marriage, that cool skepticism turns to sentimental dreams right out of *Ladies' Home Journal* or the hard-hitting pages of *Reader's Digest*. They all mouth the same vapid platitudes about finding happiness through sharing and personal fulfillment through giving (each is to give 51 percent). They have all heard about divorce, and most of them have been touched by it in some way or another. Yet they insist that their marriage will be different.

[16]   So, clutching their illusions, young girls with ecstatic screams of joy lead their awkward brooding boys through the portals of the church into the land of the Mustang, Apartment 24, Macy's, Sears, and the ubiquitous drive-in. They have become members in good standing of the adult world.

[17]   The end of most of these sentimental marriages is quite predictable. They progress, in most cases, to varying stages of marital ennui, depending on the ability of the couple to adjust to reality; most common are (1) a lackluster standoff, (2) a bitter business car-

ried on for the children, church, or neighbors, or (3) separation and divorce, followed by another search to find the right person.

[18]   Divorce rates have been rising in all Western countries. In many countries the rates are rising even faster than in the United States. In 1910 the divorce rate for the United States was 87 per 1000 marriages. In 1965 the rate had risen to an estimated figure of well over 300 per 1000 in many parts of the country. At the present time some 40 percent of all brides are between the ages of fifteen and eighteen; half of these marriages break up within five years. As our population becomes younger and the age of marriage continues to drop, the divorce rate will rise to significantly higher levels.

[19]   What do we do, what can we do, about this wretched and disappointing institution? In terms of the immediate generation, the answer probably is, not much. Even when subjected to the enormous strains I have described, the habits, customs, traditions, and taboos that make up our courtship and marriage cycle are uncommonly resistant to change. Here and there creative and courageous individuals can and do work out their own unique solutions to the problem of marriage. Most of us simply suffer without understanding and thrash around blindly in an attempt to reduce the acute pain of a romance gone sour. In time, all of these individual actions will show up as a trend away from the old and toward the new, and the bulk of sluggish moderates in the population will slowly come to accept this trend as part of social evolution. Clearly, in middle-class America, the trend is ever toward more romantic courtship and marriage, earlier premarital sexual intercourse, earlier first marriages, more extra-marital affairs, earlier first divorces, more frequent divorces and remarriages. The trend is away from stable lifelong monogamous relationships toward some form of polygamous male-female relationship. Perhaps we should identify it as serial or consecutive polygamy, simply because Americans in significant numbers are going to have more than one husband or more than one wife. Attitudes and laws that make multiple marriages (in sequence, of course) difficult for the romantic and sentimental among us are archaic obstacles that one learns to circumvent with the aid of weary judges and clever attorneys.

[20]   Now, the absurdity of much of this lies in the fact that we pretend that marriages of short duration must be contracted for life. Why not permit a flexible contract perhaps for one to two or more years, with periodic options to renew? If a couple grew disenchanted

with their life together, they would not feel trapped for life. They
would not have to anticipate and then go through the destructive
agonies of divorce. They would not have to carry about the stigma of
marital failure, like the mark of Cain[1] on their foreheads. Instead of a
declaration of war, they could simply let their contract lapse, and while
still friendly, be free to continue their romantic quest. Sexualized
romanticism is now so fundamental to American life—and is bound
to become even more so—that marriage will simply have to accommo-
date itself to it in one way or another. For a great proportion of us it
already has.

[21]   What of the children in a society that is moving inexorably
toward consecutive plural marriages? Under present arrangements in
which marriages are ostensibly lifetime contracts and then are dis-
solved through hypocritical collusions or messy battles in court, the
children do suffer. Marriage and divorce turn lovers into enemies,
and the child is left to thread his way through the emotional wreck-
age of his parents' lives. Financial support of the children, mere subsistence, is not really a problem in a society as affluent as ours. Enduring emotional support of children by loving, healthy, and friendly
adults is a serious problem in America, and it is a desperately urgent
problem in many families where divorce is unthinkable. If the bitter
and poisonous denouement of divorce could be avoided by a frank
acceptance of short-term marriages, both adults and children would
benefit. Any time husbands and wives and ex-husbands and ex-
wives treat each other decently, generously, and respectfully, their
children will benefit.

[22]   The braver and more critical among our teen-agers and youthful adults will still ask, But if the institution is so bad, why get married at all? This is a tough one to deal with. The social pressures
pushing any couple who live together into marriage are difficult to
ignore even by the most resolute rebel. It can be done, and many
should be encouraged to carry out their own creative experiments in
living together in a relationship that is wholly voluntary. If the demands of society to conform seem overwhelming, the couple should
know that simply to be defined by others as married will elicit mar-
ried-like behavior in themselves, and that is precisely what they want
to avoid.

[23]   How do you marry and yet live like gentle lovers, or at least

---

[1] *Mark of Cain,* The Bible tells us that God punished Cain, who slew his brother
Abel, by putting a brand upon his forehead.

like friendly roommates? Quite frankly, I do not know the answer to
that question.

STUDY AND DISCUSSION

Vocabulary

If you are unfamiliar with any of the following words or terms, look up
their meanings in your dictionary:

1. resolutely (para. 1)
2. transmuted (para. 3)
3. titillating (para. 4)
4. domestic grotesqueries (para. 4)
5. ambivalence (para. 7)
6. schizophrenic (para. 9)
7. to assuage (para. 9)
8. vapid platitudes (para. 15)
9. ubiquitous (para. 16)
10. ennui (para. 17)
11. polygamous (para. 19)
12. to circumvent (para. 19)
13. stigma (para. 20)
14. inexorably (para. 20)
15. ostensibly (para. 20)
16. denouement (para. 21)

Rhetoric

1. What rhetorical device does the author make heavy use of in paras. 9
   and 10? Why do you think he mentions song titles that were hits in
   the early 1940's?
2. What rhetorical method does Cadwallader use in para. 12? Is it successful?
3. How does his use of specific magazine titles in para. 15 and products
   in para. 16 further the theme of his article?
4. How does para. 18 work in the overall structure of Cadwallader's
   piece? Why must it precede para. 19? Could their order, in other words,
   have been reversed? Would the absence of either strengthen the essay,
   in your opinion?
5. What is the function of para. 23?

Content

1. For what reason(s) does the author believe that "marriage (is) a
   wretched institution"?
2. How do the purposes of marriage today differ from those of the past?
   To what end did marriage evolve over the centuries in the West—does
   the author ever say for sure?
3. What are the purposes of the institution of marriage today? Is the institution adequate to meet them?

4. What is the single most damaging aspect of modern marriage in the author's opinion?
5. In para. 9, the author mentions "the dating game"—what does it hinge on?
6. What does the author feel *responsibility* means to adolescents today?
7. What is the "rite of passage" that the author says all American adolescents undergo?
8. What is the "one area that seems exempt" from teenage skepticism?
9. What does the author propose that we do about the "wretched and disappointing institution"?

Ideas and Implications

1. In your opinion, is the author over-reacting to what most people find is one of the most—if not *the* most—rewarding areas of life?
2. Do you believe that because Mervyn Cadawallader has been married three times he is an expert on the subject? How did the mention of the author's own multi-marriages in the brief editorial introduction to this piece affect you? Or did it affect you before you heard what he had to say at all?
3. Is Cadwallader right when he says that "industrialized, urbanized America has lost the sense of community"? What effect would this have on your own life—if you agree with him? (What effect has it had?)
4. Honesty is important between two people—isn't it? Then how can Cadwallader say, as he does in para. 7, that "total exposure is always probably mutually destructive in the long run"? Isn't the aim of marriage to grow, together? Wouldn't your mate be interested in what you have learned through the trial-and-error process of growth? Can you think of any experiences, which have changed you as an individual, whose recounting to a spouse would be harmful to your marriage?
5. Both Rollo May and Mervyn Cadwallader seem to see marriage as an attempt to fill an emotional vacuum—what are some of the other reasons for marriage? Do you want to get married yourself? Why? Why not?
6. In your experience, is Cadwallader correct when he writes in para. 12 that, "the teen-ager wants to be old enough to drive, drink, screw, and travel"? Or is he over-simplifying?
7. Is the trend really "away from stable lifelong monogamous relations toward some form of (polygamy) . . ."? What do you foresee as some of the effects on society if this trend proves a reality? How would it affect your own life?

8. What happens to children if both Mommy and Daddy are engaged in "consecutive plural marriages"?
9. Cadwallader advocates, in para. 20, a flexible contract "with periodic options to renew"—but doesn't the mere notion of such an institution render marriage obsolete?
10. Ultimately, the only reason to get married in a world that no longer believes in anything is to escape the terror of being alone. Comment upon this.
11. The final paragraph is a cop-out which just goes to show that the author wrote this piece out of his own feelings of bitterness and entrapment. Comment upon this piece of opinion.

STEREOTYPE
AND
CONFLICT

UP AGAINST THE WALL,
MALE CHAUVINIST PIG!

*MORTON HUNT   In paragraph 51, the author writes, "Beneath the
civilized veneer, there resides still the animal reality of our bodies and
emotions." As far as the editors of this book can see, both of us being
male, the following essay is a plea to acknowledge the primacy of this
animal reality. As you read it, you might do well to keep asking yourself
exactly whom Morton Hunt is against—otherwise you might make the
mistake of coming to think that he is totally opposed to all the grievances and the goals of Women's Liberation . . . which he is not.*

However, this essay originally appeared in Playboy Magazine—what
*does this bit of information tell you, even before you have begun to read
the article, about the author's attitude toward Women's Lib?*

*Morton Hunt is one of the country's foremost free-lance writers whose
articles and essays regularly appear in our popular magazines. In addition, he is the author of a book entitled* The Natural History of Love.

[1]   Revolutions traditionally appear first as clouds no larger than a man's hand, easily overlooked if you're not staring at the sky. Only occasionally are they as startling and dramatic as a clap of thunder.

[2]   You might, for instance, never have noticed the tiny cloud that appeared one night last fall at a feminist Congress to Unite Women meeting in New York, a conference attended by thousands of anxious members of women's organizations ranging from Hadassah to a small radical group somewhat muscularly named Female Liberation Cell-16. When H hour struck, the girls of Cell-16 strode on stage in tight pants, polo shirts and heavy custom-made mountain boots and announced to the awe-struck thousands that they were going to "demonstrate a liberated woman."

[3]   The only woman on stage with long hair promptly stepped forward; all the others had newly cropped locks that barely covered their ears. The long-haired girl spoke plaintively about the way men related to her tresses rather than to her as a person and complained that she was still a sex object. "My long hair symbolizes a delicate Alice-in-Wonderland thing that undercuts the image of a strong human being," she said sweetly.

[4]   "No, no, don't!" came the cry from some anguished members of the throng. But the long-haired girl held up a tiny scissors and handed it to one of the members of Cell-16 drawn up behind her, their arms folded self-consciously across their chests, like pre-adolescent tomboys spoiling for a fight. She sat down on a chair and, while the shorn curls fell around her, the various girls of Cell-16 stepped forward, one by one, to tell the audience how short hair made them feel stronger and freer. Once the ceremony was over, hostility from the rest of the congress rolled over the stage like breakers over a beach. There were shouts and protests and nobody accepted the invitation to join the hair liberation.

[5]   "Women have been denied so much for so long," pleaded an older woman with coils of white hair piled above her brow, "why deny any part of our femininity that makes us feel good?"

[6]   A striking blonde in a boy's polo shirt, obviously not wearing a bra, put it more succinctly. "I want to be liberated!" she bellowed over the hubbub. "But I'm not cutting my hair just because men like hair. When I make love, men play with my breasts and I'm sure as hell not cutting *them* off!"

[7]   And so the discussion went at the front lines of *another* revolution by women. Actually, they had begun their fight before any of

today's other insurrectionary groups—in 1848, to be precise—and had seemingly won it by the 1920s and made peace.

[8]   As a revolutionary act, it sounds laughable—but Louis XVI and Marie Antoinette laughed, too, and eventually lost their heads. Modern men who cherish their own heads, and their—you know what—had better pay attention. For, since 1966, a new insurgency known as the women's liberation movement (no capital letters; it's not an organization but a phenomenon) has rapidly gained strength and is now more powerful, revolutionary, morally justifiable—and, at times, more ridiculous—than any previous wave of feminist revolution.

[9]   The ridiculousness is thoroughly misleading. While snickering at the follies of the neofeminists, one is likely to underestimate both their seriousness of purpose and the legitimacy of many of their complaints. The women's liberation movement is unique. No other recent struggle for human rights has been so frivolous and yet so earnest, so absurd and yet so justified, so obsessed on the one hand with trivia and, on the other, with the radical restructuring of male-female relationships, of family life and of society itself. It is, in short, a study in contrasts. A few examples:

[10]   *Higher education:* Eight Temple University coeds insist on their right to take R.O.T.C. courses, and go hup-two-three-fouring alongside the boys, rifles on shoulders, in winter wind and sleet; 20 Berkeley girls demand that they be admitted to the karate class and invade the men's locker room—catching some occupants dripping wet —to make their point; on a number of campuses, extremist women variously strip to the buff in lecture rooms, shout dirty words at professors or speakers they consider male chauvinists or even bite, punch and kick some of the latter, to prove that women are not necessarily weak, timid and inferior.

[11]   But there is another side to all this: Such women, kookie though they may be, are the advance scouts of a vast, slow-moving army of females pressing forward into all aspects of college life and into the world for which it presumably trains people. Two and a half times as many girls go to college today as did 20 years ago, and they now make up over 40 percent of the college population—the highest proportion in our peacetime history. Increasingly, they go to college on equal terms: Yale, Princeton and other redoubts of male privilege have opened their doors to women.

[12]   *Equal opportunities:* In the landmark year of 1969, girl

jockeys ride in the races for the first time. *The New York Times,* pestered to death by demonstrators and lawyers from NOW (the National Organization for Women), stops listing help-wanted ads according to sex. Neofeminist women march upon Wall Street, carrying placards and shouting denunciatory slogans, because it allows so few women to function as brokers and only one to hold a seat on the New York Stock Exchange. And NOW president Betty Friedan and a handful of her pals picket the Plaza Hotel, where businessmen can lunch in the Oak Room away from the sight and sound of women.

[13]   Are you amused and contemptuous? All right, but don't overlook what lies behind these frivolities—a major drive by American women, the Labor Department and the Equal Employment Opportunity Commission to give women an even break in the job market. For it is not only blacks, Jews and other minorities who are discriminated against: In nearly every part of American industry, women are systematically given, and largely limited to, the lesser jobs. Thirty-one million women work—but a third of them are secretaries and clerical workers and over a fifth are service workers (waitresses, domestics and the like); only small numbers of male workers are in either category. Not surprisingly, the average yearly income of full-time female workers is about $4150, while that of full-time male workers is $7200; only three percent of the women make over $10,000, as compared with 23 percent of the men. Apologists for discriminatory hiring often say that the discrepancies in position and income are due to the lesser abilities and lesser work drive of women, and, to some extent, this may be true. Unquestionably, the lower female *average* yearly income reflects the fact that many women drop out of the work market for marriage before they have had the opportunity to climb to a respectable annual salary. But even when men and women do the same work, and equally well, women are given lesser titles and lower pay. Women full professors, for instance, earn about ten percent less than their male counterparts and women chemists earn a half less than male chemists.

[14]   *Feminine charm:* Busloads of feminists from a number of cities disembark outside Convention Hall in Atlantic City to protest the "degrading, mindless boob-girlie symbolism" of the Miss America contest and, more generally, the exploitation and oppression of women through "sexism." The demonstrators publicly remove and burn their bras, crown their own Miss America (a sheep) and fill a "freedom trash can" with instruments of sexist enslavement: steno pads, false

eyelashes, women's magazines and copies of PLAYBOY. Before an enthralled group of neofeminists in Boston, several members of Cell-16 demonstrate the karate blows and kicks designed to keep objectionable men in their place (crumpled on the ground?) and Abby Aldrich Rockefeller provides the *pièce de résistance* by breaking a board with her forehead as effectively as any man—well, actually, on the *second* try.

[15]   Sneer at all this, if you like—but don't deceive yourself that it's nothing but the exhibitionism of a handful of neurotics, uglies and dykes. For these women are martyrs of a new faith being propagated among the multitudes. Behind the few hundred extremists there are from 5000 to 10,000—no one knows the actual figure—vociferous but less extreme women who belong to all sorts of liberation groups; and behind these thousands are millions of nonjoiners whose moderate feminism is evident in their voting, their letters to Congressmen and to editors, their reading habits, their work lives, their sexual behavior, their marriages and divorces. Not many of these millions feel the feminist rage of which the radicals speak; not many advocate, as do some of the extremists, living in female communes and avoiding men except for sex or, better yet, doing without men altogether for long periods and relying on their own hands for relief. Not many seek, as do feminists from the New Left, the total overthrow of male-dominated, sexist, family-based, capitalist-militarist society. But all of them feel at least some of the frustrations, the conflicts, the contradictions endemic in the lives of modern women, and all of them would like things to be different.

[16]   How different? They don't agree; indeed, their opinions run the gamut from moderate amelioration (better jobs, abortion reform, more child-care centers for working mothers) to a total radicalism that calls for the abolition of marriage, the transfer of child rearing from the home to communal centers and the elimination of all sex differences in clothing, education, home life, politics and manners.

[17]   Why the new feminist revolution? Didn't women win their war long ago? Oberlin, originally a men's college, first admitted them way back in 1837 and other colleges followed suit over the years. Abolitionist and prohibitionist women held the first Women's Rights Convention in Seneca Falls, New York, in 1848. In the next several decades, a number of states liberalized their divorce laws (giving women greater leverage over husbands who mistreated them); and by

1900, most states had granted women the right to handle their own property, make contracts, bring suit and, in general, be persons (rather than childlike dependents) before the law. Women entered the labor force in ever-larger numbers, making their way into factories and business offices. By the Twenties, birth-control clinics were multiplying and women began to have the freedom to use their own bodies as they chose. And, finally, women got the vote. From then on, it seemed as if they were into everything, including free love, Bolshevism, flying nuclear physics, Congress and, during World War Two, aircraft assembly lines.

[18]   There was good reason for this long, slow, sweeping change. When America was still agricultural and mercantile, women had innumerable essential functions to perform. Granted that they worked like galley slaves, had no legal rights and lived in a totally male-run society; at least what they did was absolutely necessary and gave them a clear sense of importance and achievement. In 1778, one Christopher Marshall, a thrifty and prudent Philadelphian, wrote approvingly in his diary of his wife's activities, as follows:

> [19]   From early in the morning till late at night she is constantly employed in the affairs of the family. . . . This calls for her constant attendance at getting prepared in the kitchen, baking our own bread and pies, meat &c. [and] also on the table. Her cleanliness about the house, her attendance in the orchard, cutting and drying of apples . . . her seeing to all our washing done . . . add to this her making of 20 large cheeses, besides her sewing, knitting, &c.

[20]   Mrs. Marshall, it's safe to say, suffered no role conflicts; when would she have had time to think about such things?

[21]   But as America became industrial and urban, many of woman's functions were taken away from her. Factories, canneries, public schools and hospitals made her skills unnecessary (at least if her husband had some money) and left her to fill her leisure with romantic novels, tatting, gossip and attacks of the vapors. When electricity, household machinery and refrigeration became available, her relegation to the minor chores of homemaking was almost complete and her sense of devaluation increased.

[22]   No wonder more and more women began to hunger, as the 19th Century wore on, for legal rights, the vote and the chance to do some of those interesting things men did in the outside world. No

wonder girls who had discovered in college their own mental power could envision themselves as scholars, scientists and businesswomen and tried to make their visions real. No wonder women felt liberated when they achieved control of their fertility and were no longer committed to 20-odd years of successive pregnancies. No wonder they felt, when they finally won the vote in 1920, that they had opened the gates to the man's world. With this victory, the revolutionary fervor died away until, by World War Two, writings about "the woman question" had a quaint bygone flavor, like the faded picture books of a war fought before one's time.

[23]   But it was a false peace. Woman had won a kind of liberation—but not from her own biology nor from thousands of years of tradition. Except for a handful of hard-driving careerists and a small corps of daring bohemians, almost all American women wanted, more than anything else, to marry; compared with that, careers, sexual freedom and the right to seek public office all took a back seat. After World War Two, this traditional orientation was particularly strong; home life had been so threatened by the War that women were anxious to rebuild familism and to play house once again. More girls than ever went to college—but worked only briefly afterward, quitting their jobs when they married and settling into suburban domesticity and fecundity, only to find, within a few years, that they were bored, trapped by household and maternal duties and resentful of men, who, it seemed, had somehow tricked them into all this. They wanted to be wives and mothers and had their wish, but somehow it meant less than they had thought it would; besides, they wanted to be *people,* deal with adults, use their minds, be considered interesting, *"do* something." Worst of all, after a few years of marriage, they could begin to see the long decades stretching ahead, when their children would be slipping away from them into adolescence and adulthood and they themselves would be idle and useless for 30 or 40 years; by comparison, Mrs. Marshall's daily toil seemed exhilarating.

[24]   Meanwhile, post-War domesticity was allowing the gains of the feminist movement to evaporate. The earnings gap between men and women widened: In the mid-Fifties, full-time women workers averaged 64 percent as much as men; but by the late Sixties, they averaged only 58 percent as much. In 1969, women held 50 fewer seats in state legislatures than they had a decade earlier. In 1940, they held 45 percent of all professional and technical jobs; but in 1969,

only 37 percent, though over twice as many women were so employed. In higher education, they slipped from 26 percent of faculty positions in 1920 to 22 percent in 1964.

[25]   Odder yet, even in professions where they had seemed most likely to get ahead, they had not. They continued to make up the same small proportion of physicians (six to seven percent) that they had for half a century, achieved only token representation in politics (only ten women have served in the Senate in 50 years) and made virtually no inroads into upper-echelon business and industrial management in two decades after World War Two.

[26]   The time was out of joint and Betty Friedan, like Hamlet, was born to set it right. Mrs. Friedan, a discontented homemaker and part-time magazine writer, had her celebrated book, *The Feminine Mystique,* published in 1963, the message of which was that women had been sold a bill of goods, not just for the benefit of men but for that of American industry, which stood to profit by having them stay home and *consume.* Throughout the country, women heard her message—they bought over 1,500,000 copies of the hardcover and paperback editions—and began to gird for combat. Noting the restlessness of the natives, but partly as a joke, Representative Howard W. Smith of Virginia added "sex" to the Civil Rights Bill of 1964 that banned job discrimination on the basis of race, color, religion or national origin. Congress, chuckling, passed it—but women have had the last laugh: Some 7500 of the 44,000 complaints thus far filed with the Equal Employment Opportunity Commission created by the act have involved discrimination against women and have resulted in girl jockeys, over-32 airline stewardesses, desegregated help-wanted ads and at least one female steamship yeoman.

[27]   In 1966, Betty Friedan and other feminists formally organized NOW; since then, splinter groups and other women's liberation organizations have proliferated in every major city—50 in New York, 35 in San Francisco, 25 in Boston, and so on—some sporting aggressive names such as WITCH (Women's International Terrorist Conspiracy from Hell) and WOLF (Women's Liberation Front), while others are more blandly labeled (Redstockings, New Feminists, New Women). In 1966 and 1967, NOW seemed fierce and bristling, but some of the later groups have so greatly surpassed it in their activism and their extremism that today Mrs. Friedan looks a little like an Aunt Tabby, a sort of Roy Wilkins of feminism.

[28]   Among the small feminist contingents that take the hardest lines are those formed by disillusioned and embittered young women who had expected SDS and other politically radical groups to understand their problems but discovered, to their dismay, that men of the New Left intended to do all the planning and confronting and let the chicks fix food, type, sweep and provide sex. (Stokely Carmichael once said, "The only position for a woman in SNCC is prone"—presumably, he meant supine—while one of the New Left's leaders at Berkeley, hearing of feminist discontent in the ranks, crudely paraphrased Marie Antoinette, saying, "Let 'em eat cock.")

[29]   Today's radical neofeminists have also turned away from the contemporary sexual revolution, even though their predecessors at the turn of the century had linked the women's rights movement with contraception, free love and the female's right to orgasm. Radical feminists see the present fascination with sexuality as the oppressors' effort to imprison women by making them value themselves only as sexual objects, brainwashing them into seeking to please men and, thus, eventually trapping them in the housewife-mother role. Nudity, sexual freedom in print and on film, the emphasis on sexual pleasure, the preoccupation of advertising with beauty and sex appeal, all are considered links in the chains binding women to love and to men.

[30]   In their own words, taken from miscellaneous pamphlets of radical feminist groups published in Boston, New York and Chicago:

> [31]   If your appearance is pleasing, you are sunk, for no one will ever look beyond. . . . We reject the soft, sexy, slender, stylishly clothed body. . . . [Be] inoffensively plain, thoroughly nondescript. . . . Bright colors and materials are wonderful to have around, but do you really want to decorate your body with them? On your body they cry out, "Look at me, I'm swinging, I'm sexy, I'm female." . . . You have to be prepared to be not just unattractive but actually sexually repulsive to most men, perhaps including all the men you currently admire.

[32]   In two separate issues of the feminist journal *No More Fun and Games*, Dana Densmore shot down sex itself:

> [33]   [Sex is] inconvenient, time-consuming, energy-draining and irrelevant. . . . Guerrillas don't screw. They have important things to do, things that require all their energy. . . . Erotic energy is just life energy and is quickly worked off if you are doing interesting, absorbing things. . . . [If] genital tensions persist, you can still masturbate.

Isn't that a lot easier, anyway? This is not a call for celibacy but for an acceptance of celibacy as an alternative preferable to the degradation of most male-female sexual relationships.

[34]   Procreation fares no better. A memo from SDS women in *Women: A Journal of Liberation*: "We are the baby producers, the household slaves, who should be weak and dumb and can be successful only by being 'pretty.' . . . It's all jive, a lot of bullshit."

[35]   In effect, the rallying cry of Roxanne Dunbar of Cell-16 was "Up against the wall, Mother!": "We are damaged—we women, we oppressed, we disinherited. We have the right to hate and have contempt and to kill and to scream. . . . The family is what destroys people. Women take on a slave role in the family when they have children."

[36]   Her opinion was echoed by sociologist Marlene Dixon in *Ramparts*:

> [37]   The institution of marriage is the chief vehicle for the perpetuation of the oppression of women; it is through the role of wife that the subjugation of women is maintained. . . . The Sky-God tramples through the heavens and the Earth Mother-Goddess is always flat on her back with her legs spread, putting out for one and all.

[38]   One is tempted to dismiss such women too easily as frigid or Lesbian (a few of them look and sound it, most do not), dignifying their despair with the name of revolution; one is tempted to say, condescendingly (and probably incorrectly), that all they really need is to get soundly laid. In any event, either way of dismissing them is only an *ad hominem* attack (dare I say so? Or would they scream that it is *ad feminem?*). Roxanne Dunbar, with her monkish haircut, karate postures and vicious rhetoric, or Abby Rockefeller, with her bare calloused feet and battered forehead, may not be *your* kind of girls, nor any man's, but the basic attack on the "oppressors" and the arguments for the elimination of sex-role differences deserve to be judged on their own merits.

[39]   The central argument of the neofeminists is essentially a moral one: Man has always enslaved and oppressed woman, assigning better roles to himself and worse ones to her; and since it is immoral to treat equals this way, eliminating all male-female role differences should be the goal of every fair-minded person.

[40]   The morality is flawless, but the assumptions on which the

major premise rests are hopelessly faulty. For one thing, it is assumed that men have always divided the roles in the same fashion, assigning desirable ones to themselves and undesirable ones to women; for another, it is assumed that all role differences are assigned or chosen and could, therefore, be eliminated; for a third, it is taken for granted that the elimination of all role differences would make women happier.

[41] On the first point, there is a wealth of contrary evidence in the collected data concerning the hundreds of separate primitive societies, as well as the various civilizations, that human beings have constructed around the world. From the record it is clear that men have not invariably divided roles in the same way and that what constitutes a "desirable" or male role in one society may be a female role in another or an ambisexual role in a third.

[42] It *is* true that extremely few functions have universally or very generally belonged to one sex or the other: Some years ago, anthropologist George Murdock surveyed the available data on 224 primitive societies and found that warmaking was a male job in 100 percent of them, childbearing and suckling a female job in 100 percent, and that it was almost always men who performed the far-ranging, strenuous, risky tasks, while women very generally had the more sedentary and nurturant tasks. Nor is that surprising: This much of the division of labor is a natural consequence of the physical differences between men and women, at least in cultures where human energy, rather than mechanical, is the chief way of getting things done.

[43] But beyond these generalizations, the assignment of male and female roles is far from uniform and the data belie the paranoid picture the feminists paint of human history. Trading or bartering, for instance, is most often a male job—but in 18 percent of Murdock's societies, women also participated in it, and in 13 percent, it was exclusively a female role. Food gathering was a male role in almost all hunting societies, but in agricultural societies, it was as often a woman's job as a man's. Pottery making, weaving and working with hides were quite often assigned to women, but in nearly a quarter of the societies, they were assigned only to men. Various household tasks were female work in most societies but were shared by men in about a tenth—and were wholly male functions in slightly more than that. Cooking, curiously enough, was exclusively a male function in nine percent of the cultures studied. Most important is the fact that for nearly every role, there were some cultures in which it was masculine, others in which it was feminine and some in which it was assigned to both sexes.

[44]   Apart from the qualities expressed in work, many of the personal traits we think of as female—especially those the feminists say have been thrust upon the exploited female by the oppressing male—have been male traits in at least some groups, and vice versa. In certain Philippine tribes, men have been the gossips, women the solid, sensible citizens; in various South Sea Island cultures, men have spent nearly all their time in artistic work or in debate, leaving women to do all the life-supporting work and to make all the daily decisions.

[45]   Nor is this diversity of role allotment peculiar to primitive societies. Even within our own Western civilization, there has been a broad spectrum of conceptions of the masculine and feminine natures and of their proper functions. It is quite true that much of the time these have been divided along the lines of which feminists complain—but not all of the time. In the Third and Second centuries B.C., for instance, Roman women were sturdy, tough, puritanical and business-like—and had to be, for their farmer-warrior husbands were off conquering Europe, leaving things in their wive's hands. In the Renaissance, there appears the virago (at that time, term of approbation)—a woman equal to man in her intelligence, abilities and interests: 17th Century biographer John Aubrey, describing a 16th Century virago, wrote of her, "Prodigious parts for a woman. I have heard my father's mother say that she had Chaucer at her fingers' ends. A great politician; great wit and spirit, but revengeful. Knew how to manage her estate as well as any man; understood jewels as well as any jeweler." Men, meanwhile, had new options: They could be indifferent with the sword but skillful with the pen, the crucible and retort, the brush and canvas, and still be considered manly men and lovers of women.

[46]   In the 18th Century, a male courtier could wear lace, perfume and long curls, walk with an affected sway, lisp charmingly—and be a hellion with his sword and a stud with his penis. A court lady could be a simpering confection of taffeta, high-piled hair and coy mannerisms —while secretly intriguing with her lover, openly debating intellectual issues in some fashionable salon and swaying her husband's political opinions through subtle domestic tyrannies. But in the 19th Century, the ideal middle-class woman was gentle, pure, maternal and stupid, her ideal male being strong, pure, manly and wise. In Tennyson's immortal picture of the happy couple:

> Her faith is fixt and cannot move,
> She darkly feels him great and wise,

She dwells on him with faithful eyes,
"I cannot understand; I love."

[46]   Even in the relatively short history of our own country, we have had not one but several notions of the masculine roles and of the feminine ones: Our pioneer women and their sodbusting husbands dealt with each other and with the world around them in quite different fashion from the Brahmin gentlemen and ladies of Boston, and they, in turn, from men and women in the socialist movement, in the Bible belt and in the free-love movement. As models of manliness, we have had everything from Daniel Boone to Cary Grant; as models of womanliness, everything from Dolly Madison to Raquel Welch.

[48]   Human beings have tried out a very wide range of definitions of the masculine and feminine roles. The experiments have not worked out equally well, but they have shown that all sorts of variations are possible and that the feminist doctrine—that man has always made woman his slave, sexual toy and brood mare, and granted himself the position of overlord, philosopher and stallion—is a gross distortion of human history.

[49]   Yet one must grant that in Western civilization, the balance has been tipped to one side. Despite the many variations, men have always been the warriors (Joan of Arc was a notable exception) and women the homemakers; men have generally been the rulers of society, women the rulers of the home; men have, for the most part, been the educated, the inventive, the active, the logical ones, and women the ignorant, the tradition-bound, the passive, the emotional ones. What we need to know, then, is this: Is there any biological justification for this tendency? Have the societies that deviated from it—and those eras in our own civilization in which the roles were reshuffled—been mistakes in social evolution that violated innate characteristics of male and female?

[50]   First of all, it's obvious that in all societies and eras in which greater skeletal strength, muscle power, lung capacity and stature have had survival value in fighting, food getting and other strenuous tasks, man has been by nature better equipped than woman to perform such tasks. A few of today's radical neofeminists assert that the physical differences between men and women (aside from the shape of sexual parts and hair distribution) are the product of dissimilar rearing: If girls were allowed to develop themselves in the ways boys do, they would be just as strong. This is utter nonsense. At no time and place—not

even when children have done exactly the same things—have males and females been equal in size and strength. Men always average out taller, about 50 to 60 percent stronger in muscle power, heavier boned and with heavier knobs on the ends of their long bones (to bear the greater strain of their more powerful musculature), bigger of rib cage and lung. In every society but ours—the only one in which mechanical energy vastly outstrips human muscle power—the physical differences between the sexes are important determinants of certain role allocations. And these physical differences are dictated by the chromosomes, the master chemical templates in every cell of the human being.

[51]   Even in our own society, these differences are important—not in terms of survival but in determining our psychological make-up. Little girls and little boys cannot help perceiving that boys can outrun and overpower girls, throw stones farther and hit harder—and these inevitable experiences mold their thinking about themselves. Some part of that thinking is realistic and sensible: Even in a mechanically powered society, it's true that a man can generally lift heavy burdens, carry a sleeping child and defend himself and his family against attackers better than his mate can. If this does not make man innately better than woman at operating powerful machinery, directing a steel company or running the Department of Defense, at least it so conditions men's and women's feelings about themselves that they think and act as if size and muscular strength were crucial. They may not be, but they are significant: Even if a man never raises his hand to his wife, he and she are both forever aware that he is the more powerful of the two and, in almost all cases, could win a pitched battle between them. Beneath the civilized veneer, there resides still the animal reality of our bodies and emotions.

[52]   Which is no great matter, as long as it does not impair other functions. Unfortunately, it often does—most notably, the working of intelligence. The intellectual powers of men and women, though not identical, are very similar—or would be if each were not misled by traditional prejudices. For thousands of years, most men have believed women to be mentally inferior; as Lord Chesterfield succinctly put it, "Women, then, are only children of a larger growth. . . . For solid, reasoning, good sense, I never knew in my life one that had it." But during most of these thousands of years, very few women were educated at all; and even when they were, they were taught that it was not in their natures to understand weighty matters and that they were inherently illogical and impractical.

[53]   In modern times, boys and girls are educated together and similarly; we can, therefore, put the traditional belief to the test. And we have: I.Q. testing has consistently shown girls and boys to have virtually the same average intelligence. There are minor differences, to be sure: Boys average slightly higher in such areas as mathematical reasoning, spatial perception and mechanical aptitude, while girls average slightly higher in such areas as vocabulary, verbal fluency and memory. But the differences are so small that many females have higher mechanical-aptitude scores than the average male, while many males have higher verbal-fluency scores than the average female. In any case, the average composite scores are almost identical.

[54]   Yet in ordinary life we continually experience seeming differences; try explaining to your favorite female how much you actually save when you deduct a business expense. But most of the difference in everyday intelligence is the result of our growing up in a society in which, as boys and girls, we are continually told that men are logical and women illogical and that certain kinds of problems are a man's business, others, a woman's. Girls do poorly at logical thinking when the content of the problem is culturally masculine and better when the content is culturally feminine. Based on many pieces of evidence, research psychologists have concluded that the sexual difference in reasoning ability is very small but that culture makes boys and girls suppose the difference to be large and act accordingly. Men think better because they think they can; women don't think as well because they think they can't.

[55]   In one interesting test of women's low opinion of their own intellectual powers, a team of psychologists at Connecticut College asked two groups of college girls to evaluate a series of articles on various subjects. One group of girls received the articles in booklet form, bearing male by-lines, such as John T. McKay; the other group got the same articles with female by-lines, such as Joan T. McKay. In every case, the girls reading male authors rated the articles higher than did the girls reading the same articles by female authors. Conclusion: Women are prejudiced against women.

[56]   In much the same way, it is clearly demonstrable that many of the differences between male and female personalities are learned rather than inherent and are cultural cliches rather than innate characteristics. The classic test of masculinity and femininity, created by two psychologists and called the M-F test, asks many questions about preferences in food, jobs, amusements, and so on, and assigns each answer a

certain number of points on an M-F scale, based on traditional male and female tastes. But such tastes are highly modifiable by experience: The more educated a man is, for instance, the less "masculine" is his total score, and the more educated a woman, the less "feminine" is hers.

[57]   Moreover, it has become increasingly clear in the past generation that Freud's theory of feminine psychology—on which he based his highly conservative ideas as to the proper roles for men and women in marriage and in society—was shaped by the manners and morals of the 19th Century middle-class world in which he grew up, and has little validity today. Freud sought to explain the origins of the demureness, emotionality and passivity he saw in middle-class European woman as she was at the turn of the century. He decided that the determining factor had to be her realization that nature had failed to provide her with the admirable external parts boys possess. As a result, she felt inferior, ashamed, imperfect—and adjusted to her condition by assuming a passive and submissive role in life and by emphasizing her beauty rather than her abilities. All this, Freud felt, was inevitable and therefore natural. The normal woman turned to dependency and domesticity, while the woman who sought a career was suffering from a masculinity complex and the hostile or vengeful wife was exhibiting penis envy.

[58]   A good deal of writing about female psychology has been based on this formulation and, even today, it plays a major part in the thinking of many analysts. But three or more decades ago, Karen Horney and other psychoanalysts with a more sociological outlook than Freud's began to challenge his ideas about women; and when some of them looked at woman's personality in other societies, it became clear that she was not always as Freud had seen her. In many times and places, woman has not been in the least ashamed of her lack of a penis nor forced to compensate by being pretty but dumb, sexy but helpless. Indeed, in some times and places, it's been man who was indolent and vain—even though perfectly well equipped with a male member.

[59]   Nevertheless, even if a woman's personality is in large part formed by the culture in which she grows up and if Freud's penis-envy theory applies only to women in certain times and places, it is undeniable that women have some universal tendencies differentiating them from men and that these must be due to innate biological factors.

[60]   Some differences in behavior appear in infants long before they can perceive what is expected of each sex in their society. Dr.

Howard Moss, a National Institute of Mental Health psychologist, has observed three-week-old and three-month-old infants for as much as eight hours at a time and has noted that they display striking differences: Boys sleep less, cry more, demand more attention, and so on; in short, says Dr. Moss, "Much more is happening with the male infants." Dr. Benjamin Spock points out in his new book, *Decent and Indecent*, that by the end of the first year, boys are more restless, inquisitive and striving, more interested in handling things, more fractious than girls. Girls are more compliant, quieter, can be toilet trained earlier. And these characteristics appear even in an only child, who has no models to ape. By the school years, says Dr. Stanley Yolles, director of the National Institute of Mental Health, boys are more likely to stutter, to have reading problems and to lag behind girls in their physical maturation; when they enter school, for instance, their hand muscles are markedly less mature than those of girls. Those unlearned differences can only be innate—the result of dissimilar chromosomal complements that make for different internal chemistry and, hence, for different development of the body and of the nervous system.

[61]   Dr. John Money of Johns Hopkins University has studied chromosomal abnormalities in children and found that where there is an extra female chromosome, there is a strong tendency in the young child toward maternalism and doll play; while in men with an extra male chromosome, there is a strong tendency toward aggressiveness.

[62]   There is, accordingly, at least a basic substratum of inherent masculinity and inherent femininity. Moreover, the very fact that we grow up in different bodies gives us different experiences, and these inevitably shape part of our personalities and behavior. Even if women do not necessarily feel penis envy, the existence of breasts makes a difference, even before they are suckled; the experience of ejaculation makes a difference, even when no child is conceived; the monthly experience of the menses, with its mood swings, the loss of blood and the reassuring return to normality, makes a difference; the omnipresent knowledge that, for all his power, man dies younger than woman makes a difference; in the sex act, the woman's need to allow entry of her body and the man's need to be firm, intrusive and bold make a difference; the contrast between the man's brief, careless throwing out of semen and the woman's long, careful harboring of the infant within herself makes a difference.

[63]   Thus our biological differences, and the experiences they commit us to, make for an inevitable core of masculinity and femininity

that is present in all cultures. Indeed, we can make a distinction between two categories of male and female roles: the *socially prescribed* (the fashions, prejudices and customs concerning masculinity and femininity) and the *psychobiologically determined* (the inherent and the developmental).

[64]   When we say that man is logical and woman illogical, man creative and woman fit only for routine chores, man decisive and woman vacillating, we are speaking of traits that are socially prescribed and no more central to masculinity and femininity than styles of hairdress or clothing. Most forms of work, many forms of leisure activity, most styles of dress and ornament are considered masculine by some societies but feminine by others. To the people in any one society, however, their own mores and tastes seem to be timeless, natural and right —so much so that they attribute them to their own gods and make them divine edicts: "In sorrow thou shalt bring forth children; and thy desire shall be to thy husband, and he shall rule over thee. And unto Adam He said, Because thou hast hearkened unto the voice of thy wife, and hast eaten of the tree . . . cursed is the ground for thy sake. . . . In the sweat of thy face shalt thou eat bread."

[65]   The psychobiologically determined roles, on the other hand, stem from innate differences in genetic make-up and their hormonal, neurological and structural consequences. Even in a civilized, power-energy society, men will do the heavy work, protect the women they love and sometimes beat them when angry. The sexual relationship will inevitably call for a degree of aggressiveness on the part of the male and a degree of acquiescence on the part of the female. The female's body, within which the child grows and from which, after birth, he is nourished, is better equipped, in many ways, to be tender, sensitive and responsive to the child's needs. (In an experiment performed at the animal-behavior laboratories at Rutgers University, psychologists put newborn rat pups in with virgin females and with males; after enough times with them, the virgin females and even the males began to show mothering behavior—licking, retrieving, covering—but the virgin females did so much sooner than the males. Since experience of motherhood played no part, one can only conclude that the females were neurologically more sensitive than the males to the stimuli provided by the pups.)

[66]   "Male and female created He them"—and no matter what variations human beings play on the theme of masculinity and femininity, no matter how men and women share or trade their roles, there

remains an underlying maleness and femaleness in us, as in all other animals. And those fundamental and irreducible differences between male and female are the core of a reproductive system so advantageous to the species and so gratifying to most individuals within it that we can only suppose it to be the happiest accident of the evolutionary process.

[67]   This, however, is just what the extremist wing of neofeminism denies.

[68]   The less strident, relatively reasonable neofeminists concentrate their fire on the socially determined roles: They want to erase differences between men and women in employment, politics and the law. Other than that, they want to de-emphasize or modify—but not wipe out—the differences between men and women in dress and personal adornment, manners, sexual initiative and the allocation of homemaking and parental duties.

[69]   But the fiery evangelists and raging nihilists of neofeminism want to wipe out *all* role differences—not just the socially prescribed but the psychobiologically determined as well. (They would not, however, recognize this distinction; to them, all role differences have been the arbitrary choices of the enslaving male oppressors.) As a result, they offer women (and men) some of the worst advice since the celibate Paul wrote to the Corinthians: "I say therefore to the unmarried and widows, It is good for them if they abide even as I." Their fight includes an all-out assault upon purely visual differences—the clothing, hair styles and make-up that distinguish the sexes, serve as cues to sexual interaction and, according to the radicals, maintain the enslavement of women. In part, their adoption of male dress permits self-defense and attack: "Narrow skirts and high heels were *designed* to prevent you from kicking [men]," says Abby Rockefeller. "Our recommendation is obvious." Abby herself wears denim work shirts and pants; so, presumably, will every sensible, equality-minded woman.

[70]   This rejection of distinctly feminine clothing and of the pursuit of beauty is supposed to free women from squandering their time and energy pleasing (and, thus, being subservient to) men. But as one listens to the extremists, it becomes clear that they are after bigger game —the withering away of heterosexual desire and heterosexual intercourse. Without the many subtle cues and incitements men and women offer each other through clothing and behavior, sexuality could dwindle to a relatively minor part of life; history offers a few examples of ascetic

and antisexual movements (such as the Albigenses from 11th to 13th Century France) that achieved just that. Roxanne Dunbar—termed by Marlene Dixon "one of the most impressive women in the movement"—envisions a future in which heterosexual intercourse would be unnecessary and undersirable: "Perhaps sex, as we conceive of it as 'fucking,' is doomed to die as property and power relations are changed. As for affection, we have quite enjoyable universal habits which include verbal and physical contact, which do not lead to genital intercourse, e.g., female relationships, adult and child, childhood relationships."

[71]   Nor is this antisexual future seen as any great deprivation, for it turns out that male-female sex is not only often degrading but physically unsatisfactory, as compared with other possibilities. Writes Anne Koedt, of the October 17th Movement, in *The Myth of the Vaginal Orgasm*:

> [72]   The position of the penis inside the vagina . . . does not usually stimulate an orgasm in women because the clitoris is not usually located there but, rather, externally and higher up. . . . Lesbian sexuality, in rubbing one clitoris against the other, could make an excellent case, based on anatomical data, for the extinction of the male organ. . . . It forces us to discard many "physical" arguments explaining why women go to bed with men. What is left, it seems to me, are psychological reasons why women select men [to] the exclusion of other women.

[73]   Weak-willed revolutionaries may find it difficult to live up to these austere principles if they mingle with men; it may be necessary, therefore, for them to isolate themselves from men as much as possible, even as black militants today have rejected social integration with whites. Betsy Warrior, as one Boston militant renamed herself, explains it all in *No More Fun and Games*:

> [74]   Sooner or later, if we are effective, men will become hostile. We have to be prepared to accept this fact. Not only accept it but segregate ourselves from men in many situations, to allow ourselves freedom from their criticism, opinions and dominance. . . . As long as we are entangled in personal relationships and group situations with men, we won't be able to clearly analyze our positions and will have a vested interest in not making males too hostile.

[75]   This is to be not just a temporary expedient but a new way of life. According to Ti-Grace Atkinson, a leader of the Feminists (a "Poli-

tical Organization to Annihilate Sex Roles"), marriage, at long last, is
to be destroyed, in order to set woman free:

> [76]   The institution of marriage has the same effect the institu-
> tion of slavery had. It separates people in the same category, disperses
> them, keeps them from identifying as a class. . . . To say that a woman
> is really "happy" with her home and kids is as irrelevant as saying
> that the blacks were "happy" being taken care of by Ol' Massa.

[77]   Judith Brown, in *Toward a Female Liberation Movement*,
agrees totally:

> [78]   The marriage institution, like so many others, is an an-
> achronism. . . . The married woman knows that love is, at its best, an
> inadequate reward for her unnecessary and bizarre heritage of op-
> pression. . . . She is locked into a relationship which is oppressive
> politically, exhausting physically, stereotyped emotionally and sexually
> and atrophying intellectually.

[79]   There may be some women, of course, who want to have children (the species, after all, ought not to be allowed to die out), but offspring must not be reared at home, according to the extremists, or
woman remains trapped. Says Miss Atkinson: "Children would be
raised communally; it's just not honest to talk about freedom for women
unless you get the child rearing off their backs."

[80]   But what are those who see the light only after they have acquired husbands and children to do? One answer is to change the husband's outlook and, meanwhile, find a way to get the rearing of the children done by others. A simpler answer is to ditch them—to pack one's
bag and leave husband and children, as that impressive figure Roxanne
Dunbar herself did.

[81]   It is not easy to envision society as it would be if reshaped by
the extreme neofeminists; perhaps ant or bee colonies, which consist
chiefly of sexually neutral workers, come closest to it. Given what we
know about artificial insemination and what we are rapidly learning
about parthenogenesis (fertilization of the egg without the use of
sperm), and given the possibility of state-operated child-rearing facili-
ties on a national scale in order to make family life unnecessary, such a
society might be possible. And life in it might be fulfilling and happy
for the likes of Betsy Warrior, Roxanne Dunbar and Ti-Grace Atkinson. But they are unusual women; for most others, and for nearly all
men, such a way of life might seem the worst deprivation ever visited
upon mankind.

[82]   Neofeminists are forever likening the oppression of woman to the oppression of the Negro and asserting that just as equality is both possible and desirable for the races, so it is now for the sexes. But the analogy is misleading. As far as we know, whites and blacks do not have innate biological differences of such an order as to commit them to specific and dissimilar roles in education, employment ,politics or leisure activities. Men and women, on the other hand, can eliminate all role differences only by ignoring and suppressing a vital part of their inherent natures and by accepting the frustration that results from unmet needs and unfulfilled desires.

[83]   Sex differences, as manifested in our looks, our personalities, our behavior toward each other and our division of roles within the home and without, are deeply gratifying to male and female alike. It is complementarity—the fitting together of two beings who serve and complete each other—that makes heterosexual love, both physical and emotional, so necessary and so fulfilling. And it's the central mechanism at work in heterosexual love, in which it's made doubly powerful by the complementarity of our sexual parts and biological traits and the psychological differences they produce.

[84]   The sexual and stylistic differences that attract men and women to each other ought not, therefore, be minimized; indeed, they should be emphasized, within reasonable limits. They delight us and are actually good for us. As Dr. Spock points out, psychosexual differences do not impoverish either sex but enrich both; male and female are more valuable and more pleasing to each other if they have somewhat specialized traits and somewhat specialized roles to play for each other's benefit—gifts of function, so to speak, that they can give each other.

[85]   It feels good, and is productive of well-being, for man and woman to look different, smell different, act somewhat different. Though fashions change, the changes are unimportant as long as sexual distinctions remain, offering clues, reassurances and incitements about each sex to the other. The unisex fad is dangerous and hurtful, or would be if it were to last; Rudi Gernreich, ardently promoting identical clothing and identically shaved heads for both sexes, ought to be declared a public enemy. It feels good, and is productive of well-being, for man and woman to play special roles for each other. It comforts and pleases a woman—not just the clinging-vine type but almost any woman—to have a man be strong, gallant and protective, at times; it

pleases and gratifies a man—not just the old-style patriarch but almost any man—to have a woman sometimes fuss over him, take special pains to make him comfortable and make herself beautiful for his sake. It pleases most women to have a man be romantic before going to bed but a stallion in it; it pleases most men to have a woman be a wildcat in bed but demurely seductive beforehand.

[86] It feels good, and is productive of well-being, for husbands and wives to specialize in some of the functions they perform within marriage, to take care of each other in particular ways, to handle certain duties for the two of them, so that they are not just two of a kind but a team, equal not in the sense of identical but equal in the sense of equivalent. The *Kreutzer Sonata* requires a pianist and a violinist, playing together—not two interchangeable performers but two different ones, both of them essential.

[87] On the other hand, it's perfectly clear that most of the sex-based allocations of work by our 18th and 19th Century forebears are not only unnecessary today but highly undersirable. Woman is not needed as a producer of goods in the home, but she's needed elsewhere —and is quite capable of performing nearly all the kinds of work men do in contemporary society. As long as she's childless, there's no reason she should not do so and on equal terms with men.

[88] To be sure, biology will still set a few limits upon her; heavy labor remains more suitable for men; they may more often prove qualified for mechanical occupations; and it might not be the best thing to have a Boeing 747, circling in the overcast, piloted by a woman during her premenstrual period. By and large, however, most of the world's work can be performed by either sex, and the principal differentiations should be only questions of specialization within a field. In medicine, for instance, men may make better surgeons because of their mechanical and spatial aptitudes, while women may make better psychiatrists because of their verbal ability and empathic capacity; in business, men may make tougher bargainers, women better administrators and handlers of personnel.

[89] And women do want to work—not to the exclusion of love, sex, marriage and motherhood but as part of a total way of life involving all those things. In fact, a reaction to the excessive post-War domesticity had begun even before the women's liberation movement got started. Sociologist Jessie Bernard points out that five years before Betty Friedan published her call to arms, women were beginning to delay

marriage, return to college, take graduate work, cut down on their pregnancies and hold jobs in ever-larger numbers (a third more women were
in the work force in 1969 than in 1959).

[90]   It remains true, unhappily, that they get the lesser jobs and the
lower pay and that this is, in part, due to male prejudice and exploitation. But only in part. Most of the women who use their talents and
training in a career do not give this top priority in their scheme of
things or do so only for a short time; they assign a higher priority to marriage (or, more accurately, love and marriage) and to motherhood.
They do not view marriage and career as alternatives nor as mutually
exclusive; on the contrary, every recent study of the plans of high school
and college girls indicates that they expect to be able to work out a
combination of the two—a combination in which marriage and motherhood will take precedence over career, the latter being started, stopped,
restarted or modified as need be.

[91]   While they are still in school, it may not be clear to them that
this will often seem unfair, be somewhat frustrating and make them
resentful of men. Soon enough, however, they discover that in order to
obey the desires of their bodies and emotions, they have to settle for
second-rate careers—interrupting them, sometimes for many years, in
order to bear their children and raise them at least as far as the grade
school level and, in any case, dividing their energy and attention between work and home in a way men almost never have to. The result
is considerable satisfaction—plus the exasperation of seeing themselves
fail to achieve the level of recognition and income they certainly could
have attained had they been men. Yet even if unfair and far from ideal,
this scheme is more satisfying and more workable than the existing
alternatives. Consider them:

[92]   One consists of having a full-time career, plus home and
family—the home and family being attended to by paid help. But it is
an extremely expensive answer, possible only for the women making a
good deal of money. And it may be deeply disappointing, for there is
little emotional reward in merely *having* children; the rewards come
from living with them, nourishing and shaping them.

[93]   Another alternative consists of the state's operating vast child-
care centers, in the Russian fashion or even in the manner of the Israeli
pioneer communities (*kibbutzim*), where parents visit their children
only a couple of hours a day. Either method solves the problems of
cost and scarcity of suitable help; neither, however, yields the rewards
that come from raising one's own children—indeed, these collective sys-

tems are much more detached and nonfamilial than the use of full-time help at home. They have succeeded thus far in social systems in which the need for woman's labor power is so great that personal fulfillments, such as those of family life, are considered secondary in importance. But within the American economy and culture, it seems most unlikely that the majority of women would prefer to have their children raised by others.

[94]   A third possibility consists of having husband and wife share equally in all things—each one forgoing career advancement in order to spend part of the day at home, doing household chores and tending the children. This is advocated by some neofeminists, but it is a botched answer. It greatly multiplies all sorts of practical problems (there aren't that many opportunities in the labor market for jobs that fit home-making hours); more important, it omits two essential aspects of all successful human groups—specialization of function and a system of leadership. When there is no specialization of function, there is in-efficient performance and endless decision making every day, about who is going to do what. When there is no leadership, every minor mat-ter has to be taken up as if in committee, debated and voted upon.

[95]   It fits naturally into the biology of woman's life that she play a set of roles within the family different from those played by her hus-band. When husband and wife decide to have a child, biology deter-mines which of them will have it and will be the more deeply changed by the experience. Because it is the woman whose work life is inter-rupted by pregnancy and childbirth, and whose nervous system and chemistry react more immediately and nurturantly to the infant, it's only reasonable that she become, at least for a while, the principal homemaker and child rearer; it's only reasonable that her husband provide, at least for a while, the principal support of the family.

[96]   And from this division of labor comes the second feature of successful group life—the system of leadership: In most marriages, it's logical that the husband become the head of the family, at least in eco-nomic and related areas, while the wife would make decisions in areas directly within her daily purview. This is not enslavement but democ-racy: They do discuss issues, they do have separate areas of control, but they have machinery for making everyday decisions easily and for getting work done efficiently. Psychiatrist Nathaniel Lehrman likens such a family to a tiny demoncracy; the husband is not a dictator but a president; the wife is not a slave but the speaker of the legislature. And although the man is the head, he owes much to his wife's man-

agerial support. A woman said it best: Senator Maurine Neuberger, addressing a conference on working women, commented wryly, "My greatest single need, as a Senator, is for a good 'wife.' "

[97]   Thus, for American woman today and in the foreseeable future, the most workable answer—the scheme of life that most nearly fits her own needs and those of the American man—is a combination of marriage and career in which she accepts a secondary part in the world of work and achievement in order to have a primary part in the world of love and the home. This basic choice establishes the fundamental relationship of husband and wife in the economic sphere and, thereby, in many other areas of their marriage; and all this harmonizes with the inherent biological differences between male and female. As an answer, it's unfair to women in the sense that it grants them less than they might desire in one area of life; the alternatives grant them more in that area but at a cost most women—and their men—refuse to pay.

[98]   The eradication of all sex-role differences would be disastrous for mankind, but we need hardly fear that it will come to be; nothing as joyless and contrary to our instincts is likely to become the pattern of the majority. There have always been women who found sex, marriage or both intolerable and who sought to make others find them so, too. Today, they are more vocal than ever and, in part, because they are advancing the cause of normal women as well as their own, they have captured the attention of a vast audience. In the end, however, it isn't their way that will triumph.

[99]   "We mean treason!" trumpeted one incendiary feminist. "We mean seccession, and on a thousand times greater scale than was that of the South. We are plotting revolution!" Her name was Victoria Claflin Woodhull and she has been almost wholly forgotten; she uttered these words a century ago, but, instead of revolution, there came evolution. Masculinity, femininity, heterosexual love, marriage and motherhood are still very much alive and are likely to be so many years hence, when Ti-Grace Atkinson, Roxanne Dunbar and Betsy Warrior have joined Victoria Claflin Woodhull in the discard pile of history.

STUDY AND DISCUSSION

Vocabulary
This essay is a rather involved one that covers much of the ground underneath today's social sciences. If you are not familiar with all the words and

concepts herein, don't despair: dictionaries were made for just such plights. Consult yours whenever necessary. It will do you no harm.

1. plaintively (para. 3)
2. phenomenon (para. 8)
3. redoubts (para. 11)
4. denunciatory (para. 12)
5. frivolities (para. 13)
6. *pièce de résistance* (para. 14)
7. vociferous (para. 15)
8. endemic (para. 15)
9. relegation (para. 21)
10. to gird (para. 26)
11. supine (para. 28)
12. *ad hominem* (para. 38)
13. ambisexual (para. 41)
14. nurturant (para. 42)
15. to belie (para. 43)
16. paranoid (para. 43)
17. role allotment (para. 45)
18. virago (para. 45)
19. crucible (para. 45)
20. hellion (para. 46)
21. innately (para. 51)
22. pitched battle (para. 51)
23. impair (para. 52)
24. validity (para. 57)
25. fractious (para. 60)
26. vacillating (para. 64)
27. mores (para. 64)
28. acquiescence (para. 65)
29. stimuli (para. 65) [cf. "stimulus"]
31. strident (para. 68)
32. ascetic (para. 70)
33. vested interest (para. 74)
34. anachronism (para. 78)
35. atrophying (para. 78)
36. complementarity (para. 83)
37. patriarch (para. 85)
38. empathic (para. 88)
39. purview (para. 96)

Rhetoric

1. What does this title of this essay tell you about its theme? Are titles generally important in expository writing? Why?
2. What roles do paras. 7, 8, 9, 10, 11, 12, 13, and 17 play in the overall structure of the essay?
3. Does Hunt anywhere in this essay make use of "loaded language"? If so, find examples.
4. What rhetorical techniques does Morton Hunt use in paras. 24, 25, and 26?
5. Is para. 39 necessary to this essay? Why? What would happen to Hunt's argument if it were not included, or if it were cut? Could paras. 40 and 41 exist without it?
6. In para. 61, Hunt cites Dr. John Money of Johns Hopkins University and his studies of chromosomal *abnormalities* in children. In the following paragraph, Hunt concludes—largely on the basis of Dr. Money's study of *ab*normalities—that "there is, accordingly, at least a basic substratum of inherent masculinity and inherent feminity." Is he, in your opinion, justified in making this claim about us all?

7. This is the single longest essay included in these readings. It has a definite rhythm—can you discern it? How, in other words, does Morton Hunt marshal his arguments and turn them into a single theme? Consider paras. 9, 11 and 15; 38, 39 and 40; 49 and 59 in particular.

Content

1. In para. 21, to what does Morton Hunt ascribe woman's "devaluation"?
2. Why do radical women see the present (and Hunt would maintain past and future) fascination with sex as "links in the chain binding women to love and to men"?
3. In para. 38, Hunt states that we must judge the neofeminist argument on its own merits; in para. 43, he then talks about "the paranoid picture the feminists paint of human history." What do you think he really feels about the neo-feminist movement?
4. What is the conclusion Hunt draws from the anthropological data collected by George Murdock in paras. 42, 43 and 44?
5. What notions of ideal masculine and feminine roles does Hunt say have prevailed in "the relatively short history of our country" (para. 47)?
6. What have the results of the research psychologists shown regarding sexual differences in reasoning ability (paras. 54 and 55)?
7. What distinction does Hunt draw between the socially prescribed and the psychobiologically determined roles of masculine and feminine behavior?
8. Why does Hunt say that the analogy between the plights of oppressed women and Blacks in this society is misleading? Is he right, do you think?

Ideas and Implications

1. Judging by this article and the essay by Marya Mannes entitled "Who Am I," do you believe that it is better for a writer to be emotionally engaged in or coolly detached from his subject? How do both Mannes and Hunt differ in tone from George Orwell? (To answer this question, select any one of the three Orwell essays included in this book.)
2. In your opinion, is Morton Hunt correct when he writes that the women of Cell-16 and NOW are "martyrs of a new faith" (para. 15)?
3. Roxanne Dunbar, a Women's Lib militant, says that "the family is what destroys people" (para. 35). Hunt mentions her later on in this essay— do you recall in what context? What does he reveal about her that lets you know his opinion of her? Do you agree with Roxanne Dunbar— would you have rather been raised in a state-run institution or a *kibbutz* than in your own home? Why/Why not?
4. Do women have any justifiable grievances in 1972 America? If so, what are they?

5. Some male chauvinist wit once referred to the entire neo-feminist or Women's Liberation movement as "a tempest in a C-cup"—in your opinion, are these women kicking up too much of a fuss?

6. Can any male take the issue of Women's Liberation to heart? By implication: can anyone not personally involved in an injustice really feel strongly about it? Do you, for instance, accept unquestioningly the motives and/or the sincerity of a Caucasian who is "deeply involved" with American Indian attempts to gain some parity in this society or who is committed to the Black struggle?

7. Do you agree with the author when he writes in para. 83 that "sex differences . . . are deeply gratifying to male and female alike?"

WHAT IT WOULD BE LIKE
IF WOMEN WON

GLORIA STEINEM   What distinguishes the following essay from any you have read so far is its purpose: it is an unabashed piece of utopian prose. Gloria Steinem, a staff writer for New York *magazine, is deeply involved in and committed to Women's Liberation. Throughout this essay, she is trying to present her cause in its most favorable light. More than any other writer you have yet been exposed to in this book, she is out to persuade. Therefore, you will not see her devoting a great deal of time and space to delving into the socio-political, historico-economic reasons behind the Movement; rather, she is going to base the tenor of her argument on what she feels are the most positive aspects of Women's Lib.*

We have included this piece because we feel that not only is Miss Steinem saying something that needs saying, but also because hers is a marvelous example of persuasive prose.

[1]   Any change is fearful, especially one affecting both politics and sex roles, so let me begin these utopian speculations with a fact. To break the ice.

[2]   Women don't want to exchange places with men. Male chauvinists, science-fiction writers and comedians may favor that idea for its shock value, but psychologists say it is a fantasy based on ruling-class ego and guilt. Men assume that women want to imitate them, which is just what white people assumed about blacks. An assumption so strong that it may convince the second-class group of the need to imitate, but for both women and blacks that stage has passed. Guilt produces the question: What if they could treat us as we have treated them?

[3]   That is not our goal. But we do want to change the economic system to one more based on merit. In Women's Lib Utopia, there will be free access to good jobs—and decent pay for the bad ones women have been performing all along, including housework. Increased skilled labor might lead to a four-hour workday, and higher wages would encourage further mechanization of repetitive jobs now kept alive by cheap labor.

[4]   With women as half the country's elected representatives, and a woman President once in a while, the country's *machismo*[1] problems would be greatly reduced. The old-fashioned idea that manhood depends on violence and victory is, after all, an important part of our troubles in the streets, and in Viet Nam. I'm not saying that women leaders would eliminate violence. We are not more moral than men: we are only uncorrupted by power so far. When we do acquire power, we might turn out to have an equal impulse toward aggression. Even now, Margaret Mead believes that women fight less often but more fiercely than men, because women are not taught the rules of the war game and fight only when cornered. But for the next 50 years or so, women in politics will be very valuable by tempering the idea of manhood into something less aggressive and better suited to this crowded, post-atomic planet. Consumer protection and children's rights, for instance, might get more legislative attention.

[5]   Men will have to give up ruling-class privileges, but in return they will no longer be the only ones to support the family, get drafted, bear the strain of power and responsibility. Freud to the contrary, anatomy is not destiny, at least not for more than nine months at a time. In Israel, women are drafted, and some have gone to war. In England, more men type and run switchboards. In India and Israel, a woman rules. In Sweden, both parents take care of the children. In this country, come Utopia, men and women won't reverse roles; they will be free to choose according to individual talents and preferences.

[6]   If role reform sounds sexually unsettling, think how it will change the sexual hypocrisy we have now. No more sex arranged on the barter system, with women pretending interest, and men never sure whether they are loved for themselves or for the security few women can get any other way. (Married or not, for sexual reasons or social ones, most women still find it second nature to Uncle-Tom.) No more men who are encouraged to spend a lifetime living with inferiors; with housekeepers, or dependent creatures who are still children. No more domineering wives, emasculating women, and "Jewish mothers," all of whom are simply human beings with all their normal ambition and drive confined to the home. No more unequal partnerships that eventually doom love and sex.

[7]   In order to produce that kind of confidence and individuality, child rearing will train according to talent. Little girls will no longer

[1] *machismo*, a Spanish term that describes the various feats and tests to which a male (*un macho*) must put his maleness in order to prove his masculinity.

be surrounded by air-tight, self-fulfilling prophecies of natural passivity, lack of ambition and objectivity, inability to exercise power, and dexterity (so long as special aptitude for jobs requiring patience and dexterity is confined to poorly paid jobs; brain surgery is for males).

[8] Schools and universities will help to break down traditional sex roles, even when parents will not. Half the teachers will be men, a rarity now at preschool and elementary levels: girls will not necessarily serve cookies or boys hoist up the flag. Athletic teams will be picked only by strength and skill. Sexually segregated courses like auto mechanics and home economics will be taken by boys and girls together. New courses in sexual politics will explore female subjugation as the model for political oppression, and women's history will be an academic staple, along with black history, at least until the white-male-oriented textbooks are integrated and rewritten.

[9] As for the American child's classic problem—too much mother, too little father—that would be cured by an equalization of parental responsibility. Free nurseries, school lunches, family cafeterias built into every housing complex, service companies that will do household cleaning chores in a regular, businesslike way, and more responsibility by the entire community for the children: all these will make it possible for both mother and father to work, and to have equal leisure time with the children at home. For parents of very young children, however, a special job category, created by Government and unions, would allow such parents a shorter work day.

[10] The revolution would not take away the option of being a housewife. A woman who prefers to be her husband's housekeeper and/or hostess would receive a percentage of his pay determined by the domestic relations court. If divorced, she might be eligible for a pension fund, and for a job-training allowance. Or a divorce could be treated the same way that the dissolution of a business partnership is now.

[11] If these proposals seem farfetched, consider Sweden, where most of them are already in effect. Sweden is not yet a working Women's Lib model; most of the role-reform programs began less than a decade ago, and are just beginning to take hold. But that country is so far ahead of us in recognizing the problem that Swedish statements on sex and equality sound like bulletins from the moon.

[12] Our marriage laws, for instance, are so reactionary that Women's Lib groups want couples to take a compulsory written exam

on the law, as for a driver's license, before going through with the wedding. A man has alimony and wifely debts to worry about, but a woman may lose so many of her civil rights that in the U.S. now, in important legal ways, she becomes a child again. In some states, she cannot sign credit agreements, use her maiden name, incorporate a business, or establish a legal residence of her own. Being a wife, according to most social and legal definitions, is still a 19th century thing.

[13] Assuming, however, that these blatantly sexist laws are abolished or reformed, that job discrimination is forbidden, that parents share financial responsibility for each other and the children, and that sexual relationships become partnerships of equal adults (some pretty big assumptions), then marriage will probably go right on. Men and women are, after all, physically complementary. When society stops encouraging men to be exploiters and women to be parasites, they may turn out to be more complementary in emotion as well. Women's Lib is not trying to destroy the American family. A look at the statistics on divorce—plus the way in which old people are farmed out with strangers and young people flee the home—shows the destruction that has already been done. Liberated women are just trying to point out the disaster, and build compassionate and practical alternatives from the ruins.

[14] What will exist is a variety of alternative life-styles. Since the population explosion dictates that childbearing be kept to a minimum, parents-and-children will be only one of many "families": couples, age groups, working groups, mixed communes, blood-related clans, class groups, creative groups. Single women will have the right to stay single without ridicule, without the attitudes now betrayed by "spinster" and "bachelor." Lesbians or homosexuals will no longer be denied legally binding marriages, complete with mutual-support agreements and inheritance rights. Paradoxically, the number of homosexuals may get smaller. With fewer overpossessive mothers and fewer fathers who hold up an impossibly cruel or perfectionist idea of manhood, boys will be less likely to be denied or to reject their identity as males.

[15] Changes that now seem small may get bigger:

[16] Men now suffer from more diseases due to stress, heart attacks, ulcers, a higher suicide rate, greater difficulty living alone, less adaptability to change and, in general, a shorter life span than women. There is some scientific evidence that what produces physical problems is not work itself, but the inability to choose which work, and how

much. With women bearing half the financial responsibility, and with the idea of "masculine" jobs gone, men might well feel freer and live longer.

[17]   Protestant women are already becoming ordained ministers; radical nuns are carrying out liturgical functions that were once the exclusive property of priests; Jewish women are rewriting prayers—particularly those that Orthodox Jews recite every morning thanking God they are not female. In the future, the church will become an area of equal participation by women. This means, of course, that organized religion will have to give up one of its great historical weapons: sexual repression. In most structured faiths, from Hinduism through Roman Catholicism, the status of women went down as the position of priests ascended. Male clergy implied, if they did not teach, that women were unclean, unworthy and source of ungodly temptation, in order to remove them as rivals for the emotional forces of men. Full participation of women in ecclesiastical life might involve certain changes in theology, such as, for instance, a radical redefinition of sin.

[18]   Revised sex roles will outdate more children's books than civil rights ever did. Only a few children had the problem of a *Little Black Sambo,* but most have the male-female stereotypes of "Dick and Jane." A boomlet[2] of children's books about mothers who work has already begun, and liberated parents and editors are beginning to pressure for change in the textbook industry. Fiction writing will change more gradually, but romantic novels with wilting heroines and swashbuckling heroes will be reduced to historical value. Or perhaps to the sado-masochist trade. (*Marjorie Morningstar,* a romantic novel that took the '50s by storm, has already begun to seem as unreal as its '20s predecessor, *The Sheik.*) As for the literary plots that turn on forced marriages or horrific abortions, they will seem as dated as Prohibition stories. Free legal abortions and free birth control will force writers to give up pregnancy as the *deus ex machina.*

[19]   Dress will be more androgynous, with class symbols becoming more important than sexual ones. Pro- or anti-Establishment styles may already be more vital than who is wearing them. Hardhats are just as likely to rough up antiwar girls as antiwar men in the street, and police understand that women are just as likely to be pushers or bombers. Dances haven't required that one partner lead the other for years, anyway. Chivalry will transfer itself to those who need it, or deserve re-

---

[2] *boomlet,* a word presumably coined by the author, indicating "a modest boom" or a quiet trend towards one.

spect; old people, admired people, anyone with an armload of packages. Women with normal work identities will be less likely to attach their whole sense of self to youth and appearance; thus there will be fewer nervous breakdowns when the first wrinkles appear. Lighting cigarettes and other treasured niceties will become gestures of mutual affection. "I like to be helped on with my coat," says one Women's Lib worker, "but not if it costs me $2,000 a year in salary."

[20]   For those with nostalgia for a simpler past, here is a word of comfort. Anthropologist Geoffrey Gorer studied the few peaceful human tribes and discovered one common characteristic: sex roles were not polarized. Differences of dress and occupation were at a minimum. Society, in other words, was not using sexual blackmail as a way of getting women to do cheap labor, or men to be aggressive.

[21]   Thus Women's Lib may achieve a more peaceful society on the way toward its other goals. That is why the Swedish government considers reform to bring about greater equality in the sex roles one of its most important concerns. As Prime Minister Olof Palme explained in a widely ignored speech delivered in Washington this spring: "It is *human beings* we shall emancipate. In Sweden today, if a politician should declare that the woman ought to have a different role from man's, he would be regarded as something from the Stone Age." In other words, the most radical goal of the movement is egalitarianism.

[22]   If Women's Lib wins, perhaps we all do.

STUDY AND DISCUSSION

Vocabulary
If you don't know any of the following words or terms, run (do not walk) to the dictionary nearest you:

1. utopian (para. 1)	2. tempering (para. 4)
3. barter system (para. 6)	4. domineering (para. 6)
5. emasculating (para. 6)	6. staple (para. 8)
7. reactionary (para. 12)	8. blatantly (para. 13)
9. sexist (para. 13)	10. liturgical (para. 16)
11. wilting (para. 18)	12. swashbuckling (para. 18)
13. sado-masochist (para. 18)	14. *deus ex machina* (para. 18)
15. androgynous (para. 19)	16. polarized (para. 20)
17. egalitarianism (para. 21)	

Rhetoric

1. To what does the opening word in para. 3 refer? What is its antecedent?
2. According to which rhetorical principle are paras. 6, 7, 8 and 9 organized?
3. In para. 11, how does Gloria Steinem shift her rhetorical mode?
4. What, in your mind, is the most salient detail mentioned in para. 19?

Content

1. According to Gloria Steinem, do women want to take over a "man's world" or do they just want to change it?
2. If women succeed in their revolution, in what fields might we see new legislation enacted?
3. What concessions will men have to make, comes the revolution?
4. What does the author mean by "the sexual hypocrisy we have now"?
5. Why do women "still find it second nature to Uncle-Tom"?
6. What does she feel is the "American child's classic problem"?
7. Would the revolution deprive a woman who just wants to be a mother and a housewife from these quiet joys?
8. Would the revolution put an end to marriage, in Miss Steinem's opinion?
9. What might be the effect(s) upon men once the idea of strictly "masculine jobs" goes, and once women start bearing "half the financial responsibility"?

Ideas and Implications

1. Gloria Steinem says that Women's Liberation advocates want "to change the economic system to one more based on merit." What is the system now based on?
2. No matter what anybody says, women are still going to be governed by the reproductive function that Mother Nature has laid on them. Thus, a lot of the emotion behind The Cause stems from some women's deep frustration at their biological role . . .
3. Does our society really encourage men to be exploiters and women parasites, as Steinem maintains in para. 13?
4. Women are inherently more moral than men. Discuss this assertion.
5. Do you agree that "one of (the) great historical weapons" of organized religion is sexual oppression?
6. Would the "variety of alternative life styles," mentioned in para. 14, appeal to you? Can you think of any not mentioned by Gloria Steinem? Do you feel hemmed in by the options offered you in America today?

STORY OF MRS. W----

DOROTHY PARKER   Dorothy Parker, who wrote criticism, poetry, and fiction, established a reputation early in her career for witty, satirical, cynical, and sometimes malicious views of modern life. Her publications include her collected poems, Not So Deep as a Well, *and her collected short stores,* Here Lies.

In "Story of Mrs. W----," Dorothy Parker brilliantly and succinctly depicts the empty stretch of time that spreads out around a lady who, with great resignation, lives the stereotyped existence prescribed for the genteel.

My garden blossoms pink and white,
    A place of decorous murmuring,
Where I am safe from August night
    And cannot feel the knife of Spring.

And I may walk the pretty place
    Before the curtsying hollyhocks
And laundered daisies, round of face—
    Good little girls, in party frocks.

My trees are amiably arrayed
    In pattern on the dappled sky,
And I may sit in filtered shade
    And watch the tidy years go by.

And I may amble pleasantly
    And hear my neighbors list their bones
And click my tongue in sympathy,
    And count the cracks in paving-stones.

My door is grave in oaken strength,
    The cool of linen calms my bed,
And there at night I stretch my length
    And envy no one but the dead.

STUDY AND DISCUSSION

1. The garden traditionally symbolizes paradise on earth. Is the garden used symbolically in this poem? Discuss in detail.
2. Why are pink and white especially appropriate colors for Mrs. W's---- garden?
3. What is "decorous murmuring"? Why is it appropriate to Mrs. W----?
4. She is 'safe from August night," Mrs. W---- says. But why should she want to be? What is *dangerous* about August night?
5. What is "the knife of Spring"? Why can't she feel it? Does she want to?
6. In what specific ways do the plants in her garden resemble her?
7. What are *"tidy* years"? Do you think she enjoys them?
8. In what specific ways does she waste her life?
9. What does the last stanza reveal about Mrs. W's---- existence?
10. How do you think a member of the Women's Liberation Front would respond to this poem?

Turning Points: a World in Crisis

RACE
AND
PREJUDICE

THE ENVIRONMENT OF LANGUAGE

NORMAN COUSINS In this essay, Mr. Cousins, the editor of Saturday Review, *discusses the language of prejudice. He shows in convincing detail that language not only reflects the way we think about other people—but that it* influences *the way we think about them. As you read, take careful note of the many examples.*

[1] The words men use, Julian Huxley once said, not only express but shape their ideas. Language is an instrument; it is even more an environment. It has as much to do with the philosophical and political conditioning of a society as geography or climate. The role of language in contributing to men's problems and their prospects is the subject of an imaginative and valuable study now getting under way at Pro Deo University in Rome, which is winning recognition in world university circles for putting advanced scholarship to work for the concept of a world community.

[2]   One aspect of the Pro Deo study, as might be expected, has to do with the art of conveying precise meaning from one language to another. Stuart Chase, one of America's leading semanticists, has pointed out that when an English speaker at the United Nations uses the expression "I assume," the French interpreter may say "I deduce" and the Russian interpreter may say "I consider." When Pope Paul VI sent a cable to Prime Minister Alexei Kosygin and Party Chairman Leonid Brezhnev on their accession to office, he expressed the hope that the historic aspirations of the Russian people for a fuller life would be advanced under the new leadership. As translated into Russian by the Vatican's own interpreter, the Pope's expression of hope came out in a way that made it appear that the Pope was making known his endorsement of the new regime. The eventual clarification was inevitably awkward for all concerned.

[3]   The Pro Deo study, however, will not be confined to problems of precise translation. The major emphasis has to do with something even more fundamental: the dangerous misconceptions and prejudices that take root in language and that undermine human values. The color of a man's skin, for example, is tied to plus-or-minus words that inevitably condition human attitudes. The words "black" and "white," as defined in Western culture, are heavily loaded. "Black" has all sorts of unfavorable connotations; "white" is almost all favorable. One of the more interesting papers being studied by the Pro Deo scholars is by Ossie Davis, the author and actor. Mr. Davis, a Negro, concluded on the basis of a detailed study of dictionaries and *Roget's Thesaurus* that the English language was his enemy. In *Roget's*, he counted 120 synonyms for "blackness," most of them with unpleasant connotations: blot, blotch, blight, smut, smudge, sully, begrime, soot, becloud, obscure, dingy, murky, threatening, frowning, foreboding, forbidden, sinister, baneful, dismal, evil, wicked, malignant, deadly, secretive, unclean, unwashed, foul, blacklist, black book, black-hearted, etc. Incorporated in the same listing were words such as Negro, nigger, and darky.

[4]   In the same *Roget's*, Mr. Davis found 134 synonyms for the word "white," almost all of them with favorable connotations: purity, cleanness, bright, shining, fair, blonde, stainless, chaste, unblemished, unsullied, innocent, honorable, upright, just, straightforward, genuine, trustworthy, honesty, etc. "White" as a racial designation was, of course, included in this tally of desirable terms.

[5]   No less invidious than black are some of the words associated

with the color yellow: coward, conniver, baseness, fear, effeminacy, funk, soft, spiritless, poltroonery, pusillanimity, timidity, milksop, recreant, sneak, lilylivered, etc. Oriental peoples are included in the listing.

[6] As a matter of factual accuracy, white, black, and yellow as colors are not descriptive of races. The coloration range of so-called white people may run from pale olive to mottled pink. So-called colored people run from light beige to mahogany. Absolute color designations—white, black, red, yellow—are not merely inaccurate; they have become symbolic rather than descriptive. It will be argued, of course, that definitions of color and the connotations that go with them are independent of sociological implications. There is no getting around the fact, it will be said, that whiteness means cleanliness and blackness means dirtiness. Are we to doctor the dictionary in order to achieve a social good? What this line of argument misses is that people in Western cultures do not realize the extent to which their racial attitudes have been conditioned since early childhood by the power of words to ennoble or condemn, augment or detract, glorify or demean. Negative language infects the subconscious of most Western people from the time they first learn to speak. Prejudice is not merely imparted or superimposed. It is metabolized in the bloodstream of society. What is needed is not so much a change in language as an awareness of the power of words to condition attitudes. If we can at least recognize the underpinnings of prejudice, we may be in a position to deal with the effects.

[7] To be sure, Western languages have no monopoly on words with connotations that affect judgment. In Chinese, whiteness means cleanliness, but it can also mean bloodlessness, coldness, frigidity, absence of feeling, weakness, insensitivity. Also in Chinese, yellowness is associated with sunshine, openness, beauty, flowering, etc. Similarly, the word black in many African tongues has connotations of strength, certainty, recognizability, integrity, while white is associated with paleness, anemia, unnaturalness, deviousness, untrustworthiness.

[8] The purpose of Pro Deo University in undertaking this study is not just to demonstrate that most cultures tend to be self-serving in their language. The purpose is to give educational substance to the belief that it will take all the adroitness and sensitivity of which the human species is capable if it is to be sustained. Earth-dwellers now have the choice of making their world into a neighborhood or a crema-

torium. Language is one of the factors in that option. The right words may not automatically produce the right actions but they are an essential part of the process.

STUDY AND DISCUSSION

Vocabulary
A. In your dictionary find the meaning of all the words you cannot define in context in this essay.
B. What is the difference between the *connotation* and *denotation* of a word? Choose five of the highly connotative words discussed in this essay. Look them up in your dictionary and be prepared to explain the difference between their denotation and their connotation.

Rhetoric
1. What is the main idea of this essay? Where is it stated?
2. How are paragraphs 2, 3, 4, and 5 developed?
3. What is the purpose of the first sentence in paragraph 3? What sentence serves as the topic sentence in this paragraph?

Content
1. What does the title mean? In what sense is language an environment?
2. What examples does Mr. Cousins give to show how words shape ideas?
3. How does Mr. Cousins illustrate the difficulty of conveying precise meaning from one language to another?
4. What does Mr. Cousins mean by "plus-or-minus words"? By "loaded" words?
5. Contrast the connotations of *black* and *white.*
6. What are the connotations of *yellow?*
7. When they are applied to races, how accurate *are* the words *white, black,* and *yellow?*
8. For the Chinese what does *white* connote?
9. For many African tribes what are the connotations of *black* and *white?*
10. What is the purpose of the Pro Deo study?

Ideas and Implications
1. For you, what are the connotations of *black, white,* and *yellow?* For your parents? For your grandparents?
2. What highly connotative words are sometimes applied to Blacks? To

Chinese and Japanese Americans? To Frenchmen and Italians? To Jews? Do you approve of the use of these terms?

3. How do you acquire racial prejudices? Are they based firmly on unhappy experiences? Or are they "just picked up" from the environment?

4. Have you ever been a victim of prejudice? Have you ever been discriminated against because of your pigmentation or the sound of your family name? Is there anything, in your experience, worse than how this made you feel?

5. Are you prejudiced against any group of people? If so, why? Is your prejudice justified?

6. What can be done to eliminate racial and religious prejudice? What are *you* going to do?

DISPATCH FROM WOUNDED KNEE

*CALVIN KENTFIELD   Nothing superfluous is allowed into the follow-
ing essay. Every detail is chosen with great care and intelligence. The
author is never intrusive—it is his custom to allow the people he meets
to talk about and for themselves at all times—but how Calvin Kentfield
feels about what he sees and hears is most evident. "Dispatch from
Wounded Knee" is quite simply one of the best pieces of expository
prose writing we have come across in the past decade. Among its many
impressive features is its tone, which simultaneously manages to combine
passion with the intellect, the past with the present with the future. Indeed, as you read this essay, you might do well to keep asking yourself,*
What is going to happen to the Sioux nation?

*We feel that their fate is projected quite unequivocally in this brilliant
piece of reportage.*

Calvin Kentfield, born in Iowa in 1924, is editor of Contact *magazine
and director of Angel Island Publications in Sausalito, California. He is
the author of* The Alchemist's Voyage, The Angel and the Sailor, *and,
most recently,* The Great Wandering Goony Bird.

WOUNDED KNEE, S.D.

[1]   From time to time over the years, since long before the frigid
Plains winter of 1890 when United States forces armed with Hotchkiss
machine guns mowed down men, women, children and some of their
own soldiers in the final slaughter at Wounded Knee, the Congress of
the United States has become guiltily concerned about the condition
and fate of the native American Indian. The most recent manifestation
of that concern is the House of Representatives Bill 10560, also
known as the Indian Resources Development Act of 1967, sponsored
by Representative James Haley, a Florida Democrat, and a fellow
Democrat, Representative Wayne N. Aspinall of Colorado, chairman
of the Committee on Interior and Insular Affairs with which the bill
now resides.

[2]   If enacted, the bill would allow the Indians greater freedom in
selling, mortgaging, and developing what lands they still possess, encourage them through Government loans to bring industry to the reservations, and enable them with the approval of the Interior Department's Bureau of Indian Affairs to obtain loans from private sources.

Indians in general, after years of bitter experience with Congressional maneuvers and of watching the depletion of their lands despite Federal largesse, are wary of the bill's benevolence, but most of their tribal councils have chosen to go along with it, chiefly because they hope that this time around the economic provisions will really work and because they figure that this is as good a bill as they can get at this time.

[3]   Out where the battle of Wounded Knee took place, however, the tribal elders are decidedly unenthusiastic about the bill and its Government backers. "We know they mean well," says Johnson Holy Rock, the chairman of the Tribal Council of the Oglala Sioux at Pine Ridge Reservation in South Dakota. "Their intentions in putting forth this bill are undoubtedly of the best, but they don't understand the Indian mind, and we here at Pine Ridge have simply said we won't accept it, we want to be left out, we're not ready for it, we know we'd lose more than we'd gain and we've lost too much already."

[4]   And Brice Lay, the chief of the Pine Ridge Agency of the Bureau of Indian Affairs to which an Indian must apply in order to sell or lease his land, says, "We here at the bureau know, and the council knows, that if a piece of land comes up for bids, a non-Indian's going to get it." He pointed to a chart of the reservation that showed 42 per cent of the land already in white hands. "The Indians have first choice," he went on, "but very few of them can afford it, not even the council acting for the tribe as a whole. It's simply going to go out of Indian hands, and there's nothing on earth we can do about it."

[5]   The ever-diminishing land is almost the sole source of subsistence for the inhabitants of the Pine Ridge Reservation—or, more colorfully, the Land of Red Cloud—which is the seventh largest of the 300-odd reservations in the United States. It stretches for 90 miles east from the Black Hills and about 50 miles from the northern Badlands south to the Nebraska line.

[6]   In the eastern part some of the land is fertile enough to bear wheat, oats, safflower and the like, but 99 per cent of this farm land is now and forever in the hands of the white man. The rest of the reservation consists of rolling short-grass prairie land, an enormous landscape divided into four parts: endless green grass, tall blue sky, low ridges of ponderosa pine, and a constant rustling, sighing wind. Through these great plains wander cottonwood-shaded creeks such as Bear In the Lodge, Potato, Wounded Knee, and the twisted White and

Cheyenne Rivers. In the summer, thunderclouds build up towers on the far horizons and the uninhibited sun may produce temperatures of 120 degrees; in the winter, the creeks become ice and blizzard winds such as those that froze the bodies at the massacre of Wounded Knee into such baroque and unusual shapes can bring the thermometer down to 40 below.

[7]   U.S. Highway 18 passes east-west through the southern edge of the reservation. There are miles and miles of good black-top roads kept in repair by Indians working for the Interior Department road service; and there are miles and miles of roads that are no good at all. There are modern boarding schools exclusively for Indian children as well as local public schools and a Catholic mission school, outlying clinics and a good free hospital with doctors, surgeons, dentists and a psychiatrist. There are churches of all kinds (40 percent of the Indians profess to be Catholics and more to be Protestants, but the old beliefs still lie heavily in their souls). There is an American Legion Post, a Lions Club, a Ladies' Aid, a P.-T.A. and a Boy Scout troop. Nearly all of the Sioux (or Dakotas, their own pre-reservation name for themselves) speak English as well as their native Lakota dialect, and there are still a few medicine men around, like old Frank Fools Crow who usually presides over the annual Sun Dance. The center of nearly everything—government, society, law and order, education—is Pine Ridge, a town of 1,256 people close enough to the state line to have a "suburb" in Nebraska, Whiteclay, center of shopping (three supermarkets) and entertainment (bars and dance halls).

[8]   On this reservation live, in one fashion or another, nearly 10,000 Teton Sioux of the Oglala tribe. They are not the poorest nor the richest of the country's Indians. The Hopis and some of the Apaches of the Southwest are poorer, and the inhabitants of the Agua-caliente reservation in Southern California, who more or less own Palm Springs, are richer, to say nothing of those few tribes that have oil wells. But the Oglalas range from a state of imminent starvation to fair affluence.

[9]   On the reservation itself, unemployment is 43 per cent, so some of the younger people go elsewhere for summer work. There is a new factory at Pine Ridge that employs about a hundred people to make "handmade" moccasins. A fishhook factory near Wounded Knee employs nearly 200 more, and a few more work for the Bureau of

Indian Affairs. Most of the businesses—filling stations, grocery stores —are owned by whites, and the rest of the Indians work for white ranchers or live off the land which they work themselves or lease to white ranchers. The land, though it belongs to the Indians, is held in trust by the Department of the Interior, which takes care of all the leasing arrangements and issues checks to the owners each month from a computer in Aberdeen.

[10]   Aside from Interior Department employees and a few Indian ranchers, the average annual income per family is less than $900. The 34 members of the Tribal Council, however, have voted themselves a yearly salary of $7,500, paid out of proceeds from tribal lands under grazing leases. "Those earnings are supposed to be divided up amongst us all," one man told me, "but we ain't none of us seen a pinny of it for years." Most of the money, of course, goes into the operation of the tribal government, which has charge of all municipal services—police, fire and courts—as well as the maintenance of lawyers in Rapid City and Washington to represent the tribe in all higher dealings with the Government, such as House Bill 10560. Though technically wards of the Federal Government under the guiding thumb of the Bureau of Indian Affairs, the Indians, since 1924, have enjoyed the rights and privileges of full American citizenship, including the right to fight in Vietnam and the privilege of paying income taxes. They enjoy some extra privileges as well, such as untaxed land.

[11]   "We try to help them," said Brice Lay in his office in the new air-conditioned bureau headquarters in Pine Ridge, "to make the best possible use of the land they have, but it's very hard." Like most of the non-Indian (the bureau does not use the term "white man") employees of the bureau, he is intensely sincere in his desire to help the Indian become a white man. "Here in Pine Ridge most of the people live fairly well, but you go out on the reservation—the way some of those people live!" He made a gesture of despair. "No one should have to live that way."

[12]   And, indeed, out on the windy treeless tracts of the reservation, at the end of two dirt ruts across the prairie, will be a one-room shack, possibly a log cabin, possibly a frame house walled in tarpaper, for a family of six, eight, ten people and surrounded by a circle of old car bodies that, like the bodies of U.S. soldiers killed in a battle of olden times, have been stripped and mutilated and left to rot where

they lay. An outhouse nearby. No electricity, no running water. A monthly ration of rice, flour, powdered milk, peanut butter, margarine, lard, raisins, oatmeal, cornmeal, potted meat, dried beans, dried peas, bulgur and rolled wheat, plus $50 in cash from Welfare. This kind of poverty engenders horror, pity and disgust in the Anglo-Saxon breast, but all the Oglalas are not that badly off, and many of them simply don't want some of the amenities that the Great White Father insists they must have, if possible, for their own good.

[13]   "We had one old woman out on the reservation," Brice Lay said, "that was all by herself and living in a tent, so we found a house for her, but she wouldn't move in. She said she'd die if she lived in a house, that the air in a house was bad air. Oh, she was stubborn. But finally," he concluded with a tone of great satisfaction, "we got her in there."

[14]   Out at Wounded Knee about two miles from the general store and post office lives a man in his late 50's, his wife, two married sons, six grandchildren, three dogs, two cats, some hens and a rooster. He is a full blood, very dark, though his wife is not. He owns a section of land (640 acres) through which runs Wounded Knee Creek and on which graze about 200 head of cattle and 60 or 70 horses. He has a field of alfalfa which, this year, because of the late rains, is exceptionally rich and high and, when I visited him, was ready for cutting. There are tall shade trees along the creek, plenty of water, and a small field of sweet corn nearby.

[15]   He and his wife and one orphaned grandchild live in a very old, one-room log cabin with a shade, or "squaw cooler" (though "squaw" is an insulting word these days), a kind of summer house made of poles and pine boughs that keep off the sun but let the breeze come through, making it a comfortable outdoor kitchen and sleeping place during the hot months. His sons and their families live in small asphalt-shingled houses on either side of the parental house. One son is a cowboy and works the section, the other works at the fishhook factory over the hill. Standing to one side at the edge of the alfalfa is a two-hole outhouse.

[16]   They carry their water from the creek, build their fire with wood and light their lamps with kerosene. They walk to the store and back, as they have no car. They are well and presumably happy. They are members of the Native American Church who use peyote, the hallucinatory cactus, in their services, during which, under the spell

of the drug, they chant and sing and pray to God that the day will come when all men will be at peace and all men will be brothers. Not half a mile from this man's house reside the bones in a mass hilltop grave of the victims of the massacre of Wounded Knee.

[17]   Though a Peace Sacrifice was the climax of this year's Sun Dance—"Richard "Buddy" Red Bow," the posters read, "17 years old, member of the Oglala Sioux tribe, will pray for worldwide peace by performing the traditional Sun Dance worship. Red Bow will pierce his flesh and offer his blood, praying for the safety of American Servicemen and a peaceful speedy end to war in Vietnam"—the Sioux were not always a peaceable people.

[18]   "Sioux" is short for "Nadowessioux," which is French for "Nadowessi," which is Chippewa meaning "little snakes" or, in other words, treacherous enemies. The Sioux fought everybody—the Chippewa, the Crow, the Cheyenne, the Kiowa and the white man after he came pushing onto the plains, stealing, pushing, lying, slaughtering the buffalo, always pushing. In 1866, Red Cloud, "the first and only Indian leader in the West to win a war with the United States," said to a Colonel Carrington, come to open a road to the Montana gold-fields, "You are the White Eagle who has come to steal the road! The Great Father sends us presents and wants us to sell him the road, but the White Chief comes with soldiers to steal it before the Indian says yes or no! I will talk with you no more. As long as I live I will fight you for the last hunting grounds of my people."

[19]   Red Cloud and Crazy Horse, Custer's Last Stand, Sitting Bull and Big Foot, and the final slaughter at Wounded Knee! After all that misery, bravery, and bloodshed, the Sioux, romanticized by the white man, became the Ideal Indian, the Mounted Warrior in War Bonnet, the End of the Trail, the Indian at the Medicine Show, the all-American Buffalo-Nickel Indian.

[20]   The last treaty the Sioux made with the United States Government (1868-69) set aside nearly half of South Dakota, including the sacred Black Hills, and part of North Dakota as the "Great Sioux Reserve." But white men discovered gold in the Black Hills (as Johnson Holy Rock said to me, "The Indians still don't understand gold, it's a white man's concept and the white man just can't understand that"), so an Act of Congress in 1877 removed the Black Hills from the Indians' reserve. Later, another act divided what was left of the

"Great Sioux Reserve" into five reservations with still more loss of land, settling the Oglalas at Pine Ridge. It is no wonder, indeed, that the Indian leaders look twice and twice again at Acts of Congress.

[21] The Indian Bureau demands at least one-quarter Indian blood as a prerequisite for donating its paternalistic blessings—but the Pine Ridge Tribal Council has *never* been able to decide upon who is and who is not an Indian.

[22] "The Tribal Council is ridiculous," said a man I shall call Edgar Running Bear because he has asked me not to use his real name. "Two of them are stupid women who have not even had a sixth-grade education, one of them is a hopeless alcoholic, and they're all prejudiced."

[23] We were sitting in Edgar Running Bear's house in one of the several new Pine Ridge subdivisions financed by the Public Housing Authority and built by Indian labor against the fierce objections of half-a-dozen union leaders. It is a two-bedroom house, pink and white, with a carport and a front lawn like millions of others all over America. In the living room were two modernistic armchairs, a huge radio-phonograph-television combination set in the corner. On top of the TV stood a vase of plastic flowers and on the wall opposite the picture window hung a small imitation tapestry of a roaring tiger printed in lurid colors on black velvet.

[24] It was a hot day and through the open windows we could hear the drumming and amplified chanting of one of the bands, the Oglala Juniors or the Sioux Travelers, who had gathered at the nearby campground for the four-day Sun Dance celebration, a kind of county fair, carnival and tribal get-together combined with ancient ritual which was just then beginning. The celebration is an annual rite that Edgar, at one point in our conversation, referred to scornfully as a reversion to primitivism, though he later took his children over to the campground to ride the Space-Mobile.

[25] "Why do you say they're prejudiced?" I asked. "Against whom?"

[26] "Against the mixed bloods."

[27] Both Edgar and his wife, and indeed most of the population of the reservation, are mixed bloods. The classic face of Red Cloud is seldom seen. Johnson Holy Rock himself is three-quarter Oglala and one-quarter Scotch-Irish. I mentioned this fact and elicited only a shrug from Edgar.

[28] "Do you find," I asked, "that white people on the reservation or off it show prejudice toward you because you're Indians?"

[29] "Oh, yes," Edgar's wife said quickly. "They move onto our land, look down their noses at us, and complain about our laws and our dogs and—"

[30] "When I go off the reservation," Edgar broke in, "I expect to abide by the ways of the people there. It doesn't bother me, if we don't get served one place, we'll go someplace else, but *you* could go staggering drunk down the main street of Rushville [Rushville, Neb., the nearest town of any size] and nobody'd look at you, but if *I* did—well, not me because being a policeman they know me—but if an ordinary Innun did the same thing he'd be in jail so fast. . . ."

[31] I related an incident I had witnessed in a restaurant-bar in Rushville. The television had been giving news of the aftermath of the Negro riots in Detroit and the waitress had said, "I know it's a funny attitude to take, but if one of them come in here, I just couldn't serve him. I don't know what it is, but—" Then she had given a little laugh and said, "But nobody kin accuse me of racial prejudice because I feel the same damn way about the dirty Indians."

[32] There was a moment of silence while the drums beat at the Sun Dance grounds.

[33] "Well," Edgar said, "that's the kind of thing you run into."

[34] "Well, us Innuns aren't prejudiced against the niggers," Edgar's wife said. "Of course, I wouldn't want my daughter to marry one any more than I'd want her to marry a full blood."

[35] Edgar, slouching deeply in his armchair, gave the living room wall a kick with the side of his foot. "Look at this damn house," he said. "It's coming apart already."

[36] "That's why we send our kids to public school instead of the B.I.A. Innun school," his wife went on, "because we don't want them to grow up with nothing but Innuns."

[37] "To live here, to live this life we live here," Edgar said, shaking his head, "you have to be half-drunk all the time."

[38] Until 1953, it was, as a Klamath Indian friend of mine once explained, "against the law to feed liquor to Indians." It's still against the law on Pine Ridge because the members of the tribe voted for a dry reservation, though in the "suburb" of Whiteclay there are bars and dance halls that get quite lively on a Saturday night or just after the computer has issued the Mother's Aid or Welfare check.

[39] In those resorts, there is, as well as drunkenness, a great deal

of laughter and joking and horseplay; the Oglala is a friendly and, at times, very witty creature. He loves athletic games and plays them well, and his manual deftness makes him an excellent carpenter, machinist or technician if he takes the trouble to develop his talents and possesses the courage to go into the outside world and exercise his skills. One of the commonest reasons, of course, for Indian apathy toward Government training programs is that once an Indian learns a white man's trade there is no place on the reservation where he can exercise it. He has to leave his home and relatives and work in some foreign place, and he doesn't want to. The sponsors of H.R. 10560 eagerly point out that the bill will help relieve that condition.

[40]   In one Whiteclay bar, I met a fat jolly Oglala lady who, although she has an excellent secretarial job with the bureau, also creates fine tomahawks for the ever so slightly increasing tourist trade. She has three daughters who are or are becoming registered nurses, one son who has a Ph.D. in sociology and is working with other Indians in Nebraska, and a young son who is a good-for-nothing drunk. She knows Edgar Running Bear very well.

[41]   "Pooh! You can't believe a word Ed says," she said, although she allowed that the council was, in fact, incompetent and overpaid and that Johnson Holy Rock was unfair in his recommendations for loans. In general, she felt, the Innuns on the reservation were a passably contented lot and pretty much satisfied with the way the Bureau was handling their affairs.

[42]   "This is our place," she said. "Some of us go away, but an awful lot of us come back. See those two boys over there in the ball caps? They've been in Oakland, California, making good money, but they've come back."

[43]   I asked them why they had come back. One of them laughed and said, "Hell, I don't know. I guess to play baseball."

[44]   Johnson Holy Rock told me that he had been to Washington and explained to the Interior Department people that the chief complaints they have against the Government were that the Government treated them like digits instead of human beings, that it didn't understand the Indians' attachment to their people and their land, and that the Indians themselves didn't yet understand the white man's notion of business and money and private property. "We're not ready to be let out on our own," he had told them, "but treat us like people instead of numbers."

[45]   I remarked that all of us, not just the Indians, were victims of the official digital computer, that we were all cards full of little holes. "*We've* given up," I said, but this time he didn't understand, because he means to go right on trying to keep his people what they are, more so than any other Americans I know—human beings. But I'm sure that one day he, too, will give up just as Red Cloud, in spite of his vow to fight for his lands forever, gave up, finally telling his people in tones of scornful irony:

[46]   "You must begin anew and put away the wisdom of your fathers. You must lay up food and forget the hungry. When your house is built, your storeroom filled, then look around for a neighbor whom you can take advantage of and seize all he has."

[47]   That was the way, he said, to get rich like a white man.

STUDY AND DISCUSSION

Vocabulary

We feel that you will not be able to appreciate Calvin Kentfield's essay fully if you do not know the following words; so if you are not familiar with any or all of them, consult your dictionary:

1. manifestation (para. 1)
2. depletion (para. 2)
3. largesse (para. 2)
4. uninhibited (para. 6)
5. baroque (para. 6)
6. imminent (para. 8)
7. amenities (para. 12)
8. paternalistic (para. 21)
9. reversion (para. 21)
10. primitivism (para. 21)
11. apathy (para. 39)

Rhetoric

1. What rhetorical role do the opening two paragraphs play in the overall structure of the essay?
2. What happens when you arrive at para. 3?
3. Are paras. 5-10 more like the opening two or do they come closer to para. 3 in rhetorical method? What effect does Calvin Kentfield achieve by closely juxtaposing two distinct rhetorical modes throughout this essay? What are the two rhetorical modes he relies on most heavily?
4. What effect does the invocation of names in para. 19 have upon your emotions?
5. Why does Kentfield devote almost one-seventh of his article to reporting a conversation he had with "Edgar Running Bear" and his wife (paras. 22-37)?

6. What role do the final two paragraphs play? How do they relate to: the opening sentences of this essay; the closing lines of para. 6; the closing lines of para. 10; the fifth and sixth lines of para. 12; the closing lines of para. 16; para. 19 and para. 37? Do you feel that they provide a good finale to this essay or not?

Content

1. Does the United States Government understand the Sioux?
2. How much of the farm land on the Pine Ridge Reservation is owned by Indians—that is, land fertile enough to yield crops?
3. What is the average annual income per family among Indian ranchers? How much do members of the Tribal Council earn?
4. What specific rights and privileges of full American citizenship does the author mention the Indians enjoying in para. 10?
5. Is the term "squaw" insulting to an Indian today? If so, why?
6. In para. 19, Kentfield dwells long on the names of Indian braves of the past—so long, indeed, that it seems to us almost as though he were engaged in an invocation, almost trying to invoke a mythic dimension from the past. Why should he wish to do this?
7. What, "after all that misery, bravery, and bloodshed," does Kentfield say has happened to the Sioux in para. 19?
8. What condition does "Edgar Running Bear" say is a necessary prerequisite to "live this life we live here"?
9. What is the strongest reason behind the Sioux indifference to government training programs?
10. How do the Sioux wish to be treated? How, in fact, are they treated?

Ideas and Implications

1. Again and again, throughout this essay, Calvin Kentfield returns to the massacre at Wounded Knee in 1890. Why? What does it symbolize for him?
2. Brice Lay, of the Bureau of Indian Affairs, is described as being "intensely sincere in his desire to help the Indian become a white man." How do you feel about this statement? How would Mr. Lay? How would "Edgar Running Bear" and Johnson Holy Rock? How does Calvin Kentfield?
3. What does para. 13 tell you about the Bureau of Indian Affairs? What does it imply about the Sioux' response to the U.S. Government?
4. What is the irony involved with the Bureau's being able to define who is an Indian and who is not while the Indians themselves are unable to?
5. What sort of woman is "Mrs. Edgar Running Bear"? What sort of woman is the waitress in the restaurant-bar in Rushville?
6. What do you think is going to happen to the Sioux nation in the next twenty-five years?

THE INDIANS

*GENE FOWLER   In "The Indians," Gene Fowler pictures a Mormon
museum where the mummified remains of American Indians, "the skin,
raw/canvas dried to rock," are displayed in glass cases for the amusement
of tourists. He sees "color of desert/color of distance"—but he sees beyond them too, into the American past which destroyed the Indians and
their gods. It is a poignant picture.*

*For a note on the life of the author, see the introduction to "Colors of
Love" and "Eulogy."*

i walk among
glass tombs
curled bodies

these other Americans
women, men, unformed
ones
the children

held out there
by dry desert air

now, here
in a Mormon museum
in a shade of mountains

by thermostat
& curiosity

hair
red-brown
rough as desert horses

the skin, raw
canvas dried to rock
sucked in
& welded to bone

color of desert
color of distance

the shrunken figures
curl with shocked smiles
left behind in the rock

their trust offered
once
to gods who followed
them off the plains

STUDY AND DISCUSSION

1. How do you explain the lines "by thermostat/ & curiosity"? How do they fit into the poem?
2. How is the Indians' hair described? Is it an apt description? Why? What about the description of the skin?
3. The "shrunken figures/ curl with *shocked* smiles." In your opinion, why are the smiles *shocked?* Considering the poem as a whole, how much meaning does that word imply for you?
4. What is the significance of the fact that the gods "followed/ them off the plains"?
5. What point(s) do you think Fowler is making in this poem?
6. What do you think of the kind of museum display described here?
7. In general, what do you think of the treatment Indians have received from other Americans?

THE ETHICS OF LIVING JIM CROW

RICHARD WRIGHT   Richard Wright (1902-1967) wrote a number of distinguished books, including Uncle Tom's Children, Native Son, Black Boy, *and* The Long Dream. *His subject most often was the black man's experience of America—a subject handled with sensitivity and power in the essay which follows, an autobiographical account of how Wright "learned" to live as a Black Man in the United States. Note the dexterity with which Wright sets scenes, chooses effective details, and reconstructs dialogue.*

I

[1]   My first lesson in how to live as a Negro came when I was quite small. We were living in Arkansas. Our house stood behind the railroad tracks. Its skimpy yard was paved with black cinders. Nothing green ever grew in that yard. The only touch of green we could see was far away, beyond the tracks, over where the white folks lived. But cinders were good enough for me and I never missed the green growing things. And anyhow, cinders were fine weapons. You could always have a nice hot war with huge black cinders. All you had to do was crouch behind the brick pillars of a house with your hands full of gritty ammunition. And the first woolly black head you saw pop out from behind another row of pillars was your target. You tried your very best to knock it off. It was great fun.

[2]   I never fully realized the appalling disadvantages of a cinder environment till one day the gang to which I belonged found itself engaged in a war with the white boys who lived beyond the tracks. As usual we laid down our cinder barrage, thinking that this would wipe the white boys out. But they replied with a steady bombardment of broken bottles. We doubled our cinder barrage, but they hid behind trees, hedges, and the sloping embankments of their lawns. Having no such fortifications, we retreated to the brick pillars of our homes. During the retreat a broken milk bottle caught me behind the ear, opening a deep gash which bled profusely. The sight of blood pouring over my face completely demoralized our ranks. My fellow-combatants

left me standing paralyzed in the center of the yard, and scurried for their homes. A kind neighbor saw me and rushed me to a doctor, who took three stitches in my neck.

[3]   I sat brooding on my front steps, nursing my wound and waiting for my mother to come from work. I felt that a grave injustice had been done me. It was all right to throw cinders. The greatest harm a cinder could do was leave a bruise. But broken bottles were dangerous; they left you cut, bleeding, and helpless.

[4]   When night fell, my mother came from the white folks' kitchen. I raced down the street to meet her. I could just feel in my bones that she would understand. I knew she would tell me exactly what to do next time. I grabbed her hand and babbled out the whole story. She examined my wound, then slapped me.

[5]   "How come yuh didn't hide?" she asked me. "How come yuh awways fightin'?"

[6]   I was outraged, and bawled. Between sobs I told her that I didn't have any trees or hedges to hide behind. There wasn't a thing I could have used as a trench. And you couldn't throw very far when you were hiding behind the brick pillars of a house. She grabbed a barrel stave, dragged me home, stripped me naked, and beat me till I had a fever of one hundred and two. She would smack my rump with the stave, and, while the skin was still smarting, impart to me gems of Jim Crow wisdom. I was never to throw cinders any more. I was never to fight any more wars. I was never, never, under any conditions, to fight *white* folks again. And they were absolutely right in clouting me with the broken milk bottle. Didn't I know she was working hard every day in the hot kitchens of the white folks to make money to take care of me? When was I ever going to learn to be a good boy? She couldn't be bothered with my fights. She finished by telling me that I ought to be thankful to God as long as I lived that they didn't kill me.

[7]   All that night I was delirious and could not sleep. Each time I closed my eyes I saw monstrous white faces suspended from the ceiling, leering at me.

[8]   From that time on, the charm of my cinder yard was gone. The green trees, the trimmed hedges, the cropped lawns grew very meaningful, became a symbol. Even today when I think of white folks, the hard, sharp outlines of white houses surrounded by trees, lawns, and hedges

are present somewhere in the background of my mind. Through the years they grew into an overreaching symbol of fear.

[9]   It was a long time before I came in close contact with white folks again. We moved from Arkansas to Mississippi. Here we had the good fortune not to live behind the railroad tracks, or close to white neighborhoods. We lived in the very heart of the local Black Belt. There were black churches and black preachers; there were black schools and black teachers; black groceries and black clerks. In fact, everything was so solidly black that for a long time I did not even think of white folks, save in remote and vague terms. But this could not last forever. As one grows older one eats more. One's clothing costs more. When I finished grammar school I had to go to work. My mother could no longer feed and clothe me on her cooking job.

[10]   There is but one place where a black boy who knows no trade can get a job, and that's where the houses and faces are white, where the trees, lawns, and hedges are green. My first job was with an optical company in Jackson, Mississippi. The morning I applied I stood straight and neat before the boss, answering all his questions with sharp yessirs and nosirs. I was very careful to pronounce my *sirs* distinctly, in order that he might know that I was polite, that I knew where I was, and that I knew he was a *white* man. I wanted that job badly.

[11]   He looked me over as though he were examining a prize poodle. He questioned me closely about my schooling, being particularly insistent about how much mathematics I had had. He seemed very pleased when I told him I had had two years of algebra.

[12]   "Boy, how would you like to try to learn something around here?" he asked me.

[13]   "I'd like it fine, sir," I said, happy. I had visions of "working my way up." Even Negroes have those visions.

[14]   "All right," he said. "Come on."

[15]   I followed him to the small factory.

[16]   "Pease," he said to a white man of about thirty-five, "this is Richard. He's going to work for us."

[17]   Pease looked at me and nodded.

[18]   I was then taken to a white boy of about seventeen.

[19]   "Morrie, this is Richard, who's going to work for us."

[20]   "Whut yuh sayin' there, boy!" Morrie boomed at me.

[21]   "Fine!" I answered.

[22]   The boss instructed these two to help me, teach me, give me jobs to do, and let me learn what I could in my spare time.

[23]   My wages were five dollars a week.

[24]   I worked hard, trying to please. For the first month I got along O.K. Both Pease and Morrie seemed to like me. But one thing was missing. And I kept thinking about it. I was not learning anything and nobody was volunteering to help me. Thinking they had forgotten that I was to learn something about the mechanics of grinding lenses, I asked Morrie one day to tell me about the work. He grew red.

[25]   "Whut yuh tryin' t' do, nigger, git smart?" he asked.

[26]   "Naw; I ain' tryin' t' git smart," I said.

[27]   "Well, don't, if yuh know whut's good for yuh!"

[28]   I was puzzled. Maybe he just doesn't want to help me, I thought. I went to Pease.

[29]   "Say, are you crazy, you black bastard?" Pease asked me, his gray eyes growing hard.

[30]   I spoke out, reminding him that the boss had said I was to be given a chance to learn something.

[31]   "Nigger, you think you're *white,* don't you?"

[32]   "Naw, sir!"

[33]   "Well, you're acting mighty like it!"

[34]   "But, Mr. Pease, the boss said . . ."

[35]   Pease shook his fist in my face.

[36]   "This is a *white* man's work around here, and you better watch yourself!"

[37]   From then on they changed toward me. They said good-morning no more. When I was just a bit slow in performing some duty, I was called a lazy black son-of-a-bitch.

[38]   Once I thought of reporting all this to the boss. But the mere idea of what would happen to me if Pease and Morrie should learn that I had "snitched" stopped me. And after all, the boss was a white man, too. What was the use?

[39]   The climax came at noon one summer day. Pease called me to his work-bench. To get to him I had to go between two narrow benches and stand with my back against a wall.

[40]   "Yes sir," I said.

[41]   "Richard, I want to ask you something," Pease began pleasantly, not looking up from his work.

[42]   "Yes, sir," I said again.

[43]   Morrie came over, blocking the narrow passage between the benches. He folded his arms, staring at me solemnly.

[44]   I looked from one to the other, sensing that something was coming.

[45]   "Yes sir," I said for the third time.

[46]   Pease looked up and spoke very slowly.

[47]   "Richard, *Mr.* Morrie here tells me you called me *Pease.*"

[48]   I stiffened. A void seemed to open up in me. I knew this was the show-down.

[49]   He meant that I had failed to call him *Mr.* Pease. I looked at Morrie. He was gripping a steel bar in his hands. I opened my mouth to speak, to protest, to assure Pease that I had never called him simply *Pease,* and that I had never had any intentions of doing so, when Morrie grabbed me by the collar, ramming my head against the wall.

[50]   "Now, be careful, nigger!" snarled Morrie, baring his teeth. "*I* heard yuh call 'im *Pease!* 'N' if yuh say yuh didn't, yuh're callin' me a *lie,* see?" He waved the steel bar threateningly.

[51]   If I had said: No, sir, Mr. Pease, I never called you *Pease,* I would have been automatically calling Morrie a liar. And if I had said: Yes, sir, Mr. Pease, I called you *Pease,* I would have been pleading guilty to having uttered the worst insult that a Negro can utter to a southern white man. I stood hesitating, trying to frame a neutral reply.

[52]   "Richard, I asked you a question!" said Pease. Anger was creeping into his voice.

[53]   "I don't remember calling you *Pease,* Mr. Pease," I said cautiously. "And if I did, I sure didn't mean . . ."

[54]   "You black son-of-a-bitch! You called me *Pease,* then!" he spat, slapping me till I bent sideways over a bench. Morrie was on top of me, demanding:

[55]   "Didn't yuh call 'im *Pease*? If yuh say yuh didn't, I'll rip yo' gut string loose with this bar, yuh black granny dodger! Yuh can't call a white man a lie 'n' git erway with it, you black son-of-a-bitch!"

[56]   I wilted. I begged them not to bother me. I knew what they wanted. They wanted me to leave.

[57]   "I'll leave," I promised. "I'll leave right *now.*"

[58]   They gave me a minute to get out of the factory. I was warned not to show up again, or tell the boss.

[59]   I went.

[60]   When I told the folks at home what had happened, they called

me a fool. They told me that I must never again attempt to exceed my boundaries. When you are working for white folks, they said, you got to "stay in your place" if you want to keep working.

II

[61]   My Jim Crow education continued on my next job, which was portering in a clothing store. One morning, while polishing brass out front, the boss and his twenty-year-old son got out of their car and half dragged and half kicked a Negro woman into the store. A policeman standing at the corner looked on, twirling his nightstick. I watched out of the corner of my eye, never slackening the strokes of my chamois upon the brass. After a few minutes, I heard shrill screams coming from the rear of the store. Later the woman stumbled out, bleeding, crying, and holding her stomach. When she reached the end of the block, the policeman grabbed her and accused her of being drunk. Silently, I watched him throw her into a patrol wagon.

[62]   When I went to the rear of the store, the boss and his son were washing their hands at the sink. They were chuckling. The floor was bloody and strewn with wisps of hair and clothing. No doubt I must have appeared pretty shocked, for the boss slapped me reassuringly on the back.

[63]   "Boy, that's what we do to niggers when they don't want to pay their bills," he said, laughing.

[64]   His son looked at me and grinned.

[65]   "Here, hava cigarette," he said.

[66]   Not knowing what to do, I took it. He lit his and held the match for me. This was a gesture of kindness, indicating that even if they had beaten the poor old woman, they would not beat me if I knew enough to keep my mouth shut.

[67]   "Yes, sir," I said, and asked no questions.

[68]   After they had gone, I sat on the edge of a packing box and stared at the bloody floor till the cigarette went out.

[69]   That day at noon, while eating in a hamburger joint, I told my fellow Negro porters what had happened. No one seemed surprised. One fellow, after swallowing a huge bite, turned to me and asked:

[70]   "Huh! Is tha' all they did t' her?"

[71]   "Yeah. Wasn't tha' enough?" I asked.

[72]   "Shucks! Man, she's a lucky bitch!" he said, burying his lips

deep into a juicy hamburger. "Hell, it's a wonder they didn't lay her when they got through."

III

[73]   I was learning fast, but not quite fast enough. One day, while I was delivering packages in the suburbs, my bicycle tire was punctured. I walked along the hot, dusty road, sweating and leading my bicycle by the handle-bars.

[74]   A car slowed at my side.

[75]   "What's the matter boy?" a white man called.

[76]   I told him my bicycle was broken and I was walking back to town.

[77]   "That's too bad," he said. "Hop on the running board."

[78]   He stopped the car. I clutched hard at my bicycle with one hand and clung to the side of the car with the other.

[79]   "All set?"

[80]   "Yes, sir," I answered. The car started.

[81]   It was full of young white men. They were drinking. I watched the flask pass from mouth to mouth.

[82]   "Wanna drink, boy?" one asked.

[83]   I laughed as the wind whipped my face. Instinctively obeying the freshly planted percepts of my mother, I said:

[84]   "Oh, no!"

[85]   The words were hardly out of my mouth before I felt something hard and cold smash me between the eyes. It was an empty whisky bottle. I saw stars, and fell backwards from the speeding car into the dust of the road, my feet becoming entangled in the steel spokes of my bicycle. The white men piled out and stood over me.

[86]   "Nigger, ain' yuh learned no better sense'n tha' yet?" asked the man who hit me. "Ain' yuh learned t' say *sir* t' a white man yet?"

[87]   Dazed, I pulled to my feet. My elbows and legs were bleeding. Fists doubled, the white man advanced, kicking my bicycle out of the way.

[88]   "Aw, leave the bastard alone. He's got enough," said one.

[89]   They stood looking at me. I rubbed my shins, trying to stop the flow of blood. No doubt they felt a sort of contemptuous pity, for one asked:

[90]   "Yah wanna ride t' town now, nigger? Yuh reckon yuh know enough t' ride now?"

[91] "I wanna walk," I said, simply.

[92] Maybe it sounded funny. They laughed.

[93] "Well, walk, yuh black son-of-a-bitch!"

[94] When they left they comforted me with:

[95] "Nigger, yuh sho better be damn glad it wuz us yuh talked t' tha' way. Yuh're a lucky bastard, 'cause if yuh'd said tha' t' somebody else, yuh might've been a dead nigger now."

IV

[96] Negroes who have lived South know the dread of being caught alone upon the streets in white neighborhoods after the sun has set. In such a simple situation as this the plight of the Negro in America is graphically symbolized. While white strangers may be in these neighborhoods trying to get home, they can pass unmolested. But the color of a Negro's skin makes him easily recognizable, makes him suspect, converts him into a defenseless target.

[97] Late one Saturday night I made some deliveries in a white neighborhood. I was pedaling my bicycle back to the store as fast as I could, when a police car, swerving toward me, jammed me into the curbing.

[98] "Get down and put up your hands!" the policemen ordered.

[99] I did. They climbed out of the car, guns drawn, faces set, and advanced slowly.

[100] "Keep still!" they ordered.

[101] I reached my hands higher. They searched my pockets and packages. They seemed dissatisfied when they could find nothing incriminating. Finally, one of them said:

[102] "Boy, tell your boss not to send you out in white neighborhoods after sundown."

[103] As usual, I said:

[104] "Yes, sir."

V

[105] My next job was as hall-boy in a hotel. Here my Jim Crow education broadened and deepened. When the bell-boys were busy, I was often called to assist them. As many of the rooms in the hotel were occupied by prostitutes, I was constantly called to carry them liquor and cigarettes. These women were nude most of the time. They did not bother about clothing, even for bell-boys. When you went into their

rooms, you were supposed to take their nakedness for granted, as though it startled you no more than a blue vase or a red rug. Your presence awoke in them no sense of shame, for you were not regarded as human. If they were alone, you could steal sidelong glimpses at them. But if they were receiving men, not a flicker of your eyelids could show. I remember one incident vividly. A new woman, a huge, snowy-skinned blonde, took a room on my floor. I was set to wait upon her. She was in bed with a thick-set man; both were nude and uncovered. She said she wanted some liquor and slid out of bed and waddled across the floor to get her money from a dresser drawer. I watched her.

[106]   "Nigger, what in hell you looking at?" the white man asked me, raising himself upon his elbows.

[107]   "Nothing," I answered, looking miles deep into the blank wall of the room.

[108]   "Keep your eyes where they belong, if you want to be healthy!" he said.

[109]   "Yes, sir."

VI

[110]   One of the bell-boys I knew in this hotel was keeping steady company with one of the Negro maids. Out of a clear sky the police descended upon his home and arrested him, accusing him of bastardy. The poor boy swore he had had no intimate relations with the girl. Nevertheless, they forced him to marry her. When the child arrived, it was found to be much lighter in complexion than either of the two supposedly legal parents. The white men around the hotel made a great joke of it. They spread the rumor that some white cow must have scared the poor girl while she was carrying the baby. If you were in their presence when this explanation was offered, you were supposed to laugh.

VII

[111]   One of the bell-boys was caught in bed with a white prostitute. He was castrated and run out of town. Immediately after this all the bell-boys and hall-boys were called together and warned. We were given to understand that the boy who had been castrated was a "mighty, mightly lucky bastard." We were impressed with the fact that next time the management of the hotel would not be responsible for the lives of "trouble-makin' niggers." We were silent.

VIII

[112]   One night, just as I was about to go home, I met one of the Negro maids. She lived in my direction, and we fell in to walk part of the way home together. As we passed the white night-watchman, he slapped the maid on her buttock. I turned around, amazed. The watch-man looked at me with a long, hard, fixed-under stare. Suddenly he pulled his gun and asked:

[113]   "Nigger, don't yuh like it?"

[114]   I hesitated.

[115]   "I asked yuh don't yuh like it?" he asked again, stepping forward.

[116]   "Yes, sir," I mumbled.

[117]   "Talk like it, then!"

[118]   "Oh, yes, sir!" I said with as much heartiness as I could muster.

[119]   Outside, I walked ahead of the girl, ashamed to face her. She caught up with me and said:

[120]   "Don't be a fool! Yuh couldn't help it!"

[121]   This watchman boasted of having killed two Negros in self-defense.

[122]   Yet, in spite of all this, the life of the hotel ran an amazing smoothness. It would have been impossible for a stranger to detect anything. The maids, the hall-boys, and the bell-boys were all smiles. They had to be.

IX

[123]   I had learned my Jim Crow lessons so thoroughly that I kept the hotel job till I left Jackson for Memphis. It so happened that while in Memphis I applied for a job at a branch of the optical company. I was hired. And for some reason, as long as I worked there, they never brought my past against me.

[124]   Here my Jim Crow education assumed quite a different form. It was no longer brutally cruel, but subtly cruel. Here I learned to lie, to steal, to dissemble. I learned to play that dual role which every Negro must play if he wants to eat and live.

[125]   For example, it was almost impossible to get a book to read. It was assumed that after a Negro had imbibed what scanty schooling the state furnished he had no further need for books. I was always borrowing books from men on the job. One day I mustered enough cour-

age to ask one of the men to let me get books from the library in his name. Surprisingly, he consented. I cannot help but think that he consented because he was a Roman Catholic and felt a vague sympathy for Negroes, being himself an object of hatred. Armed with a library card, I obtained books in the following manner: I would write a note to the librarian, saying: "Please let this nigger boy have the following books." I would then sign it with the white man's name.

[126]   When I went to the library, I would stand at the desk, hat in hand, looking as unbookish as possible. When I received the books desired I would take them home. If the books listed in the note happened to be out, I would sneak into the lobby and forge a new one. I never took any chances guessing with the white librarian about what the fictitious white man would want to read. No doubt if any of the white patrons had suspected that some of the volumes they enjoyed had been in the home of a Negro, they would not have tolerated it for an instant.

[127]   The factory force of the optical company in Memphis was much larger than that in Jackson, and more urbanized. At least they liked to talk, and would engage the Negro help in conversation whenever possible. By this means I found that many subjects were taboo from the white man's point of view. Among the topics they did not like to discuss with Negros were the following: American white women; the Ku Klux Klan; France, and how Negro soldiers fared while there; French women; Jack Johnson; the entire northern part of the United States; the Civil War; Abraham Lincoln; U. S. Grant; General Sherman; Catholics; the Pope; Jews; the Republican Party; slavery; social equality; Communism; Socialism; the 13th and 14th Amendments to the Constitution; or any topic calling for positive knowledge or manly self-assertion on the part of the Negro. The most accepted topics were sex and religion.

[128]   There were many times when I had to exercise a great deal of ingenuity to keep out of trouble. It is a southern custom that all men must take off their hats when they enter an elevator. And especially did this apply to us blacks with rigid force. One day I stepped into an elevator with my arms full of packages. I was forced to ride with my hat on. Two white men stared at me coldly. Then one of them very kindly lifted my hat and placed it upon my armful of packages. Now the most accepted response for a Negro to make under such circumstances is to look at the white man out of the corner of his eye and grin. To have said: "Thank you!" would have made the white man *think* that you *thought* you were receiving from him a personal service.

For such an act I have seen Negroes take a blow in the mouth. Finding the first alternative distasteful, and the second dangerous, I hit upon an acceptable course of action which fell safely between these two poles. I immediately—no sooner than my hat was lifted—pretended that my packages were about to spill, and appeared deeply distressed with keeping them in my arms. In this fashion I evaded having to acknowledge his service, and, in spite of adverse circumstances, salvaged a slender shred of personal pride.

[129]   How do Negroes feel about the way they have to live? How do they discuss it when alone among themselves? I think this question can be answered in a single sentence. A friend of mine who ran an elevator once told me:

[130]   "Lawd, man! Ef it wuzn't fer them polices 'n' them ol' lynch-mobs, there wouldn't be nothin' but uproar down here!"

STUDY AND DISCUSSION

Vocabulary
Check the meaning of each of the following words in your dictionary:

1. Jim Crow (para. 6)   2. leering (para. 7)
3. symbol (para. 8)   4. castrated (para. 111)
5. dissemble (para. 124)   6. imbibed (para. 125)
7. urbanized (para. 127)   8. fared (para. 127)
9. ingenuity (para. 128)

Rhetoric
1. In your own words, state the thesis of this essay.
2. What method of organization is used throughout this essay?
3. What techniques of development are used most extensively in this essay?

Content
1. Explain how Wright learned his first lesson in how to live as a Black man in a white world. What did he learn?
2. Why did his mother beat him so brutally when he told her how he had been injured?
3. What do the cinders symbolize? What do trees, hedges, and lawns symbolize for Wright?
4. Why were the white employees of the optical company offended by Wright? What lesson did he learn there?

5. What did Wright learn on his next job about the "ethics of living Jim Crow"? What lesson did he learn in scene III? In scene IV?
6. According to Wright, why did the white prostitutes not bother with clothes when a bell-boy came into their rooms? What other lessons did Wright learn when he was employed at the hotel?
7. After he moved to Memphis, Wright tells us, his "Jim Crow" education "was no longer brutally cruel, but subtly cruel." He tells us that he learned to play a "dual role." Explain what he means by these two statements.

Ideas and Implications
1. Discuss the last two sentences in relation to the essay as a whole and as a comment on the current state of race relations in America.
2. In what ways do the Caucasians described in this essay emasculate the Black male? Do such forms of emasculation still occur? Are there other ways in which the manhood of the Black male may still be stripped from him?
3. Some sociologists have said that Blacks in America live in a matriarchal culture. Discuss that idea in relation to this essay.

INCIDENT

COUNTEE CULLEN *Countee Cullen (1903-1946), a distinguished Black poet, was educated at New York University and at Harvard. His publications include several books of poetry*—Color, Copper Sun, On These I Stand, The Ballad of the Brown Girl, *and* The Black Christ—*as well as a novel,* One Way to Heaven.

. .*"Incident," from* On These I Stand, *is an exquisite account of a sensitive young man's first experience of racial prejudice. The poem speaks so openly and so poignantly for itself that little can be said about it in the way of discussion or explanation; thus "Incident" stands alone without the usual questions for study and discussion.*

Once riding in old Baltimore,
    Heart-filled, head-filled with glee,
I saw a Baltimorean
    Keep looking straight at me.

Now I was eight and very small,
    And he was no whit bigger,
And so I smiled, but he poked out
    His tongue, and called me, "Nigger."

I saw the whole of Baltimore
    From May until December;
Of all the things that happened there
    That's all that I remember.

SON IN THE AFTERNOON

JOHN A. WILLIAMS "Son in the Afternoon" is a deceptive story: on the surface, easy, relaxed, almost random in structure; underneath, tense with compelling revelations of a Black man's soul. Wendell, the narrator, tells us about going to Couchmans' house to pick up Nora, his mother, who has spent most of her life working as a domestic in wealthy white families. "It was hot and I'm a bitch when it's hot," he tells us in the first sentence of the story. Then, seething with racial hatred and a touching, totally credible jealousy of all those white children who have received his mother's love, Wendell proceeds to behave like a "bitch." At the end, he feels as though he might throw up—he can almost hate himself—as he looks at the little boy, Ronnie; but he can still think, "There, you little bastard, there."

The author of this finely wrought story is John A. Williams. Mr. Williams has published five novels—The Angry Ones, Night Song, Sissie, The Man Who Cried I Am, and Sons of Darkness, Sons of Light. He is also the editor of The Angry Black and Beyond the Angry Black.

[1] It was hot and I'm a bitch when it's hot. I goosed the Ford over Sepulveda Boulevard toward Santa Monica until I got stuck in the traffic that pours from Elay[1] into the surrounding towns. I'd had a lousy day at the studio.

[2] I was—and still am—a writer and this studio had hired me to check scripts and films with Negroes in them to make sure the Negro movie-goer wouldn't be offended. I'm a Negro writer, you see. Anyway, the day had been tough because of a couple of verbs—slink and walk. One of those Yale guys had done a script calling for a Negro waiter to slink away from this table where a dinner party was glaring at him. I had said the waiter shouldn't slink, but walk. This Yale guy said it was essential to the plot that the waiter slink, because later on he becomes a hero. I said you don't slink one minute and be a hero the next; there has to be some consistency. The actor who played the waiter agreed with me, and so did the director. I knew this Yale guy's stuff. It was all the same, that one subtle scene packed with prejudice that usually registered subliminally. I wondered how come the guy didn't hate himself, but then, I heard he did.

[1] Elay: residents of Los Angeles frequently refer to it as L. A.

[3]   Anyway . . . hear me out now. I was on my way to Santa Monica
to pick up my mother, Nora. Sometimes I call her mother; sometimes I
call her Nora. It was a long haul for such a hot day. I had planned a
quiet evening; a nice shower, fresh clothes, and then I would have dinner at the Watkins and talk with some of the musicians making it on
the scene for a quick one before they cut out to their sets to blow. After,
I was going by the Pigalle down on Figueroa and catch Earl Grant. The
boy really plays; he'll make it big one day. And still later, if nothing
exciting happened, I'd pick up Scottie and make it to the Lighthouse
on the Beach or to the Strollers and listen to some sounds. I looked
forward to hearing Sleepy Stein's show on the way out. So you see, this
picking up Nora was a little inconvenient because we had to drive all
the way into West Los Angeles. My mother was a maid for the Couchmans. Ronald Couchman was an architect, a good one I understood
from Nora who has a fine sense for this sort of thing; you don't work in
some hundred-odd houses during your life and not get some idea of the
way a house or even a building should be laid out, if you're Nora.
Couchman's wife, Kay, was a playgirl who drove a white Jaguar from
one elbow-bending function to another. My mother didn't like her
much; she didn't seem to care much for her son, Ronald, junior. The
Couchmans lived in a real fine residential section, of course. In the
neighborhood there also lived a number of actors my mother knew
quite well, like the guy who used to play Dagwood.
[4]   Somehow it is very funny. I mean that the maids and butlers
know everything about these people and these people, like the Yale
guy, know nothing about butlers or maids. Through Nora we knew
who was laying whose wife; who had money and who *really* had money;
we knew about the wild parties hours before the police, and we knew
who smoked marijuana, when they smoked it and where they got it. We
knew all about them.
[5]   To get to the Couchmans' driveway I had to go three blocks up
one side of a palm-planted center strip and back down the other. The
drive bent gently, swept out of sight of the main road. The house, shel-
tered by slim palms, looked like a transplanted Colonial only with ugly
brown shingles. I parked and walked to the kitchen door, skirting the
growling Great Dane tied to a tree. I don't like kitchen doors. Entering
people's houses by them, I mean. I'd done this sort of thing most of my
life when I called at the places where Nora worked to pick up the
patched sheets or the half-used meats and tarnished silver—the fringe
benefits of a housemaid. As a teenager I'd told Nora I was through with

that crap; that I was not going through anybody's kitchen door. She only laughed and said I'd learn. One day I called for her—I was still a kid—and without knocking walked through the front door of this house, right through the living room. I was almost out of the room when I saw feet behind a couch. I leaned over and there was Mr. Jorgensen and his wife making out like crazy. I guess it hit them sort of sudden and they went at it like the Hell-bomb was due to drop any minute. I've been like that too, mostly in the Spring. Of course, when Mr. Jorgensen looked over his shoulder and saw me, you know what happened. I was thrown out and Nora was right behind me. In the middle of winter, the old man sick and the coal bill three months overdue. Nora was right; I learned.

[6] My mother saw me before I could ring the bell. She opened the door. "Hello," she said. She was breathing hard like she was out of breath. "Come in and sit down. I don't know *where* that Kay is. Little Ronald is sick and she's problly out gittin' drunk again." She left me and half-walked, half-ran back through the house, I guess to be with Ronnie. I disliked the combination of her white nylon uniform, her dark brown face and the streaks of gray in her hair. Nora had married this guy from Texas a few years after the old man died. He was all right, I guess, and he made out okay. Nora didn't have to work, but she couldn't be still; she always had to be doing something. I suggested she quit work, but like her husband, I had little luck. It would have been good for her to take an extended trip around the country visiting my brothers and sisters, and once she got to Philly, she'd probably go right out to the cemetery and sit awhile with the old man.

[7] I walked through the house. I liked Couchman's library. I thought if I knew him I'd like him. The room made me feel like that. I left it and went into the big living room. You could tell Couchman had let his wife do it. Everything in it was fast, moving, dart-like with no sense of ease. But on the walls were several of Couchman's conceptions of buildings and homes. His lines were neat, well-paced and functional.

[8] My mother walked rapidly through the room and without looking at me said, "Just be patient, Wendell. She should be here real soon."

[9] "Yeah," I said, "with a snootfull." I had turned back to the drawings when Ronnie scampered into the room, his face twisted with rage.

[10] "Nora!" he tried to roar, perhaps as he'd seen the parents of some of his friends roar at their maids; I'm quite sure Kay didn't shout at Nora, and I don't think Couchman would. But then, no one shouts

at Nora. That is implicit in her posture, her speech and manner. "Nora you come right back here this minute!" and the little bastard stamped and pointed to a spot on the floor where my mother was supposed to come to roost.

[11]   I have a nasty temper. Sometimes it lies dormant for ages and at other times, like when the weather is hot and nothing seems to be going right, it stands poised on a springboard. It dived off. "Don't talk to *my* mother like that you little——!" I said sharply, breaking off just before I cursed. I took a step forward, wishing he'd been big enough for me to strike. "How'd you like for me to talk to *your* mother like that?"

[12]   The nine-year-old looked up at me in surprise and confusion. He hadn't expected me to say anything; I was just another piece of furniture or something. Tears rose in his eyes and spilled out onto his pale cheeks. He put his hands behind him, twisted them. He moved backwards, away from me. He looked at my mother with a "Nora, come help me," look. And sure, there was Nora, speeding back across the room, gathering the kid in her arms, tucking his robe together.

[13]   I was almost too angry to feel hatred for myself.

[14]   Ronnie was the Couchmans' only kid. Nora loved him; I suppose that was the trouble, she loved him. Couchman was gone ten, twelve hours a day; the mother didn't stay around the house any longer than necessary, so Ronnie had only my mother. You know, I think kids should have someone to love, and Nora wasn't a bad sort. But somehow, when the six of us were growing up we never had her. She was gone, out scuffling to get those crumbs to put into our mouths and shoes for our feet and praying for something to happen so that all the space in between would be taken care of. Nora's affection for us took the form of rushing out into the morning's five o'clock blackness to wake some silly bitch and get her coffee; took form in her trudging five miles home every night instead of taking the streetcar because we always needed tablets for school, we said. But the truth was all of us liked to draw and we went through a tablet in a couple of hours every day. Can you imagine? There's not a goddamn artist among us. We never had the physical affection, the pat on the head, the quick, smiling kiss, the "gimmee a hug" routine. All of this Ronnie was getting.

[15]   He buried his little blond head in Nora's breast and sobbed. "There, there now," Nora said. "Don't you cry, Ronnie. Ol' Wendell is just jealous, and he hasn't got much sense either. He didn't mean nuthin'."

[16]   I left the room. Nora had hit it of course; hit it and passed on. I looked back. It didn't look so incongruous, the white and black together, I mean. Ronnie was still sobbing, his head now on Nora's shoulder. The only time I ever got that close to her was when she trapped me with a bearhug so she could whale the daylights out of me after I put an iceball through Mrs. Grant's window.

[17]   I walked outside and lighted a cigarette. When Ronnie was in the hospital the month before Nora got me to run her way the hell over in Hollywood every night to see him. I didn't like it worth a damn. All right, I'll admit it; it did upset me. All that affection I didn't get nor my brothers and sisters going to that little white boy who without a doubt, when away from her called her "our nigger maid." I spat at the Great Dane. He snarled and then I bounced a rock off his fanny. "Lay down you bastard," I muttered. He strained at his leash. It was a good thing he was tied up.

[18]   I heard the low cough of the Jaguar slapping against the road. The car was throttled down and with a muted roar swung into the driveway. The woman aimed it for me. I didn't move. At the last moment, grinning, she swung the wheel over and braked to a jolting stop. She bounded out of the car like a tennis player vaulting over a net. "Hi," she said. She tugged at her shorts.

[19]   "Hello."

[20]   "You're Nora's boy?"

[21]   "I'm Nora's son." I can't stand the word "boy."

[22]   We stood looking at each other while the dog whined. Kay had a nice tan, a nice body. She was high. Looking at her, I could feel myself going into my sexy-looking bastard role; sometimes I can swing it great, and I guess this was one of the times. Maybe it all had to do with the business inside. Kay took off her sunglasses and took a good look at me.

[23]   "May I have a cigarette?"

[24]   I gave her one and lighted it.

[25]   "Nice tan," I said. Most white people I know think it's a big, big deal if a Negro compliments them on their tans. It's a large laugh, honest. You have all this volleyball about color and come summer you can't hold the white folks back from the beaches and the country, anyplace where they can get sun. And of course, the blacker they get, the more pleased they are. Crazy.

[26]   "You like it?" she asked. She was pleased. She placed her arm next to mine. "Almost the same color," she said.

[27]   "Ronnie isn't feeling well," I said.

[28]   "Oh, the poor kid. I'm so glad we have Nora. She's such a charm. I'll run right in and look at him. Have a drink in the bar. Fix me one too."

[29]   Kay skipped inside and I went to the bar and poured out two drinks. I made hers three times stronger than mine. She was back soon. "Nora was trying to put him to sleep and she made me stay out." She giggled. I leaned over the bar and peered down her breasts as she gulped her drink. "Fix me another, would you?" For one second I was angry; I wasn't her damned servingman. I held my temper.

[30]   While I was fixing her drink she was saying how amazing it was for Nora to have a son who was a writer. What she was really saying was that it was amazing for a servant to have a son who was not also a servant. "Anything can happen in a democracy," I said. "Servant's sons drink with the madam and so on."

[31]   "Oh, Nora isn't a servant," Kay said. "She's part of the family."

[32]   Yeah, I thought. Where and how many times had I heard *that* jazz before? We were silent again and she said after it, "You like my tan, huh?"

[33]   This time I went close to her, held her arm and we compared the colors.

[34]   I placed one arm around her. She pretended not to see or feel it, but she wasn't trying to get away either. In fact, while trying to appear not to, she pressed just a bit closer and the register in my brain which tells me I've got it made clicked and inwardly I grinned. I looked at her. She was very high. I put both arms around her and she wrapped her arms around me, running her hands up and down the back of my neck. Then I kissed her; she responded quickly, completely.

[35]   "Mom!"

[36]   "Ronnie, come to bed," I heard Nora shout from the other room. We could hear Ronnie out there too, running over the rug. Kay tried to get away from me, push me to one side because Ronnie was coming right for the bar. "Oh, *please*," she said, "don't let him see us." I wouldn't let her push me away. "Stop!" she hissed. "He'll *see* us!" We stopped struggling, just for an instant, and we listened to the echo of the word *see*. She gritted her teeth and renewed her efforts to get away.

[37]   Me? I had the scene laid right out before me. The kid breaks in and sees his mother in this real wriggly clinch with this nigger who's just hollered at him and no matter how his mother explains it away, the kid has the image for the rest of his life.

[38]   That's the way it happened. The kid's mother hissed under her breath, *"You're crazy!"* and she looked at me as though she were seeing me or something about me for the very first time. I'd released her as soon as Ronnie, romping into the bar, saw us and came to a full, open-mouthed halt. Kay went to him. He looked first at me, then at his mother. Kay turned to me, but she couldn't speak.

[39]   Outside in the main room my mother called with her clear, loud voice, "Wendell, where are you? We can go now."

[40]   I started to move past Kay and Ronnie. I wasn't angry any longer; I felt as though I might throw up. I was beginning to feel sorry for it all, but I made my self think, *"There, you little bastard, there."*

[41]   My mother thrust her face inside the door and said, "Goodbye, Mrs. Couchman, see you tomorrow. 'Bye, Ronnie."

[42]   "Yes, Nora," Kay said, sort of stunned. "Tomorrow." She was reaching for Ronnie's hand as we left. I turned and saw that the kid was slapping her hand away. I hurried quickly after Nora.

STUDY AND DISCUSSION

1. How does the narrator's job affect his feelings about himself? (What *exactly* does he do, for instance?)
2. How does his job affect his actions in this story? Discuss in detail.
3. Analyze what you learn about Ronald Couchman. What point is there in having him seem to be a very decent person, especially when compared with his wife?
4. In para. 4, the narrator says, "We knew all about them." To what extent does that statement seem to be true? To what extent does it seem to be a reflection of the narrator's own prejudice?
5. Why does the narrator dislike kitchen doors? Is that typical of him? Why? What has the narrator learned about kichen doors?
6. How does the narrator feel about his mother? Explain in detail.
7. What is the turning point in this story—the decisive moment that causes Wendell to act as he does in the end?
8. Is it true that "Ol' Wendell is just jealous" (para. 15)?
9. Why does Wendell go into his "sexy-looking bastard role" when Kay arrives? Why does he flirt with her? Why does he refuse to let her go when Ronnie enters the room?
10. What is Kay's attitude toward Wendell? Toward Nora? Toward Ronnie?

11. What satisfaction does Wendell get out of the scene with Kay and Ronnie? What are Wendell's motives? Is he justified in doing what he does?

12. Discuss the title in relation to the story as a whole.

EARTH, FIRE, AIR, WATER

MORTGAGING THE OLD HOMESTEAD

LORD RITCHIE-CALDER   Lord Peter Ritchie-Calder, who began his career as a police court reporter in Dundee, Scotland, has served as science advisor to the United Nations. In this essay, which bristles with illustration and factual detail, he discusses the destruction of the environment as an international problem, a problem confounded by the "ignorance" of scientists and decision-makers. Lord Ritchie-Calder's works include From Magic to Medicine, The Birth of the Future, The Wonderful World of Medicine, Common Sense about a Starving World, *and* Living with the Atom. *Currently he is Edinburgh University Professor of International Relations.*

[1]   Past civilizations are buried in the graveyards of their own mistakes, but as each died of its greed, its carelessness or its effeteness an-

other took its place. That was because such civilizations took their character from a locality or region. Today ours is a global civilization; it is not bounded by the Tigris and the Euphrates nor even the Hellespont and the Indus; it is the whole world. Its planet has shrunk to a neighborhood round which a man-made satellite can patrol sixteen times a day, riding the gravitational fences of Man's family estate. It is a community so interdependent that our mistakes are exaggerated on a world scale.

[2] For the first time in history, Man has the power of veto over the evolution of his own species through a nuclear holocaust. The overkill is enough to wipe out every man, woman and child on earth, together with our fellow lodgers, the animals, the birds and the insects, and to reduce our planet to a radioactive wilderness. Or the Doomsday Machine could be replaced by the Doomsday Bug. By gene-manipulation and man-made mutations, it is possible to produce, or generate, a disease against which there would be no natural immunity; by "generate" is meant that even if the perpetrators inoculated themselves protectively, the disease in spreading round the world could assume a virulence of its own and involve them too. When a British bacteriologist died of the bug he had invented, a distinguished scientist said, "Thank God he didn't sneeze; he could have started a pandemic against which there would have been no immunity."

[3] Modern Man can outboast the Ancients, who in the arrogance of their material achievements built pyramids as the gravestones of their civilizations. We can blast our pyramids into space to orbit through all eternity round a planet which perished by our neglect.

[4] A hundred years ago Claude Bernard, the famous French physiologist, enjoined his colleagues, "True science teaches us to doubt and in ignorance to refrain." What he meant was that the scientist must proceed from one tested foothold to the next (like going into a minefield with a mine-detector). Today we are using the biosphere, the living space, as an experimental laboratory. When the mad scientist of fiction blows himself and his laboratory skyhigh, that is all right, but when scientists and decision-makers act out of ignorance and pretend that it is knowledge, they are putting the whole world in hazard. Anyway, science at best is not wisdom; it is knowledge, while wisdom is knowledge tempered with judgment. Because of overspecialization, most scientists are disabled from exercising judgments beyond their own sphere.

[5] A classic example was the atomic bomb. It was the Physicists'

Bomb. When the device exploded at Alamogordo on July 16, 1945, and made a notch-mark in history from which Man's future would be dated, the safe-breakers had cracked the lock of the nucleus before the locksmiths knew how it worked. (The evidence of this is the billions of dollars which have been spent since 1945 on gargantuan machines to study the fundamental particles, the components of the nucleus; and they still do not know how they interrelate.)

[6]   Prime Minister Clement Attlee, who concurred with President Truman's decision to drop the bomb on Hiroshima, later said: "We knew nothing whatever at that time about the genetic effects of an atomic explosion. I knew nothing about fall-out and all the rest of what emerged after Hiroshima. As far as I know, President Truman and Winston Churchill knew nothing of those things either, nor did Sir John Anderson who coordinated research on our side. Whether the scientists directly concerned knew or guessed, I do not know. But if they did, then so far as I am aware, they said nothing of it to those who had to make the decision."[1]

[7]   That sounds absurd, since as long before as 1927, Herman J. Muller had been studying the genetic effects of radiation, work for which he was awarded the Nobel Prize in 1946. But it is true that in the whole documentation of the British effort, before it merged in the Manhattan Project, there is only one reference to genetic effects—a Medical Research Council minute which was not connected with the bomb they were intending to make; it concerned the possibility that the Germans might, short of the bomb, produce radioactive isotopes as a form of biological warfare. In the Franck Report, the most statesmanlike document ever produced by scientists, with its percipience of the military and political consequences of unilateral use of the bomb (presented to Secretary of War Henry L. Stimson even before the test bomb exploded), no reference is made to the biological effects, although one would have supposed that to have been a very powerful argument. The explanation, of course, was that it was the Physicists' Bomb and military security restricted information and discussion to the bombmakers, which excluded the biologists.

[8]   The same kind of breakdown in interdisciplinary consultation was manifest in the subsequent testing of fission and fusion bombs. Categorical assurances were given that the fallout would be confined to the testing area, but the Japanese fishing-boat *Lucky Dragon* was

[1] "Twilight of Empire," by Clement Attlee with Francis Williams. New York: Barnes, 1961, p. 74.

"dusted" well outside the predicted range. Then we got the story of radiostrontium. Radiostrontium is an analogue of calcium. Therefore in bone-formation an atom of natural strontium can take the place of calcium and the radio-active version can do likewise. Radiostrontium did not exist in the world before 1945; it is a man-made element. Today every young person, anywhere in the world, whose bones are forming during the massive bomb-testing in the atmosphere, carries this brand-mark of the Atomic Age. The radiostrontium in their bones is medically insignificant, but, if the test ban (belated recognition) had not pre-vented the escalation of atmospheric testing, it might not have been.

[9]   Every young person everywhere was effected, and why? Because those responsible for H-bomb testing miscalculated. They assumed that the upthrust of the H-bomb would punch a hole in the stratosphere and that the gaseous radioactivity would dissipate itself. One of those gases was radioactive krypton, which quickly decays into radiostrontium, which is a particulate. The technicians had been wrongly briefed about the nature of the troposphere, the climatic ceiling which would, they maintained, prevent the fall-back. But between the equatorial tropo-sphere and the polar troposphere there is a gap, and the radiostrontium came back through this fanlight into the climatic jet-stream. It was swept all round the world to come to earth as radioactive rain, to be deposited on foodcrops and pastures, to be ingested by animals and to get into milk and into babies and children and adolescents whose growing bones were hungry for calcium or its equivalent strontium, in this case radio-active. Incidentally, radiostrontium was known to the biologists before it "hit the headlines." They had found it in the skin burns of animals exposed on the Nevada testing ranges and they knew its sinister nature as a "bone-seeker." But the authorities clapped security on their work, classified it as "Operation Sunshine" and cynically called the units of radiostrontium "Sunshine Units"—an instance not of ignorance but of deliberate non-communication.

[10]   One beneficial effect of the alarm caused by all this has been that the atoms industry is, bar none, the safest in the world for those working on it. Precautions, now universal, were built into the code of practice from the beginning. Indeed it can be admitted that the safety margins in health and in working conditions are perhaps excessive in the light of experience, but no one would dare to modify them. There can, however, be accidents in which the public assumes the risk. At Windscale, the British atomic center in Cumberland, a reactor burned out. Radioactive fumes escaped from the stacks in spite of the filters.

They drifted over the country. Milk was dumped into the sea because radioactive iodine had covered the dairy pastures.

[11]   There is the problem of atomic waste disposal, which persists in the peaceful uses as well as in the making of nuclear explosives. Low energy wastes, carefully monitored, can be safely disposed of. Trash, irradiated metals and laboratory waste can be embedded in concrete and dumped in the ocean deeps—although this practice raises some misgivings. But high-level wastes, some with elements the radioactivity of which can persist for *hundreds of thousands* of years, present prodigious difficulties. There must be "burial grounds" (or euphemistically "farms"), the biggest of which is at Hanford, Washington. It encloses a stretch of the Columbia River in a tract covering 575 square miles, where no one is allowed to live or to trespass.

(12]   There, in the twentieth century Giza, it has cost more, much more, to bury live atoms than it cost to entomb the sun-god Kings of Egypt. The capital outlay runs into hundreds of millions of dollars and the maintenance of the U.S. sepulchres is over $6 million a year. (Add to that the buried waste of the U.S.S.R., Britain, Canada, France and China, and one can see what it costs to bury live atoms.) And they are very much alive. At Hanford they are kept in million-gallon carbon-steel tanks. Their radioactive vitality keeps the accompanying acids boiling like a witches' cauldron. A cooling system has to be maintained continuously. The vapors from the self-boiling tanks have to be condensed and "scrubbed" (radioactive atoms removed); otherwise a radioactive miasma would escape from the vents. The tanks will not endure as long as the pyramids and certainly not for the hundreds of thousands of years of the long-lived atoms. The acids and the atomic ferments erode the toughest metal, so the tanks have to be periodically decanted. Another method is to entomb them in disused salt mines. Another is to embed them in ceramics, lock them up in glass beads. Another is what is known as "hydraulic fraction": a hole is drilled into a shale formation (below the subsoil water); liquid is piped down under pressure and causes the shale to split laterally. Hence the atoms in liquid cement can be injected under enormous pressure and spread into the fissures to set like a radiocative sandwich.

[13]   This accumulating waste from fission plants will persist until the promise, still far from fulfilled, of peaceful thermonuclear power comes about. With the multiplication of power reactors, the wastes will increase. It is calculated that by the year 2000, the number of six-ton nuclear "hearses" in transit to "burial grounds" at any given time on the

highways of the United States will be well over 3,000 and the amount of radioactive products will be about a billion curies, which is a mighty lot of curies to be roaming around a populated country.

[14]   The alarming possibilities were well illustrated by the incident at Palomares, on the coast of Spain, when there occurred a collision of a refueling aircraft with a U.S. nuclear bomber on "live" mission. The bombs were scattered. There was no explosion, but radioactive materials broke loose and the contaminated beaches and farm soil had to be scooped up and taken to the United States for burial.

[15]   Imagine what would have happened if the *Torrey Canyon*, the giant tanker which was wrecked off the Scilly Isles, had been nuclear-powered. Some experts make comforting noises and say that the reactors would have "closed down," but the *Torrey Canyon* was a wreck and the Palomares incident showed what happens when radioactive materials break loose. All those oil-polluted beaches of southwest England and the coasts of Brittany would have had to be scooped up for nuclear burial.

II

[16]   The *Torrey Canyon* is a nightmarish example of progress for its own sake. The bigger the tanker the cheaper the freightage, which is supposed to be progress. This ship was built at Newport News, Virginia, in 1959 for the Union Oil Company: it was a giant for the time— 810 feet long and 104 feet beam—but, five years later, that was not big enough. She was taken to Japan to be "stretched." The ship was cut in half amidship and a mid-body section inserted. With a new bow, this made her 974 feet long, and her beam was extended 21 feet. She could carry 850,000 barrels of oil, twice her original capacity.

[17]   Built for Union Oil, she was "owned" by the Barracuda Tanker Corporation, the head office of which is a filing cabinet in Hamilton, Bermuda. She was registered under the Liberian flag of convenience and her captain and crew were Italians, recruited in Genoa. Just to complicate the international triangle, she was under charter to the British Petroleum Tanker Company to bring 118,000 tons of crude oil from Kuwait to Milford Haven in Wales, via the Cape of Good Hope. Approaching Lands End, the Italian captain was informed that if he did not reach Milford Haven by 11 p.m. Saturday night, he would miss highwater and would not be able to enter the harbor for another five days, which would have annoyed his employers. He took a shortcut, setting course between Seven Stones rocks and the Scilly Isles, and he

finished up on Pollard Rock, in an area where no ship of that size should ever have been.

[18]   Her ruptured tanks began to vomit oil and great slicks spread over the sea in the direction of the Cornish holiday beaches. A Dutch tug made a dash for the stranded ship, gambling on the salvage money. (Where the salvaged ship could have been taken one cannot imagine since no place would offer harborage to a leaking tanker). After delays and a death in the futile salvage effort, the British Government moved in with the navy, the air force and, on the beaches, the army. They tried to set fire to the floating oil which, of course, would not volatilize. They covered the slicks with detergents (supplied at a price by the oil companies), and then the bombers moved in to try to cut open the deck and, with incendiaries, to set fire to the remaining oil in the tanks. Finally the ship foundered and divers confirmed that the oil had been effectively consumed.

[19]   Nevertheless the result was havoc. All measures had had to be improvised. Twelve thousand tons of detergents went into the sea. Later marine biologists found that the cure had been worse than the complaint. The oil was disastrous for seabirds, but marine organic life was destroyed by the detergents. By arduous physical efforts, with bull-dozers and flame-throwers and, again, more detergents, the beaches were cleaned up for the holiday-makers. Northerly winds swept the oil slicks down Channel to the French coast with even more serious conse-quences, particularly to the valuable shellfish industry. With even big-ger tankers being launched, this affair is a portentous warning.

[20]   Two years after *Torrey Canyon* an offshore oil rig erupted in the Santa Barbara Channel. The disaster to wildlife in this area, which has island nature reserves and is on the migratory route of whales, seals and seabirds, was a repetition of the *Torrey Canyon* oil-spill. And the operator of the lethal oil rig was Union Oil.

III

[21]   Another piece of stupidity shows how much we are at the mercy of ignorant men pretending to be knowledgeable. During the Interna-tional Geophysical Year, 1957-58, the Van Allen Belt was discovered. This is an area of magnetic phenomena. Immediately it was decided to explode a nuclear bomb in the Belt to see whether an artificial aurora could be produced. The colorful draperies and luminous skirts of the aurora borealis are caused by the drawing in of cosmic particles through

the rare bases of the upper atmosphere—ionization it is called; it is like passing electrons through the vacuum tubes of our common fluorescent lighting. The name Rainbow Bomb was given it in anticipation of the display it was expected to produce. Every eminent scientist in the field of cosmology, radio-astronomy or physics of the atmosphere protested at this irresponsible tampering with a system which we did not understand. And typical of the casual attitude toward this kind of thing, the Prime Minister of the day, answering protests in the House of Commons that called on him to intervene with the Americans, asked what all the fuss was about. After all, they hadn't known that the Van Allen Belt even existed a year before. This was the cosmic equivalent of Chamberlain's remark about Czechoslovakia, at the time of Munich, about that distant country of which we knew so little. They exploded the bomb. They got their pyrotechnics and we still do not know the cost we may have to pay for this artificial magnetic disturbance.

[22]   In the same way we can look with misgivings on those tracks— the white tails of the jets, which are introducing into our climatic system new factors, the effects of which are immensurable. Formation of rain clouds depends upon water vapor having a nucleus on which to form. That is how artificial precipitation is introduced—the so-called rain-making. So the jets, criss-crossing the weather system, playing noughts and crosses with it, can produce a man-made change.

[23]   In the longer term we can foresee even more drastic effects from Man's unthinking operations. At the United Nations Science and Technology Conference in Geneva in 1963 we took stock of the effects of industrialization on our total environment thus far. The atmosphere is not only the air which humans, animals and plants breathe; it is also the envelope which protects living things from harmful radiation from the sun and outer space. It is also the medium of climate, the winds and the rain. Those are inseparable from the hydrosphere—the oceans, covering seven-tenths of the globe, with their currents and extraordinary rates of evaporation; the biosphere, with its trees and their transpiration; and, in terms of human activities, the minerals mined from the lithosphere, the rock crust. Millions of years ago the sun encouraged the growth of the primeval forests, which became our coal, and the plant growth of the seas, which became our oil. Those fossil fuels, locked away for aeons of time, are extracted by man and put back into the atmosphere from the chimney stacks and the exhaust pipes of modern engineering. About 6 billion tons of carbon are mixed with the atmosphere annually. During the past century, in the process of indus-

trialization, with its release of carbon by the burning of fossil fuels, more than 400 billion tons of carbon have been artificially introduced into the atmosphere. The concentration in the air we breathe has been increased by approximately 10 percent, and if all the known reserves of coal and oil were burnt at once, the concentration would be ten times greater.

[24]   This is something more than a public health problem, more than a question of what goes into the lungs of an individual, more than a question of smog. The carbon cycle in nature is a self-adjusting mechanism. Carbon dioxide is, of course, indispensable for plants and is, therefore, a source of life, but there is a balance which is maintained by excess carbon being absorbed by the seas. The excess is now taxing this absorption and it can seriously disturb the heat balance of the earth because of what is known as the "greenhouse effect." A greenhouse lets in the sun's rays but retains the heat. Carbon dioxide, as a transparent diffusion, does likewise. It keeps the heat at the surface of the earth and in excess modifies the climate.

[25]   It has been estimated that, at the present rate of increase, the mean annual temperature all over the world might increase by 3.6 degrees centigrade in the next forty to fifty years. The experts may argue about the time factor and even about the effects, but certain things are apparent, not only in the industrialized Northern Hemisphere but in the Southern Hemisphere also. The North-polar icecap is thinning and shrinking. The seas, with their blanket of carbon dioxide, are changing their temperature, with the result that marine plant life is increasing and is transpiring more carbon dioxide. As a result of the combination, fish are migrating, changing even their latitudes. On land the snow line is retreating and glaciers are melting. In Scandinavia, land which was perennially under snow and ice is thawing, and arrow heads of over 1,000 years ago, when the black soils were last exposed, have been found. The melting of sea ice will not affect the sea level, because the volume of floating ice is the same as the water it displaces, but the melting of icecaps or glaciers, in which the water is locked up, will introduce additional water to the sea and raise the level. Rivers originating in glaciers and permanent snow fields will increase their flow; and if ice dams, such as those in the Himalayas, break, the results in flooding may be catastrophic. In this process the patterns of rainfall will change, with increased precipitation in some areas and the possibility of aridity in now fertile regions. One would be well advised not to take ninety-nine year leases on properties at present sea level.

IV

[26]   At that same conference, there was a sobering reminder of mistakes which can be writ large, from the very best intentions. In the Indus Valley in West Pakistan, the population is increasing at the rate of ten more mouths to be fed every five minutes. In that same five minutes in that same place, an acre of land is being lost through waterlogging and salinity. This is the largest irrigated region in the world. Twenty-three million acres are artificially watered by canals. The Indus and its tributaries, the Jhelum, the Chenab, the Ravi, the Beas and the Sutlej, created the alluvial plains of the Punjab and the Sind. In the nineteenth century, the British began a big program of farm development in lands which were fertile but had low rainfall. Barrages and distribution canals were constructed. One thing which, for economy's sake, was not done was to line the canals. In the early days, this genuinely did not matter. The water was being spread from the Indus into a thirsty plain and if it soaked in so much the better. The system also depended on what is called "inland delta drainage," that is to say, the water spreads out like a delta and than drains itself back into the river. After independence, Pakistan, with external aid, started vigorously to extend the Indus irrigation. The experts all said the soil was good and would produce abundantly once it got the distributed water. There were plenty of experts, but they all overlooked one thing—the hydrological imperatives. The incline from Lahore to the Rann of Kutch—700 miles—is a foot a mile, a quite inadequate drainage gradient. So as more and more barrages and more and more lateral canals were built, the water was not draining back into the Indus. Some 40 percent of the water in the unlined canals seeped underground, and in a network of 40,000 miles of canals that is a lot of water. The result was that the watertable rose. Low-lying areas became waterlogged, drowning the roots of the crops. In other areas the water crept upwards, leaching salts which accumulated in the surface layers, poisoning the crops. At the same time the irrigation regime, which used just 1½ inches of water a year in the fields, did not not sluice out those salts but added, through evaporation, its own salts. The result was tragically spectacular. In flying over large tracts of this area one would imagine that it was an Arctic landscape because the white crust of salt glistens like snow.

[27]   The situation was deteriorating so rapidly that President Ayub appealed in person to President Kennedy, who sent out a high-powered mission which encompassed twenty disciplines. This was backed by the computers at Harvard. The answers were pretty grim. It would take

twenty years and $2 billion to repair the damage—more than it cost to create the installations that did the damage. It would mean using vertical drainage to bring up the water and use it for irrigation, and also to sluice out the salt in the surface soil. If those twenty scientific disciplines had been brought together in the first instance it would not have happened.

[28]   One more instance of the far-flung consequences of men's localized mistakes: No insecticides or pesticides have ever been allowed into the continent of Antarctica. Yet they have been found in the fauna along the northern coasts. They have come almost certainly from the Northern Hemisphere, carried from the rivers of the farm-states into the currents sweeping south. In November 1969, the U.S. Government decided to "phase out" the use of DDT.

[29]   Pollution is a crime compounded of ignorance and avarice. The great achievements of *Homo sapiens* become the disaster-ridden blunders of Unthinking Man—poisoned rivers and dead lakes, polluted with the effluents of industries which give something called "prosperity" at the expense of posterity. Rivers are treated like sewers and lakes like cesspools. These natural systems—and they are living systems—have struggled hard. The benevolent microorganisms which cope with reasonable amounts of organic matter have been destroyed by mineral detergents. Witness our foaming streams. Lake Erie did its best to provide the oxygen to neutralize the pickling acids of the great steel works. But it could not contend. It lost its oxygen in the battle. Its once rich commercial fishing industry died and its revitalizing microorganic life gave place to anaerobic organisms which do not need oxygen but give off foul smells, the mortuary smells of dead water. As one Erie industrialist retorted, "It's not our effluent; it's those damned dead fish."

[30]   We have had the Freedom from Hunger Campaign; presently we shall need a Freedom from Thirst Campaign. If the International Hydrological Decade does not bring us to our senses we will face a desperate situation. Of course it is bound up with the increasing population but also with the extravagances of the technologies which claim that they are serving that population. There is a competition between the water needs of the land which has to feed the increasing population and the domestic and industrial needs of that population. The theoretical minimum to sustain living standards is about 300 gallons a day per person. This is the approximate amount of water needed to produce grain for 2½ pounds of bread, but a diet of 2 pounds of

bread and 1 pound of beef would require about 2,500 gallons. And that is nothing compared with the gluttonous requirements of steel-making, paper-making and the chemical industry.

[31]   Water—just H_2O—is as indispensable as food. To die of hunger one needs more than fifteen days. To die of thirst one needs only three. Yet we are squandering, polluting and destroying water. In Los Angeles and neighboring Southern California, a thousand times more water is being consumed than is being precipitated in the locality. They have preempted the water of neighboring states. They are piping it from Northern California and there is a plan to pipe it all the way from Canada's North-West Territories, from the Mackenzie and the Liard which flow northwards to the Arctic Ocean, to turn them back into deserts.

V

[32]   Always and everywhere we come back to the problem of population—more people to make more mistakes, more people to be the victims of the mistakes of others, more people to suffer Hell upon Earth. It is appalling to hear people complacently talking about the population explosion as though it belonged to the future, or world hunger as though it were threatening, when hundreds of millions can testify that it is already here—swear it with panting breath.

[33]   We know to the exact countdown second when the nuclear explosion took place—5:30 A.M., July 16, 1945, when the first device went off in the desert of Alamogordo, New Mexico. The fuse of the population explosion had been lit ten years earlier—February 1935. On that day a girl called Hildegarde was dying of generalized septicaemia. She had pricked her finger with a sewing needle and the infection had run amok. The doctors could not save her. Her desperate father injected a red dye into her body. Her father was Gerhard Domagk. The red dye was prontosil which he, a pharmaceutical chemist, had produced and had successfully used on mice lethally infected with streptococci, but never before on a human. Prontosil was the first of the sulfa drugs—chemotherapeutics, which could attack the germ within the living body. Thus was prepared the way for the rediscovery of penicillin—rediscovery because although Fleming had discovered it in 1928, it had been ignored because neither he nor anybody else had seen its supreme virtue of attacking germs within the living body. That is the operative phrase, for while medical science and the medical profession had used antiseptics for surface wounds

and sores, they were always labeled "Poison, not to be taken internally." The sulfa drugs had shown that it was possible to attack specific germs within the living body and had changed this attitude. So when Chain and Florey looked again at Fleming's penicillin in 1938, they were seeing it in the light of the experience of the sulfas.

[34]   A new era of disease-fighting had begun—the sulfas, the antibiotics, DDT insecticides. Doctors could now attack a whole range of invisible enemies. They could master the old killer diseases. They proved it during the war, and when the war ended there were not only stockpiles of the drugs, there were tooled up factories to produce them. So to prevent the spread of the deadly epidemics which follow wars, the supplies were made available to the war-ravaged countries with their displaced persons, and then to the developing countries. Their indigenous infections and contagions and insect-born diseases were checked.

[35]   Almost symbolically, the first clinical use of prontosil had been in dealing with puerperal sepsis, childbed fever. It had spectacularly saved mothers' lives in Queen Charlotte's Hospital, London. Now its successors took up the story. Fewer mothers died in childbirth, to live and have more babies. Fewer infants died, fewer toddlers, fewer adolescents. They lived to marry and have children. Older people were not killed off by, for instance, malaria. The average life-span increased.

[36]   Professor Kingsley Davis of the University of California at Berkeley, the authority on urban development, has presented a hair-raising picture from his survey of the world's cities. He has shown that 38 percent of the world's population is already living in what are defined as urban places. Over one-fifth of the world's population is living in cities of 100,000 or more. And over one-tenth of the world's population is now living in cities of a million or more inhabitants. In 1968, 375 million people were living in million-and-over cities. The proportions are changing so quickly that on present trends it would take only 16 years for half the world's population to be living in cities and only 55 years for it to reach 100 percent.

[37]   Within the lifetime of a child born today, Kingsley Davis foresees, on present trends of population-increase, 15 billion people to be fed and housed—nearly five times as many as now. The whole human species would be living in cities of a million-and-over inhabitants, and —wait for it!—the biggest city would have 1.3 billion inhabitants. That means 186 times as many as there are in Greater London.

[38]   For years the Greek architect Doxiadis has been warning us

about such prospects. In his Ecumenopolis—World City—one urban area like confluent ulcers would ooze into the next. The East Side of World City would have as its High Street the Eurasian Highway stretching from Glasgow to Bangkok, with the Channel Tunnel as its subway and a built-up area all the way. On the West Side of World City, divided not by the tracks but by the Atlantic, the pattern is already emerging, or rather, merging. Americans already talk about Boswash, the urban development of a built-up area stretching from Boston to Washington; and on the West Coast, apart from Los Angeles, sprawling into the desert, the realtors are already slurring one city into another all along the Pacific Coast from the Mexican Border to San Francisco. We don't need a crystal ball to foresee what Davis and Doxiadis are predicting; we can already see it through smog-covered spectacles; a blind man can smell what is coming.

[39]   The danger of prediction is that experts and men of affairs are likely to plan for the predicted trends and confirm these trends. "Prognosis" is something different from "prediction." An intelligent doctor having diagnosed your symptoms and examined your condition does not say (except in novelettes), "You have six months to live." An intelligent doctor says, "Frankly, your condition is serious. Unless you do so-and-so, and I do so-and-so, it is bound to deteriorate." The operative phrase is "do so-and-so." We don't have to plan for trends; if they are socially undesirable our duty is to plan away from them; to treat the symptoms before they become malignant.

[40]   We have to do this on the local, the national, and the international scale, through intergovernmental action, because there are no frontiers in present-day pollution and destruction of the biosphere. Mankind shares a common habitat. We have mortgaged the old homestead and nature is liable to foreclose.

STUDY AND DISCUSSION

Vocabulary

If you don't know what any or all of the following words mean, then consult your dictionary:

1. effeteness (para. 1)   2. holocaust (para. 2)
3. mutations (para. 2)   4. pandemic (para. 2)
5. biosphere (para. 4)   6. isotopes (para. 7)

7. percipience (para. 7)
8. categorical assurances (para. 8)
9. particulate (para. 9)
10. prodigious (para. 11)
11. Giza (para. 12)
12. miasma (para. 12)
13. curies (para. 13)
14. portentous (para. 19)
15. aeons (para. 23)
16. diffusion (para. 24)
17. salinity (para. 26)
18. alluvial (para. 26)
19. microorganism (para. 29)
20. indigenous (para. 34)

Rhetoric
1. What is the thesis statement for this essay?
2. Why are words like "stupidity," "ignorance," and "mistakes" repeated frequently in the essay?
3. What types of development are found in paras. 6, 7, 8, 9, 12, 16-19, 23?
4. Assume paras. 24 and 25 are one paragraph. Analyze for topic sentence, major and minor supports.
5. The essay is divided into five parts. Why?

Content
1. What does the author mean when he applies the term "ignorance" to scientists and decision-makers?
2. What instances of "stupidity" in regard to the environment does the author present to make his point "how much we are at the mercy of ignorant men pretending to be knowledgeable"?
3. Some mistakes are results of good intentions; others are compounded by avarice. Support your explanation with illustrations.
4. What are the origins of the population explosion?
5. Where will the predicted throngs of people live?
6. What does the author suggest we do if we are to prevent nature from foreclosing the mortgage on "the old homestead"?

Ideas and Implications
1. Has this world become a "community so interdependent that our mistakes are exaggerated on a world scale"?
2. If so, what would you propose be done to curtail or eliminate such "mistakes"?
3. In para. 4 the author claims that much of the trouble, the "mistakes", result from overspecialization on the part of the scientist. What are the requirements for a bachelor's degree in science? From your findings, do you conclude that the author is correct?
4. If he is correct, then what do you propose be done to make the scientist less narrow?

5. Are scientists the only ones who are so "narrow"? If not, what should be done about the curriculum in the other disciplines?

6. Considering the author's stance on matters such as nuclear energy, bigger oil tankers, longer life expectancy, might he be accused of being anti-progress?

7. How much of the environmental problem might be solved if there were a world-wide program of birth control?

THE PROBLEM

PAUL EHRLICH   What is in store for this world—perhaps even the solar system—if population continues to double at the present rate? In this selection, Stanford Professor Paul Ehrlich impresses the reader with the dire urgency of the population problem in a fact-laden analysis of its causes as well as its effects. Dr. Ehrlich's book, The Population Bomb, *from which this excerpt is taken, has been the most widely read book on overpopulation since Malthus' Essay.*

[1]   I have understood the population explosion intellectually for a long time. I came to understand it emotionally one stinking hot night in Delhi a couple of years ago. My wife and daughter and I were returning to our hotel in an ancient taxi. The seats were hopping with fleas. The only functional gear was third. As we crawled through the city, we entered a crowded slum area. The temperature was well over 100, and the air was a haze of dust and smoke. The streets seemed alive with people. People eating, people washing, people sleeping. People visiting, people arguing, and screaming. People thrusting their hands through the taxi window, begging. People defecating and urinating. People clinging to buses. People herding animals. People, people, people, people. As we moved slowly through the mob, hand horn squawking, the dust, noise, heat, and cooking fires gave the scene a hellish aspect. Would we ever get to our hotel? All three of us were, frankly, frightened. It seemed that anything could happen—but, of course, nothing did. Old India hands will laugh at our reaction. We were just some overprivileged tourists, unaccustomed to the sights and sounds of India. Perhaps, but since that night I've known the *feel* of over-population.

TOO MANY PEOPLE

[2]   Americans are beginning to realize that the undeveloped countries of the world face an inevitable population-food crisis. Each year food production in undeveloped countries falls a bit further behind burgeoning population growth, and people go to bed a little bit

hungrier. While there are temporary or local reversals of this trend, it now seems inevitable that it will continue to its logical conclusion: mass starvation. The rich are going to get richer, but the more numerous poor are going to get poorer. Of these poor, a minimum of three and one-half million will starve to death this year, mostly children. But this is a mere handful compared to the numbers that will be starving in a decade or so. And it is now too late to take action to save many of those people.

[3]   There is a temptation to stun the reader with an avalanche of statistics. I'll spare you most, but not all, of that. After all, no matter how you slice it, population is a numbers game. Perhaps the best way to impress you with numbers is to tell you about the "doubling time"— the time necessary for the population to double in size.

[4]   It has been estimated that the human population of 6000 B.C. was about five million people, taking perhaps one million years to get there from two and a half million. The population did not reach 500 million until almost 8,000 years later—about 1650 A.D. This means it doubled roughly once every thousand years or so. It reached a billion people around 1850, doubling in some 200 years. It took only 80 years or so for the next doubling, as the population reached two billion around 1930. We have not completed the next doubling to four billion yet, but we now have well over three billion people. The doubling time at present seems to be about 37 years.[1] Quite a reduction in doubling times: 1,000,000 years, 1,000 years, 200 years, 80 years, 37 years. Perhaps the meaning of a doubling time of around 37 years is best brought home by a theoretical exercise. Let's examine what might happen on the absurd assumption that the population continued to double every 37 years into the indefinite future.

[5]   If growth continued at that rate for about 900 years, there would be some 60,000,000,000,000,000 people on the face of the earth. Sixty million billion people. This is about 100 persons for each square yard of the Earth's surface, land and sea. A British physicist, J. H. Fremlin,[2] guessed that such a multitude might be housed in a continuous 2,000-story building covering our entire planet. The upper 1,000 stories would contain only the apparatus for running this gigantic warren. Ducts, pipes, wires, elevator shafts, etc., would occupy about half of the space in the bottom 1,000 stories. This would leave three or four yards of floor space for each person. I will leave to your imagination the physical details of existence in this ant heap, except to point out that all would not be black. Probably each person would be limited in

his travel. Perhaps he could take elevators through all 1,000 residential stories but could travel only within a circle of a few hundred yards' radius on any floor. This would permit, however, each person to choose his friends from among some ten million people! And, as Fremlin points out, entertainment on the worldwide TV should be excellent, for at any time "one could expect some ten million Shakespeares and rather more Beatles to be alive."

[6]   Could growth of the human population of the Earth continue beyond that point? Not according to Fremlin. We would have reached a "heat limit." People themselves, as well as their activities, convert other forms of energy into heat which must be dissipated. In order to permit this excess heat to radiate directly from the top of the "world building" directly into space, the atmosphere would have been pumped into flasks under the sea well before the limiting population size was reached. The precise limit would depend on the technology of the day. At a population size of one billion billion people, the temperature of the "world roof" would be kept around the melting point of iron to radiate away the human heat generated.

[7]   But, you say, surely Science (with a capital "S") will find a way for us to occupy the other planets of our solar system and eventually of other stars before we get all that crowded? Skip for a moment the virtual certainty that those planets are uninhabitable. Forget also the insurmountable logistic problems of moving billions of people off the Earth. Fremlin has made some interesting calculations on how much time we could buy by occupying the planets of the solar system. For instance, at any given time it would take only about 50 years to populate Venus, Mercury, Mars, the moon, and the moons of Jupiter and Saturn to the same population density as Earth.[3]

[8]   What if the fantastic problems of reaching and colonizing the other planets of the solar system, such as Jupiter and Uranus, can be solved? It would take only about 200 years to fill them "Earth-full." So we could perhaps gain 250 years of time for population growth in the solar system after we had reached an absolute limit on Earth. What then? We can't ship our surplus to the stars. Professor Garrett Hardin[4] of the University of California at Santa Barbara has dealt effectively with this fantasy. Using extremely optimistic assumptions, he has calculated that Americans, by cutting their standard of living down to 18% of its present level, could in *one year* set aside enough capital to finance the exportation to the stars of *one day's* increase in the population of the world.

[9]   Interstellar transport for surplus people presents an amusing prospect. Since the ships would take generations to reach most stars, the only people who could be transported would be those willing to exercise strict birth control. Population explosions on space ships would be disastrous. Thus we would have to export our responsible people leaving the irresponsible at home on Earth to breed.

[10]   Enough of fantasy. Hopefully, you are convinced that the population will have to stop growing sooner or later and that the extremely remote possibility of expanding into outer space offers no escape from the laws of population growth. If you still want to hope for the stars, just remember that, at the current growth rate, in a few thousand years everything in the visible universe would be converted into people, and the ball of people would be expanding with the speed of light![5] Unfortunately, even 900 years is much too far in the future for those of us concerned with the population explosion. As you shall see, the next *nine* years will probably tell the story.

[11]   Of course, population growth is not occurring uniformly over the face of the Earth. Indeed, countries are divided rather neatly into two groups: those with rapid growth rates, and those with relatively slow growth rates. The first group, making up about two-thirds of the world population, coincides closely with what are known as the "undeveloped countries" (UDCs). The UDCs are not industrialized, tend to have inefficient agriculture, very small gross national products, high illiteracy rates and related problems. That's what UDCs are technically, but a short definition of undeveloped is "starving." Most Latin American, African, and Asian countries fall into this category. The second group consists, in essence, of the "developed countries" (DCs). DCs are modern, industrial nations, such the the United States, Canada, most European countries, Israel, Russia, Japan, and Australia. Most people in these countries are adequately nourished.

[12]   Doubling times in the UDCs range around 20 to 35 years. Examples of these times (from the 1968 figures just released by the Population Reference Bureau) are Kenya, 24 years; Nigeria, 28; Turkey, 24; Indonesia, 31; Philippines, 20; Brazil, 22; Costa Rica, 20; and El Salvador, 19. Think of what it means for the population of a country to double in 25 years. In order just to keep living standards at the present inadequate level, the food available for the people must be doubled. Every structure and road must be duplicated. The amount of power must be doubled. The capacity of the transport system must be doubled. The number of trained doctors, nurses, teachers, and ad-

ministrators must be doubled. This would be a fantastically difficult job in the United States—a rich country with a fine agricultural system, immense industries, and rich natural resources. Think of what it means to a country with none of these.

[13] Remember also that in virtually all UDCs, people have gotten the word about the better life it is possible to have. They have seen colored pictures in magazines of the miracles of Western technology. They have seen automobiles and airplanes. They have seen American and European movies. Many have seen refrigerators, tractors, and even TV sets. Almost all have heard transistor radios. They *know* that a better life is possible. They have what we like to call "rising expectations." If twice as many people are to be happy, the miracle of doubling what they now have will not be enough. It will only maintain today's standard of living. There will have to be a tripling or better. Needless to say, they are not going to be happy.

[14] Doubling times for the populations of the DCs tend to be in the 50-to-200-year range. Examples of 1968 doubling times are the United States, 63 years; Austria, 175; Denmark, 88; Norway, 88; United Kingdom, 140; Poland, 88; Russia, 63; Italy, 117; Spain, 88; and Japan, 63. These are industrialized countries that have undergone the so-called demographic transition—a transition from high to low growth rate. As industrialization progressed, children became less important to parents as extra hands to work on the farm and as support in old age. At the same time they became a financial drag—expensive to raise and educate. Presumably these are the reasons for a slowing of population growth after industrialization. They boil down to a simple fact—people just want to have fewer children.

[15] This is not to say, however, that population is not a problem for the DCs. First of all, most of them are overpopulated. They are overpopulated by the simple criterion that they are not able to produce enough food to feed their populations. It is true that they have the money to buy food, but when food is no longer available for sale they will find the money rather indigestible. Then, too, they share with the UDCs a serious problem of population distribution. Their urban centers are getting more and more crowded relative to the countryside. This problem is not as severe as it is in the UDCs (if current trends should continue, which they cannot, Calcutta could have 66 million inhabitants in the year 2000). As you are well aware, however, urban concentrations are creating serious problems even in America. In the United States, one of the more rapidly growing DCs, we hear con-

stantly of the headaches caused by growing population: not just gar-
bage in our environment, but overcrowded highways, burgeoning
slums, deteriorating school systems, rising crime rates, riots, and other
related problems.

[16]   From the point of view of a demographer, the whole problem
is quite simple. A population will continue to grow as long as the birth
rate exceeds the death rate—if immigration and emigration are not
occurring. It is, of course, the balance between birth rate and death
rate that is critical. The birth rate is the number of births per thousand
people per year in the population. The death rate is the number of
deaths per thousand people per year.[6] Subtracting the death rate from
the birth rate, and ignoring migration, gives the rate of increase. If
the birth rate is 30 per thousand per year, and the death rate is 10 per
thousand per year, then the rate of increase is 20 per thousand per
year (30 − 10 = 20). Expressed as a percent (rate per hundred
people), the rate of 20 per thousand becomes 2%. If the rate of increase is 2%, then the doubling time will be 35 years. Note that if
you simply added 20 people per thousand per year to the population,
it would take 50 years to add a second thousand people (20 × 50 =
1,000). But the doubling time is actually much less because populations grow at compound interest rates. Just as interest dollars themselves earn interest, so people added to populations produce more
people. It's growing at compound interest that makes populations
double so much more rapidly than seems possible. Look at the relationship between the annual percent increase (interest rate) and the
doubling time of the population (time for your money to double):

Annual percent increase	Doubling time
1.0	70
2.0	35
3.0	24
4.0	17

[17]   Those are all the calculations—I promise. If you are interested
in more details on how demographic figuring is done, you may enjoy
reading Thompson and Lewis's excellent book, *Population Problems.*[7]

[18]   There are some professional optimists around who like to greet
every sign of dropping birth rates with wild pronouncements about the
end of the population explosion. They are a little like a person who,
after a low temperature of five below zero on December 21, interprets
a low of only three below zero on December 22 as a cheery sign of

approaching spring. First of all, birth rates, along with all demographic statistics, show short-term fluctuations caused by many factors. For instance, the birth rate depends rather heavily on the number of women at reproductive age. In the United States the current low birth rates soon will be replaced by higher rates as more post World War II "baby boom" children move into their reproductive years. In Japan, 1966, the Year of the Fire Horse, was a year of very low birth rates. There is widespread belief that girls born in the Year of the Fire Horse make poor wives, and Japanese couples try to avoid giving birth in that year because they are afraid of having daughters.

[19]   But, I repeat, it is the relationship between birth rate and death rate that is most critical. Indonesia, Laos, and Haiti all had birth rates around 46 per thousand in 1966. Costa Rica's birth rate was 41 per thousand. Good for Costa Rica? Unfortunately, not very. Costa Rica's death rate was less than nine per thousand, while the other countries all had death rates above 20 per thousand. The population of Costa Rica in 1966 was doubling every 17 years, while the doubling times of Indonesia, Laos, and Haiti were all above 30 years. Ah, but, you say, it was good for Costa Rica—fewer people per thousand were dying each year. Fine for a few years perhaps, but what then? Some 50% of the people in Costa Rica are under 15 years old. As they get older, they will need more and more food in a world with less and less. In 1983 they will have twice as many mouths to feed as they had in 1966, if the 1966 trend continues. Where will the food come from? Today the death rate in Costa Rica is low in part because they have a large number of physicians in proportion to their population. How do you suppose those physicians will keep the death rate down when there's not enough food to keep people alive?

[20]   One of the most ominous facts of the current situation is that roughly 40% of the population of the undeveloped world is made up of people *under 15 years old*. As that mass of young people moves into its reproductive years during the next decade, we're going to see the greatest baby boom of all time. Those youngsters are the reason for all the ominous predictions for the year 2000. They are the gunpowder for the population explosion.

[21]   How did we get into this bind? It all happened a long time ago, and the story involves the process of natural selection, the development of culture, and man's swollen head. The essence of success in evolution is reproduction. Indeed, natural selection is simply defined as differential reproduction of genetic types. That is, if people with blue eyes have

more children on the average than those with brown eyes, natural selection is occurring. More genes for blue eyes will be passed on to the next generation than will genes for brown eyes. Should this continue, the population will have progressively larger and larger proportions of blue-eyed people. This differential reproduction of genetic types is the driving force of evolution; it has been driving evolution for billions of years. Whatever types produced more offspring became the common types. Virtually all populations contain very many different genetic types (for reasons that need not concern us), and some are always outreproducing others. As I said, reproduction is the key to winning the evolutionary game. Any structure, physiological process, or pattern of behavior that leads to greater reproductive success will tend to be perpetuated. The entire process by which man developed involves thousands of millennia of our ancestors being more successful breeders than their relatives. Facet number one of our bind—the urge to reproduce has been fixed in us by billions of years of evolution.

[22] Of course through all those years of evolution, our ancestors were fighting a continual battle to keep the birth rate ahead of the death rate. That they were successful is attested to by our very existence, for, if the death rate had overtaken the birth rate for any substantial period of time, the evolutionary line leading to man would have gone extinct. Among our apelike ancestors, a few million years ago, it was still very difficult for a mother to rear her children successfully. Most of the offspring died before they reached reproductive age. The death rate was near the birth rate. Then another factor entered the picture—cultural revolution was added to biological evolution.

[23] Culture can be loosely defined as the body of nongenetic information which people pass from generation to generation. It is the accumulated knowledge that, in the old days, was passed on entirely by word of mouth, painting, and demonstration. Several thousand years ago the written word was added to the means of cultural transmission. Today culture is passed on in these ways, and also through television, computer tapes, motion pictures, records, blueprints, and other media. Culture is all the information man possesses except for that which is stored in the chemical language of his genes.

[24] The large size of the human brain evolved in response to the development of cultural information. A big brain is an advantage when dealing with such information. Big-brained individuals were able to deal more successfully with the culture of their group. They were thus more successful reproductively than their smaller-brained relatives.

They passed on their genes for big brains to their numerous offspring. They also added to the accumulating store of cultural information, increasing slightly the premium placed on brain size in the next generation. A self-reinforcing selective trend developed—a trend toward increased brain size.[8]

[25] But there was, quite literally, a rub. Babies had bigger and bigger heads. There were limits to how large a woman's pelvis could conveniently become. To make a long story short, the strategy of evolution was not to make a woman bell-shaped and relatively immobile, but to accept the problem of having babies who were helpless for a long period while their brains grew after birth.[9] How could the mother defend and care for her infant during its unusually long period of helplessness? She couldn't, unless Papa hung around. The girls are still working on that problem, but an essential step was to get rid of the short, well-defined breeding season characteristic of most mammals. The year-round sexuality of the human female, the long period of infant dependence on the female, the evolution of the family group, all are at the roots of our present problem. They are essential ingredients in the vast social phenomenon that we call sex. Sex is not simply an act leading to the production of offspring. It is a varied and complex cultural phenomenon penetrating into all aspects of our lives—one involving our self-esteem, our choice of friends, cars, and leaders. It is tightly interwoven with our mythologies and history. Sex in man is necessary for the production of young, but it also evolved to ensure their successful rearing. Facet number two of our bind—our urge to reproduce is hopelessly entwined with most of our other urges.

[26] Of course, in the early days the whole system did not prevent a very high mortality among the young, as well as among the older members of the group. Hunting and food-gathering is a risky business. Cavemen had to throw very impressive cave bears out of their caves before the men could move in. Witch doctors and shamans had a less than perfect record at treating wounds and curing disease. Life was short, if not sweet. Man's total population size doubtless increased slowly but steadily as human populations expanded out of the African cradle of our species.

[27] Then about 8,000 years ago a major change occurred—the agricultural revolution. People began to give up hunting food and settled down to grow it. Suddenly some of the risk was removed from life. The chances of dying of starvation diminished greatly in some human groups. Other threats associated with the nomadic life were also

reduced, perhaps balanced by new threats of disease and large-scale warfare associated with the development of cities. But the overall result was a more secure existence than before, and the human population grew more rapidly. Around 1800, when the standard of living in what are today the DCs was dramatically increasing due to industrialization, population growth really began to accelerate. The development of medical science was the straw that broke the camel's back. While lowering death rates in the DCs was due in part to other factors, there is no question that "instant death control," exported by the DCs, has been responsible for the drastic lowering of death rates in the UDCs. Medical science, with its efficient public health programs, has been able to depress the death rate with astonishing rapidity and at the same time drastically increase the birth rate; healthier people have more babies.

[28]   The power of exported death control can best be seen by an examination of the classic case of Ceylon's assault on malaria after World War II. Between 1933 and 1942 the death rate due directly to malaria was *reported* as almost two per thousand. This rate, however, represented only a portion of the malaria deaths, as many were reported as being due to "pyrexia."[10] Indeed, in 1934-1935 a malaria epidemic may have been directly responsible for fully half of the deaths on the island. In addition, malaria, which infected a large portion of the population, made people susceptible to many other diseases. It thus contributed to the death rate indirectly as well as directly.

[29]   The introduction of DDT in 1946 brought rapid control over the mosquitoes which carry malaria. As a result, the death rate on the island was halved in less than a decade. The death rate in Ceylon in 1945 was 22. It dropped 34% between 1946 and 1947 and moved down to ten in 1954. Since the sharp postwar drop it has continued to decline and now stands at eight. Although part of the drop is doubtless due to the killing of other insects which carry disease and to other public health measures, most of it can be accounted for by the control of malaria.

[30]   Victory over malaria, yellow fever, smallpox, cholera, and other infectious diseases has been responsible for similar plunges in death rate throughout most of the UDCs. In the decade 1940-1950 the death rate declined 46% in Puerto Rico, 43% in Formosa, and 23% in Jamaica. In a sample of 18 undeveloped areas the average decline in death rate between 1945 and 1950 was 24%.

[31]   It is, of course, socially very acceptable to reduce the death rate.

Billions of years of evolution have given us all a powerful will to live. Intervening in the birth rate goes against our evolutionary values. During all those centuries of our evolutionary past, the individuals who had the most children passed on their genetic endowment in greater quantities than those who reproduced less. Their genes dominate our heredity today. All our biological urges are for more reproduction, and they are all too often reinforced by our culture. In brief, death control goes with the grain, birth control against it.

[32]   In summary, the world's population will continue to grow as long as the birth rate exceeds the death rate; it's as simple as that. When it stops growing or starts to shrink, it will mean that either the birth rate has gone down or the death rate has gone up or a combination of the two. Basically, then, there are only two kinds of solutions to the population problem. One is a "birth rate solution," in which we find ways to lower the birth rate. The other is a "death rate solution," in which ways to raise the death rate—war, famine, pestilence—*find us.* The problem could have been avoided by *population control,* in which mankind consciously adjusted the birth rate so that a "death rate solution" did not have to occur.

NOTES

1. Since this was written, 1968 figures have appeared, showing that the doubling time is now 35 years.
2. J. H. Fremlin, "How Many People Can the World Support?" *New Scientist,* October 29, 1964.
3. To understand this, simply consider what would happen if we held the population constant at three billion people by exporting all the surplus people. If this were done for 37 years (the time it now takes for one doubling) we would have exported three billion people—enough to populate a twin planet of the Earth to the same density. In two doubling times (74 years) we would reach a total human population for the solar system of 12 billion people, enough to populate the Earth and three similar planets to the density found on Earth today. Since the areas of the planets and moons mentioned above are not three times that of the Earth, they can be populated to equal density in much less than two doubling times.
4. "Interstellar Migration and the Population Problem." *Heredity* 50: 68–70, 1959.
5. I. J. Cook, *New Scientist,* September 8, 1966.
6. The birth rate is more precisely the total number of births in a country during a year, divided by the total population at the midpoint of the year, multiplied by 1,000. Suppose that there were 80 births in Lower Slobbovia during 1967, and that the population of Lower Slobbovia was 2,000 on July 1, 1967. Then the birth rate would be:

$$\text{Birth rate} = \frac{80 \ (\text{total births in L. Slobbovia in 1967})}{2,000 \ (\text{total population, July 1, 1967})} \times 1,000$$

$$= .04 \times 1,000 = 40$$

Similarly if there were 40 deaths in Lower Slobbovia during 1967, the death
rate would be:

Death rate =
40 (total deaths in L. Slobbovia in 1967)
2,000 (total population, July 1, 1967)
$\times$ 1,000
= .02 $\times$ 1,000 = 20

Then the Lower Slobbovian birth rate would be 40 per thousand, and the
death rate would be 20 per thousand. For every 1,000 Lower Slobbovians alive
on July 1, 1967, 40 babies were born and 20 people died. Subtracting the death
rate from the birth rate gives us the rate of natural increase of Lower Slobbovia
for the year 1967. That is, $40 - 20 = 20$; during 1967 the population grew at a
rate of 20 people per thousand per year. Dividing that rate by ten expresses the
increase as a percent (the increase per hundred per year). The increase in 1967
in Lower Slobbovia was two percent. Remember that this rate of increase ignores
any movement of people into and out of Lower Slobbovia.

7. McGraw-Hill Book Company, Inc., New York. 1965.
8. Human brain size increased from an apelike capacity of about 500 cubic centi-
meters (cc) in *Australopithecus* to about 1,500 cc in modern *Homo sapiens*.
Among modern men small variations in brain size do not seem to be related to
significant differences in the ability to use cultural information, and there is no
particular reason to believe that our brain size will continue to increase. Further
evolution may occur more readily in a direction of increased efficiency rather
than increased size.
9. This is, of course, an oversimplified explanation. For more detail see Ehrlich and
Holm, *The Process of Evolution*, McGraw-Hill Book Company, Inc., New York.
1963.
10. These data and those that follow on the decline of death rates are from Kingsley
Davis's "The Amazing Decline of Mortality in Underdeveloped Areas," *The
American Economic Review*, Vol. 46, pp. 305–318.

STUDY AND DISCUSSION

Vocabulary

Check the meaning of any of the following words you do not know in a
dictionary of probity and repute:

1. defecating (para. 1)   2. burgeoning (para. 2)
3. warren (para. 5)   4. dissipated (para. 6)
5. demographic (para. 14)   6. demographer (para. 16)
7. differential (para. 21)   8. genetic (para. 21)
9. mythologies (para. 25)   10. facet (para. 25)
11. nomadic (para. 27)

Rhetoric

1. Why will para. 1 probably grab reader interest?
2. What types of development does the author use in paras. 4, 5, 11, 14,
16, 19?

3. What kind of paragraph is para. 3?
4. Sometimes the topic sentence for a paragraph is found in the previous one. What are the topic sentences for paras. 4 and 5?
5. Analyze para. 4 for topic sentence, major and minor supports. What is the function of the next-to-last sentence in para. 4? Also analyze paras. 11 and 15 for topic sentence, major and minor supports. Paras. 11, 15, 21-25 follow what patttern of organization?
6. List the transitional terms in the first sentences of paras. 7, 11, 13, 15, 19, 25, 26, 31.

Content
1. Why does Ehrlich see mass starvation as inevitable in underdeveloped countries?
2. At what rate through history has the world's population doubled?
3. What will happen to living space if population continues to double at the present rate for the next 900 years?
4. Why couldn't the earth continue to support such a population increase beyond that point? Actually how much time does Ehrlich feel we really have left to do something about the problem?
5. Is there any hope that we might relieve population pressure on earth by occupying planets of the solar system?
6. Just how badly are the UDCs and the DCs overpopulated right now? What does the doubling of population mean in terms of the economy of an underdeveloped country?
7. Explain in detail why the relationship between birth rate and death rate is so critical.
8. What was there about the evolution of man that produced the population problem?
9. What are the two alternative solutions, one of which Ehrlich sees as inevitable?

Ideas and Implications
1. Many people feel that Dr. Ehrlich's predictions are much exaggerated; the world is not really in any great danger of overpopulation; ways have "always been found to feed people and we can develop new ways"; that "there is plenty of empty land—say in Nevada or Arizona—that could be cultivated." Do you find these arguments persuasive?
2. In the face of dire projections of what we can expect from the current population explosion, why do certain individuals, groups, even institutions, still deplore birth control or homosexuality? Do you find any validity in such arguments?
3. Why not withdraw aid to the UDCs in the hope that disease, etc., would make their population growth less rapid?

4. Do the chances for war including a world war increase as population rises so sharply in the UDCs? Explain.
5. What will happen to the dignity of man in those DCs which have always regarded it so highly should the present population trend continue for the next 900 years?
6. Why does Dr. Ehrlich say that the next nine years will tell the story about the population explosion?

WILDERNESS AND HUMANITY

ASHLEY MONTAGU "To be cut off from the wilderness is to suffer a *spiritual impoverishment and curtailment of life which the understanding and appreciation of the wilderness and the kinship with nature and everything in it, brings. It is not the notion of the wilderness for its own sake that is of value, but the awareness of one's relatedness to it, one's unity with it, that deepens and extends the scope of human life," writes the renowned British anthropologist Ashley Montagu in the fourteenth paragraph of the following essay which, we feel, cannot help but involve you with the urgent need our species has to get back to its roots.*

Among Ashley Montagu's most famous books are: The Direction of Human Development, Education and Human Relations, On Being Human, The Natural Superiority of Women, *and* The Humanization of Man.

[1]   Some weeks ago a cartoonist, clearly painfully aware of what has been going on around him, produced a cartoon showing two obviously opulent men standing amidst a host of oil derricks and the splintered remnants of trees by a pool filled with oil slick and debris. With evident pride one of these instruments of destruction, surveying the devastation they had jointly wrought, remarks to the other, "And to think that only a few weeks ago all this was wilderness."

[2]   That cartoon faithfully recorded an incident which must have been repeated scores of thousands of times in the United States alone, not to mention other lands. A short time ago I read in the *New York Times* an account of a developer who had announced his intention of erecting a housing project on one of the last remaining woods in Long Island. The residents, revolted by the threatened destruction, called a meeting of protest at which the developer presented his case. He failed to understand, he said, how there could possibly be the last objection to his proposed leveling of the woodland, and with a sincerity that could only have sprung from the deepest conviction, he pleadingly said, "But, look what beautiful houses, streets, roadways and gas stations there would be where now there is only wilderness." It was, in its way, really quite touching, for I am informed that he had a catch in his voice. He doubtless felt as Milton might have done had his *Paradise Lost* been

rejected by an uncomprehending editor. What the outcome of the meeting was I do not know, but I suspect that the developer won out, and
that for him the destruction of the woodland and its replacement by a
development assumed the form of *Paradise Regained*. Like Peter Bell:

> *A primrose by a river's brim*
> *A yellow primrose was to him,*
> *And it was nothing more.*

[3]   There can be little doubt that there are among us, in numbers
saddening to reflect upon, many who when they see a blade of grass or
a tree immediately feel how nice it would be if it could be bulldozed
out of existence and a surface of asphalt put in its place. Wilderness is
equated to wasteland, and with the pressures of population being what
they are, there remain few among us who seem able to contemplate
with equanimity good land going to what they consider waste.

[4]   Wherever one may live, it is not necessary to travel far to observe
the human and natural devastation that is everywhere about us, the
debasement of the human spirit, the disinheritance of the birthright of
millions of human beings, the disengagement from humanity, the
progression from cruelty to callousness to indifferences to unawareness.
This is a condition of millions of human beings, the product of over-
population, of what inevitably occurs when human beings uncon-
trolledly, thoughtlessly, unfeelingly, and irresponsibly do as they please.

[5]   If the human landscape has been devastated, what shall one say
of the rapine and spoilation of the natural landscape, of the wilderness,
the congenial environment in which man once lived? Here there has
been not only destruction of the natural beauties of the land but also
an unspeakable transmogrification and uglification of it. The living
creatures that once inhabited the land are everywhere threatened with
extinction. Numberless animals, every day, birds and butterflies, beautiful and enhancing, cease to be before the onrushing masses of re-
duplicating human beings and the poisons they produce. The air, the
land, rivers, lakes, and streams are unconscionably polluted, while the
silent spring bears poignant testimony to the degradation of the human
spirit. As Aldous Huxley remarked after reading Rachel Carson's book,
we are exterminating half the basis of English poetry. And as the editor of the *Architectural Forum* put it in the title of a significant book,
we are turning God's Own Country into *God's Own Junkyard*, as anyone who travels along our highways may see for himself.

[6]   Perhaps the greatest havoc wrought by the pressures of popula-

tion has been the damage of the human spirit, disabling millions of human beings from the ability to perceive and to feel as human beings. Conditioned in a world which places an exaggerated value upon things, these persons take such things for granted, perceiving what they see only as things, not in the least in the context of the human situation, in the context of the necessity of beauty, and scarcely ever being humanly affronted by them. On the other hand, they rejoice in the great highways and freeways that have brought about the destruction of millions of trees, the annihilation of parklands, farmlands, meadows, orchards, and the wilderness. And to what end? So that the slums of the immediate future may replace them in order to house the millions who will require the sewers, the gasoline stations, shopping centers, hot dog stands, drive-ins, and other desecrations of the landscape which, like a cancerous growth, spread over the length and breadth of the land destroying everything beautiful or potentially beautiful in their path.

[7]   These desecrations are a cancer from which a great part of the inhabited world is increasingly suffering. Unless we quickly learn to understand the causes of this disorder, we shall be overcome by our own misguided thrust toward survival. This is no empty Jeremiad, for man's survival depends on his ability to care for and use his natural resources.

[8]   Contemporary man in relation to the wilderness is well described in A. E. Housman's "improvement" on Frances Cornford's poem "To a Fat Lady Seen from the Train."

> *O why do you walk through the fields in boots,*
> *Missing so much and so much?*
> *O fat white person whom nobody shoots,*
> *Why do you walk through the fields in boots,*
> *When the grass is soft as the breast of coots*
> *And shivering-sweet to the touch?*
> *O why do you walk through the field in boots,*
> *Missing so much and so much?*

[9]   It was not always so. Man has been on this earth for about two million years, and for almost the whole of that time he lived in the wilderness; it was his home and his world. And of that world he considered himself a natural part. He was a food gatherer and hunter, and he saw and experienced the world as a web of intricate interrelationships of which he, in common with every other living thing—everything indeed, in nature—was an inseparable and connected part.

[10]   Such people, living as close to nature as they do, entertain a

wholly different conception of their relation to the world in which they live from that of the town dweller of civilized societies. Indeed, the modern urbanite is so far removed from the world of nature, while his views of his own relation to the world in which he finds himself differ so profoundly from those of peoples living closer to nature that he usually finds it difficult, if not impossible, to understand the meaning of such peoples' beliefs. He, therefore, tends to treat them as odd, curious, esoteric, primitive, savage, wild, and strange. So far as urban man departed from life in the wilderness that he comes to regard it as something crude and rude, "wild" in the worser meaning of that word. Like his conception of "wild" animals, his view of the wilderness is as far removed from the realities as it could possibly be. A strong case might, in fact, be made for civilized man being the only "wild" animal in existence. Animals in the state of nature do not make war upon their own kind; they have no Attilas or Hitlers. They seldom exhibit the kind of savagery that civilized men exhibit toward one another. Civilized man, especially in the western world, has projected an image of his own violent self upon the screen of nature. Without in any way wishing to diminish the great contribution of Darwin toward our understanding of nature, his view of nature, as Patrick Geddes was the first to point out, was substantially a projection of conditions prevailing in 19th Century industrial Europe upon the backdrop of nature. One of Darwin's favorite phrases in *The Origin of Species* was "the warfare of Nature." It was an idea that Darwin inherited from earlier thinkers and from his environment. The conception of nature as a gladiatorial show is one which the followers of Darwin even more than Darwin himself helped to perpetuate. For most people today the idea of nature as the "wild," the "jungle," in the Darwinian sense, is the only idea of nature they know.

[11]   The myth of the beast and the myth of the jungle (as the mythological beliefs relating to wild animals and nature may be called) profoundly affect the attitudes and conduct of those who adhere to such myths toward the "wilderness." Seen through the distorting glass of their prejudices, the wilderness is something to be civilized, brought under control. The best way to do that is, of course, to get rid of it and to turn its "useless" acres to profitable use. Under the pressures of expanding populations, this has everywhere been the history of the destruction of the wilderness. Under the increasing accelerating pressures of population everywhere in the inhabited world, millions of acres of wilderness are destined to be destroyed. It is, therefore, all the more

necessary to do what we can now to make clear to everyone what such devastation is likely to do to humanity. In this way, perhaps, we may yet be able to save some remnants of the wilderness and also help to revitalize and renew man's necessary relationship to it.

[12]   Man, it cannot too often be pointed out, is a wild animal who has, in civilized societies, domesticated himself. Urban man especially lives under highly artificial conditions, in most cases far removed from the wilderness. Millions of such dwellers have never seen an apple on a tree, and the only animals they know are domestic ones and those they may have seen in zoos. This virtual complete separation from nature leads to a view of it which is wholly disengaged, even alienated, and frequently hostile. This is a pathological state, a morbid dissociation from what should have been a vital involvement in relation to the whole of nature. Man's two million or so years spent in close interrelationship with the wilderness helped to form him and make possible everything he has since done, and yet I believe with Benjamin Rush, that, "Man is naturally a wild animal . . . taken from the woods, he is never happy . . . till he returns to them again." This should not be taken to mean that there exists anything like an archetypal species memory, but what I think it should be taken to mean is that man is a part of the wilderness, a part of nature, and that his relation to it is not merely one of natural harmony and ecologic necessity, but also of civilized health. A healthy relationship to the wilderness is not in the least incompatible with civilized living. Indeed, I believe it to be an indispensable condition thereof; that no man is truly civilized unless he is involved in and cares for the wilderness. To live in the city can be quite wonderful and enlarging, but not if it renders one insensitive to the meaning of the wilderness. Detachment from the wilderness means detachment from the world of nature, an exchange of the one for attachment to the world of things. Most people feel this and hence the strong urge that so often comes upon them to return to the wilderness. The enormous number of people who enjoy camping with their families in the wilderness, and even those who prefer more sophisticated reversions to the wilderness such as a country or seashore hotel, or those Isles of Illusion, Palm Springs and Las Vegas, constitute a significant testimony not merely to the desire for a change of scene, but to the deep-seated need to get out into the open. It is a feeling beautifully expressed in Keats' sonnet,

> To one who has been long in city pent,
> 'Tis very sweet to look into the fair
> And open face of heaven—to breathe a prayer

> Full in the smile of the blue firmament.
> Who is more happy, when, with heart's content,
>   Fatigued he sinks into some pleasant lair
>   Of wavy grass, and reads a debonair
> And gentle tale of love and languishment?
> Returning home at evening, with an ear
>   Catching the notes of Philomel—an eye
> Watching the sailing cloudlet's bright career,
>   He mourns that day so soon has glided by:
> E'en like the passage of an angel's tear
>   That falls through the clear ether silently.

[13]   Perhaps no other poet has put it better than Wordsworth in his "Lines Composed a Few Miles Above Tintern Abbey, on Revisiting the Banks of the Wye During a Tour, July 13, 1798."

>   For I have learned
>   To look on nature, not as in the hour
>   Of thoughtless youth, but hearing oftentimes
>   The still sad music of humanity,
>   Nor harsh nor grating, though of ample power
>   To chasten and subdue. And I have felt
>   A presence that disturbs me with the joy
>   Of elevated thoughts; a sense sublime
>   Of something far more deeply interfused,
>   Whose dwelling is the light of setting suns,
>   And the round ocean, and the living air,
>   And the blue sky, and in the mind of man,
>   A motion and a spirit, that impels
>   All thinking things, all objects of all thought,
>   And rolls through all things. Therefore am I still
>   A lover of the meadows and the woods,
>   And mountains; and of all that we behold
>   From this green earth; of all the mighty world
>   Of eye and ear, both what they half create,
>   And what perceive; well pleased to recognize
>   In nature and the language of the sense,
>   The anchor of my purest thoughts, the nurse,
>   The guide, the guardian of my heart, and soul
>   Of all my moral being.

[14]   To be cut off from the wilderness is to suffer a spiritual im-

poverishment and curtailment of life which the understanding and appreciation of the wilderness and the kinship with nature and everything in it, brings. It is not the notion of the wilderness for its own sake that is of value, but the awareness of one's relatedness to it, one's unity with it, that deepens and extends the scope of human life. The esthetic life and the enjoyment of the merely picturesque often lead to a sybaritic self-indulgence rather than to spiritual exaltation. And neither the one nor the other are enough, for what is necessary is the recognition of the simple fact that our wholeness as human beings depends upon the depth of our awareness of the fact that we are a part of the wholeness of nature, and that the standards of dominance we have erected for ourselves in relation to nature are artificial and destructive. As Immanuel Kant remarked, evolution has been anthropocentrically envisaged as "a very long ladder, created by man to place himself on the highest rung." And so we have created categories of "higher" and "lower" animals, a kind of race prejudice from the folly of which the "highest" so-called may justifiably do with the "lowest" so-called whatever they opportunistically desire. It is alleged that man is made in God's image, but that the beast is made in the image of the brute. Man, it is alleged, is loving and intelligent, the most successful of all creatures, and therefore superior to all other creatures, who act from instinct and not from intelligence, from selfish appetite and not from love. These are among the most entrenched beliefs of the learned as well as of the ignorant.

[15] It is all very well awarding ourselves prizes for extreme, even excessive, ingenuity, but if that ingenuity leads to the kind of destructiveness that man has been practicing in the recent period, man's ingenuity may yet prove itself to have been the most selectively disadvantageous trait that any creature has yet developed.

[16] Man prides himself upon the variety of his inventiveness, but the variety of animated nature is far greater than that achieved by man. If man would simply have the grace and the humility to acknowledge himself the made-over ape that he is, he might be able to see the world of which he is a part in truer perspective. Like most self-made men, man, who has made himself, is an outstanding example of unskilled labor, a very imperfect creature, indeed. Man is, in fact, the only example of 150-pound nonlinear servomechanism that can be wholly reproduced by unskilled labor—and the lack of skill he exhibits in the making of human beings is prodigious. Indeed, that lack of skill threatens to put an end to us all. What man has made of man and of the world

in which he lives is a sorry story. What animal, indeed, has created as much devastation? It is written in the Book of Job:

Ask now the beasts and they shall teach thee; and the fowls of the air, and they shall teach thee:
Or speak to the earth, and it shall teach thee and the fishes of the sea shall declare unto thee.
Who knoweth not in all these that the hand of the Lord hath wrought this?
In whose hand is the soul of every living thing, and the breath of all mankind.

And in the Koran it is written,

There is no beast on earth nor fowl that flieth, but the same are a people like unto you, and to God they shall return.

[17]   Without accepting these words in their literal sense, the fundamental truths they express are beyond dispute, namely, that we can learn from these other "peoples," and that we ought to love and respect them for what they are, our kin.

[18]   Who but a few have ever given any attention to the profound meaning of those words? Saint Francis of Assisi, whose love for all living creatures is a part of our tradition, is regarded as an eccentric who carried things too far, and to whom, at best, we offer up the smoke of incense as before an empty shrine.

[19]   Man may yet restore himself to health if he will learn to understand himself in relation to the world of nature in which he evolved as an integral part, and to appreciate the nature of his relationship to the world of nature. He has for too long diminished himself by his prejudiced and false views of himself in relation to that nature, and in so doing he has diminished and devastated so much of the rest of the world. He has everything to gain from taking a fresh look at the world of nature and making it a part of life as essential to him as he is essential to it. The lessons man may learn from the study of nature are of at least as great significance as any he can learn from the purely human tradition, for as Wordsworth said in the poem already quoted:

> *Nature never did betray*
> *The heart that loved her; 'tis her privilege*
> *Through all the years of this our life, to lead*
> *From joy to joy: for she can so inform the mind*
> *The mind that is within us, so impress*
> *With quietness and beauty, and so feed*

With lofty thoughts, that neither evil tongues,
Rash judgments, nor the sneers of selfish men,
Nor greetings where no kindness is, nor all
The dreary intercourses of daily life,
Shall e'er prevail against us, or disturb
Our cheerful faith that all which we behold
Is full of blessings.

STUDY AND DISCUSSION

Vocabulary
Support your local dictionary . . .

1. opulent (para. 1)
2. equanimity (para. 3)
3. devastation (para. 3)
4. debasement (para. 3)
5. rapine (para. 5)
6. transmogrification (para. 5)
7. enhancing (para. 5)
8. unconscionably (para. 5)
9. poignant (para. 5)
10. degradation (para. 5)
11. havoc (para. 6)
12. wrought (para. 6)
13. annihilation (para. 6)
14. desecrations (para. 6)
15. Jeremiad (para. 7)
16. urbanite (para. 10)
17. esoteric (para. 10)
18. pathological (para. 12)
19. archetypal species memory (para. 12)
20. incompatible (para. 12)
21. sybaritic self-indulgence (para. 14)
22. anthropocentrically (para. 14)
23. entrenched (para. 14)

Rhetoric
1. How do the opening two paragraphs set the stage for Ashley Montagu's argument? Consider, too, the use of the three lines of poetry by Peter Bell—is Montagu consistent in his use of poetic quotes throughout the article?
2. What effect does Montagu's frequent "appeal to poetry" have on (a) his essay as a whole, (b) you? Is this, in other words, a valid rhetorical device? This article originally appeared in a publication of The Sierra Club—do you think that Montagu's knowing specifically how his audience already felt about the subject of ecology freed him to ground so much of his argument in poetry? In other words, could Montagu "get away" with so much poetry if he was writing for a magazine like *Sports Illustrated* or like *Fortune*? Why/why not?

3. On the basis of the following quotations (from paras. 4, 10 and 16), what can you say about Montagu's style? Does it, in other words, fit his theme? Or is it merely some kind of artificial decoration?

> ". . . the debasement of the human spirit, the disinheritance of the birthright of millions of human beings, the disengagement from humanity, the progression from cruelty to callousness to indifference to unawareness . . ."

> (The modern urbanite) "therefore, tends to treat them as odd, curious, esoteric, primitive, savage, wild, and strange."

> "It is written in the book of Job: *Ask now the beasts and they shall teach thee . . .*"

> "And in the Koran it is written: *There is no beast on earth nor foul that flieth, but the same are people like unto you . . .*"

4. What role does para. 9 play in the overall strategy of the essay?
5. What role does para. 19 play? Is it, in your opinion, a successful one?

Content

1. In the eyes of real-estate speculators, what is "wilderness" equated with?
2. What does Ashley Montagu feel is "the greatest havoc wrought" by the pressures of over-population?
3. What conception of nature does the author say that Darwin and his followers perpetuated? What effect has it had on our attitude toward nature? What is the probable outcome of this attitude as regards the future of our species?
5. What are we, in Montagu's eyes? How does he define us?
6. What does Montagu say we exchange for our "detachment from the world of nature"? What happens to us once we are cut off from the wilderness?

Ideas and Implications

1. Montagu is too hard on us. He forgets just how callously indifferent to our fate "Nature" is. Choking blizzards, blinding rains, parching droughts, devastating hurricanes, murderous earthquakes—all these are part of nature, too. (To say nothing of sharks, the bacterial diseases, and the various blood-sucking insects.) Nature fights us every inch of the way, and what we have achieved has come at a tremendous price, because "Mother Nature" is out to kill us . . .
2. Montagu is dead right/dead wrong when he says, in para. 10, that "animals in the state of nature do not make war upon their own kind . . ."

3. "It is not the notion of wilderness for its own sake that is of value, but the awareness of one's relatedness to it, one's unity with it, that deepens and extends the scope of human life. . . ." Montagu is right—I wish I'd never heard of indoor plumbing, electricity, and antibiotics. (Comment upon this attitude.)

4. It's all very well and good for Montagu to define us as "a made-over ape" and as an "example of (a) 150-pound nonlinear servomechanism that can be wholly reproduced by unskilled labor . . ." but I know in my heart that we human beings are basically innocent and good. (Comment upon this assertion.)

The Classical Mode:
Essays for Further Reading

THAT WE ARE TO AVOID PLEASURES, EVEN AT THE EXPENSE OF LIFE.

MICHEL DE MONTAIGNE Michel Eyquem de Montaigne (1533-1592) was born in Périgord, in the south of France, to a family of wealth and refinement. His father ordered the entire household to speak only Latin to the boy until he was six, and arranged for him to be awakened each morning by the sounds of sweet music. Montaigne was educated in law and became counselor at the Parliament of Bordeaux, where he remained until he retired in 1570 to a secluded life in his château. There he devoted himself to study and reflection. His thoughts were recorded in his Essais, the first two books of which appeared in 1580 and the third in 1588. In the Essais Montaigne appears as a skeptic who asks himself, "Que sais-je?" (What do I really know?"). The answer, in brief, is that all human knowledge is relative and that human reason is fallible. Hence the necessity of tolerance—of avoiding excesses of opinion and behavior and of living peacefully with one's fellow men. Montaigne's important contributions to the development of the essay form are universally acknowledged.

[1] I had long ago observed most of the opinions of the ancients to concur in this, that it is high time to die, when there is more ill than

good in living, and that to preserve life to our own torment and inconvenience, is contrary to the very rules of nature, as these old laws instruct us.

> Ἢ ζῆν ἀλύπως, ἢ θανεῖν εὐδαιμόνως.
> Καλὸν τὸ θνήσκειν οἷς ὕβριν τὸ ζῆν φέρει.
> Κρεῖσσον τὸ μὴ ζῆν ἐστιν ἢ ζῆν ἀθλίως.[1]

[2]   But to push this contempt of death so far as to employ it to the removing our thoughts from the honors, riches, dignities, and other favors, and goods, as we call them, of fortune, as if reason were not sufficient to persuade us to avoid them, without adding this new injunction, I had never seen it either commanded or practiced, till this passage of Seneca[2] fell into my hands; who advising Lucilius, a man of great power and authority about the emperor, to alter his voluptuous and magnificent way of living, and to retire himself from this worldly vanity and ambition, to some solitary, quiet, and philosophical life, and the other alleging some difficulties: "I am of opinion," says he, "either that thou leave that life of thine, or life itself; I would, indeed, advise thee to the gentle way, and to untie, rather than to break, the knot thou hast indiscreetly knit, provided, that if it be not otherwise to be untied, thou resolutely break it. There is no man so great a coward, that had not rather once fall than to be always falling." I should have found this counsel conformable enough to the Stoical roughness: but it appears the more strange, for being borrowed from Epicurus, who writes the same thing upon the like occasion to Idomeneus. And I think I have observed something like it, but with Christian moderation, among our own people.

[3]   St. Hilary, Bishop of Poictiers, that famous enemy of the Arian heresy, being in Syria had intelligence thither sent him, that Abra his only daughter, whom he left at home under the eye and tuition of her mother, was sought in marriage by the greatest nobleman of the country, as being a virgin virtuously brought up, fair, rich, and in the flower of her age; whereupon he wrote to her (as appears upon record), that she should remove her affection from all the pleasures and advantages proposed to her; for that he had in his travels found out a much greater and more worthy fortune for her, a husband of much greater power and magnificence, who would present her with robes and jewels

---

[1]"Either tranquil life, or happy death. It is well to die when life is wearisome. It is better to die than to live miserable."—STOBAEUS, *Serm.*, xx.
[2]*Ep.*, 22.

of inestimable value; wherein his design was to dispossess her of the appetite and use of worldly delights, to join her wholly to God; but the nearest and most certain way to this, being, as he conceived, the death of his daughter; he never ceased, by vows, prayers, and orisons, to beg of the Almighty, that He would please to call her out of this world, and to take her to Himself; as accordingly it came to pass; for soon after his return, she died, at which he expressed a singular joy. This seems to outdo the other, forasmuch as he applies himself to this means at the outset, which they only take subsidiarily; and, besides, it was toward his only daughter. But I will not omit the latter end of this story, though it be from my purpose; St. Hilary's wife, having understood from him how the death of their daughter was brought about by his desire and design, and how much happier she was, to be removed out of this world than to have stayed in it, conceived so vivid an apprehension of the eternal and heavenly beatitude, that she begged of her husband, with the extremest importunity, to do as much for her; and God, at their joint request, shortly after calling her to Him, it was a death embraced with singular and mutual content.

OF LOVE

FRANCIS BACON   Francis Bacon (1561-1626) was born in London. He was a lawyer, politician, judge, scientist, and writer. Bacon's public career ended in 1621, when he was found guilty of accepting bribes as a judge. Although he admitted to "corruption and neglect," he denied having been influenced by the bribes and consequently escaped severe punishment. He spent the rest of his life doing the literary and scientific writing for which he is best known.

The most famous of Bacon's literary works is his Essays, *which appeared in three editions: that of 1597, which contained ten essays; that of 1612, which contained thirty-eight essays; and that of 1625, which contained fifty-eight essays. Bacon's essays, for the most part, offer advice for successful living. They are written in an elegant, varied, aphoristic style.*

[1]   The stage is more beholding to love than the life of man. For as to the stage, love is ever matter of comedies, and now and then of tragedies; but in life it doth much mischief—sometimes like a siren, sometimes like a fury. You may observe that, amongst all the great and worthy persons (whereof the memory remaineth either ancient or recent), there is not one that hath been transported to the mad degree of love; which shows that great spirits and great business do keep out this weak passion. You must except, nevertheless, Marcus Antonius, the half-partner of the empire of Rome, and Appius Claudius, the decemvir and law-giver; whereof the former was indeed a voluptous man, and inordinate; but the latter was an austere and wise man; and, therefore, it seems (though rarely) that love can find entrance, not only into an open heart, but also into a heart well fortified, if watch be not well kept. It is a poor saying of Epicurus: *Satis magnum alter alteri theatrum sumus;*[1] as if man, made for the contemplation of heaven and all noble objects, should do nothing but kneel before a little idol and make himself subject, though not of the mouth (as beasts are), yet of the eye, which was given him for higher purposes. It is a strange thing to note the excess of this passion, and how it braves the nature and value of things; by this, that the speaking in a perpetual hyperbole is comely in nothing but in love. Neither is it merely in the phrase; for whereas it hath been well said "That the arch-flatterer, with whom all the petty

[1] *Satis magnum,* etc. Latin for "We are, to one another, a theatre sufficiently large."

flatterers have intelligence," is a man's self, certainly the lover is more. For there was never proud man thought so absurdly well of himself as the lover doth of the person loved; and therefore it was well said, that it is impossible to love and to be wise. Neither doth this weakness appear to others only, and not to the party loved, but to the loved most of all, except the love be reciproque; for it is a true rule, that love is ever rewarded either with the reciproque or with an inward and secret contempt. By how much the more men ought to beware of this passion, which loseth not only other things, but itself. As for the other losses, the poet's relation doth well figure them; that he that preferred Helena quitted the gifts of Juno and Pallas, for whosoever esteemeth too much of amorous affection quitteth both riches and wisdom. This passion hath its floods in the very times of weakness, which are, great prosperity and great adversity, though this latter hath been less observed; both which times kindle love and make it more fervent, and therefore show it to be the child of folly. They do best who, if they cannot but admit love, yet make it keep quarter, and sever it wholly from their serious affairs and actions of life; for if it check once with business it troubleth men's fortunes, and maketh men that they can no ways be true to their own ends. I know not how, but martial men are given to love. I think it is, but as they are given to wine; for perils commonly ask to be paid in pleasures. There is in man's nature a secret inclination and motion towards love of others, which, if it be not spent upon some one or a few, doth naturally spread itself towards many, and maketh men become humane and charitable, as it is seen sometimes in friars. Nuptial love maketh mankind; friendly love perfecteth it; but wanton love corrupteth and embaseth it.

A BUSY LIFE   (The *Spectator*, No. 317.—Addison. Tuesday, March 4, 1711-12.)

*JOSEPH ADDISON   Joseph Addison (1672-1719), son of an English clergyman, was a politician, poet, dramatist, and essayist. He is best known for the essays he contributed to several periodicals—*The Tatler *(1709-1711),* The Spectator *(1711-1714), and* The Guardian *(1713). Covering every aspect of London life, Addison's essays ranged widely and easily from cosmetics to lap dogs, from superstitions to Milton's* Paradise Lost. *Addison's clear, simple, precise, colloquial style profoundly influenced later essayists; and it was used as a model for student writing, in both England and America, well into the twentieth century.*

——Fruges consumere nati.[1]
—*Horace.*

[1]   Augustus, a few moments before his death, asked his friends who stood about him if they thought he had acted his part well; and upon receiving such an answer as was due to his extraordinary merit, Let me then, says he, go off the stage with your applause, using the expression with which the Roman actors made their exit at the conclusion of a dramatic piece. I could wish that men, while they are in health, would consider well the nature of the part they are engaged in, and what figure it will make in the minds of those they leave behind them: whether it was worth coming into the world for, whether it be suitable to a reasonable being; in short, whether it appears graceful in this life, or will turn to an advantage in the next. Let the sycophant, or buffoon, the satirist, or the good companion, consider with himself, when his body shall be laid in the grave, and his soul pass into another state of existence, how much it will redound to his praise to have it said of him that no man in England eat better, that he had an admirable talent at turning his friends into ridicule, that nobody outdid him at an ill-natured jest, or that he never went to bed before he had dispatched his third bottle. These are, however, very common funeral orations, and eulogiums on deceased persons who have acted among mankind with some figure and reputation.

[2]   But if we look into the bulk of our species, they are such as are not likely to be remembered a moment after their disappearance. They

[1]"Born but to feed."—*Sir Theodore Martin.*

leave behind them no traces of their existence, but are forgotten as though they had never been. They are neither wanted by the poor, regretted by the rich, nor celebrated by the learned. They are neither missed in the common-wealth, nor lamented by private persons. Their actions are of no significancy to mankind, and might have been performed by creatures of much less dignity than those who are distinguished by the faculty of reason. An eminent French author speaks somewhere to the following purpose: I have often seen from my chamber window two noble creatures, both of them of an erect countenance, and endowed with reason. These two intellectual beings are employed, from morning to night, in rubbing two smooth stones one upon another; that is, as the vulgar phrase it, in polishing marble.

[3] My friend, Sir Andrew Freeport, as we were sitting in the Club last night, gave us an account of a sober citizen who died a few days since. This honest man, being of greater consequence in his own thoughts than in the eye of the world, had for some years past kept a journal of his life. Sir Andrew showed us one week of it. Since the occurrences set down in it mark out such a road of action as that I have been speaking of, I shall present my reader with a faithful copy of it; after having first informed him that the deceased person had in his youth been bred to trade, but finding himself not so well turned for business, he had for several years last past lived altogether upon a moderate annuity.

[4] MONDAY, Eight o'clock. I put on my clothes and walked into the parlor.

[5] Nine o'clock, ditto. Tied my knee-strings, and washed my hands.

[6] Hours ten, eleven, and twelve. Smoked three pipes of Virginia. Read the *Supplement* and *Daily Courant*. Things go ill in the north. Mr. Nisby's opinion thereupon.

[7] One o'clock in the afternoon. Chid Ralph for mislaying my tobacco-box.

[8] Two o'clock. Sat down to dinner. Mem.[2] Too many plums, and no suet.

[9] From three to four. Took my afternoon's nap.

[10] From four to six. Walked into the fields. Wind, S.S.E.

[11] From six to ten. At the Club. Mr. Nisby's opinion about the peace.

[12] Ten o'clock. Went to bed, slept sound.

---

[2] *mem.*: abbreviation of Latin *memento*, "reminder to oneself"

[13] TUESDAY, BEING HOLIDAY, Eight o'clock. Rose as usual.

[14] Nine o'clock. Washed hands and face, shaved, put on my double soled shoes.

[15] Ten, eleven, twelve. Took a walk to Islington.

[16] One. Took a pot of Mother Cob's Mild.

[17] Between two and three. Returned, dined on a knuckle of veal and bacon. Mem. Sprouts wanting.

[18] Three. Nap as usual.

[19] From four to six. Coffee house. Read the news. A dish of twist. Grand Vizier strangled.

[20] From six to ten. At the Club. Mr. Nisby's account of the Great Turk.

[21] Ten. Dream of the Grand Vizier. Broken sleep.

[22] WEDNESDAY, Eight o'clock. Tongue of my shoe-buckle broke. Hands, but not face.

[23] Nine. Paid off the butcher's bill. Mem. To be allowed for the last leg of mutton.

[24] Ten, eleven. At the coffee house. More work in the north. Stranger in a black wig asked me how stocks went.

[25] From twelve to one. Walked in the fields. Wind to the south.

[26] From one to two. Smoked a pipe and a half.

[27] Two. Dined as usual. Stomach good.

[28] Three. Nap broke by the falling of a pewter-dish. Mem. Cook-maid in love, and grown careless.

[29] From four to six. At the coffee house. Advice from Smyrna, that the Grand Vizier was first of all strangled, and afterwards beheaded.

[30] Six o'clock in the evening. Was half an hour in the Club before anybody else came. Mr. Nisby of opinion that the Grand Vizier was not strangled the sixth instant.

[31] Ten at night. Went to bed. Slept without waking till nine next morning.

[32] THURSDAY, Nine o'clock. Stayed within till two o'clock for Sir Timothy, who did not bring me my annuity according to his promise.

[33] Two in the afternoon. Sat down to dinner. Loss of appetite. Small beer sour. Beef overcorned.

[34] Three. Could not take my nap.

[35] Four and five. Gave Ralph a box on the ear. Turned off my cookmaid. Sent a message to Sir Timothy. Mem. I did not go to the Club tonight. Went to bed at nine o'clock.

[36] FRIDAY. Passed the morning in meditation upon Sir Timothy, who was with me a quarter before twelve.

[37] Twelve o'clock. Bought a new head to my cane, and a tongue to my buckle. Drank a glass of purl to recover appetite.

[38] Two and three. Dined, and slept well.

[39] From four to six. Went to the coffee house. Met Mr. Nisby there. Smoked several pipes. Mr. Nisby of opinion that laced coffee is bad for the head.

[40] Six o'clock. At the Club as steward. Sat late.

[41] Twelve o'clock. Went to bed, dreamt that I drank small beer with the Grand Vizier.

[42] SATURDAY. Waked at eleven, walked in the fields. Wind N.E.

[43] Twelve. Caught in a shower.

[44] One in the afternoon. Returned home, and dried myself.

[45] Two. Mr. Nisby dined with me. First course marrow-bones. Second ox-cheek, with a bottle of Brook's and Hellier.

[46] Three o'clock. Overslept myself.

[47] Six. Went to the Club. Like to have fallen into a gutter. Grand Vizier certainly dead, etc.

[48] I question not but the reader will be surprised to find the above-mentioned journalist taking so much care of a life that was filled with such inconsiderable actions and received so very small improvements; and yet, if we look into the behavior of many whom we daily converse with, we shall find that most of their hours are taken up in those three important articles of eating, drinking, and sleeping. I do not suppose that a man loses his time, who is not engaged in public affairs, or in an illustrious course of action. On the contrary, I believe our hours may very often be more profitably laid out in such transactions as make no figure in the world than in such as are apt to draw upon them the attention of mankind. One may become wiser and better by several methods of employing one's self in secrecy and silence, and do what is laudable without noise or ostentation. I would, however, recommend to every one of my readers the keeping a journal of their lives for one week, and setting down punctually their whole series of employments during that space of time. This kind of self-examination would give them a true state of themselves, and incline them to consider seriously what they are about. One day would rectify the omissions of another, and make a man weigh all those indifferent actions, which, though they are easily forgotten, must certainly be accounted for.

A MODEST PROPOSAL   For Preventing the Children of Poor People From Being a Burthen to Their Parents or Country, and for Making Them Beneficial to the Public.

JONATHAN SWIFT   Jonathan Swift (1667-1745), born in Dublin of English parents, was a poet, essayist, and clergyman of great distinction. Gulliver's Travels (1726) remains his most popular work, but he wrote other satirical masterpieces, including A Tale of a Tub (1704), Battle of the Books (1704), and "A Modest Proposal" (1729). Most of Swift's work is characterized by a grim, bitter, ironic humor; they often seem deeply cynical and misanthropic. But many critics feel that this surface disguises a profound love for humanity—a possibility that has still to be settled to the satisfaction of everyone, however. Swift's prose style is marked by ease, grace, and lucidity.

[1]   It is a melancholy object to those who walk through this great town, or travel in the country, when they see the streets, the roads, and cabin-doors crowded with beggars of the female sex, followed by three, four, or six children, *all in rags*, and importuning every passenger for an alms. These mothers, instead of being able to work for their honest livelihood, are forced to employ all their time in strolling, to beg sustenance for their helpless infants, who, as they grow up, either turn thieves for want of work, or leave their dear Native Country to fight for the Pretender in Spain, or sell themselves to the Barbadoes.

[2]   I think it is agreed by all parties that this prodigious number of children, in the arms, or on the backs, or at the heels of their mothers, and frequently of their fathers, is in the present deplorable state of the kingdom a very great additional grievance; and therefore whoever could find out a fair, cheap, and easy method of making these children sound useful members of the common-wealth would deserve so well of the public as to have his statue set up for a preserver of the nation.

[3]   But my intention is very far from being confined to provide only for the children of professed beggars; it is of a much greater extent, and shall take in the whole number of infants at a certain age who are born of parents in effect as little able to support them as those who demand our charity in the streets.

[4]   As to my own part, having turned my thoughts, for many years,

upon this important subject, and maturely weighed the several schemes of other projectors, I have always found them grossly mistaken in their computation. It is true a child, just dropped from its dam, may be supported by her milk for a solar year with little other nourishment, at most not above the value of two shillings, which the mother may certainly get, or the value in scraps, by her lawful occupation of begging, and it is exactly at one year old that I propose to provide for them, in such a manner as, instead of being a charge upon their parents, or the parish, or wanting food and raiment for the rest of their lives, they shall, on the contrary, contribute to the feeding and partly to the clothing of many thousands.

[5]   There is likewise another great advantage in my scheme, that it will prevent those voluntary abortions, and that horrid practice of women murdering their bastard children, alas, too frequent among us, sacrificing the poor innocent babes, I doubt, more to avoid the expense than the shame, which would move tears and pity in the most savage and inhuman breast.

[6]   The number of souls in this kingdom being usually reckoned one million and a half, of these I calculate there may be about two hundred thousand couple whose wives are breeders, from which number I subtract thirty thousand couple who are able to maintain their own children, although I apprehend there cannot be so many under the present distresses of the kingdom, but this being granted, there will remain an hundred and seventy thousand breeders. I again subtract fifty thousand for those women who miscarry, or whose children die by accident or disease within the year. There only remain an hundred and twenty thousand children of poor parents annually born: The question therefore is, how this number shall be reared, and provided for, which, as I have already said, under the present situation of affairs, is utterly impossible by all the methods hitherto proposed, for we can neither employ them in handicraft, or agriculture; we neither build houses (I mean in the country), nor cultivate land: they can very seldom pick up a livelihood by stealing till they arrive at six years old, except where they are of towardly parts, although I confess they learn the rudiments much earlier, during which time they can however be properly looked upon only as *probationers*, as I have been informed by a principal gentleman in the County of Cavan, who protested to me that he never knew above one or two instances under the age of six, even in a part of the kingdom so renowned for the quickest proficiency in that art.

[7]   I am assured by our merchants that a boy or a girl, before twelve years old, is no saleable commodity, and even when they come to this age, they will not yield above three pounds, or three pounds and half-a-crown at most on the Exchange, which cannot turn to account either to the parents of the kingdom, the charge of nutriment and rags having been at least four times that value.

[8]   I shall now therefore humbly propose my own thoughts, which I hope will not be liable to the least objection.

[9]   I have been assured by a very knowing American of my acquaintance in London, that a young healthy child well nursed is at a year old a most delicious, nourishing, and wholesome food, whether stewed, roasted, baked, or boiled, and I make no doubt that it will equally serve in a fricassee, or a ragout.

[10]   I do therefore humbly offer it to public consideration, that of the hundred and twenty thousand children already computed, twenty thousand may be reserved for breed, whereof only one fourth part to be males, which is more than we allow to sheep, black-cattle, or swine, and my reason is that these children are seldom the fruits of marriage, a circumstance not much regarded by our savage, therefore one male will be sufficient to serve four females. That the remaining hundred thousand may at a year old be offered in sale to the persons of quality, and fortune, through the kingdom, always advising the mother to let them suck plentifully in the last month, so as to render them plump, and fat for a good table. A child will make two dishes at an entertainment for friends, and when the family dines alone, the fore or hind quarters will make a reasonable dish, and seasoned with a little pepper or salt will be very good boiled on the fourth day, especially in winter.

[11]   I have reckoned upon a medium, that a child just born will weigh 12 pounds, and in a solar year if tolerably nursed increaseth to 28 pounds.

[12]   I grant this food will be somewhat dear, and therefore very proper for landlords, who, as they have already devoured most of the parents, seem to have the best title to the children.

[13]   Infant's flesh will be in season throughout the year, but more plentiful in March, and a little before and after, for we are told by a grave author, an eminent French physician, that fish being a prolific diet, there are more children born in Roman Catholic countries about nine months after Lent than at any other season; therefore reckoning a year after Lent, the markets will be more glutted than usual, because

the number of Popish infants is at least three to one in this kingdom, and therefore it will have one other collateral advantage by lessening the number of Papists among us.

[14]   I have already computed the charge of nursing a beggar's child (in which list I reckon all cottagers, labourers, and four-fifths of the farmers) to be about two shillings *per annum*, rags included, and I believe no gentleman would repine to give ten shillings for the carcass of a good fat child, which, as I have said, will make four dishes of excellent nutritive meat, when he hath only some particular friend or his own family to dine with him. Thus the Squire will learn to be a good landlord, and grow popular among his tenants, the mother will have eight shillings net profit, and be fit for work till she produces another child.

[15]   Those who are more thrifty (as I must confess the times require) may flay the carcass; the skin of which, artificially dressed, will make admirable gloves for ladies, and summer boots for fine gentlemen.

[16]   As to our City of Dublin, shambles may be appointed for this purpose, in the most convenient parts of it, and butchers we may be assured will not be wanting, although I rather recommend buying the children alive, and dressing them hot from the knife, as we do roasting pigs.

[17]   A very worthy person, a true lover of this country, and whose virtues I highly esteem, was lately pleased, in discoursing on this matter, to offer a refinement upon my scheme. He said that many gentlemen of this kingdom, having of late destroyed their deer, he conceived that the want of venison might be well supplied by the bodies of young lads and maidens, not exceeding fourteen years of age, nor under twelve, so great a number of both sexes in every country being now ready to starve, for want of work and service: and these to be disposed of by their parents if alive, or otherwise by their nearest relations. But with due deference to so excellent a friend, and so deserving a patriot, I cannot be altogether in his sentiments; for as to the males, my American acquaintance assured me from frequent experience that their flesh was generally tough and lean, like that of our schoolboys, by continual exercise, and their taste disagreeable, and to fatten them would not answer the charge. Then as to the females, it would, I think with humble submission, be a loss to the public, because they soon would become breeders themselves: And besides, it is not improbable that some scrupulous people might be apt to censure such a practice (al-

though indeed very unjustly) as a little bordering upon cruelty, which, I confess, hath always been with me the strongest objection against any project, however so well intended.

[18]   But in order to justify my friend, he confessed that this expedient was put into his head by the famous Psalmanazer, a native of the island Formosa, who came from thence to London, above twenty years ago, and in conversation told my friend that in his country when any young person happened to be put to death, the executioner sold the carcass to persons of quality, as a prime dainty, and that, in his time, the body of a plump girl of fifteen, who was crucified for an attempt to poison the emperor, was sold to his Imperial Majesty's Prime Minister of State, and other great Mandarins of the Court, in joints from the gibbet, at four hundred crowns. Neither indeed can I deny that if the same use were made of several plump young girls in this town, who, without one single groat to their fortunes, cannot stir abroad without a chair, and appear at the playhouse, and assemblies in foreign fineries, which they never will pay for, the kingdom would not be the worse.

[19]   Some persons of a desponding spirit are in great concern about that vast number of poor people, who are aged, diseased, or maimed, and I have been desired to employ my thoughts what course may be taken to ease the nation of so grievous an encumbrance. But I am not in the least pain upon that matter, because it is very well known that they are every day dying, and rotting, by cold, and famine, and filth, and vermin, as fast as can be reasonably expected. And as to the younger labourers they are now in almost as hopeful a condition. They cannot get work, and consequently pine away for want of nourishment, to a degree, that if at any time they are accidentally hired to common labour, they have not strength to perform it; and thus the country and themselves are happily delivered from the evils to come.

[20]   I have too long digressed, and therefore shall return to my subject. I think the advantages by the proposal which I have made are obvious and many, as well as of the highest importance.

[21]   For first, as I have already observed, it would greatly lessen the number of Papists, with whom we are yearly over-run, being the principal breeders of the nation, as well as our most dangerous enemies, and who stay at home on purpose with a design to deliver the kingdom to the Pretender, hoping to take their advantage by the absence of so many good Protestants, who have chosen rather to leave their country than

stay at home, and pay tithes against their conscience to an Episcopal curate.

[22]   Secondly, the poorer tenants will have something valuable of their own, which by law be made liable to distress, and help to pay their landlord's rent, their corn and cattle being already seized and *money a thing unknown.*

[23]   Thirdly, Whereas the maintenance of an hundred thousand children, from two years old, and upwards, cannot be computed at less than ten shillings a piece *per annum*, the nation's stock will be thereby increased fifty thousand pounds *per annum*, besides the profit of a new dish, introduced to the tables of all gentlemen of fortune in the kingdom, who have any refinement in taste, and the money will circulate among ourselves, the goods being entirely of our own growth and manufacture.

[24]   Fourthly, The constant breeders, besides the gain of eight shillings sterling *per annum*, by the sale of their children, will be rid of the charge of maintaining them after the first year.

[25]   Fifthly, This food would likewise bring great custom to taverns, where the vintners will certainly be so prudent as to procure the best receipts for dressing it up to perfection, and consequently have their houses frequented by all the fine gentlemen, who justly value themselves upon their knowledge in good eating; and a skillful cook, who understands how to oblige his guests, will contrive to make it as expensive as they please.

[26]   Sixthly, This would be a great inducement to marriage, which all wise nations have either encouraged by rewards, or enforced by laws and penalties. It would increase the care and tenderness of mothers toward their children, when they were sure of a settlement for life, to the poor babes, provided in some sort by the public to their annual profit instead of expense. We should see an honest emulation among the married women, which of them could bring the fattest child to the market, men would become as fond of their wives, during the time of their pregnancy, as they are now of their mares in foal, their cows in calf, or sows when they are ready to farrow, nor offer to beat or kick them (as it is too frequent a practice) for fear of a miscarriage.

[27]   Many other advantages might be enumerated: For instance, the addition of some thousand carcasses in our exportation of barrelled beef; the propagation of swine's flesh, and improvement in the art of making good bacon, so much wanted among us by the great destruction

of pigs, too frequent at our tables, which are no way comparable in taste or magnificence to a well-grown, fat yearling child, which roasted whole will make a considerable figure at a Lord Mayor's feast, or any other public entertainment. But this and many others I omit, being studious of brevity.

[28]   Supposing that one thousand families in this city would be constant customers for infants' flesh, besides others who might have it at merry-meetings, particularly weddings and christenings, I compute that Dublin would take off annually about twenty thousand carcasses, and the rest of the kingdom (where probably they will be sold somewhat cheaper) the remaining eighty thousand.

[29]   I can think of no one objection that will possibly be raised against this proposal, unless it should be urged that the number of people will be thereby much lessened in the kingdom. This I freely own, and it was indeed one principal design in offering it to the world. I desire the reader will observe, that I calculate my remedy for this one individual *Kingdom of Ireland, and for no other that ever was, is, or, I think, ever can be upon earth.* Therefore let no man talk to me of other expedients: *Of taxing our absentees at five shillings a pound: Of using neither clothes, nor household furniture, except what is of our own growth and manufacture: Of utterly rejecting the materials and instruments that promote foreign luxury: Of curing the expensiveness of pride, vanity, idleness, and gaming in our women: Of introducing a vein of parsimony, prudence, and temperance: Of learning to love our Country, wherein we differ even from* LAPLANDERS, *and the inhabitants of* TOPINAMBOO: *Of quitting our animosities and factions, nor act any longer like the Jews, who were murdering one another at the very moment their city was taken: Of being a little cautious not to sell our country and consciences for nothing: Of teaching landlords to have at least one degree of mercy toward their tenants. Lastly, of putting a spirit of honesty, industry, and skill into our shopkeepers, who, if a resolution could now be taken to buy only our native goods, would immediately unite to cheat and exact upon us in the price, the measure, and the goodness, nor could ever yet be brought to make one fair proposal of just dealing, though often and earnestly invited to it.*

[30]   Therefore I repeat, let no man talk to me of these and the like expedients, till he hath at least some glimpse of hope that there will ever be some hearty and sincere attempt to put them in practice.

[31]   But as to myself, having been wearied out for many years with offering vain, idle, visionary thoughts, and at length utterly despairing

of success, I fortunately fell upon this proposal, which as it is wholly new, so it hath something solid and real, of no expense and little trouble, full in our own power, and whereby we can incur no danger in *disobliging* ENGLAND. For this kind of commodity will not bear exportation, the flesh being too tender a consistence to admit a long continuance in salt, *although perhaps I could name a country which would be glad to eat up our whole nation without it.*

[32]   After all I am not so violently bent upon my own opinion as to reject any offer, proposed by wise men, which shall be found equally innocent, cheap, easy, and effectual. But before something of that kind shall be advanced in contradiction to my scheme, and offering a better, I desire the author, or authors, will be pleased maturely to consider two points. First, as things now stand, how they will be able to find food and raiment for an hundred thousand useless mouths and backs. And secondly, there being a round million of creatures in human figure, throughout this kingdom, whose whole subsistence put into a common stock would leave them in debt two millions of pounds sterling; adding those, who are beggars by profession, to the bulk of farmers, cottagers, and labourers with their wives and children, who are beggars in effect. I desire those politicians, who dislike my overture, and may perhaps be so bold to attempt an answer, that they will first ask the parents of these mortals whether they would not at this day think it a great happiness to have been sold for food at a year old, in the manner I prescribe, and thereby have avoided such a perpetual scene of misfortunes as they have since gone through, by the oppression of landlords, the impossibility of paying rent without money or trade, the want of common sustenance, with neither house nor clothes to cover them from the inclemencies of the weather, and the most inevitable prospect of entailing the like, or greater miseries upon their breed for ever.

[33]   I profess in the sincerity of my heart that I have not the least personal interest in endeavoring to promote this necessary work, having no other motive than the *public good of my country, by advancing our trade, providing for infants, relieving the poor, and giving some pleasure to the rich.* I have no children by which I can propose to get a single penny; the youngest being nine years old, and my wife past childbearing.

LAST THINGS from *The Rambler*, No. 207. Tuesday,
10 March 1752.

*SAMUEL JOHNSON   Samuel Johnson (1709-1784), born at Lichfield,
England, started life inauspiciously as the son of an obscure, impoverished
bookdealer. He became a scholar, poet, editor, biographer, critic, lexicographer, conversationalist, and essayist of tremendous power and influence. In 1739, accompanied by his pupil David Garrick—who was to
become a very great actor—Johnson moved to London, his home for the
rest of his life. In 1738 he published his poem* London. *In 1744 he published a superlative biography of his friend Richard Savage, with whom
Johnson had shared the fierce poverty of his early years in London. His
best known and most influential later work includes his poem,* The Vanity
of Human Wishes *(1749);* A Dictionary of the English Language *(1755);*
Rasselas, Prince of Abyssinia *(1759); an edition of Shakespeare (1765);
and* Lives of the Poets *(1779-1781). Besides producing this work, Johnson
also established a reputation as the finest essayist in the last half of the
eighteenth century by writing over two hundred essays for his periodical*
The Rambler *(1750-1752). He also contributed essays to* The Idler *(1758-
1760) and numerous other periodicals.*

*   It is impossible to estimate Johnson's work accurately and fairly without
giving it detailed attention. The most recent critical opinion, however,
affirms that Johnson was a great prose stylist and a profoundly influential
man of letters. His prose style is marked by elegant, Latinate diction,
rather long and highly rhythmical sentences, and a distinct feeling of
strength and manliness.*

> *Solve senescentem mature sanus equum, ne*
> *Peccet ad extremum ridendus.*
>
> Horace, EPISTLES, 1.1.8–9.

> The voice of reason cries with winning force,
> Loose from the rapid car your aged horse,
> Lest, in the race derided, left behind,
> He drag his jaded limbs and burst his wind.
>
> Francis.

[1]   Such is the emptiness of human enjoyment, that we are always
impatient of the present. Attainment is followed by neglect, and possession by disgust; and the malicious remark of the Greek epigrammatist
on marriage may be applied to every other course of life, that its two
days of happiness are the first and the last.

[2]   Few moments are more pleasing than those in which the mind

is concerting measures for a new undertaking. From the first hint that wakens the fancy, till the hour of actual execution, all is improvement and progress, triumph and felicity. Every hour brings additions to the original scheme, suggests some new expedient to secure success, or discovers consequential advantages not hitherto foreseen. While preparations are made, and materials accumulated, day glides after day through elysian prospects, and the heart dances to the song of hope.

[3]   Such is the pleasure of projecting, that many content themselves with a succession of visionary schemes, and wear out their allotted time in the calm amusement of contriving what they never attempt or hope to execute.

|4]   Others, not able to feast their imagination with pure ideas, advance somewhat nearer to the grossness of action, with great diligence collect whatever is requisite to their design, and, after a thousand researches and consultations, are snatched away by death, as they stand *in procinctu*[1] waiting for a proper opportunity to begin.

[5]   If there were no other end of life, than to find some adequate solace for every day, I know not whether any condition could be preferred to that of the man who involves himself in his own thoughts, and never suffers experience to shew him the vanity of speculation; for no sooner are notions reduced to practice, than tranquillity and confidence forsake the breast; every day brings its task, and often without bringing abilities to perform it: Difficulties embarrass, uncertainity perplexes, opposition retards, censure exasperates, or neglect depresses. We proceed, because we have begun; we complete our design, that the labour already spent may not be vain; but as expectation gradually dies away, the gay smile of alacrity disappears, we are compelled to implore severer powers, and trust the event to patience and constancy.

[6]   When once our labour has begun, the comfort that enables us to endure it is the prospect of its end; for though in every long work there are some joyous intervals of self-applause, when the attention is recreated by unexpected facility, and the imagination soothed by incidental excellencies; yet the toil with which performance struggles after idea, is so irksome and disgusting, and so frequent is the necessity of resting below that perfection which we imagined within our reach, that seldom any man obtains more from his endeavours than a painful conviction of his defects, and a continual resuscitation of desires which he feels himself unable to gratify.

[1] *in procinctu,* Latin for "at the ready; nearby"

[7]   So certainly is weariness the concomitant of our undertakings, that every man, in whatever he is engaged, consoles himself with the hope of change; if he has made his way by assiduity to publick employment, he talks among his friends of the delight of retreat; if by the necessity of solitary application he is secluded from the world, he listens with a beating heart to distant noises, longs to mingle with living beings, and resolves to take hereafter his fill of diversions, or display his abilities on the universal theatre, and enjoy the pleasure of distinction and applause.

[8]   Every desire, however innocent, grows dangerous, as by long indulgence it becomes ascendent in the mind. When we have been much accustomed to consider any thing as capable of giving happiness, it is not easy to restrain our ardour, or to forbear some precipitation in our advances, and irregularity in our persuits. He that has cultivated the tree, watched the swelling bud and opening blossom, and pleased himself with computing how much every sun and shower add to its growth, scarcely stays till the fruit has obtained its maturity, but defeats his own cares by eagerness to reward them. When we have diligently laboured for any purpose, we are willing to believe that we have attained it, and, because we have already done much, too suddenly conclude that no more is to be done.

[9]   All attraction is encreased by the approach of the attracting body. We never find ourselves so desirous to finish, as in the latter part of our work, or so impatient of delay, as when we know that delay cannot be long. This unseasonable importunity of discontent may be partly imputed to langour and weariness, which must always oppress those more whose toil has been longer continued; but the greater part usually proceeds from frequent contemplation of that ease which is now considered as within reach, and which, when it has once flattered our hopes, we cannot suffer to be withheld.

[10]   In some of the noblest compositions of wit, the conclusion falls below the vigour and spirit of the first books; and as a genius is not to be degraded by the imputation of human failings, the cause of this declension is commonly sought in the structure of the work, and plausible reasons are given why in the defective part less ornament was necessary, or less could be admitted. But, perhaps, the author would have confessed, that his fancy was tired, and his perseverance broken; that he knew his design to be unfinished, but that, when he saw the end so near, he could no longer refuse to be at rest.

[11]   Against the instillations of this frigid opiate, the heart should

be secured by all the considerations which once concurred to kindle the ardour of enterprize. Whatever motive first incited action, has still greater force to stimulate perseverance; since he that might have lain still at first in blameless obscurity, cannot afterwards desist but with infamy and reproach. He, whom a doubtful promise of distant good, could encourage to set difficulties at defiance, ought not to remit his vigour, when he has almost obtained his recompence. To faint or loiter, when only the last efforts are required, is to steer the ship through tempests, and abandon it to the winds in sight of land; it is to break the ground and scatter the seed, and at last to neglect the harvest.

[12] The masters of rhetorick direct, that the most forcible arguments be produced in the latter part of an oration, lest they should be effaced or perplexed by supervenient images. This precept may be justly extended to the series of life: Nothing is ended with honour, which does not conclude better than it begun. It is not sufficient to maintain the first vigour; for excellence loses its effect upon the mind by custom, as light after a time ceases to dazzle. Admiration must be continued by that novelty which first produced it, and how much soever is given, there must always be reason to imagine that more remains.

[13] We not only are most sensible of the last impressions, but such is the unwillingness of mankind to admit transcendent merit, that, though it be difficult to obliterate the reproach of miscarriages by any subsequent achievement, however illustrious, yet the reputation raised by a long train of success, may be finally ruined by a single failure, for weakness or error will be always remembered by that malice and envy which it gratifies.

[14] For the prevention of that disgrace, which lassitude and negligence may bring at last upon the greatest performances, it is necessary to proportion carefully our labour to our strength. If the design comprises many parts, equally essential, and therefore not to be separated, the only time for caution is before we engage; the powers of the mind must be then impartially estimated, and it must be remembered, that not to complete the plan, is not to have begun it; and, that nothing is done, while any thing is omitted.

[15] But, if the task consists in the repetition of single acts, no one of which derives its efficacy from the rest, it may be attempted with less scruple, because there is always opportunity to retreat with honour. The danger is only lest we expect from the world the indulgence with which most are disposed to treat themselves; and in the hour of listlessness imagine, that the diligence of one day will atone for the idleness of

another, and that applause begun by approbation will be continued by habit.

[16]   He that is himself weary will soon weary the public. Let him therefore lay down his employment, whatever it be, who can no longer exert his former activity or attention; let him not endeavour to struggle with censure, or obstinately infest the stage till a general hiss commands him to depart.

THE SUPERANNUATED MAN

CHARLES LAMB   Charles Lamb (1775-1824), the English essayist and critic, lived a quiet life devoted to the care of his mentally ill sister. Early in his career he wrote poetry, some of which was published with that of Coleridge. Then he turned to plays, but with little success. With his sister he wrote Tales From Shakespeare, *and then, alone, he wrote* Specemins of English Dramatic Poets Who Lived about the Time of Shakespeare, *the book that laid the foundation for his reputation as a critic. Shortly afterward came "Essays of Elia," published in* London Magazine *upon which perhaps his greatest fame rests. His refined and exquisite humor, genuine pleasantry, and delicate pathos assure him of a place among the essayists beside Montaigne, Addison and Steele. His great contribution to literature is in reviving interest in the dramatic writers of the Shakespearean age.*

Sera tamen respexit
Libertas.   VIRGIL.[1]

A Clerk I was in London gay.—O'KEEFE.

[1]   If peradventure, Reader, it has been thy lot to waste the golden years of thy life—thy shining youth—in the irksome confinement of an office; to have thy prison days prolonged through middle age down to decrepitude and silver hairs, without hope of release or respite; to have lived to forget that there are such things as holidays, or to remember them but as the prerogatives of childhood; then, and then only, will you be able to appreciate my deliverance.

[2]   It is now six-and-thirty years since I took my seat at the desk in Mincing Lane. Melancholy was the transition at fourteen from the abundant playtime, and the frequently-intervening vacations of school days, to the eight, nine, and sometimes ten hours' a day attendance at the counting-house. But time partially reconciles us to anything. I gradually became content—doggedly contented, as wild animals in cages.

[3]   It is true I had my Sundays to myself; but Sundays, admirable as the institution of them is for purposes of worship, are for that very reason the very worst adapted for days of unbending and recreation.

[1] Sera tamen respexit/Libertas: "Freedom, though late (in coming), has looked (in) upon me."

In particular, there is a gloom for me attendant upon a city Sunday, a weight in the air. I miss the cheerful cries of London, the music, and the ballad-singers—the buzz and stirring murmur of the streets. Those eternal bells depress me. The closed shops repel me. Prints, pictures, all the glittering and endless succession of knacks and gewgaws, and ostentatiously displayed wares of tradesmen, which make a week-day saunter through the less busy parts of the metropolis so delightful—are shut out. No book-stalls deliciously to idle over—No busy faces to recreate the idle man who contemplates them ever passing by—the very face of business a charm by contrast to his temporary relaxation from it. Nothing to be seen but unhappy countenances—or half-happy at best—of emancipated 'prentices and little tradesfolks, with here and there a servant-maid that has got leave to go out, who, slaving all the week, with the habit has lost almost the capacity of enjoying a free hour; and livelily expressing the hollowness of a day's pleasuring. The very strollers in the fields on that day look anything but comfortable.

[4]   But besides Sundays, I had a day at Easter, and a day at Christmas, with a full week in the summer to go and air myself in my native fields of Hertfordshire. This last was a great indulgence; and the prospect of its recurrence, I believe, alone kept me up through the year, and made my durance tolerable. But when the week came round, did the glittering phantom of the distance keep touch with me? or rather was it not a series of seven uneasy days, spent in restless pursuit of pleasure, and a wearisome anxiety to find out how to make the most of them? Where was the quiet, where the promised rest? Before I had a taste of it, it was vanished. I was at the desk again, counting upon the fifty-one tedious weeks that must intervene before such another snatch would come. Still the prospect of its coming threw something of an illumination upon the darker side of my captivity. Without it, as I have said, I could scarcely have sustained my thraldom.

[5]   Independently of the rigours of attendance, I have ever been haunted with a sense (perhaps a mere caprice) of incapacity for business. This, during my latter years, had increased to such a degree, that it was visible in all the lines of my countenance. My health and my good spirits flagged. I had perpetually a dread of some crisis, to which I should be found unequal. Besides my daylight servitude, I served over again all night in my sleep, and would awake with terrors of imaginary false entries, errors in my accounts, and the like. I was fifty years of age, and no prospect of emancipation presented itself. I had grown to my desk, as it were; and the wood had entered into my soul.

[6] My fellows in the office would sometimes rally me upon the trouble legible in my countenance; but I did not know that it had raised the suspicions of any of my employers, when, on the fifth of last month, a day ever to be remembered by me, L——, the junior partner in the firm, calling me on one side, directly taxed me with my bad looks, and frankly inquired the cause of them. So taxed, I honestly made confession of my infirmity, and added that I was afraid I should eventually be obliged to resign his service. He spoke some words of course to hearten me, and there the matter rested. A whole week I remained labouring under the impression that I had acted imprudently in my disclosure; that I had foolishly given a handle against myself, and had been anticipating my own dismissal. A week passed in this manner, the most anxious one, I verily believe, in my whole life, when on the evening of the 12th of April, just as I was about quitting my desk to go home (it might be about eight o'clock) I received an awful summons to attend the presence of the whole assembled firm in the formidable back parlour. I thought now my time is surely come, I have done for myself, I am going to be told that they have no longer occasion for me. L——, I could see, smiled at the terror I was in, which was a little relief to me, —when to my utter astonishment B——, the eldest partner, began a formal harangue to me on the length of my services, my very meritorious conduct during the whole of the time (the deuce, thought I, how did he find out that? I protest I never had the confidence to think as much). He went on to descant on the expediency of retiring at a certain time of life (how my heart panted!), and asking me a few questions as to the amount of my own property, of which I have a little, ended with a proposal, to which his three partners nodded a grave assent, that I should accept from the house, which I had served so well, a pension for life to the amount of two-thirds of my accustomed salary—a magnificent offer! I do not know what I answered between surprise and gratitude, but it was understood that I accepted their proposal, and I was told that I was free from that hour to leave their service. I stammered out a bow, and at just ten minutes after eight I went home—for ever. This noble benefit—gratitude forbids me to conceal their names—I owe to the kindness of the most munificent firm in the world—the house of Boldero, Merryweather, Bosanquet, and Lacy.

Esto perpetua![2]

[7] For the first day or two I felt stunned, overwhelmed. I could

[2] *Esto perpetua!* "May it endure forever!"

only apprehend my felicity; I was too confused to taste it sincerely. I
wandered about, thinking I was happy, and knowing that I was not. I
was in the condition of a prisoner in the old Bastile, suddenly let loose
after a forty years' confinement. I could scarce trust myself with myself. It was like passing out of Time into Eternity—for it is a sort of
Eternity for a man to have his Time all to himself. It seemed to me
that I had more time on my hands than I could ever manage. From a
poor man, poor in Time, I was suddenly lifted up into a vast revenue;
I could see no end of my possessions; I wanted some steward, or judi-
cious bailiff, to manage my estates in Time for me. And here let me
caution persons grown old in active business, not lightly, nor without
weighing their own resources, to forego their customary employment
all at once, for there may be danger in it. I feel it by myself, but I know
that my resources are sufficient; and now that those first giddy rap-
tures have subsided, I have a quiet home-feeling of the blessedness of
my condition. I am in no hurry. Having all holidays, I am as though
I had none. If Time hung heavy upon me, I could walk it away; but
I do *not* walk all day long, as I used to do in those old transient holidays, thirty miles a day, to make the most of them. If Time were
troublesome, I could read it away; but I do *not* read in that violent
measure, with which, having no Time in my own but candlelight Time,
I used to weary out my head and eyesight in bygone winters. I walk,
read, or scribble (as now), just when the fit seizes me. I no longer
hunt after pleasure; I let it come to me. I am like the man

> — — — that's born, and has his years come to him,
> In some green desert.

[8]   "Years!" you will say; "what is this superannuated simpleton
calculating upon, He has already told us he is past fifty."

[9]   I have indeed lived nominally fifty years, but deduct out of them
the hours which I have lived to other people, and not to myself, and
you will find me still a young fellow. For *that* is the only true Time,
which a man can properly call his own, that which he has all to himself; the rest, though in some sense he may be said to live it, is other
people's Time, not his. The remnant of my poor days, long or short,
is at least multiplied for me threefold. My ten next years, if I stretch
so far, will be as long as any preceding thirty. 'Tis a fair rule-of-three
sum.

[10]   Among the strange fantasies which beset me at the commence-
ment of my freedom, and of which all traces are not yet gone, one was,

that a vast tract of time had intervened since I quitted the Counting House. I could not conceive of it as an affair of yesterday. The partners, and the clerks with whom I had for so many years, and for so many hours in each day of the year, been closely associated—being suddenly removed from them—they seemed as dead to me. There is a fine passage, which may serve to illustrate this fancy, in a Tragedy by Sir Robert Howard, speaking of a friend's death:—

> ——— 'Twas but just now he went away;
> I have not since had time to shed a tear;
> And yet the distance does the same appear
> As if he had been a thousand years from me.
> Time takes no measure in Eternity.

[11]   To dissipate this awkward feeling, I have been fain to go among them once or twice since; to visit my old desk-fellows—my co-brethren of the quill—that I had left below in the state militant. Not all the kindness with which they received me could quite restore to me that pleasant familiarity, which I had heretofore enjoyed among them. We cracked some of our old jokes, but methought they went off but faintly. My old desk; the peg where I hung my hat, were appropriated to another. I knew it must be, but I could not take it kindly. D——l take me, if I did not feel some remorse—beast, if I had not—at quitting my old compeers, the faithful partners of my toils for six-and-thirty years, that smoothed for me with their jokes and conundrums the ruggedness of my professional road. Had it been so rugged then, after all? or was I a coward simply? Well, it is too late to repent; and I also know that these suggestions are a common fallacy of the mind on such occasions. But my heart smote me. I had violently broken the bands betwixt us. It was at least not courteous. I shall be some time before I get quite reconciled to the separation. Farewell, old cronies, yet not for long, for again and again I will come among ye, if I shall have your leave. Farewell, Ch——, dry, sarcastic, and friendly! Do——, mild, slow to move, and gentlemanly! Pl——, officious to do, and to volunteer, good services!—and thou, thou dreary pile, fit mansion for a Gresham or a Whittingham of old, stately house of Merchants; with thy labyrinthine passages, and light-excluding, pent-up offices, where candles for one-half the year supplied the place of the sun's light; unhealthy contributor to my weal, stern fosterer of my living, farewell! In thee remain, and not in the obscure collection of some wandering bookseller, my "works"! There let them rest, as I do

from my labours, piled on thy massy shelves, more MSS, in folio than
ever Aquinas left, and full as useful! My mantle I bequeath among ye.

[12]   A fortnight has passed since the date of my first communication. At that period I was approaching to tranquillity, but had not
reached it. I boasted of a calm indeed, but it was comparative only.
Something of the first flutter was left; an unsettling sense of novelty;
the dazzle to weak eyes of unaccustomed light. I missed my old chains,
forsooth, as if they had been some necessary part of my apparel. I was
a poor Carthusian, from strict cellular discipline suddenly by some
revolution returned upon the world. I am now as if I had never been
other than my own master. It is natural to me to go where I please,
to do what I please. I find myself at eleven o'clock in the day in Bond
Street, and it seems to me that I have been sauntering there at that
very hour for years past. I digress into Soho, to explore a book-stall.
Methinks I have been thirty years a collector. There is nothing strange
nor new in it. I find myself before a fine picture in the morning. Was
it ever otherwise? What is become of Fish Street Hill? Where is Fen-
church Street? Stones of old Mincing Lane, which I have worn with
my daily pilgrimage for six-and-thirty years, to the footsteps of what
toil-worn clerk are your everlasting flints now vocal? I indent the
gayer flags of Pall Mall. It is 'Change time, and I am strangely among
the Elgin marbles. It was no hyperbole when I ventured to compare
the change in my condition to a passing into another world. Time
stands still in a manner to me. I have lost all distinction of season. I
do not know the day of the week or of the month. Each day used to
be individually felt by me in its reference to the foreign post days; in
its distance from, or propinquity to, the next Sunday. I had my Wednesday feelings, my Saturday nights' sensations. The genius of each day
was upon me distinctly during the whole of it, affecting my appetite,
spirits, etc. The phantom of the next day, with the dreary five to
follow, sate as a load upon my poor Sabbath recreations. What charm
has washed that Ethiop white? What is gone of Black Monday? All
days are the same. Sunday itself—that unfortunate failure of a holiday, as it to often proved, what with my sense of its fugitiveness, and
over-care to get the greatest quantity of pleasure out of it—is melted
down into a week day. I can spare to go to church now, without
grudging the huge cantle which it used to seem to cut out of the
holiday. I have Time for everything. I can visit a sick friend. I can
interrupt the man of much occupation when he is busiest. I can insult
over him with an invitation to take a day's pleasure with me to Windsor

this fine May-morning. It is Lucretian pleasure to behold the poor drudges, whom I have left behind in the world, carking and caring; like horses in a mill, drudging on in the same eternal round—and what is it all for? A man can never have too much Time to himself, nor too little to do. Had I a little son, I would christen him NOTHING-TO-DO; he should do nothing. Man, I verily believe, is out of his element as long as he is operative. I am altogether for the life contemplative. Will no kindly earthquake come and swallow up those accursed cotton mills? Take me that lumber of a desk there, and bowl it down

As low as to the fiends.

[13] I am not longer * * * * *, clerk to the Firm of, etc. I am Re-tired Leisure. I am to be met with in trim gardens. I am already come to be known by my vacant face and careless gesture, perambulating at no fixed pace, nor with any settled purpose. I walk about; not to and from. They tell me, a certain *cum dignitate*[3] air, that has been buried so long with my other good parts, has begun to shoot forth in my person. I grow into gentility perceptibly. When I take up a newspaper, it is to read the state of the opera. *Opus operatum est.*[4] I have done all that I came into this world to do. I have worked task-work, and have the rest of the day to myself.

[3] *cum dignitate,* "with dignity"
[4]*Opus operatum est,* "my work is done"

MORAL PERFECTION

BENJAMIN FRANKLIN   A printer, publisher, essayist, inventor, scientist and statesman, Benjamin Franklin (1706-1790) was a man of fantastic energy and enormous accomplishment. He combined wit and warmth with an orderly mind and a desire to help his fellow man. Aside from his famous maxims, Franklin wrote a great number of essays: one was believed to have influenced the makers of the Treaty of Paris, 1763; others presented the American view of the troubles with Great Britain. Franklin's influence both as author and statesman, enormous in his own time, extends even into the 20th century. At the center of events that led to the founding of this country, Franklin in addition invented many of the terms still used in discussing electricity: for instance "positive," "negative," "battery", and "conductor." His work and thought are relevant today in so many areas that it is nothing less than astonishing.

[1]   It was about this time I conceiv'd the bold and arduous project of arriving at moral perfection. I wish'd to live without committing any fault at any time; I would conquer all that either natural inclination, custom, or company might lead me into. As I knew, or thought I knew, what was right and wrong, I did not see why I might not always do the one and avoid the other. But I soon found I had undertaken a task of more difficulty than I had imagined. While my care was employ'd in guarding against one fault, I was often surprised by another; habit took the advantage of inattention; inclination was sometimes too strong for reason. I concluded, at length, that the mere speculative conviction that it was our interest to be completely virtuous, was not sufficient to prevent our slipping; and that the contrary habits must be broken, and good ones acquired and established, before we can have any dependence on a steady, uniform rectitude of conduct. For this purpose I therefore contrived the following method.

[2]   In the various enumerations of the moral virtues I had met with in my reading, I found the catalogue more or less numerous, as different writers included more or fewer ideas under the same name. Temperance, for example, was by some confined to eating and drinking, while by others it was extended to mean the moderating every other pleasure, appetite, inclination, or passion, bodily or mental, even to our avarice and ambition. I propos'd to myself, for the sake of clearness, to use rather more names, with fewer ideas annex'd to each, than

a few names with more ideas; and I included under thirteen names of virtues all that at that time occurr'd to me as necessary or desirable, and annexed to each a short precept, which fully express'd the extent I gave to its meaning.

[3] These names of virtues, with their precepts, were:

1. TEMPERANCE
Eat not to dullness; drink not to elevation.

2. SILENCE
Speak not but what may benefit others or yourself; avoid trifling conversation.

3. ORDER
Let all your things have their places; let each part of your business have its time.

4. RESOLUTION
Resolve to perform what you ought; perform without fail what you resolve.

5. FRUGALITY
Make no expense but to do good to others or yourself; *i.e.,* waste nothing.

6. INDUSTRY
Lose no time; be always employ'd in something useful; cut off all unnecessary actions.

7. SINCERITY
Use no hurtful deceit; think innocently and justly, and, if you speak, speak accordingly.

8. JUSTICE
Wrong none by doing injuries, or omitting the benefits that are your duty.

9. MODERATION
Avoid extreams; forbear resenting injuries so much as you think they deserve.

10. CLEANLINESS
Tolerate no uncleanliness in body, cloaths, or habitation.

11. TRANQUILLITY
Be not disturbed at trifles, or at accidents common or unavoidable.

12. CHASTITY

Rarely use venery but for health or offspring, never to dulness, weakness, or the injury of your own or another's peace or reputation.

13. HUMILITY

Imitate Jesus and Socrates.

[4]   My intention being to acquire the *habitude* of all these virtues, I judg'd it would be well not to distract my attention by attempting the whole at once, but to fix it on one of them at a time; and, when I should be master of that, then to proceed to another, and so on, till I should have gone thro' the thirteen; and, as the previous acquisition of some might facilitate the acquisition of certain others, I arrang'd them with that view, as they stand above. Temperance first, as it tends to procure that coolness and clearness of head, which is so necessary where constant vigilance was to be kept up, and guard maintained against the unremitting attraction of ancient habits, and the force of perpetual temptations. This being acquir'd and establish'd, Silence would be more easy; and my desire being to gain knowledge at the same time that I improv'd in virtue, and considering that in conversation it was obtain'd rather by the use of the ears than of the tongue, and therefore wishing to break a habit I was getting into of prattling, punning, and joking, which only made me acceptable to trifling company, I gave *Silence* the second place. This and the next, *Order,* I expected would allow me more time for attending to my project and my studies. *Resolution,* once become habitual, would keep me firm in my endeavors to obtain all the subsequent virtues; *Frugality* and Industry freeing me from my remaining debt, and producing affluence and independence, would make more easy the practice of Sincerity and Justice, etc., etc. Conceiving then, that, agreeably to the advice of Pythagoras in his Golden Verses, daily examination would be necessary, I contrived the following method for conducting that examination.

[5]   I made a little book, in which I allotted a page for each of the virtues. I rul'd each page with red ink, so as to have seven columns, one for each day of the week, marking each column with a letter for the day. I cross'd these columns with thirteen red lines, marking the beginning of each line with the first letter of one of the virtues, on which line, and in its proper column, I might mark, by a little black spot, every fault I found upon examination to have been committed respecting that virtue upon that day.

FORM OF THE PAGES

TEMPERANCE

Eat not to Dulness.
Drink not to Elevation.

	SUN.	MON.	TUES.	WED.	THURS.	FRI.	SAT.
T [Temperance]							
S [Silence]	• •	•		•		•	
O [Order]	•	•	•		•	•	•
R [Resolution]			•			•	
F [Frugality]		•			•		
I [Industry]			•				
S [Sincerity]							
J [Justice]							
M [Moderation]							
Cl. [Cleanliness]							
T [Tranquility]							
Ch. [Chastity]							
H [Humility]							

[6]   I determined to give a week's strict attention to each of the virtues successively. Thus, in the first week, my great guard was to avoid every the least offence against *Temperance,* leaving the other virtues to their ordinary chance, only marking every evening the faults of the day. Thus, if in the first week I could keep my first line, marked T, clear of spots, I suppos'd the habit of that virtue so much strengthen'd, and its opposite weaken'd, that I might venture extending my attention to include the next, and for the following week keep both lines clear of spots. Proceeding thus to the last, I could go thro' a course compleat in thirteen weeks, and four courses in a year. And like him who, having a garden to weed, does not attempt to eradicate all the bad herbs at once, which would exceed his reach and his strength, but works on one of the beds at a time, and, having accomplish'd the first, proceeds to a second, so I should have, I hoped, the encouraging pleasure of seeing on my pages the progress I made in virtue, by clearing successively my lines of their spots, till in the end, by a number of courses, I should be happy in viewing a clean book, after a thirteen weeks' daily examination.

[7]   This my little book had for its motto these lines from Addison's *Cato*:

> "Here will I hold. If there's a power above us
> (And that there is, all nature cries aloud
> Thro' all her works), He must delight in virtue;
> And that which he delights in must be happy."

[8]   Another from Cicero,

> "O vitae Philosophia dux! O virtutum indagatrix expultrixque vitiorum! Unus dies, bene et ex praeceptis tuis actus, peccanti immortalitati est anteponendus."[1]

[9]   Another from the Proverbs of Solomon, speaking of wisdom or virtue:

> "Length of days is in her right hand, and in her left hand riches and honour. Her ways are ways of pleasantness, and all her paths are peace." iii. 16, 17.

[10]   And conceiving God to be the fountain of wisdom, I thought it right and necessary to solicit his assistance for obtaining it; to this

---

[1]*O vitae Philosophia* . . . "Oh, Philosophy, sweet guide of life! Oh, explorer of virtues and scourge of vice! One single day lived according to your rules ought to be preferred to an eternal life of sinning."

end I formed the following little prayer, which was prefix'd to my tables of examination, for daily use.

> "O powerful Goodness! bountiful Father! merciful Guide! Increase in me that wisdom which discovers my truest interest. Strengthen my resolutions to perform what that wisdom dictates. Accept my kind offices to thy other children as the only return in my power for thy continual favours to me."

[11]   I used also sometimes a little prayer which I took from Thomson's Poems, viz.:

> "Father of light and life, thou Good Supreme!
> O teach me what is good; teach me Thyself!
> Save me from folly, vanity, and vice,
> From every low pursuit; and fill my soul
> With knowledge, conscious peace, and virtue pure;
> Sacred, substantial, never-fading bliss!"

[12]   The precept of *Order* requiring that *every part of my business should have its allotted time,* one page in my little book contain'd the following scheme of employment for the twenty-four hours of a natural day.

THE MORNING *Question.* What good shall I do this day?	5 6 7	Rise, wash and address *Powerful Goodness!* Contrive day's business, and take the resolution of the day; prosecute the present study, and breakfast.
	8 9 10 11	Work.
NOON.	12 1	Read, or overlook my accounts, and dine.
	2 3 4 5	Work.
EVENING. *Question.* What good have I done to-day?	6 7 8 9	Put things in their places. Supper. Music or diversion, or conversation. Examination of the day.

	10	
	11	
	12	
NIGHT.	1	Sleep.
	2	
	3	
	4	

[13]   I enter'd upon the execution of this plan for self-examination, and continu'd it with occasional intermissions for some time. I was surpris'd to find myself so much fuller of faults than I had imagined; but I had the satisfaction of seeing them diminish. To avoid the trouble of renewing now and then my little book, which, by scraping out the marks on the paper of old faults to make room for new ones in a new course, became full of holes, I transferr'd my tables and precepts to the ivory leaves of a memorandum book, on which the lines were drawn with red ink, that made a durable stain, and on those lines I mark'd my faults with a black-lead pencil, which marks I could easily wipe out with a wet sponge. After a while I went thro' one course only in a year, and afterward only one in several years, till at length I omitted them entirely, being employ'd in voyages and business abroad, with a multiplicity of affairs that interfered; but I always carried my little book with me.

[14]   My scheme of ORDER gave me the most trouble; and I found that, tho' it might be practicable where a man's business was such as to leave him the disposition of his time, that of a journeyman printer, for instance, it was not possible to be exactly observed by a master, who must mix with the world, and often receive people of business at their own hours. *Order,* too, with regard to places for things, papers, etc., I found it extreamly difficult to acquire. I had not been early accustomed to it, and, having an exceeding good memory, I was not so sensible of the inconvenience attending want of method. This article, therefore, cost me so much painful attention, and my faults in it vexed me so much, and I made so little progress in amendment, and had such frequent relapses, that I was almost ready to give up the attempt, and content myself with a faulty character in that respect, like the man who, in buying an ax of a smith, my neighbour, desired to have the whole of its surface as bright as the edge. The smith consented to grind it bright for him if he would turn the wheel; he turn'd, while the smith press'd the broad face of the ax hard and heavily on the stone,

which made the turning of it very fatiguing. The man came every now and then from the wheel to see how the work went on, and at length would take his ax as it was, without farther grinding. "No," said the smith, "turn on, turn on; we shall have it bright by-and-by; as yet, it is only speckled." "Yes," says the man, *"but I think I like a speckled ax best."* And I believe this may have been the case with many, who, having, for want of some such means as I employ'd, found the difficulty of obtaining good and breaking bad habits in other points of vice and virtue, have given up the struggle, and concluded that *"a speckled ax was best";* for something, that pretended to be reason, was every now and then suggesting to me that such extream nicety as I exacted of myself might be a kind of foppery in morals, which, if it were known, would make me ridiculous; that a perfect character might be attended with the inconvenience of being envied and hated; and that a benevolent man should allow a few faults in himself, to keep his friends in countenance.

[15]   In truth, I found myself incorrigible with respect to Order; and now I am grown old, and my memory bad, I feel very sensibly the want of it. But, on the whole, tho' I never arrived at the perfection I had been so ambitious of obtaining, but fell far short of it, yet I was, by the endeavor, a better and a happier man than I otherwise should have been if I had not attempted it; as those who aim at perfect writing by imitating the engraved copies, tho' they never reach the wish'd-for excellence of those copies, their hand is mended by the endeavor, and is tolerable while it continues fair and legible.

[16]   It may be well my posterity should be informed that to this little artifice, with the blessing of God, their ancestor ow'd the constant felicity of his life, down to his 79th year, in which this is written. What reverses may attend the remainder is in the hand of Providence; but, if they arrive, the reflection on past happiness enjoy'd ought to help his bearing them with more resignation. To Temperance he ascribes his long-continued health, and what is still left to him of a good constitution; to Industry and Frugality, the early easiness of his circumstances and acquisition of his fortune, with all that knowledge that enabled him to be a useful citizen, and obtained for him some degree of reputation among the learned; to Sincerity and Justice, the confidence of his country, and the honorable employs it conferred upon him; and to the joint influence of the whole mass of the virtues, even in the imperfect state he was able to acquire them, all that evenness

of temper, and that cheerfulness in conversation, which makes his company still sought for, and agreeable even to his younger acquaintance. I hope, therefore, that some of my descendants may follow the example and reap the benefit.

[17]   It will be remark'd that, tho' my scheme was not wholly without religion, there was in it no mark of any of the distinguishing tenets of any particular sect. I had purposely avoided them; for, being fully persuaded of the utility and excellency of my method, and that it might be serviceable to people in all religions, and intending some time or other to publish it, I would not have any thing in it that should prejudice any one, of any sect, against it. I purposed writing a little comment on each virtue, in which I would have shown the advantages of possessing it, and the mischiefs attenting its opposite view; and I should have called my book THE ART OF VIRTUE, [Nothing so likely to make a man's fortune as virtue.] because it would have shown the means and manner of obtaining virtue, which would have distinguished it from the mere exhortation to be good, that does not instruct and indicate the means, but is like the apostle's man of verbal charity, who only without showing to the naked and hungry how or where they might get clothes or victuals, exhorted them to be fed and clothed. —James ii. 15, 16.

[18]   But it so happened that my intention of writing and publishing this comment was never fulfilled. I did, indeed, from time to time, put down short hints of the sentiments, reasonings, etc., to be made use of in it, some of which I have still by me; but the necessary close attention to private business in the earlier part of my life, and public business since, have occasioned my postponing it; for, it being connected in my mind with *a great and extensive project,* that required the whole man to execute, and which an unforeseen succession of employs prevented my attending to, it has hitherto remain'd unfinish'd.

[19]   In this piece it was my design to explain and enforce this doctrine, that vicious actions are not hurtful because they are forbidden, but forbidden because they are hurtful, the nature of man alone considered; that it was, therefore, every one's interest to be virtuous who wish'd to be happy even in this world; and I should, from this circumstance (there being always in the world a number of rich merchants, nobility, states, and princes, who have need of honest instruments for the management of their affairs, and such being so rare), have endeavored to convince young persons that no qualities were so likely to make a poor man's fortune as those of probity and integrity.

[20]   My list of virtues contain'd at first but twelve; but a Quaker friend having kindly informed me that I was generally thought proud; that my pride show'd itself frequently in conversation; that I was not content with being in the right when discussing any point, but was overbearing, and rather insolent, of which he convinc'd me by mentioning several instances; I determined endeavoring to cure myself, if I could, of this vice or folly among the rest, and I added *Humility* to my list, giving an extensive meaning to the word.

[21]   I cannot boast of much success in acquiring the *reality* of this virtue, but I had a good deal with regard to the *appearance* of it. I made it a rule to forbear all direct contradiction to the sentiments of others, and all positive assertion of my own. I even forbid myself, agreeably to the old laws of our Junto, the use of every word or expression in the language that imported a fix'd opinion, such as *certainly, undoubtedly*, etc., and I adopted, instead of them, *I conceive, I apprehend*, or *I imagine* a thing to be so or so; or it *so appears to me at present*. When another asserted something that I thought an error, I deny'd myself the pleasure of contradicting him abruptly, and of showing immediately some absurdity in his proposition; and in answering I began by observing that in certain cases or circumstances his opinion would be right, but in the present case there *appear'd* or *seem'd* to me some difference, etc. I soon found the advantage of this change in my manner; the conversations I engag'd in went on more pleasantly. The modest way in which I propos'd my opinions procur'd them a readier reception and less contradiction; I had less mortification when I was found to be in the wrong, and I more easily prevail'd with others to give up their mistakes and join with me when I happened to be in the right.

[22]   And this mode, which I at first put on with some violence to natural inclination, became at length so easy, and so habitual to me, that perhaps for these fifty years past no one has ever heard a dogmatical expression escape me. And to this habit (after my character of integrity) I think it principally owing that I had early so much weight with my fellow-citizens when I proposed new institutions, or alterations in the old, and so much influence in public councils when I became a member; for I was but a bad speaker, never eloquent, subject to much hesitation in my choice of words, hardly correct in language, and yet I generally carried my points.

[23]   In reality, there is, perhaps, no one of our national passions so hard to subdue as *pride*. Disguise it, struggle with it, beat it down,

stifle it, mortify it as much as one pleases, it is still alive, and will every now and then peep out and show itself; you will see it, perhaps, often in this history; for, even if I could conceive that I had compleatly overcome it, I should probably be proud of my humility.

CIVIL DISOBEDIENCE

HENRY DAVID THOREAU   Most people know that Thoreau lived by Walden Pond for two years but not much more. Henry David Thoreau (1817-1862), philosopher and writer, loved the countryside around his birthplace, Concord, Massachusetts. He felt that one should pursue money only to the extent demanded by necessity or community betterment; that the work week should be reversed; that a man should labor just one day each week using the other six to expand his soul. And he went to Walden to prove his point. When he felt the point proved, he went back to Concord, back to his lecturing and his writing. Naturalist as well as philosopher, Thoreau's most lasting influence may be in his contributions to the science of ecology. His studies of the relation of plants, birds, animals, and man to the environment are as important as his addresses, "Civil Liberty," "Life Without Principle," and "Civil Disobedience." An intense individualist, Thoreau's spiritual and intellectual radicalism are as challenging in the 20th century as to the period immediately preceding the Civil War.

[1]   I heartily accept the motto,—"That government is best which governs least;" and I should like to see it acted up to more rapidly and systematically. Carried out, it finally amounts to this, which also I believe,—"That government is best which governs not at all;" and when men are prepared for it, that will be the kind of government which they will have. Government is at best but an expedient; but most governments are usually, and all governments are sometimes, inexpedient. The objections which have been brought against a standing army, and they are many and weighty, and deserve to prevail, may also at last be brought against a standing government. The standing army is only an arm of the standing government. The government itself, which is only the mode which the people have chosen to execute their will, is equally liable to be abused and perverted before the people can act through it. Witness the present Mexican war, the work of comparatively a few individuals using the standing government as their tool; for, in the outset, the people would not have consented to this measure.

[2]   This American government,—what is it but a tradition, though a recent one, endeavoring to transmit itself unimpaired to posterity, but each instant losing some of its integrity? It has not the vitality and force of a single living man; for a single man can bend it to his will.

It is a sort of wooden gun to the people themselves. But it is not the less necessary for this; for the people must have some complicated machinery or other, and hear its din, to satisfy that idea of government which they have. Governments show thus how successfully men can be imposed on, even impose on themselves, for their own advantage. It is excellent, we must all allow. Yet this government never of itself furthered any enterprise, but by the alacrity with which it got out of its way. *It* does not keep the country free. *It* does not settle the West. *It* does not educate. The character inherent in the American people has done all that has been accomplished; and it would have done somewhat more, if the government had not sometimes got in its way. For government is an expedient by which men would fain succeed in letting one another alone; and, as has been said, when it is most expedient, the governed are most let alone by it. Trade and commerce, if they were not made of India-rubber, would never manage to bounce over the obstacles which legislators are continually putting in their way; and, if one were to judge these men wholly by the effects of their actions and not partly by their intentions, they would deserve to be classed and punished with those mischievous persons who put obstructions on the railroads.

[3]   But, to speak practically and as a citizen, unlike those who call themselves no-government men, I ask for, not at once no government, but *at once* a better government. Let every man make known what kind of government would command his respect, and that will be one step toward obtaining it.

[4]   After all, the practical reason why, when the power is once in the hands of the people, a majority are permitted, and for a long period continue, to rule is not because they are most likely to be in the right, nor because this seems fairest to the minority, but because they are physically the strongest. But a government in which the majority rule in all cases cannot be based on justice, even as far as men understand it. Can there not be a government in which majorities do not virtually decide right and wrong, but conscience?—in which majorities decide only those questions to which the rule of expediency is applicable? Must the citizen ever for a moment, or in the least degree, resign his conscience to the legislator? Why has every man a conscience, then? I think that we should be men first, and subjects afterward. It is not desirable to cultivate a respect for the law, so much as for the right. The only obligation which I have a right to assume is to do at any time

what I think right. It is truly enough said, that a corporation has no conscience; but a corporation of conscientious men is a corporation *with* a conscience. Law never made men a whit more just; and, by means of their respect for it, even the well-disposed are daily made the agents of injustice. A common and natural result of an undue respect for law is, that you may see a file of soldiers, colonel, captain, corporal, privates, powder-monkeys, and all, marching in admirable order over hill and dale to the wars, against their wills, ay, against their common sense and consciences, which makes it very steep marching indeed, and produces a palpitation of the heart. They have no doubt that it is a damnable business in which they are concerned; they are all peaceably inclined. Now, what are they? Men at all? or small movable forts and magazines, at the service of some unscrupulous man in power? Visit the Navy-Yard, and behold a marine, such a man as an American government can make, or such as it can make a man with its black arts,— a mere shadow and reminiscence of humanity, a man laid out alive and standing, and already, as one may say, buried under arms with funeral accompaniments, though it may be,—

> "Not a drum was heard, not a funeral note,
>   As his corse to the rampart we hurried;
> Not a soldier discharged his farewell shot
>   O'er the grave where our hero we buried."

[5]   The mass of men serve the state thus, not as men mainly, but as machines, with their bodies. They are the standing army, and the militia, jailers, constables, posse comitatus, etc. In most cases there is no free exercise whatever of the judgment or of the moral sense; but they put themselves on a level with wood and earth and stones; and wooden men can perhaps be manufactured that will serve the purpose as well. Such command no more respect than men of straw or a lump of dirt. They have the same sort of worth only as horses and dogs. Yet such as these even are commonly esteemed good citizens. Others—as most legislators, politicians, lawyers, ministers, and office-holders— serve the state chiefly with their heads; and, as they rarely make any moral distinctions, they are as likely to serve the Devil, without *intending* it, as God. A very few, as heroes, patriots, martyrs, reformers in the great sense, and *men*, serve the state with their consciences also, and so necessarily resist it for the most part; and they are commonly treated as enemies by it. A wise man will only be useful as a man, and will not

submit to be "clay," and "stop a hole to keep the wind away," but leave that office to his dust at least:

> "I am too high-born to be propertied,
> To be a secondary at control,
> Or useful serving-man and instrument
> To any sovereign state throughout the world."

[6]   He who gives himself entirely to his fellow-men appears to them useless and selfish; but he who gives himself partially to them is pronounced a benefactor and philanthropist.

[7]   How does it become a man to behave toward this American government to-day? I answer, that he cannot without disgrace be associated with it. I cannot for an instant recognize that political organization as *my* government which is the *slave's* government also.

[8]   All men recognize the right of revolution; that is, the right to refuse allegiance to, and to resist, the government, when its tyranny or its inefficiency are great and unendurable. But almost all say that such is not the case now. But such was the case, they think, in the Revolution of '75. If one were to tell me that this was a bad government because it taxed certain foreign commodities brought to its ports, it is most probable that I should not make an ado about it, for I can do without them. All machines have their friction; and possibly this does enough good to counterbalance the evil. At any rate, it is a great evil to make a stir about it. But when the friction comes to have its machine, and oppression and robbery are organized, I say, let us not have such a machine any longer. In other words, when a sixth of the population of a nation which has undertaken to be the refuge of liberty are slaves, and a whole country is unjustly overrun and conquered by a foreign army, and subjected to military law, I think that it is not too soon for honest men to rebel and revolutionize. What makes this duty the more urgent is the fact that the country so overrun is not our own, but ours is the invading army.

[9]   Paley, a common authority with many on moral questions, in his chapter on the "Duty of Submission to Civil Government," resolves all civil obligation into expediency; and he proceeds to say, "that so long as the interest of the whole society requires it, that is, so long as the established government cannot be resisted or changed without public inconveniency, it is the will of God that the established government be obeyed, and no longer. . . . This principle being admitted, the justice of every particular case of resistance is reduced to a computation of the

quantity of the danger and grievance on the one side, and of the probability and expense of redressing it on the other." Of this, he says, every man shall judge for himself. But Paley appears never to have contemplated those cases to which the rule of expediency does not apply, in which a people, as well as an individual, must do justice, cost what it may. If I have unjustly wrested a plank from a drowning man, I must restore it to him though I drown myself. This, according to Paley, would be inconvenient. But he that would save his life, in such case, shall lose it. This people must cease to hold slaves, and to make war on Mexico, though it cost them their existence as a people.

[10]   In their practice, nations agree with Paley; but does any one think that Massachusetts does exactly what is right at the present crisis?

> "A drab of state, a cloth-o'-silver slut,
> To have her train borne up, and her soul trail in the dirt."

Practically speaking, the opponents to a reform in Massachusetts are not a hundred thousand politicians at the South, but a hundred thousand merchants and farmers here, who are more interested in commerce and agriculture than they are in humanity, and are not prepared to do justice to the slave and to Mexico, *cost what it may*. I quarrel not with far-off foes, but with those who, near at home, cooperate with, and do the bidding of, those far away, and without whom the latter would be harmless. We are accustomed to say, that the mass of men are unprepared; but improvement is slow, because the few are not materially wiser or better than the many. It is not so important that many should be as good as you, as that there be some absolute goodness somewhere; for that will leaven the whole lump. There are thousands who are *in opinion* opposed to slavery and to the war, who yet in effect do nothing to put an end to them; who, esteeming themselves children of Washington and Franklin, sit down with their hands in their pockets, and say that they know not what to do, and do nothing; who even postpone the question of freedom to the question of free-trade, and quietly read the prices-current along with the latest advices from Mexico, after dinner, and, it may be, fall asleep over them both. What is the price-current of an honest man and patriot to-day? They hesitate, and they regret, and sometimes they petition; but they do nothing in earnest and with effect. They will wait, well disposed, for others to remedy the evil, that they may no longer have it to regret. At most, they give only a cheap vote, and a feeble countenance and Godspeed, to the right, as it goes by them. There are nine hundred and ninety-nine patrons of virtue to one virtuous man. But it is easier to deal with the real possessor of a thing than with the temporary guardian of it.

[11]   All voting is a sort of gaming, like checkers or backgammon, with a slight moral tinge to it, a playing with right and wrong, with moral questions; and betting naturally accompanies it. The character of the voters is not staked. I cast my vote, perchance, as I think right; but I am not vitally concerned that that right should prevail. I am willing to leave it to the majority. Its obligation, therefore, never exceeds that of expediency. Even voting *for the right* is *doing* nothing for it. It is only expressing to men feebly your desire that it should prevail. A wise man will not leave the right to the mercy of chance, nor wish it to prevail through the power of the majority. There is but little virtue in the action of masses of men. When the majority shall at length vote for the abolition of slavery, it will be because they are indifferent to slavery, or because there is but little slavery left to be abolished by their vote. *They* will then be the only slaves. Only *his* vote can hasten the abolition of slavery who asserts his own freedom by his vote.

[12]   I hear of a convention to be held at Baltimore, or elsewhere, for the selection of a candidate for the Presidency, made up chiefly of editors, and men who are politicians by profession; but I think, what is it to any independent, intelligent, and respectable man what decision they may come to? Shall we not have the advantage of his wisdom and honesty, nevertheless? Can we not count upon some independent votes? Are there not many individuals in the country who do not attend conventions? But no: I find that the respectable man, so called, has immediately drifted from his position, and despairs of his country, when his country has more reason to despair of him. He forthwith adopts one of the candidates thus selected as the only *available* one, thus proving that he is himself *available* for any purposes of the demagogue. His vote is of no more worth than that of any unprincipled foreigner or hireling native, who may have been bought. O for a man who is a *man*, and, as my neighbor says, has a bone in his back which you cannot pass your hand through! Our statistics are at fault: the population has been returned too large. How many *men* are there to a square thousand miles in this country? Hardly one. Does not America offer any inducement for men to settle here? The American has dwindled into an Odd Fellow,—one who may be known by the development of his organ of gregariousness, and a manifest lack of intellect and cheerful self-reliance; whose first and chief concern, on coming into the world, is to see that the Almshouses are in good repair; and, before yet he has law-

fully donned the virile garb, to collect a fund for the support of the windows and orphans that may be; who, in short, ventures to live only by the aid of the Mutual Insurance company, which has promised to bury him decently.

[13]   It is not a man's duty, as a matter of course, to devote himself to the eradication of any, even the most enormous wrong; he may still properly have other concerns to engage him; but it is his duty, at least, to wash his hands of it, and, if he gives it no thought longer, not to give it practically his support. If I devote myself to other pursuits and contemplations, I must first see, at least, that I do not pursue them sitting upon another man's shoulders. I must get off him first, that he may pursue his contemplations too. See what gross inconsistency is tolerated. I have heard some of my townsmen say, "I should like to have them order me out to help put down an insurrection of the slaves, or to march to Mexico;—see if I would go;" and yet these very men have each, directly by their allegiance, and so indirectly, at least, by their money, furnished a substitute. The soldier is applauded who refuses to serve in an unjust war by those who do not refuse to sustain the unjust government which makes the war; is applauded by those whose own act and authority he disregards and sets at naught; as if the state were penitent to that degree that it hired one to scourge it while it sinned, but not to that degree that it left off sinning for a moment. Thus, under the name of Order and Civil Government, we are all made at last to pay homage to and support our own meanness. After the first blush of sin comes its indifference; and from immoral it becomes, as it were, *un*-moral, and not quite unnecessary to that life which we have made.

[14]   The broadest and most prevalent error requires the most disinterested virtue to sustain it. The slight reproach to which the virtue of patriotism is commonly liable, the noble are most likely to incur. Those who, while they disapprove of the character and measures of a government, yield to it their allegiance and support are undoubtedly its most conscientious supporters, and so frequently the most serious obstacles to reform. Some are petitioning the state to dissolve the Union, to disregard the requisitions of the President. Why do they not dissolve it themselves,—the union between themselves and the state,—and refuse to pay their quota into its treasury? Do not they stand in the same relation to the state that the state does to the Union? And have not the same reasons prevented the state from resisting the Union which have prevented them from resisting the state?

[15]   How can a man be satisfied to entertain an opinion merely, and

enjoy *it*? Is there any enjoyment in it, if his opinion is that he is ag-grieved? If you are cheated out of a single dollar by your neighbor, you do not rest satisfied with knowing that you are cheated, or with saying that you are cheated, or even with petitioning him to pay you your due; but you take effectual steps at once to obtain the full amount, and see that you are never cheated again. Action from principle, the perception and the performance of right, changes things and relations; it is essen-tially revolutionary, and does not consist wholly with anything which was. It not only divides states and churches, it divides families; ay, it divides the *individual*, separating the diabolical in him from the divine.

[16]   Unjust laws exist: shall we be content to obey them, or shall we endeavor to amend them, and obey them until we have succeeded, or shall we transgress them at once? Men generally, under such a govern-ment as this, think that they ought to wait until they have persuaded the majority to alter them. They think that, if they should resist, the remedy would be worse than the evil. But it is the fault of the govern-ment itself that the remedy *is* worse than the evil. *It* makes it worse. Why is it not more apt to anticipate and provide for reform? Why does it not cherish its wise minority? Why does it cry and resist before it is hurt? Why does it not encourage its citizens to be on the alert to point out its faults, and *do* better than it would have them? Why does it al-ways crucify Christ, and excommunicate Copernicus and Luther, and pronounce Washington and Franklin rebels?

[17]   One would think, that a deliberate and practical denial of its authority was the only offense never contemplated by government; else, why has it not assigned its definite, its suitable and proportionate pen-ality? If a man who has no property refuses but once to earn nine shillings for the state, he is put in prison for a period unlimited by any law that I know, and determined only by the discretion of those who placed him there; but if he should steal ninety times nine shillings from the state, he is soon permitted to go at large again.

[18]   If the injustice is part of the necessary friction of the machine of government, let it go, let it go: perchance it will wear smooth,—cer-tainly the machine will wear out. If the injustice has a spring, or a pulley, or a rope, or a crank, exclusively for itself, then perhaps you may consider whether the remedy will not be worse than the evil; but if it is of such a nature that it requires you to be the agent of injustice to another, then, I say, break the law. Let your life be a counter friction to stop the machine. What I have to do is to see, at any rate, that I do not lend myself to the wrong which I condemn.

[19]   As for adopting the ways which the state has provided for remedying the evil, I know not of such ways. They take too much time, and a man's life will be gone. I have other affairs to attend to. I came into this world, not chiefly to make this a good place to live in, but to live in it, be it good or bad. A man has not everything to do, but something; and because he cannot do *everything*, it is not necessary that he should do *something* wrong. It is not my business to be petitioning the Governor or the Legilature any more than it is theirs to petition me; and if they should not hear my petition, what should I do then? But in this case the state has provided no way: its very Constitution is the evil. This may seem to be harsh and stubborn and unconciliatory; but it is to treat with the utmost kindness and consideration the only spirit that can appreciate or deserves it. So is all change for the better, like birth and death, which convulse the body.

[20]   I do not hesitate to say, that those who call themselves Abolitionists should at once effectually withdraw their support, both in person and property, from the government of Massachusetts, and not wait till they constitute a majority of one, before they suffer the right to prevail through them. I think that it is enough if they have God on their side, without waiting for that other one. Moreover, any man more right than his neighbors constitutes a majority of one already.

[21]   I meet this American government, or its representative, the state government, directly, and face to face, once a year—no more—in the person of its tax-gatherer; this is the only mode in which a man situated as I am necessarily meets it; and it then says distinctly, Recognize me; and the simplest, the most effectual, and, in the present posture of affairs, the indispensablest mode of treating with it on this head, of expressing your little satisfaction with and love for it, is to deny it then. My civil neighbor, the tax-gatherer, is the very man I have to deal with, —for it is, after all, with men and not with parchment that I quarrel,— and he has voluntarily chosen to be an agent of the government. How shall he ever know well what he is and does as an officer of the government, or as a man, until he is obliged to consider whether he shall treat me, his neighbor, for whom he has respect, as a neighbor and well-disposed man, or as a maniac and disturber of the peace, and see if he can get over this obstruction to his neighborliness without a ruder and more impetuous thought or speech corresponding with his action. I know this well, that if one thousand, if one hundred, if ten men whom I could name,—if ten *honest* men only,—ay, if *one* HONEST man, in this State of Massachusetts, *ceasing to hold slaves*, were actually to

withdraw from this copartnership, and be locked up in the county jail therefor, it would be the abolition of slavery in America. For it matters not how small the beginning may seem to be: what is once well done is done forever. But we love better to talk about it: that we say is our mission. Reform keeps many scores of newspapers in its service, but not one man. If my esteemed neighbor, the State's ambassador, who will devote his days to the settlement of the question of human rights in the Council Chamber, instead of being threatened with the prisons of Carolina, were to sit down the prisoner of Massachusetts, that State which is so anxious to foist the sin of slavery upon her sister,—though at present she can discover only an act of inhospitality to be the ground of a quarrel with her,—the Legislature would not wholly waive the subject the following winter.

[22] Under a government which imprisons any unjustly, the true place for a just man is also a prison. The proper place to-day, the only place which Massachusetts has provided for her freer and less despond-ing spirits, is in her prisons, to be put out and locked out of the State by her own act, as they have already put themselves out by their prin-ciples. It is there that the fugitive slave, and the Mexican prisoner on parole, and the Indian come to plead the wrongs of his race should find them; on that separate, but more free and honorable ground, where the State places those who are not *with* her, but *against* her,—the only house in a slave State in which a free man can abide with honor. If any think that their influence would be lost there, and their voices no longer afflict the ear of the State, that they would not be as an enemy within its walls, they do not know by how much truth is stronger than error, nor how much more eloquently and effectively he can combat injustice who has experienced a little in his own person. Cast your whole vote, not a strip of paper merely, but your whole influence. A minority is power-less while it conforms to the majority; it is not even a minority then; but it is irresistible when it clogs by its whole weight. If the alternative is to keep all just men in prison, or give up war and slavery, the State will not hesitate which to choose. If a thousand men were not to pay their tax-bills this year, that would not be a violent and bloody measure, as it would be to pay them, and enable the State to commit violence and shed innocent blood. This is, in fact, the definition of a peaceable revolution, if any such is possible. If the tax-gatherer, or any other public officer, asks me, as one has done, "But what shall I do?" my answer is, "If you really wish to do anything, resign your office." When the subject has re-fused allegiance, and the officer has resigned his office, then the revolu-

tion is accomplished. But even suppose blood should flow. Is there not a sort of blood shed when the conscience is wounded? Through this wound a man's real manhood and immortality flow out, and he bleeds to an everlasting death. I see this blood flowing now.

[23]   I have contemplated the imprisonment of the offender, rather than the seizure of his goods,—though both will serve the same purpose,—because they who assert the purest right, and consequently are most dangerous to a corrupt State, commonly have not spent much time in accumulating property. To such the State renders comparatively small service, and a slight tax is wont to appear exorbitant, particularly if they are obliged to earn it by special labor with their hands. If there were one who lived wholly without the use of money, the State itself would hesitate to demand it of him. But the rich man—not to make any invidious comparison—is always sold to the institution which makes him rich. Absolutely speaking, the more money, the less virtue; for money comes between a man and his objects, and obtains them for him; and it was certainly no great virtue to obtain it. It puts to rest many questions which he would otherwise be taxed to answer; while the only new question which it puts is the hard but superfluous one, how to spend it. Thus his moral ground is taken from under his feet. The opportunities of living are diminished in proportion as what are called the "means" are increased. The best thing a man can do for his culture when he is rich is to endeavor to carry out those schemes which he entertained when he was poor. Christ answered the Herodians according to their condition. "Show me the tribute-money," said he;—and one took a penny out of his pocket;—if you use money which has the image of Caesar on it, which he has made current and valuable, that is, *if you are men of the State*, and gladly enjoy the advantages of Caesar's government, then pay him back some of his own when he demands it. "Render therefore to Caesar that which is Caesar's, and to God those things which are God's,"—leaving them no wiser than before as to which was which; for they did not wish to know.

[24]   When I converse with the freest of my neighbors, I perceive that, whatever they may say about the magnitude and seriousness of the question, and their regard for the public tranquillity, the long and the short of the matter is, that they cannot spare the protection of the existing government, and they dread the consequences to their property and families of disobedience to it. For my own part, I should not like to think that I ever rely on the protection of the State. But, if I deny the authority of the State when it presents its tax-bill, it will soon take

and waste all my property, and so harass me and my children without
end. This is hard. This makes it impossible for a man to live honestly, and at the same time comfortably, in outward respects. It will
not be worth the while to accumulate property; that would be sure to
go again. You must hire or squat somewhere, and raise but a small
crop, and eat that soon. You must live within yourself, and depend
upon yourself always tucked up and ready for a start, and not have
many affairs. A man may grow rich in Turkey even, if he will be
in all respects a good subject of the Turkish government. Confucius
said: "If a state is governed by the principles of reason, poverty and
misery are subjects of shame; if a state is not governed by the principles
of reason, riches and honors are the subjects of shame." No: until I
want the protection of Massachusetts to be extended to me in some
distant Southern port, where my liberty is endangered, or until I am
bent solely on building up an estate at home by peaceful enterprise,
I can afford to refuse allegiance to Massachusetts, and her right to my
property and life. It costs me less in every sense to incur the penalty
of disobedience to the State than it would to obey. I should feel as if
I were worth less in that case.

[25]   Some years ago, the State met me in behalf of the Church, and
commanded me to pay a certain sum toward the support of a clergyman
whose preaching my father attended, but never I myself. "Pay," it
said, "or be locked up in the jail." I declined to pay. But, unfortunately, another man saw fit to pay it. I did not see why the schoolmaster should be taxed to support the priest, and not the priest the
schoolmaster; for I was not the State's schoolmaster, but I supported
myself by voluntary subscription. I did not see why the lyceum should
not present its tax-bill, and have the State to back its demand, as well
as the Church. However, at the request of the selectmen, I con-
descended to make some such statement as this in writing: — "Know
all men by these presents, that I, Henry Thoreau, do not wish to be
regarded as a member of any incorporated society which I have not
joined." This I gave to the town clerk; and he has it. The State,
having thus learned that I did not wish to be regarded as a member
of that church, has never made a like demand on me since; though
it said that it must adhere to its original presumption that time. If I
had known how to name them, I should then have signed off in detail
from all the societies which I never signed on to; but I did not know
where to find a complete list.

[26]   I have paid no poll-tax for six years. I was put into a jail once

on this account, for one night; and, as I stood considering the walls of
solid stone, two or three feet thick, the door of wood and iron, a foot
thick, and the iron grating which strained the light, I could not help
being struck with the foolishness of that institution which treated me
as if I were mere flesh and blood and bones, to be locked up. I wondered that it should have concluded at length that this was the best
use it could put me to, and had never thought to avail itself of my
services in some way. I saw that, if there was a wall of stone between me and my townsmen, there was a still more difficult one to
climb or break through before they could get to be as free as I was.
I did not for a moment feel confined, and the walls seemed a great
waste of stone and mortar. I felt as if I alone of all my townsmen
had paid my tax. They plainly did not know how to treat me, but
behaved like persons who are underbred. In every threat and in every
compliment there was a blunder; for they thought that my chief desire
was to stand the other side of that stone wall. I could not but smile
to see how industriously they locked the door on my meditations,
which followed them out again without let or hindrance, and *they* were
really all that was dangerous. As they could not reach me, they had
resolved to punish my body; just as boys, if they cannot come at some
person against whom they have a spite, will abuse his dog. I saw that
the State was half-witted, that it was timid as a lone woman with her
silver spoons, and that it did not know its friends from its foes, and
I lost all my remaining respect for it, and pitied it.

[27]   Thus the State never intentionally confronts a man's sense, intellectual or moral, but only his body, his senses. It is not armed with
superior wit or honesty, but with superior physical strength. I was not
born to be forced. I will breathe after my own fashion. Let us see who
is the strongest. What force has a multitude? They only can force me
who obey a higher law than I. They force me to become like themselves.
I do not hear of *men* being *forced* to live this way or that by masses of
men. What sort of life were that to live? When I meet a government
which says to me, "Your money or your life," why should I be in haste
to give it my money? It may be in a great strait, and not know what
to do: I cannot help that. It must help itself; do as I do. It is not
worth the while to snivel about it. I am not responsible for the successful working of the machinery of society. I am not the son of the
engineer. I perceive that, when an acorn and a chestnut fall side by
side, the one does not remain inert to make way for the other, but
both obey their own laws, and spring and grow and flourish as best

they can, till one, perchance, overshadows and destroys the other. If a plant cannot live according to its nature, it dies; and so a man.

[28]   The night in prison was novel and interesting enough. The prisoners in their shirt-sleeves were enjoying a chat and the evening air in the doorway, when I entered. But the jailer said, "Come, boys, it is time to lock up;" and so they dispersed, and I heard the sound of their steps returning into the hollow apartments. My room-mate was introduced to me by the jailer as "a first-rate fellow and a clever man." When the door was locked, he showed me where to hang my hat, and how he managed matters there. The rooms were whitewashed once a month; and this one, at least, was the whitest, most simply furnished, and probably the neatest apartment in the town. He naturally wanted to know where I came from, and what brought me there; and, when I had told him, I asked him in my turn how he came there, presuming him to be an honest man, of course; and, as the world goes, I believe he was. "Why," said he, "they accuse me of burning a barn; but I never did it." As near as I could discover, he had probably gone to bed in a barn when drunk, and smoked his pipe there; and so a barn was burnt. He had the reputation of being a clever man, had been there some three months waiting for his trial to come on, and would have to wait as much longer; but he was quite domesticated and contented, since he got his board for nothing, and thought that he was well treated.

[29]   He occupied one window, and I the other; and I saw that if one stayed there long, his principal business would be to look out the window. I had soon read all the tracts that were left there, and examined where former prisoners had broken out, and where a grate had been sawed off, and heard the history of the various occupants of that room; for I found that even here there was a history and a gossip which never circulated beyond the walls of the jail. Probably this is the only house in the town where verses are composed, which are afterward printed in a circular form, but not published. I was shown quite a long list of verses which were composed by some young men who had been detected in an attempt to escape, who avenged themselves by singing them.

[30]   I pumped my fellow-prisoner as dry as I could, for fear I should never see him again; but at length he showed me which was my bed, and left me to blow out the lamp.

[31]   It was like traveling into a far country, such as I had never expected to behold, to lie there for one night. It seemed to me that I never

had heard the town-clock strike before, nor the evening sounds of the village; for we slept with the windows open, which were inside the grating. It was to see my native village in the light of the Middle Ages, and our Concord was turned into a Rhine stream, and visions of knights and castles passed before me. They were the voices of old burghers that I heard in the streets. I was an involuntary spectator and auditor of whatever was done and said in the kitchen of the adjacent village-inn,—a wholly new and rare experience to me. It was a closer view of my native town. I was fairly inside of it. I never had seen its institutions before. This is one of its peculiar institutions; for it is a shire town. I began to comprehend what its inhabitants were about.

[32]   In the morning, our breakfasts were put through the hole in the door, in small oblong-square tin pans, made to fit, and holding a pint of chocolate, with brown bread, and an iron spoon. When they called for the vessels again, I was green enough to return what bread I had left; but my comrade seized it, and said that I should lay that up for lunch or dinner. Soon after he was let out to work at haying in a neighboring field, whither he went every day, and would not be back till noon; so he bade me good-day, saying that he doubted if he should see me again.

[33]   When I came out of prison,—for some one interfered, and paid that tax,—I did not perceive that great changes had taken place on the common, such as he observed who went in a youth and emerged a tottering and gray-headed man; and yet a change had to my eyes come over the scene,—the town, and State, and country,—greater than any that mere time could effect. I saw yet more distinctly the State in which I lived. I saw to what extent the people among whom I lived could be trusted as good neighbors and friends; that their friendship was for summer weather only; that they did not greatly propose to do right; that they were a distinct race from me by their prejudices and superstitions, as the Chinamen and Malays are; that in their sacrifices to humanity they ran no risks, not even to their property; that after all they were not so noble but they treated the thief as he had treated them, and hoped, by a certain outward observance and a few prayers, and by walking in a particular straight though useless path from time to time, to save their souls. This may be to judge my neighbors harshly; for I believe that many of them are not aware that they have such an institution as the jail in their village.

[34]   It was formerly the custom in our village, when a poor debtor

came out of jail, for his acquaintances to salute him, looking through their fingers, which were crossed to represent the grating of a jail window, "How do ye do?" My neighbors did not thus salute me, but first looked at me, and then at one another, as if I had returned from a long journey. I was put into jail as I was going to the shoemaker's to get a shoe which was mended. When I was let out the next morning, I proceeded to finish my errand, and, having put on my mended shoe, joined a huckleberry party, who were impatient to put themselves under my conduct; and in half an hour,—for the horse was soon tackled,—was in the midst of a huckleberry field, on one of our highest hills, two miles off, and then the State was nowhere to be seen.

[35]   This is the whole history of "My Prisons."

[36]   I have never declined paying the highway tax, because I am as desirous of being a good neighbor as I am of being a bad subject; and as for supporting schools, I am doing my part to educate my fellow-countrymen now. It is for no particular item in the tax-bill that I refuse to pay it. I simply wish to refuse allegiance to the State, to withdraw and stand aloof from it effectually. I do not care to trace the course of my dollar, if I could, till it buys a man or a musket to shoot one with,—the dollar is innocent,—but I am concerned to trace the effects of my allegiance. In fact, I quietly declare war with the State, after my fashion, though I will still make what use and get what advantage of her I can, as is usual in such cases.

[37]   If others pay the tax which is demanded of me, from a sympathy with the State, they do but what they have already done in their own case, or rather they abet injustice to a greater extent than the State requires. If they pay the tax from a mistaken interest in the individual taxed, to save his property, or prevent his going to jail, it is because they have not considered wisely how far they let their private feelings interfere with the public good.

[38]   This, then, is my position at present. But one cannot be too much on his guard in such a case, lest his action be biased by obstinacy or an undue regard for the opinions of men. Let him see that he does only what belongs to himself and to the hour.

[39]   I think sometimes, Why, this people mean well, they are only ignorant; they would do better if they knew how: why give your neighbors this pain to treat you as they are not inclined to? But I think again, This is no reason why I should do as they do, or permit others to suffer much greater pain of a different kind. Again, I sometimes say

to myself, When many millions of men, without heat, without ill will, without personal feeling of any kind, demand of you a few shillings only, without the possibility, such is their constitution, of retracting or altering their present demand, and without the possibility, on your side, of appeal to any other millions, why expose yourself to this over- whelming brute force? You do not resist cold and hunger, the winds and the waves, thus obstinately; you quietly submit to a thousand similar necessities. You do not put your head into the fire. But just in proportion as I regard this as not wholly a brute force, but partly a human force, and consider that I have relations to those millions as to so many millions of men, and not of mere brute or inanimate things, I see that appeal is possible, first and instantaneously, from them to the Maker of them, and, secondly, from them to themselves. But if I put my head deliberately into the fire, there is no appeal to fire or to the Maker of fire, and I have only myself to blame. If I could con- vince myself that I have any right to be satisfied with men as they are, and to treat them accordingly, and not according, in some respects, to my requisitions and expectations of what they and I ought to be, then, like a good Mussulman and fatalist, I should endeavor to be satisfied with things as they are, and say it is the will of God. And, above all, there is this difference between resisting this and a purely brute or natural force, that I can resist this with some effect; but I cannot expect, like Orpheus, to change the nature of the rocks and trees and beasts.

[40]   I do not wish to quarrel with any man or nation. I do not wish to split hairs, to make fine distinctions, or set myself up as better than my neighbors. I seek rather, I may say, even an excuse for conforming to the laws of the land. I am but too ready to conform to them. In- deed, I have reason to suspect myself on this head; and each year, as the tax-gatherer comes round, I find myself disposed to review the acts and position of the general and State governments, and the spirit of the people, to discover a pretext for conformity.

> "We must affect our country as our parents,
> And if at any time we alienate
> Our love or industry from doing it honor,
> We must respect effects and teach the soul
> Matter of conscience and religion,
> And not desire of rule or benefit."

I believe that the State will soon be able to take all my work of this sort out of my hands, and then I shall be no better a patriot than my fellow-countrymen. Seen from a lower point of view, the Constitution, with all its faults, is very good; the law and the courts are very respectable; even this State and this American government are, in many respects, very admirable, and rare things, to be thankful for, such as a great many have described them; but seen from a point of view a little higher, they are what I have described them; seen from a higher still, and the highest, who shall say what they are, or that they are worth looking at or thinking of at all?

[41]   However, the government does not concern me much, and I shall bestow the fewest possible thoughts on it. It is not many moments that I live under a government, even in this world. If a man is thought-free, fancy-free, imagination-free, that which *is not* never for a long time appearing *to be* to him, unwise rulers or reformers cannot fatally interrupt him.

[42]   I know that most men think differently from myself; but those whose lives are by profession devoted to the study of these or kindred subjects content me as little as any. Statesmen and legislators, standing so completely within the institution, never distinctly and nakedly behold it. They speak of moving society, but have no resting-place without it. They may be men of a certain experience and discrimination, and have no doubt invented ingenious and even useful systems, for which we sincerely thank them; but all their wit and usefulness lie within certain not very wide limits. They are wont to forget that the world is not governed by policy and expediency. Webster never goes behind government, and so cannot speak with authority about it. His words are wisdom to those legislators who contemplate no essential reform in the existing government; but for thinkers, and those who legislate for all time, he never once glances at the subject. I know of those whose serene and wise speculations on this theme would soon reveal the limits of his mind's range and hospitality. Yet, compared with the cheap professions of most reformers, and the still cheaper wisdom and eloquence of politicians in general, his are almost the only sensible and valuable words, and we thank Heaven for him. Comparatively, he is always strong, original, and, above all, practical. Still, his quality is not wisdom, but prudence. The lawyer's truth is not Truth, but consistency or a consistent expediency. Truth is always in harmony with herself, and is not concerned chiefly to reveal the justice that may consist with wrong-doing. He well deserves to be called, as he has been called, the Defender of the Constitution. There are really no blows to be given by him but defensive ones. He is

not a leader, but a follower. His leaders are the men of '87. "I have never made an effort," he says, "and never propose to make an effort; I have never countenanced an effort, and never mean to countenance an effort, to disturb the arrangement as originally made, by which the various States came into the Union." Still thinking of the sanction which the Constitution gives to slavery, he says, "Because it was a part of the orginal compact,—let it stand." Notwithstanding his special acuteness and ability, he is unable to take a fact out of its merely political relations, and behold it as it lies absolutely to be disposed of by the intellect,—what, for instance, it behooves a man to do here in America to-day with regard to slavery,—but ventures, or is driven, to make some such desperate answer as the following, while professing to speak absolutely, and as a private man,—from which what new and singular code of social duties might be inferred? "The manner," says he, "in which the governments of those States where slavery exists are to regulate it is for their own consideration, under their responsibility to their constituents, to the general laws of propriety, humanity, and justice, and to God. Associations formed elsewhere, springing from a feeling of humanity, or any other cause, have nothing whatever to do with it. They have never received any encouragement from me, and they never will."

[43]   They who know of no purer sources of truth, who have traced up its stream no higher, stand, and wisely stand, by the Bible and the Constitution, and drink at it there with reverence and humility; but they who behold where it comes trickling into this lake or that pool, gird up their loins once more, and continue their pilgrimage toward its fountain-head.

[44]   No man with a genius for legislation has appeared in America. They are rare in the history of the world. There are orators, politicians, and eloquent men, by the thousand; but the speaker has not yet opened his mouth to speak who is capable of settling the much-vexed questions of the day. We love eloquence for its own sake, and not for any truth which it may utter, or any heroism it may inspire. Our legislators have not yet learned the comparative value of free-trade and of freedom, of union, and of rectitude, to a nation. They have no genius or talent for comparatively humble questions of taxation and finance, commerce and manufactures and agriculture. If we were left solely to the wordy wit of legislators in Congress for our guidance, uncorrected by the seasonable experience and the effectual complaints of the people, America would not long retain her rank among the

nations. For eighteen hundred years, though perchance I have no right to say it, the New Testament has been written; yet where is the legislator who has wisdom and practical talent enough to avail himself of the light which it sheds on the science of legislation?

[45]   The authority of government, even such as I am willing to submit to,—for I will cheerfully obey those who know and can do better than I, and in many things even those who neither know nor can do so well,—is still an impure one: to be strictly just, it must have the sanction and consent of the governed. It can have no pure right over my person and property but what I concede to it. The progress from an absolute to a limited monarchy, from a limited monarchy to a democracy, is a progress toward a true respect for the individual. Even the Chinese philosopher was wise enough to regard the individual as the basis of the empire. Is a democracy, such as we know it, the last improvement possible in government? Is it not possible to take a further step towards recognizing and organizing the rights of man? There will never be a really free and enlightened State until the State comes to recognize the individual as a higher and independent power, from which all its own power and authority are derived, and treats him accordingly. I please myself with imagining a State at last which can afford to be just to all men, and to treat the individual with respect as a neighbor; which even would not think it inconsistent with its own repose if a few were to live aloof from it, not meddling with it, nor embraced by it, who fulfilled all the duties of neighbors and fellow-men. A State which bore this kind of fruit, and suffered it to drop off as fast as it ripened, would prepare the way for a still more perfect and glorious State, which also I have imagined, but not yet anywhere seen.